THE COMPLEATED
AUTOBIOGRAPHY
by Benjamin Franklin

THE COMPLEATED AUTOBIOGRAPHY
by Benjamin Franklin

Compiled and edited by

MARK SKOUSEN, PH.D.

Since 1947
REGNERY PUBLISHING, INC.
An Eagle Publishing Company • Washington, DC

Cataloging-in-Publication data on file with the Library of Congress

ISBN 0-89526-033-6

Published in the United States by
Regnery Publishing, Inc.
One Massachusetts Avenue, NW
Washington, DC 20001

Printed on acid-free paper

www.regnery.com

Distributed to the trade by
National Book Network
Lanham, MD 20706
Manufactured in the United States of America

10 9 8 7 6 5 4 3 2 1

Books are available in quantity for promotional or premium use. Write to Director of Special Sales, Regnery Publishing, Inc., One Massachusetts Avenue NW, Washington, DC 20001, for information on discounts and terms or call (202) 216-0600.

DEDICATED TO

My wife, Jo Ann Skousen,

our five children,
Valerie Lee, Timothy Mark, Lesley Ann,
Todd Franklin, *and* Hayley Elizabeth,

and all other descendants of Benjamin Franklin

⁓⧉⧉⧉⁓

Contents

The Compleated Autobiography:
A Continuation of the Account of My Life

Appendix

Acknowledgments

*"If you would not be forgotten, as soon as you are dead and rotten,
either write things worth reading, or do things worth the writing."*

—BEN FRANKLIN

Finishing the *Autobiography* of Benjamin Franklin has been a long-time adventure. Many people have been involved in this project over the years, and I would like to acknowledge them here.

First, appreciation goes to the editors and staff at Yale University in charge of compiling and editing the *Papers of Benjamin Franklin.* In particular, the current editor, Ellen Cohn, answered many questions and provided me the Franklin Papers Reader CD that contains virtually the entire collection of published and unpublished Franklin papers, including a translation of many of Franklin's letters in French, an invaluable tool in compiling and editing this manuscript. I wish to thank Yale University, the American Philosophical Society, and the Library of Congress, among others, for granting permission to publish copies of the original documents related to Franklin.

The staff at the various libraries at Columbia University were also helpful in locating materials related to Franklin's autobiographical writings. Thanks also to the historian Carl Van Doren, who not only wrote the definitive biography *Benjamin Franklin* (New York: Viking Press, 1938), but collected *Benjamin Franklin's Autobiographical Writings* (New York: Viking Press, 1945), which I found useful in my own efforts. I also depended on Thomas Fleming's excellent compilation, *Benjamin Franklin: A Biography in His Own Words* (New York: Harper

& Row, 1972); Claude-Anne Lopez's *Mon Cher Papa, Franklin and the Ladies of Paris* (New Haven: Yale University Press, 1990); and *The Private Franklin: The Man and His Family*, by Claude-Anne Lopez and Eugenia W. Herbert (New York: W. W. Norton, 1975).

I would like to thank my mother, Helen Louise McCarty Skousen, for passing down the legend of our family's relationship to Ben Franklin. She is responsible for my early fascination with Franklin's life and work. As a young man, I collected proverbs from *Poor Richard's Almanac,* and as an adult, I gained a great deal of pleasure posing as Franklin from time to time, visiting the Franklin House in Philadelphia and Craven Street in London, and writing a little book, *The Wit and Wisdom of Benjamin Franklin* (London: Pickering & Chatto, 1996).

Special appreciation also goes to my wife and lifelong editor, Jo Ann Skousen, who taught me years ago how to "know a participle from a predicate." Her professional editing and arranging skills helped make this work, and all of my writings, flow smoothly and naturally. Without her extraordinary efforts, this work would have remained unfinished.

Lastly, I would like to thank Jeff Carneal, president of Eagle Publishing; Marji Ross, the publisher; and Stephen Thompson, the senior editor, who recognized at once the value of bringing to life the final thirty-three years of Franklin's illustrious career in a challenging new format.

To all these, I quote the words of Franklin, "a true friend is the best possession."

MARK SKOUSEN
New York, New York

List of Illustrations

Frontispiece

Benjamin Franklin by Joseph Siffred Duplessis: National Portrait Gallery, Smithsonian Institution /Art Resource.

Text Illustrations

COLOR ILLUSTRATIONS

Benedict Arnold, 19th century steel engraving: The Granger Collection, New York.

John Jay by Gilbert Stuart: The Granger Collection, New York.

George Washington by Charles Willson Peale: The Granger Collection, New York.

Marquis de Lafayette and James Armistead Lafayette, contemporary French engraving by Noel le Mire: The Granger Collection, New York.

Madame Brillon, as played by Elaine Comparone, Robert Blake after Jan Vermeer: courtesy of Harpsichord Unlimited.

Franklin Urging the Claims of the American Colonies before Louis XVI by George Peter Alexander Healy: The American Philosophical Society.

Hotel de Valentinois at Passy, court and garden, attributed to Antoine Perignon: Réunion des Musées Nationaux/Art Resource.

Treaty of Paris, the American Peace commissioners John Jay, John Adams, Benjamin Franklin, Henry Laurens, and William Temple Franklin; unfinished painting (because the British commissioners refused to pose) by Benjamin West: The Granger Collection, New York.

U.S. Constitution (scene at signing) by Howard Chandler Christy: The Granger Collection, New York.

Benjamin Franklin by Jacques Thouron: Réunion des Musées Nationaux /Art Resource.

Introduction

"Had Franklin been able to write about every period of his life and all of his achievements, his Autobiography *would have been one of the most remarkable documents ever produced."*

—ROBERT W. MOORE

"And yet he by no means left the great remainder of his life untold."

—CARL VAN DOREN*

As a young reader, I was fascinated with Benjamin Franklin's success as an entrepreneur, inventor, civil servant, and philosopher-wit. When I came to the end of his unfinished *Autobiography*, I wanted desperately to read about his life in London as a colonial agent, his role in the Declaration of Independence, his service as America's first ambassador to France, and his part in creating a new constitution and a new nation. But it was not to be. The official autobiography of Benjamin Franklin ends abruptly in 1757, when he was just 51 years old. Another 33 years of his life were still to be recorded when he died in 1790, leaving out the most eventful years of his illustrious political career. What occurred over the next three decades made him a famous man, whom one biographer called "the most beloved and celebrated American of his age, or indeed of any age."[†]

That Franklin intended to complete his memoirs is without question. On the second day of writing his *Autobiography*, while visiting the Jonathan Shipley family in Twyford, near Winchester, England, he

---

* Carl Van Doren, ed., *Benjamin Franklin's Autobiographical Writings* (New York: Viking Press, 1945), v.
† H. W. Brands, *The First American* (New York: Doubleday, 2000), jacket.

made an outline of his entire career (see appendix). He divided each manuscript page into two columns, leaving the right-hand columns blank for making future additions and changes. Franklin addressed the material he had written so far to the "more general use [of] young readers" in pursuing a "life of business."* By 1757, Franklin was already known as an accomplished figure who had achieved fame and fortune as a publisher, postmaster, scientist, inventor, and public citizen of Philadelphia, and he desired to pass along his "prudent and imprudent" experiences to future generations. But the hard lessons he learned as a diplomat and revolutionary were left unrecorded when Franklin's mortal pen stopped on April 17TH, 1790, at the age of 84.

William Temple Franklin recognized soon after the death of his grandfather the need for a completed autobiography, and he in fact attempted to compile the remaining account, hoping to draw on Franklin's extensive outline, his journals, copies of letters, and published materials to finish the job. The result was the publication, after endless delays, of *Memoirs of the Life and Writings of Benjamin Franklin* in three volumes in 1817–18.

Now, generations later, I make another attempt. I conceived the idea of finishing the *Autobiography* while reading *The Papers of Benjamin Franklin*, a joint project of the American Philosophical Society and Yale University, and published by Yale University Press. While perusing his papers, I made a remarkable discovery: Franklin had virtually written—albeit in bits and pieces—the remainder of his illustrious life through his journals, essays, and letters to his relatives and friends about family life, politics, science, business, literature, and philosophy. As Carl Van Doren, Franklin's premier biographer, explains, "For Franklin, the most widely read of autobiographers, was an autobiographer by instinct and habitual prac-

---

* Franklin Papers Reader (FPR) 46:u112, BF to Duke de La Rochefoucauld, October 24, 1788.

tice."* There was much to work with. Franklin kept a series of diaries. In letters to his close friends and relatives, he gave charming details of his domestic existence, and related many behind-the-scenes political maneuvers in London and Paris. In one instance, Franklin wrote a three-page letter to Lord Kames, summarizing his two years in America, 1762–64. Not all his letters survive, but those that do paint a full picture of the man and his colorful career and character.

In addition to these letters, Franklin composed three important chapters he intended to include, in whole or in part, in his *Autobiography*: First, his *Tract Relative to the Affair of Hutchinson's Letters*; second, an *Account of the Negotiations in London for Effecting a Reconciliation between Great Britain and the American Colonies;* and third, *Journal of the Negotiation for Peace with Great Britain* from March 21ST to July 1ST, 1782. He showed the second of these papers to Thomas Jefferson in March 1790, as a sample of the history of his own life Franklin was preparing. All three were written after he wrote the first part of the *Autobiography* (in 1771), and he no doubt was planning to incorporate them when he reached the years in which these events took place. I have included all three monographs in condensed form in the *Compleated Autobiography*.[†]

It is important to note that these three essays were "further fragments of a work which is itself a fragment."[‡] Van Doren makes this important point, one that should not be overlooked by those who think completing Franklin's *Autobiography* is an impossible or inappropriate task. Franklin frequently revised the *Autobiography*,

---

* Carl Van Doren, *Franklin's Autobiographical Writings*, vi.

[†] I do not think the spirit of Franklin's history was violated in condensing these three lengthy monographs. As Franklin wrote the Duc de La Rochefoucauld regarding the memoirs, "I am persuaded there are many things that would, in case of publication, be best omitted" (FPR 46:u351, Nov. 13, 1789).

[‡] Carl Van Doren, *Franklin's Autobiographical Writings*, v.

and in some ways, the entire book should be considered an unfinished work, in need of further revisions.

THE MAKING OF THE *COMPLEATED AUTOBIOGRAPHY*

From the beginning of this project, my objective was to create a work entirely in the hand and voice of Franklin. After extensive research into his life and papers, I became more and more optimistic that my lofty goal could be achieved. Now, at the end of this journey, I have the happiness to conclude that Franklin's entire personal history can be told in his own words.

Yet it was not an easy task. Given the complexity, disparity, and mammoth volume of Franklin's writings, the construction of the *Compleated Autobiography* required considerable judgment as to what should be included and what should not. Finishing his memoirs entailed much more than simply gathering and reprinting his papers. He left behind hundreds of thousands of documents, which, when finally gathered and published, will exceed fifty printed volumes. My edited compilation probably represents less than two percent of his writings. Yet it is in large measure a complete story. All along, I felt as though I was assembling a giant jigsaw puzzle, not knowing precisely what the final image would be. Now, after months of effort, I see the big picture. . . . a smiling Franklin.

After reading through his papers and major biographies, I tried to put myself into Franklin's way of thinking and sought to imitate his selection process, as seen in his autobiographical writings. Like Franklin himself, I decided to "omit . . . facts and transactions that may not have a tendency to benefit the . . . reader, . . . [hoping] that the book will be found entertaining, interesting, and useful."*

---

* FPR 46:u111, BF to Benjamin Vaughan, October 24, 1788.

I have relied on Franklin's detailed outline of his memoirs, which he referred to himself when writing the *Autobiography*. Just as he injected historical events into his account to make a philosophical or moral point, so too have I inserted Franklin's stories into the *Compleated Autobiography*. And like Franklin in his memoirs, I have omitted his published essays, such as *The Way to Wealth*, and focused on his personal commentaries on events, individuals, ideas, and pursuits.

In a few cases, I have relied on letters from friends about Franklin rather than by him. For example, it is unfortunate that few if any documents survive about his involvement in the Declaration of Independence in 1776 and the Constitutional Convention in 1787. He apparently chose not to write about these singular events, privately or publicly, much to our loss. So I have had to rely mostly on several third party sources for Franklin's perspective. Franklin's lengthy commentary on the American Revolution, for example, comes from the diary of Arthur Lee, one of the commissioners to France, who spent an evening reminiscing and discussing with Franklin the events of the year and a half following the signing of the Declaration of Independence, and then recorded the conversation in his own diary.*

Sometimes I discovered a reference Franklin made of an important event, such as his wife's death, written years after the fact and buried in some obscure letter to a friend or relative. In these and other cases, a paragraph in *The Compleated Autobiography* may draw from several sources in order to create a chronologically accurate and full record of Franklin's life. As the reader will note in the citations at the end of the book, I often drew upon a half dozen references to tell the full

---

* The editors of *The Papers of Benjamin Franklin* considered this source so Franklinesque that they have included it in the *Papers*. See PBF 25:100-02. The original appeared in Richard Henry Lee, *Life of Arthur Lee* (Boston: Wells and Lilly, 1829), 343–46.

story of an incident. In short, *The Compleated Autobiography* is thoroughly Franklin.

Some have wondered if it might be better simply to reprint Franklin's letters and essays rather than attempt to finish his autobiography in a single volume, which only he could do to his complete satisfaction.   Indeed, many of his famous letters, journals, and essays have been reprinted as appendages to the *Autobiography* in various editions, or as Franklin anthologies.* Yet most of these anthologies are out of print, while the *Autobiography* continues to be reprinted and sold in bookstores. In my mind, it suggests a need for a newly fashioned memoir as a better way of recording the colorful and controversial later years of the charismatic, wise, and clever Dr. Franklin.

I have corrected much of the spelling, grammar, and sentence structure to reflect modern English usage, and have made structural changes in tense and person to create a seamless flow of writing. In no circumstances do these minor changes affect the meaning or style of Franklin's prose. At the same time, I have maintained some of the old English spelling and abbreviations that Franklin used, to give the work a sense of history. Occasionally, I insert clearly identified footnotes, brackets and short historical summaries to provide needed background. I have also included an alphabetized "Cast of Characters" at the end of the book. The sources of Franklin's writings are provided at the end of the book for those interested in locating the exact citation for further study. PBF refers to *The Papers of Benjamin Franklin*, published by Yale University Press, followed by volume and

---

* In addition to Carl Van Doren, ed., *Benjamin Franklin's Autobiographical Writings* (op. cit.), see Esmond Wright, ed., *Benjamin Franklin: His Life as He Wrote It* (Boston: Harvard University Press, 1989); Thomas Fleming, *Benjamin Franklin: A Biography in His Own Words* (New York: Harper & Row, 1972); and Walter Isaacson, ed., *A Benjamin Franklin Reader* (New York: Simon & Schuster, 2003).

page number; the letter "u" before a page number refers to the unpublished papers of Franklin found in the "Franklin Papers Reader" (FPR), a CD made available by the Papers of Benjamin Franklin Project at Yale University. The letter "t" refers to a translation of documents from French into English on the CD by the staff at Yale.

"A MAN WHO BOASTS OF HIS ANCESTORS"

What drove me to finish Ben Franklin's memoirs? I've had a lifelong interest in the "grandfather" of our nation. I find him the most creative, successful, entertaining, and approachable of the Founding Fathers. His multifaceted career and personal life are endlessly fascinating, and Franklin would be famous today even without the role he played in the American Revolution.

My personal interest in Franklin goes back to a long standing tradition in my mother's family of being descendants of Franklin through his daughter, Sally. My mother even looks like Franklin's profile. For years no one knew exactly how we were related other than the fact that it was rumored to be through an illegitimate line. In the late 1970s, I decided to do some genealogical work and discovered a will proving that we were direct descendants through Ben Franklin's grandson Louis Bache, who, according to his will, had two "natural sons" from an unmarried servant, one of whom was also named Louis. This Louis Jr. was raised by his father (shades of Ben and his illegitimate son William), and is my direct ancestor. It turns out that Ben Franklin is my eighth-generation grandfather through the Louis Bache line. Coincidentally, my career has sometimes followed Franklin's as a publisher, author, financial advisor, teacher, father, public servant, and world traveler. Several years ago I wrote a little book, *The Wit and Wisdom of Ben Franklin*, and on several occasions I have appeared as Ben Franklin, escorted to the podium by two lovely "French" ladies. Nonetheless, when I think of being related to such a famous Founding Father, I am always reminded of Poor Richard's refrain, "A man who makes boast of his ancestors doth but advertise his own insignificance."

Still, I would like to think that old grandpa Ben would find this work by one of his descendants to be "most agreeable," especially as it is presented in honor of the 300th year of his birth.

Benjamin Franklin and His *Autobiography*

A Summary

"Benjamin Franklin was perhaps the most beloved and celebrated American of his age, or indeed of any age."

—H. W. BRANDS*

"Benjamin Franklin was the most versatile genius in all of history."

—MICHAEL H. HART†

Benjamin Franklin (1706–1790) was the quintessential man of the eighteenth century Enlightenment and the most famous American of his age—a world renowned inventor, essayist, philosopher, diplomat, wit and the only founding father to sign the Declaration of Independence, the Treaty of Paris, and the U.S. Constitution. The youngest of ten sons of a Boston soap and candle maker, Franklin was born January 17, 1706, in Puritan Boston and became apprenticed as a printer. At seventeen he ran away to Philadelphia, where he became so successful publishing almanacs, pamphlets, and newspapers that he was able to retire in his early forties, to become a gentleman of leisure engaged in scientific pursuits and civic affairs. For the next forty years, Franklin

---

* H. W. Brands, *The First American: The Life and Times of Benjamin Franklin* (New York: Doubleday, 2000), jacket.

† Michael H. Hart, *The 100: A Ranking of the Most Influential Persons in History*, 2nd ed. (New York: Kensington Publishing, 1992), 516–17.

would devote himself largely to politics and diplomacy, becoming the first postmaster general and representing the colonies on two missions to England. He received many honorary degrees and was referred to as "Dr. Franklin." He repudiated the Stamp Act before the English Parliament, then returned home to become a leading revolutionary in the Continental Congress and signer of the Declaration of Independence. In the fall of 1776, he became America's first ambassador, negotiating an alliance with France, where he became the toast of French society. France's resultant support of America in its war of independence from Great Britain may have been the deciding factor in achieving victory in 1781. After negotiating a peace treaty, Franklin returned to America triumphantly in 1785 and inspired the delegates at the Constitutional Convention to adopt the Constitution before he died in 1790.

WRITING HIS MEMOIRS

Franklin worked on his much-anticipated *Autobiography* at four different times of his adult life. He wrote all or most of Part One during a two-week stay at the house of Bishop Jonathan Shipley near Twyford in Hampshire, England, in August 1771. He was then 65 and colonial agent to England. These memoirs cover his birth in 1706 through 1730. He wrote Part Two (including his list of virtues) in 1784 in Paris, where he was minister to France, at age 78. Part Three (covering 1732–57) was written in 1788, when Franklin, age 82, was living in Philadelphia. And Part Four, only a few pages long, discusses his first few months as colonial agent in London and was written when he was between 83 and 84 years old, between November 1789, and March 1790, soon before his death. He made additions and corrections to the manuscripts at various times. The original manuscript is located at the Henry E. Huntington Library in San Marino, California.

INFLUENCE OF FRANKLIN'S *AUTOBIOGRAPHY*

Franklin's memoir is considered the most popular autobiography ever written, and certainly the most read. Part One was addressed to his son, William, and more generally to his descendants with the intention "of gratifying the suppos'd curiosity of my son."[*] But Franklin quickly saw that the *Autobiography* could be much more than a genealogical record. He saw it as a guide "to benefit the young reader, by showing him from my example, and my success in emerging from poverty, and acquiring some degree of wealth, power, and reputation, the advantages of certain modes of conduct which I observed, and of avoiding the errors which were prejudicial to me."[†] In many ways it was a Horatio Alger tale of a gifted young man emerging from poverty to wealth through "industry, frugality, and prudence," Franklin's trilogy of virtues. Franklin's "bold and arduous project of arriving at moral perfection," found in Part Two, was impressed upon the minds of all young people growing up in nineteenth-century America.[‡]

The *Autobiography* is largely an account of the private Franklin, pursuing financial independence, developing and maintaining friendships, and improving the community. The *Compleated Autobiography* is primarily an account of the political Franklin, becoming a revolutionary and an international diplomat. But like the original, it reveals a private Franklin, expressing his wit, wisdom, and worries

---

[*] Gordon S. Wood, *The Americanization of Benjamin Franklin* (New York: Penguin, 2004), 139.

[†] Franklin Papers Reader (FPR) 46:u112, letter to the Duc de La Rochefoucauld, Oct. 24, 1788.

[‡] *The Autobiography of Benjamin Franklin*, 2nd ed. (New Haven: Yale University Press, 1964), 148. Franklin hoped to write a book entitled *The Art of Virtue* on the subject; the *Autobiography* is the closest he came to finishing it.

on wide-ranging themes of family life and religion, friends and enemies, science and philosophy, health and wealth, and politics and
economics.

There are over a dozen editions of the original *Autobiography* in
print. The editors of the *Papers of Benjamin Franklin* published a
definitive edition in paperback (Yale University Press, 1964). Scholars may prefer *The Autobiography of Benjamin Franklin: A Genetic
Text,* edited by J. A. Leo Lemay and P. M. Zall (University of Tennessee Press, 1981).

The Compleated Autobiography
(1757–90)

"*Life, like a dramatic piece,* should not only be conducted with regularity, but methinks it should finish handsomely. Being now in the last act, I begin to cast about for something fit to end with. Or if mine be more properly compar'd to an epigram, as some of its few lines are but barely tolerable, I am very desirous of concluding with a bright point."

—Benjamin Franklin, *July 2, 1756*

A Continuation of the Account of My Life

Preface

1789

Philadelphia, Penns.

To the Public,

Having now done with public affairs, which have hitherto taken up so much of my time, I now endeavour to enjoy, during the small remainder of life that is left to me, some of the pleasures of conversing with my old friends and compleating the personal history of my life.

I have been persuaded by my friends Messrs Benjamin Vaughan, M. Le Veillard, Mr. James of Philadelphia, and some others, that a life written by myself may be useful to the rising generation.

The Memoirs have now been brought down to my fiftieth first year, to 1757. It seems to me that what is done will be of more general use to young readers; as exemplifying strongly the effect of prudent and imprudent conduct in the commencement of a life of business. To shorten the work, as well as for other reasons, I omit all facts and transactions that may not have a tendency to benefit the young reader, by showing him from my example, and my success in emerging from poverty, and acquiring some degree of wealth, power, and reputation, the advantages of certain modes of conduct which I observed, and of avoiding the errors which were prejudicial to me. If a writer can judge properly of his own work, I fancy, on reading over what is already done, that the book will be found entertaining, interesting, and useful, more than I expected when I began it. What is to follow will be of more important transactions.

My malady renders my sitting up to write rather painful to me. For my own personal ease, I should have died two years ago; but, tho' those years have been spent in excruciating pain, I am pleas'd that I have lived with them, since they have brought me to see our present situation. Hitherto this long life has been tolerably happy; and if I were allowed to live it over again, I should make no objection, only wishing for leave to do, what authors do in a second edition of their works, correct some of my errata.

In writing the memoirs of my life, I have been so interrupted by extreme pain, which obliges me to have recourse to opium, that, between the effects of both, I have but little time in which I can write anything. My grandson, Benny, has copied what is done, which was sent to a few friends for their candid opinion, whether I had better expunge or alter my writings. I have relied on their opinions, for I am now grown so old and feeble in mind, as well as body, that I cannot place any confidence in my own judgment.

Here in hand is a full account of my life which I propose to leave behind me. I am now finishing my 84TH year, and probably with it my career in this life; but in whatever state of existence I am plac'd hereafter, if I retain any memory of what has pass'd here, I shall with it retain the esteem, respect, and affection, with which I have long been, my dear friends,

Yours most affectionately,

B FRANKLIN

Editor's Note:

In 1757, at the age of 51, Franklin was commissioned by the Pennsylvania Assembly to act as an agent in London to petition the Crown in the Assembly's dispute with the proprietors, the Penn family. The Assembly had passed a money bill to defend Pennsylvania in the French and Indian War by levying taxes on the lands of the proprietors. However, the Penns, as founders of Pennsylvania, adamantly insisted on their long-standing exemption from paying property taxes. Franklin went to London to plead the Assembly's case. Leaving behind his wife Deborah and daughter Sally, he took with him his son William and his servants Peter and King. Franklin's *Autobiography* ends shortly after his arrival in England in July 1757, and a summary of the battle over taxation of the proprietary estates, which was ultimately won by Franklin and the Pennsylvania Assembly. However, the Penns used a variety of delaying tactics for several years, leaving Franklin no choice but to spend time making the Assembly's case before the public through newspaper correspondence and meetings with prominent citizens. In his leisure time, he pursued a wide variety of scientific and philosophical interests, including extensive travel throughout the British Isles and the Continent. This part of Franklin's life covers his first mission to London, from 1757 until his return to Philadelphia in 1762.

Chapter One

First Mission to London,
1757–62

We safely arriv'd in England on the 17TH of July 1757 after having been chas'd several times on our passage by privateers. But we outsail'd everything, and in thirty days had good soundings. We met with no accident except the night before our arrival, when we narrowly escap'd running ashore on the rocks of Scilly, owing to our not having discover'd the lights ashore till it was almost too late to avoid them. The bell ringing for church, we went thither immediately, and with hearts full of gratitude, returned sincere thanks to God for the mercies we had received: were I a Roman Catholic, perhaps I should on this occasion have vowed to build a chapel to some saint; but as I am not, if I were to vow at all, it should have been to build a lighthouse.

My son and I arriv'd in London the 27TH of July. Having settled lodging near Charing Cross, I found many amusements there to pass the time agreeably. 'Tis true, the regard and friendship I met with from persons of worth, and the conversation of ingenious men, gave me no small pleasure; but at that time of life, domestic comforts afforded the most solid satisfaction, and my uneasiness at being absent from my family, and longing desire to be with them, made me often sigh in the midst of cheerful company.

London was one great smoky house

At Craven Street in Westminster everything about us was pretty gen-teel. We had four rooms furnished, but living in London was in every respect very expensive. The hackney coaches at that end of the town, where most people kept their own, was the worst in the whole city, miserable, dirty, broken shabby things, unfit to go into when dress'd clean, and such as one would be asham'd to get out of at any gentle-man's door. The whole town was one great smoky house, and every street a chimney, the air full of floating sea coal soot, and you never got a sweet breath of what was pure, without riding some miles for it into the country. As to burning wood, it answered no end, unless one could furnish all one's neighbours and the whole city with the same. I slept in a short Callico bed gown with close sleeves and flannel close-footed trowsers; for without them I got no warmth at night.*

I have a thousand times wished my wife with me

I found that every time I walk'd out, I got fresh cold. My illness con-tinued nearly eight weeks. I had a violent cold and something of a fever. I was now and then a little delirious: they cupped me on the back of the head,† which seemed to ease me for a while. I took a great deal of bark‡, both in substance and infusion, and too soon thinking

---

* This last passage was omitted in early editions of Franklin's letters "because the editors felt such details were indelicate and unworthy of a Father of the Country." See Claude-Anne Lopez and Eugenia W. Herbert, *The Private Franklin: the Man and His Family* (New York: Norton, 1975), 88.

† "Cupping" refers to bloodletting, a standard medical practice at the time.

‡ "Bark" is quinine, frequently prescribed to fight fever and malaria. Franklin had a constitution tough enough to withstand such toxic treatment.

myself well, I ventured out twice, to do a little business and forward the service I was engaged in, and both times got fresh cold and fell down again. I took so much bark in various ways that I began to abhor it; I durst not take a vomit, for fear of my head; but at last I was seized one morning with a vomiting and purging, the latter of which continued the greater part of the day. My good doctor grew very angry with me for acting so contrary to his cautions and directions, and oblig'd me to promise more obser-

Franklin took rooms in the home of Margaret Stevenson, in Craven Street, near Charing Cross Station.

vance for the future. He attended me very carefully and affectionately; and the good lady of the house, Mrs. Stevenson, nursed me kindly; Billy was also of great service to me, in going from place to place, where I could not go myself, and my servant Peter* was very diligent and attentive. Yet I have a thousand times wished my wife with me, and my little Sally with her ready hands and feet to do, and go, and come, and get what I wanted. There is a great difference in sickness being nurs'd with that tender attention which proceeds from sincere love.

---

* Franklin brought with him to London two slaves as household servants, Peter and King. Franklin owned slaves on and off for thirty years, but was one of the first Founding Fathers to abandon the practice and advocate the complete abolition of slavery. See chapter 11.

My friend Mr. Strahan* offered to lay me a considerable wager that a letter he wrote to my wife would bring her immediately over to England. He fanc'd his rhetoric and art would certainly bring her over, but I was sure there was no inducement strong enough to prevail with her to cross the seas.[†] I spent an evening in conversation with him on the subject. He was very urgent with me to stay in England and prevail with my wife to remove thither with Sally. He propos'd several advantageous schemes to me which appear'd reasonably founded. His family was a very agreeable one; Mrs. Strahan a sensible and good woman, the children of amiable characters and particularly the young man, who was sober, ingenious and industrious, and a desirable person.[‡] In point of circumstances there could be no objection, Mr. Strahan being in so thriving a way, as to lay up a thousand pounds every year from the profits of his business, after maintaining his family and paying all the charges. But I gave him two reasons why I could not think of removing thither: One, my affection to Pennsylvania, and

---

* Franklin's long-time friend, although their friendship was severely strained during the American Revolution.

[†] In addition to allaying her fears of the sea, William Strahan wrote Deborah informing her "that Mr. F. has the good fortune to lodge with a very discreet good gentlewoman [Mrs. Stevenson], who is particularly careful of him, who attended him during a very severe cold he was some time ago seized with, with an assiduity, concern, and tenderness, which perhaps only yourself could equal: so that I don't think you could have a better substitute till you come over to take him under your own protection ... There are many ladies here that would make no objection to sailing twice as far after him." See PBF 7:297-98, Strahan to Deborah Franklin, December 13, 1757. Debbie's answer to Strahan is lost, but Franklin's comment on it suggests that both her fear of the ocean and her trust in Franklin's fidelity remained unshaken. See PBF 8:93, BF to Deborah Franklin, June 10, 1758.

[‡] Strahan and Franklin entertained the idea of marriage between Strahan's son Billy and Franklin's daughter Sally. Nothing ever came of it. See PBF 7:297n.

long established friendships and connections there; the other, my wife's invincible aversion to crossing the seas.

ANOTHER OF MY FANCIES: SILK BLANKETS!

I mentioned to my wife another of my fancyings, viz. a pair of silk blankets, very fine. They were of a new kind, just taken in a French prize [privateering], and such as were never seen in England before: they were called blankets; but I thought would be very neat to cover a summer bed instead of a quilt or counterpain. While in London, I had several trunks of silk consign'd to me for sale, and I remember it fetched at a public sale as high a price within 6d. in the pound weight, as the Italian sold at the same time. I had not the least doubt but that, by perseverance, this valuable produce could be established in our province in America. And in my journey from Philadelphia to Boston in the summer of 1763, I had the pleasure of meeting with sundry persons in different places who were attempting the production of silk from the encouragement of the Society of Arts.

DECEIVED, CHEATED, AND BETRAYED

Once recovered from my long illness, I found myself engag'd in an affair that took much more time than I expected. The repeated exemptions of the Penns, proprietors of Pennsylvania, from bearing a part of our colony's heavy taxes appeared unreasonable to those who bore the burden of the American war* (where our proprietaries had so large an interest to defend) as well as for the more immediate defense of their own estates. I insisted on a conference with the proprietaries. Mr. Thomas Penn stated that we [the Pennsylvania

---

* The French and Indian War (1754–60), also known as the Seven Years War, between France and England.

Assembly] were only a kind of corporation acting by a charter from the crown and could have no privileges or rights but what was granted by that charter, in which no such privilege as we then claimed was any where mentioned.

"But," *said I*, "your father's charter expressly says that the Assembly of Pennsylvania shall have all the power and privileges of an assembly according to the rights of the freeborn subjects of England, and as is usual in any of the British Plantations in America."

"Yes," *said he*, "but if my father granted privileges he was not by the Royal Charter empowered to grant, nothing can be claim'd by such grant."

I said, "If then your father had no right to grant the privileges he pretended to grant, and to publish all over Europe as granted, then those who came to settle in the province upon the faith of that grant and in expectation of enjoying the privileges contained in it, were deceived, cheated and betrayed."

He answered, "They should have themselves looked to that, the Royal Charter was no secret; they who came into the province on my father's offer of privileges, if they were deceiv'd, it was their own fault."

And that he said with a kind of triumphing laughing insolence, such as a low jockey might do when a purchaser complained that he had cheated him in a horse. I was astonished to see him thus meanly give up his father's character and conceived that moment a more cordial and thorough contempt for him than I had ever before felt for any man living—a contempt that I cannot express in words, but I believe my countenance expressed it strongly. His brother was looking at me and must have observed it.

I reported to the Assembly that a petition expressing their dislike to the proprietary government, and praying the Crown to get rid of the proprietary government and take the province under its immediate government and protection, would be very favourably heard. Of myself, having no longer any hopes of an accommodation, I have never since desired an audience of the proprietaries.

A Journey to Cambridge

I depend chiefly on journeys into the country for the establishment of my health. In the summer of 1758, as all the great folks were out of town, and public business at a stand, Billy and I travelled over a great part of England; we took a journey to Cambridge, being entertained with great kindness by the principal people, and shown all the curiosities of the place. I found the journey advantageous to both my health and spirits. We were present at all the commencement ceremonies, dined every day in their halls, and my vanity was not a little gratified by the particular regard shown me by the chancellor and vice chancellor of the university, and heads of colleges.

The possibility of freezing a man to death on a warm summer's day

While at Cambridge, I mentioned in conversation with Dr. John Hadley, professor of chemistry, an experiment for cooling bodies by evaporation that I had, by repeatedly wetting the thermometer with common spirits, brought the mercury down five or six degrees. Dr. Hadley proposed repeating the experiments with ether, instead of common spirits, as the ether is much quicker in evaporation. We accordingly went to his chamber, where he had both ether and a thermometer. By dipping first the ball of the thermometer into the ether, it appeared that the ether was precisely of the same temperament with the thermometer, which stood then at 65; for it made no alteration in the height of the little column of mercury. But when the thermometer was taken out of the ether, and the ether with which the ball was wet, began to evaporate, the mercury sank several degrees.

The wetting was then repeated by a feather that had been dipped into the ether, when the mercury sunk still lower. We continued this operation, one of us wetting the ball, and another of the company blowing on it with the bellows, to quicken the evaporation, the mercury sinking all the time, till it came down to 7, which is 25 degrees below the freezing point, when we left off. Soon after it passed the freezing point, a thin coat of ice began to cover the ball. Whether this was water collected or condensed by the coldness of the ball, from the moisture in the air, or from our breath; or whether the feather, when dipped into the ether, might not sometimes go through it, and bring up some of the water that was under it, I was not certain. The ice continued increasing till we ended the experiment, when it appeared near a quarter of an inch thick all over the ball, with a number of small specula pointing outwards. From this experiment one may see the possibility of freezing a man to death on a warm summer's day, if he were to stand in a passage thro' which the wind blew briskly, and to be wet frequently with ether, a spirit that is more inflammable than brandy, or common spirits of wine.

COOLING BODIES BY EVAPORATION...
A POWER OF NATURE

It is but within these few years, that the European philosophers seem to have known this power in nature, of cooling bodies by evaporation. Even our common sailors seem to have had some notion of this property. I remember that, being at sea, when I was a youth, I observed one of the sailors, during a calm in the night, often wetting his finger in his mouth, and then holding it up in the air, to discover, as he said, if the air had any motion, and from which side it came; and this he expected to do, by finding one side of his finger grow suddenly cold, and from that side he should look for the next wind; which I then laughed at as a fancy.

During the hot Sunday at Philadelphia, in June 1750, when the thermometer was up at 100 in the shade, I sat in my chamber without exercise, only reading or writing, with no other clothes on than a shirt, and a pair of long linen drawers, the windows all open, and a brisk wind blowing through the house, the sweat running off the backs of my hands, and my shirt was often so wet, as to induce me to call for dry ones to put on. But my body never grew so hot as the air that surrounded it, or the inanimate bodies immers'd in the same air. May this not be a reason why our reapers in Pennsylvania, working in the open field in the clear hot sunshine common in our harvest time, find themselves well able to go through that labour without being much incommoded by the heat while they continue to sweat, and while they supply matter for keeping up that sweat by drinking frequently of a thin evaporable liquor, water mixed with rum? But if the sweat stops, they drop, and sometimes die suddenly if the sweating is not again brought on by drinking that liquor, or, as some rather choose in that case, a kind of hot punch made of water mixed with honey and a considerable proportion of vinegar.

THE VILLAGE WHERE MY FATHER WAS BORN

Billy and I travelled over a great part of England; and among other places visited the town my father was born in and found some relations in that part of the country still living (Thomas Franklin in Leicestershire, and his daughter Sally Franklin, who later lived with me in London).* We went to Ecton, being the village where my father was born, and where his father, grandfather, and great-grandfather had lived. We went first to see the old house and grounds; the land is now added to another farm, and a school kept in the house:

---

* Franklin describes his ancestors in more detail in the *Autobiography* (New Haven: Yale University Press, 1964), 45–51.

it is a decayed old stone building, but still known by the name of Franklin House. Thence we went to visit the rector of the parish, who lives close by the church, a very ancient building. He entertained us very kindly, and showed us the old church register, in which were the births, marriages, and burials of our ancestors for 200 years, recorded as early as his book began. His wife, a good-natured chatty old lady, remembered a great deal about the family. She entertained and diverted us highly with stories of Thomas Franklin, who was a conveyancer, something of a lawyer, clerk of the county court, and clerk to the archdeacon, in his visitations; a very leading man in all county affairs, and much employed in public business. He set on foot a subscription for erecting chimes in their steeple, and completed it, and we heard them play. He found out an easy method of saving their village meadows from being drowned, as they used to be sometimes by the river, which method is still in being. When first proposed, nobody could conceive how it could be; but however, they said, if Franklin says he knows how to do it, it will be done. His advice and opinion was sought for on all occasions, by all sorts of people, and he was looked upon, she said, by some as something of a conjurer. He died just four months before I was born.

THE BEST ROOM IN THE HOUSE IS CHARITY

While there, I came across a little book called *None but Christ,* presented by an old uncle Josiah to his daughter Jane. I sent the following poem from the book to my sister Jane, which for namesake's sake, as well as the good advice it contains, I transcribed:

> Illuminated from on high,
> And shining brightly in your sphere
> Ne'er faint, but keep a steady eye

Expecting endless pleasures there
Flee vice, as you'd a serpent flee,
Raise faith and hope three stories higher
And let Christ's endless love to thee
Ne'er cease to make thy love aspire.
Kindness of heart by words express
Let your obedience be sincere,
In prayer and praise your God address
Ne'er cease 'til he can cease to hear.

After professing truly that I have a great esteem and veneration for the pious author, permit me a little to play the commentator and critic on these lines. *Faith, hope* and *charity* have been called the three steps of Jacob's ladder, reaching from Earth to Heaven. The Author calls them *stories*, likening religion to a building, and those the three stories of the Christian edifice. *Faith* is then the ground-floor, *hope* is up one pair of stairs. My advice: Don't delight so much to dwell in these lower rooms, but get as fast as you can into the garret; for in truth the best room in the house is *charity*. For my part, I wish the house was turn'd upside down; 'tis so difficult (when one is fat) to get up stairs; and not only so, but I imagine *hope* and *faith* may be more firmly built on *charity*, than *charity* upon *faith* and *hope*. However that be, I think it is better reading to say "Raise faith and hope *one story* higher." Correct it boldly and I'll support the alteration. For when you are up two stories already, if you raise your building three stories higher, you will make five in all, which is two more than there should be; you expose your upper rooms to the winds and storms; and besides I am afraid the foundation will hardly bear them, unless indeed you build with such light stuff as straw and stubble, and that, you know, won't stand fire.

Again where the author says "Kindness of heart by words express," strike out *words* and put in *deeds*. The world is too full of compliments already; they are the rank growth of every soil, and choke the good plants of Benevolence. Nor do I pretend to be the first in this comparison of words and actions to plants; an ancient poet whose words we have all studied and copy'd at school, said long ago,

A man of words and not of deeds,
Is like a garden full of weeds.

Tis pity that *good works* among some sorts of people are so little valued, and *good words* admired in their stead; I mean seemingly *pious discourses* instead of *humane benevolent actions*. These they almost put out of countenance, by calling morality *rotten morality*, righteousness, *ragged righteousness* and even filthy rags; and when you mention *virtue*, they pucker up their noses as if they smelt a stink; at the same time they eagerly snuff up an empty canting harangue, as if it was a posey of the choicest flowers. So they have inverted the good old verse, and say now

A man of deeds and not of words
Is like a garden full of—

I have forgot the rhyme, but remember 'tis something the very reverse of a perfume.

MY FAVORITE COUNTRY

No part of our journey afforded us a more pleasing remembrance than Scotland. The many civilities, favours and kindnesses heap'd upon us while we were there made the most lasting impressions on our minds, and have endeared that country to us beyond express. On the whole, I must say, I think the time we spent there, was six weeks of the densest happiness I have met with in any part of my life. And the agreeable and instructive society we found there in such plenty, has left so pleasing an impression on my memory that did not strong connections draw me elsewhere, I believe Scotland would be the country I should choose to spend the remainder of my days in.

The following February I was honoured to receive a Doctorate of Laws from the University of St. Andrews at Edinburgh, the oldest university in Scotland, for my inventions and experiments in electricity, and another Doctorate of Civil Law from Oxford University in 1762 that was conferred the summer following.*

THE JUNTO: I FIND I LOVE COMPANY

Returning to London, I was grieved to learn that two of the former members of the Junto† had departed this life, Stephen Potts and William Parsons. Odd characters, both of them. Parsons, a wise man, that often acted foolishly; Potts, a wit, that seldom acted wisely. If *enough* were the means to make a man happy, one had always the means of happiness without ever enjoying the thing; the other had always the thing without ever possessing the means. Parsons, even in his prosperity, always fretting! Potts, in the midst of his poverty, ever laughing! It seems, then, that happiness in this life rather depends on internals than externals; and that, besides the natural effects of wisdom and virtue, vice and folly, there is such a thing as being of a happy or an unhappy constitution. They were both friends, and lov'd us. They had their virtues as well as their foibles; they were both honest

---

* After receiving an honorary doctorate of laws from the University of St. Andrews in 1759, it soon became customary for friends and correspondents to address him formally as "Doctor Franklin," a title he carried the rest of his life.

† In 1727 in Philadelphia, Franklin created the Junto, a "club for mutual improvement" composed of enterprising tradesmen and artisans who gathered on Friday evenings to discuss scientific pursuits, schemes for self-improvement, and philosophical topics. See the *Autobiography* (Yale University Press, 1964), 116–18.

men, and that alone, as the world goes, is one of the greatest of characters. They were old acquaintances, in whose company I formerly enjoy'd a great deal of pleasure, and I cannot think of losing them, without concern and regret. For my own part, I find I love company, chat, a laugh, a glass, and even a song, as well as ever; and at the same time relish better than I us'd to do, the grave observations and wise sentences of old men's conversations. Death begins to make breaches in the little Junto of old friends, and it must be expected he will soon pick us all off one after another. I therefore have always hoped that it would not be discontinued as long as we are able to crawl together. Loss of friends and near and dear relatives, is one of the taxes we pay for the advantage of long life, and a heavy tax it is!

Unsizable subjects and insufficient lords

In April 1759, it gave me great pleasure to learn that the bill taxing the proprietary estate would pass. A few months later a book relating to the affairs of Pennsylvania was published.* In it the author wrote: "And who or what are these proprietaries? In the province, unsizable subjects and insufficient lords. At home, gentlemen it is true, but gentlemen so very private that in the herd of gentry they are hardly to be found; not in court, not in office, not in Parliament." The proprietor Mr. Penn was enrag'd. When I met him anywhere there appeared in his wretched countenance a strange mixture of hatred, anger, fear, and vexation. He supposed me to be the author, but was mistaken. I had no hand in it. I look'd over the manuscript, but was not permitted to alter every thing I did not fully approve. And, upon the whole, I think it was a work that was of good use in England, by giving the Parliament and Ministry a clearer knowledge and truer notion of our dis-

---

* An Historical Review of the Constitution and Government of Pennsylvania, by Richard Jackson (1759).

putes; and of lasting use in Pennsylvania as it afforded a close and connected view of our public affairs. On these accounts, I agreed to encourage the publication by engaging for the expense.

PERFECTING A NEW MUSICAL INSTRUMENT CALLED THE ARMONICA

After my chief business was over, I amus'd myself with the contriving and bringing to a considerable degree of perfection a new musical instrument, which has afforded me and my friends a great deal of pleasure. As it is an instrument that seems peculiarly adapted to Italian music, especially that of the soft and plaintive kind, I have called it the Armonica. This instrument is played upon, by sitting before the middle of the set of glasses as before the keys of a harpsichord, turning them with the foot, and wetting them now and then with a sponge and clean water. The fingers should first be a little soaked in water and quite free from all greasiness; a little fine chalk upon them is sometimes useful, to make them catch the glass and bring out the tone more readily. Both hands are used, by which means different parts are played together. The advantages of the instrument are that its tones are incomparably sweet beyond those of any other; that they may be swelled and softened at pleasure by stronger or weaker pressures of the finger, and continued to any length; and that the instrument, being once well tuned, never again wants tuning.

I SAW NO SIGNS OF GOD'S JUDGMENTS

From the summer of 1761 'til toward the end of September, I took the opportunity of the vacation of business in the public office in London, to make a tour of Holland and Flanders with my son. When I travelled in Flanders I thought of the excessively strict observation of Sunday in Connecticut; and that a man could hardly travel on that day without hazard of punishment; while where I was in Flanders, every one travell'd, if he pleas'd, or diverted himself any other way; and in the afternoon both high and low went to the play or the opera, where there was plenty of singing, fiddling and dancing. I look'd round for God's judgments but saw no signs of them. The cities were well built and full of inhabitants, the markets fill'd with plenty, the people well favour'd and well clothed; the fields well till'd; the cattle fat and strong; the fences, houses and windows all in repair; and *no Old Tenor* anywhere in the country; which would almost make one suspect that the Diety is not so angry at that offence as a New England justice.

Having seen almost all the principal places and things worth notice in these two countries, we returned to London, arriving in time to witness the Coronation of the new King. My business being compleat, I made plans to return home to Philadelphia. I nevertheless regretted extremely the leaving of a country in which I receiv'd so much friendship, and friends whose conversations were so agreeable and so improving to me.

THE FUTURE GRANDEUR AND STABILITY OF THE BRITISH EMPIRE LIE IN AMERICA

And thus in the summer of 1762, I departed the old world for the new, leaving Billy behind a little longer. I fancied a little like dying saints who part with those they love in this world: grief at the parting; fear of the passage; hope of the future. I had in America connections of the most engaging kind, and happy as I had been in the friendships contracted in this happy island, those in America promised me greater and more lasting felicity. I have long been of the opinion that the foundations of the future grandeur and stability of the British Empire lie in America; and though, like other foundations, they are low and little seen, they are nevertheless broad and strong enough to support the greatest political structure human wisdom ever yet erected.

Chapter Two

⟨⟩

My Return to Philadelphia, 1762–64

A PLEASANT PASSAGE TO AMERICA

I left England about the end of August 1762, in company with ten sail of merchant ships under convoy of a Man of War to protect us against the French.* We had a pleasant passage to Madeira, an island and colony belonging to Portugal, where we were kindly receiv'd and entertain'd, our nation being then in high honour with them on account of the protection it was at that time affording their Mother Country from the united invasions of France and Spain. 'Tis a fertile island, and the different heights and situations among its mountains afford such different temperaments of air that all the fruits of Northern and Southern countries are produc'd there—corn, grapes, apples, peaches, oranges, lemons, plantains, bananas, &c. Here we furnish'd ourselves with fresh provisions and refreshments of all kinds, and after a few days proceeded on our voyage, running southward till we got into the trade winds, and then with them westward till we drew near the coast of America. The weather was so favorable, that there were few days in which we could not visit from ship to ship, dining with each other and on board the Man of War, which made the time

---

* As noted earlier, the English were still in conflict with the French following the French and Indian War.

pass agreeably, much more so than when one goes in a single ship, for this was like traveling in a moving village, with all one's neighbours about one. The reason of our being so long at sea was that, sailing with a convoy, we could none of us go faster than the slowest, being oblig'd every day to shorten sail or lay by till they came up; this was the only inconvenience of our having company, which was abundantly made up to us by the sense of greater security, the mutual good offices daily exchanged, and the other pleasures of society.

On the first of November, I arriv'd safe and well at my own house, after an absence of near six years, and found my wife and daughter perfectly well, the latter grown quite a woman, with many amiable accomplishments acquir'd in my absence. I had the pleasure to find all false that Dr. William Smith had reported about the diminution of my friends, who were as hearty and affectionate as ever. My house was fill'd with a succession of them from morning to night ever since I landed to congratulate me on my return; and I never experience'd greater cordiality among them.

The expense of living was greatly advanc'd in America

I found the city of Philadelphia greatly increas'd in building, and they said it was so in numbers of inhabitants. But to me the streets seemed thinner of people, owing perhaps to my being so long accustom'd to the bustling crowded streets of London. The expense of living was greatly advanc'd in my absence; it was more than double in most articles; and in some 'twas treble. This was by some ascrib'd to the scarcity of labourers and thence the dearness of labour; but I think the dearness of labour, as well as of other things such as rent of old houses, and value of lands, which are trebled in the last six years, are in great measure owing to the enormous plenty of money among us. There is such an over proportion of money to the demand for a medium of trade in these countries that it seems from plenty to have lost much of its value.

I also found notorious the number of taverns, alehouses and dram-shops that increased beyond all measure or necessity in Pennsylvania. They were placed so near to each other that they ruined one another; and two thirds of them were not merely useless, but had become a pest to society. Very few of them were able to provide the necessary conveniences for entertaining travellers, or accommodating the people either in country or city; and this was entirely owing to that weak policy in a former Assembly, of making it the interest of a governor to encourage and promote immorality and vice among the people. Many bills had been presented to the late governors, to lessen the number, and to regulate those nurseries of idleness and debauchery, but without success.

I was elected to the Assembly

While I was on the sea, my fellow citizens had, at the annual election, chosen me unanimously, as they had done every year while I was in England, to be their representative in Assembly; and would, they said, if I had not disappointed them by coming privately to town before they heard of my landing, have met me with 500 horses. I had been chosen yearly during my absence to represent the city of Philadelphia in our provincial assembly, and on my appearance in the House they voted me £3000 sterling for my services in England and their thanks delivered by the Speaker. It had been industriously reported that I had lived very extravagantly in England, and wasted a considerable sum of the public money which I had received out of the Treasury for the province; but the Assembly, when they came to examine my accounts and allow me for my services, found themselves two thousand two hundred and fourteen pounds 10s.7d. sterling to my debt.

In February following, my son arriv'd, with my new daughter, for, with my consent and approbation he married soon after I left England,* a very agreeable West Indian lady, with whom he is very happy. I accompanied him to his government in New Jersey,† where he met with the kindest reception from the people of all ranks.

A tour of the post offices

In the spring of 1763 I set out on a tour thro' all the northern colonies, to inspect and regulate the post offices in the several provinces, we being under the necessity of making frequent and long journeys in person to see things with our own eyes, regulate what was amiss, and direct the necessary improvements. One of our goals was to expedite the communication between Boston and New York, as we had already that between New York and Philadelphia, by making the mails travel by night as well as day. It passes now between Philadelphia and New York so quick that a letter can be sent from one place to another, and an answer received the day following, which before took a week. In this journey I spent the summer, traveled about 1600 miles, and did not get home till the beginning of November.

The simple beauty of Scottish tunes

Having return'd home my daughter Sally endeavored to collect some of the music of this country production, to send to Miss Janet Dick in Scotland, in return for her most acceptable present of Scotch songs,

---

* Franklin never mentioned it, but his son followed in his footsteps by also fathering an illegitimate son while in London, called William Temple Franklin. Ben Franklin helped to raise and educate Temple.

† William Franklin was appointed royal governor of New Jersey from 1762 until 1776.

music being a new art with us. Sally sang the songs to her harpsichord, and I played some of the softest tunes on my armonica, with which entertainment our people were quite charmed, and conceived the Scottish tunes to be the finest in the world. And indeed, there is so much simple beauty in many of them that it is my opinion they will never die, but in all ages find a number of admirers among those whose taste is not debauch'd by art.

I give it my opinion that the reason why the Scotch tunes have lived so long, and will probably live forever (if they escape being stifled in modern affected ornament) is merely this, that they are really compositions of melody and harmony united, or rather that their melody is harmony. By this I mean the simple tunes sung by a single voice. As this will appear paradoxical I must explain my meaning. In common acceptation, only an agreeable succession of sounds is called melody, and only the co-existence of agreeing sounds, harmony. But since the memory is capable of retaining for some moments a perfect idea of the pitch of a past sound, so as to compare it with it the pitch of a succeeding sound, and judge truly of their agreement or disagreement, there may and does arise from thence a sense of harmony between present and past sounds, equally pleasing with that between two present sounds. Now the construction of the old Scotch tunes is that almost every succeeding emphatic note, is a third, a fifth, an octave, or in short some note that is in concord with the preceding note. Thirds are chiefly used, which are very pleasing concords.

A HIGHER OPINION OF THE BLACK RACE

While home, I also visited the Negro School in Philadelphia in company with the Reverend Mr. Sturgeon, and had the children thoroughly examin'd. They appear'd all to have made considerably progress in reading for the time they had respectively been in the school, and most of them answer'd readily and well the questions of the Catechism; they behav'd very orderly, showed a proper respect and ready obedience to the mistress, and seem'd very attentive to, and a good deal affected by, a serious exhortation with which Mr. Sturgeon concluded our visit. I was on the whole much pleas'd, and from what I then saw, have conceiv'd a higher opinion of the natural capacities of the black race, than I had ever before entertained. Their apprehension seems as quick, their memory as strong, and their docility in every respect equal to that of white children.

Just before I left London, a gentleman requested I would sit for a picture to be drawn of me for him by a painter of his choosing. I did so, and the portrait was reckon'd a very fine one.* Since I came to Philadelphia, the painter had a print done for it, of which he sent a parcel to America for sale. I took a dozen of them and sent them to friends in Boston, which I believed would be the only way which I would likely visit them.

The Assembly sitting thro' the following winter, and warm disputes arising between them and the governor, I became wholly engag'd in public affairs. Our old Speaker, Mr. Isaac Norris, had been long declining in his health. During the winter session he was unable to come to the statehouse, and the House met at his lodging. After some days he wrote to the House that he could no longer meet with them, and requested they choose another Speaker, upon which they were pleas'd unanimously to choose your humble servant.

Besides my duty as an assemblyman, I had another trust to execute, that of being one of the commissioners appointed by law to dispose of the public money appropriate to the raising and paying an

---

* This popular painting of Franklin, quill in hand and lightning in the
background, was done by Mason Chamberlain in 1762. Engraver
Edward Fisher made a mezzotint print, from which hundreds of copies
were made and distributed by Franklin and his son William to friends in
New England and in England. See PBF 10:frontispiece, xv.

army to act against the Indians and defend the frontiers. It was well known that I had no love of the governor, and he did not love me. Our totally different tempers forbid it. And yet I consider'd government as government, paid him all respect, gave him on all occasions my best advice, and promoted in the Assembly a ready compliance with everything he propos'd or recommended.

The Paxton boys and the Indian massacres

Then in December 1763 we had two insurrections of the back inhabitants of our province, by whom 20 poor Indians were murdered who had from the first settlement of the province lived among us and under the protection of our government. On Wednesday, the 14ᵀᴴ of December, 1763, fifty-seven men from some of our frontier townships came, all well-mounted and armed with firelocks, hangers and hatchets, having travelled through the country in the night, to Conestogoe Manor. There they surrounded the small village of Indian huts, and just at break of day broke into them all at once. Only three men, two women, and a boy were found at home. These poor defenseless creatures were immediately fired upon, stabbed and hatcheted to death. All of them were scalped, and otherwise horribly mangled. Then their huts were set on fire and most of them burnt down. When the shocking news arrived in town, a proclamation was issued by the governor, forbidding all persons to molest or injure the Indians. Notwithstanding this proclamation, those cruel men again assembled themselves, and hearing that the remaining fourteen Indians were in the workhouse at Lancaster, went directly to the workhouse, and by violence broke open the door, and entered with the utmost fury in their countenances. When the poor wretches saw they had no protection nigh, nor could possibly escape, and being without the least weapon for defense, they divided into their little families, the children clinging to the parents; they fell on their knees, protesting their innocence, declaring their love to the English, and that, in their whole lives, they had never done them injury; and in this posture they all received the hatchet. Men, women and little children were every one inhumanly murdered in cold blood.

As the rioters threatened further mischief, and their actions seem'd to be approv'd by an increasing party, I wrote a pamphlet entitled *A Narrative of the Late Massacres** to strength the hands of our weak government, by rendering the proceedings of the rioters unpopular and odious. This had a good effect; and afterwards when a great body of them with arms march'd towards the capital in defiance of the government, with an avowed resolution to put to death 140 Indian converts then under its protection, I form'd an association at the governor's request, for his and their defense, we having no militia. Near 1,000 of the citizens accordingly took arms; the governor offer'd me the command of them, but I chose to carry a musket, and strengthened his authority by setting an example of obedience to his orders. Governor Penn made my house for some time his head quarters, and did everything by my advice, so that for about 48 hours I was a very great man, as I had been once some years before in a time of public danger. I was a common soldier, a counsellor, a kind of dictator, an ambassador to the country mob, and on their returning home, *nobody* again. All this happened in a few weeks!

But the fighting face we put on, and the reasonings we us'd with the insurgents (for I went at the request of the governor and council with three others to meet and discourse them) having turn'd them back, and restor'd quiet to the city, I became a less man than ever: for I had by these transactions made myself many enemies among the populace; and the governor (with whose family our public disputes

---

* *A Narrative of the Late Massacres in Lancaster County, of a Number of Indians, Friends of This Province* (January 1764). The attackers were known as the "Paxton boys."

had long plac'd me in an unfriendly light, and the services I had lately render'd him not being the kind that make a man acceptable) thinking it a favourable opportunity, join'd the whole weight of the proprietary interest to vote me out of the Assembly, which was accordingly effected at the last election, by a "majority" of about 25 in 4,000 voters.

THE PROPRIETARY GOVERNMENT WAS WEAK

The House, however, when they met in October, approv'd of my resolutions when I was Speaker to petition the Crown for a change of government, having given up all hope of the proprietary government serving the people. The Assembly's petition was as follows:

> To the King's most excellent majesty, in council: The petition of the representatives of the freemen of the province of Pennsylvania, in General Assembly met,
>
> Most humbly sheweth
>
> That the government of this province by proprietaries has by long experience been found inconvenient, attended with many difficulties and obstructions to your Majesty's service, arising from the intervention of the proprietary private interests in public affairs, and disputes concerning those interests.
>
> That the said proprietary government is weak, unable to support its own authority and maintain the common internal peace of the province, great riots having lately arisen therein, armed mobs marching from place to place, and committing violent outrages, and insults on the government with impunity, to the great terror of your Majesty's subjects. And these evils are not likely to receive any remedy here, the continual disputes between the proprietaries and people, and the mutual jealousies and dislikes preventing.

We do therefore most humbly pray that your Majesty would be graciously pleased to resume the government of this province, making such compensation to the proprietaries for the same as to your Majesty's wisdom and goodness shall appear just and equitable, and permitting your dutiful subjects therein to enjoy under your Majesty's more immediate care and protection, the privileges that have been granted to them, by and under your royal predecessors.

Signed by Order of the House

For my own part, I thought it impossible to go longer with the proprietary government. Thus the Assembly requested me to return to England to prosecute that petition; which service I accordingly undertook, and embark'd the beginning of November 1764, being accompany'd to the ship, 16 miles, by a cavalcade of three hundred of my friends, who fill'd our sails with good wishes.

Return to London

When in America, I promised myself the pleasure of a regular correspondence with many of the ingenious gentlemen that composed the Club of Honest Whigs. But after so long an absence from my family and affairs, I found so much occupation that philosophical matters could not be attended to; and my last summer was almost wholly taken up in long journeys. I wrote letters to Mr. Strahan and others expressing my interest to conveniently remove to England, but I was never able to persuade the good woman to cross the seas, she always having an invincible aversion to it, even with the help of friends.

Chapter Three

Second Mission to England, 1764-75

OLD FRIENDS IN LONDON

On sea we had terrible weather, and I often was thankful that my dear daughter Sally was not with me. Arriving in Portsmouth after 30 days, I traveled 72 miles to London in a short winter day, and think I must have practis'd flying. But the roads in England were so good, with *post chaises* and fresh horses every ten or twelve miles, that it was no difficult matter. A lady that I know came from Edinburgh to London, being 400 miles, in three days and half.

I once more had the pleasure of living at Craven Street. Mrs. Stevenson was not home, and the maid could not tell where to find her, so I sat me down and waited her return, and when she arrived she was a good deal surpris'd to find me in her parlour. I had the pleasure of finding my old friend Strahan and all his family well and happy. Those of my old friends who were in town gave me a most cordial welcome, but many were yet in the country, the Parliament not meeting till the 10ᵀᴴ of January.

GOD IS VERY GOOD TO US IN MANY RESPECTS

Immediately upon my arrival, for 10 or 12 days I was severely handled by a most violent cold that worried me extremely. By February,

I was almost well, with the cough quite gone, and my arms continued mending,* so that I could put on and off my clothes, though it
still hurt a little. I also had a visitation from that friend (or enemy),
the gout, that confin'd me near a fortnight. By June I was in perfect
health and wrote my dear Debby on the great share of health we had
both enjoyed, tho' going in the fourth score.

I wrote, "God has been very good to us in many respects. Therefore, let us enjoy his favours with a thankful and cheerful heart; and,
as we can make no direct return to him, show our sense of his goodness to us, by continuing to do good to our fellow creatures, without
regarding the returns they make us, whether good or bad. For they
are all his children, tho' they may sometimes be our enemies. The
friendships of this world are changeable, uncertain transitory things;
but his favour, if we can secure it, is an inheritance forever."

Magic squares ... and magic circles

In my younger days, having once some leisure (which I still think I
might have employed more usefully), I had amused myself in making magic squares, and, at length, had acquired such a knack of it,
that I could fill the cells of any magic square of reasonable size, with
a series of numbers as fast as I could write them, disposed in such a
manner as that the sums of every row, horizontal, perpendicular, or
diagonal, should be equal; I enclose one of 4 on the next page.

But not being satisfied with these, which I looked on as common
and easy things, I had imposed on myself more difficult tasks, and
succeeded in making other magic squares, with a variety of properties, and much more curious. I did not, however, end with squares,
but composed also a magic circle, consisting of 8 concentric circles

---

* Franklin suffered a shoulder injury while touring the post offices a year
   earlier.

and 8 radial rows, filled with a series of numbers, from 12 to 75, inclusive, so disposed as that the numbers of each circle, or each radial row, being added to the central number 12, they made exactly 360, the number of degrees in a circle; and this circle had, moreover, all the properties of the square of 8. I enclose this magical circle of circles.

34

16	3	2	13
5	10	11	8
9	6	7	12
4	15	14	1

A "magic square" I devised.

At Craven Street, in correspondence with friends in Pennsylvania, I revis'd the magic circles I had made many years before, and with some improvements. I made it as distinct as I could, by using inks of different colours for the several sets of interwoven circles; and yet the whole made so complex an appearance, that I doubted whether the

"At Craven Street, in correspondence with friends in Pennsylvania, I revis'd the magic circles I had made many years before, and with some improvements."

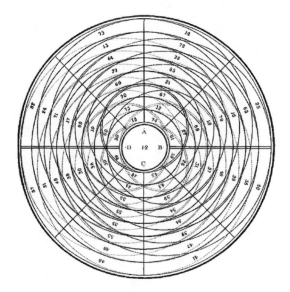

eyes could in all cases easily trace the circle of numbers one might examine, through the maze of circles intersected by it: I therefore, in the middle circle, marked the centers of the green, red, yellow, and blue sets, so that when the numbers in any circle of any of those colours were cast up, if one fixed one foot of the compass in the center of the same colour, and extended the other foot to any number in that circle, it would pass round over all the rest successively. This magic circle had more properties than are mention'd in the description of it, some of them curious and even surprising; but I could not mark them all without occasioning more confusion in the figure, nor easily describe them without too much writing.

The Stamp Act, the mother of mischief

As to business, I was immediately engag'd in public affairs related to America and in the petition to change the government in Pennsylvania. But the unsettled state of the ministry ever since the Parliament passed the Stamp Act had stop'd all proceedings in public affairs and ours among the rest. Every step in the law, every newspaper, advertisement and Almanac was to be severely tax'd, falling particularly hard on us lawyers and printers.

At first I was not much alarm'd about Parliament's schemes of raising money on the colonies, thinking that the government would take care for their own sakes not to lay greater burdens on us than we could bear; for they could not hurt us without hurting themselves. All our profits centered with England, and the more they took from us, the less we could lay out to them.

How the Stamp Act came to be

As to the true history of the Stamp Act, the facts are these: Some time in the winter of 1763–64 Mr. Grenville had called together the

George Grenville: "I am sure he would have obtained more money from the colonies by their voluntary grants than he himself expected from his stamps."

agents of the several colonies, and told them that he purposed to draw a revenue from America, and to that end his intention was to levy a stamp duty on the colonies by act of Parliament in the ensuing session, and if any other duty equally productive would be more agreeable to them, they might let him know it.

I was a member of the Assembly of Pennsylvania when this notification came to hand. In a resolution, we observed that the ancient, established, and regular method of drawing aids from the colonies was that the sovereign would direct his Secretary of State to write circular letters to the several governors, who would lay them before their assemblies; that upon their satisfaction, the assemblies would grant such sums as should be suitable to their abilities, loyalty and zeal for his service; that the colonies had always granted liberally on such requisitions, and so liberally during the previous war that the king, sensible they had granted much more than their proposition, had recommended it to Parliament five years successively to make them some compensation, and the Parliament accordingly returned them £200,000 a year to be divided among them; and that the proposition of taxing them in Parliament was therefore both cruel and unjust. I went soon after to England, and took with me an authentic copy of this resolution, which I presented to Mr. Grenville before he brought in the Stamp Act. I asserted in the House of Commons (Mr. Grenville being present) that I had done so, and he did not deny it. Other colonies made similar resolutions. And had Mr. Grenville instead of that Act applied to the King in council for such requisitional letters to be circulated by the Secretary of State, I am sure he would have obtained more money from the colonies by their voluntary grants than he himself expected from his stamps. But he chose compulsion rather than persuasion, and would not receive from their good will what he thought he could obtain without it. And thus the Golden Bridge which the ingenious author thinks the Americans unwisely and unbecomingly refused to hold out to the minister and Parliament was actually held out to them, but they refused to walk over it.

WE MIGHT AS WELL HAVE HINDERED THE SUN'S SETTING

I took every step in my power to prevent the passing of the Stamp Act; nobody could have been more concern'd in interest than myself to oppose it, sincerely and heartedly. But the tide was too strong against us. The nation was provoked by American claims of independence, and all parties joined in resolving by this Act to settle the point. We might as well have hindered the sun's setting. That we could not do. But since 'tis down, we could still light candles. As I wrote in "Father Abraham's Speech," frugality and industry will go a great way towards indemnifying us. Idleness and pride tax us with a heavier hand than kings and parliaments; if we can get rid of the former we may easily bear the latter.* For we are taxed twice as much by our *idleness*, three times as much by our *pride*, and four times as much by our *folly*. Mr. Hall wrote me about the ferment in the colonies over the Stamp Act; that Mr. Oliver, the stamp officer, was hanged in effigy in Boston; that a house was pulled down, which was supposed to have been erected for the business of the Stamp Office; that the spirit of the people was violently against everyone they thought had the least concern with the Stamp law; and that many had imbibed the false notion that I had a hand in the framing of the Stamp Act, which occasion'd me many enemies. He reported that all the papers on the American Continent, except our *Pennsylvania Gazette*, were full of spirited papers against the Stamp law, and that because he did not publish those papers likewise, he was much blamed, got a great deal of ill-will, and that some of our customers had stopped subscribing on that account. I told him that he had acted very prudently in omitting the pieces that were printed in other papers, and I would have been equally averse to printing them even if I had held no office under the crown.

---

* On board the ship coming over to England, Franklin completed an essay entitled "Father Abraham's Speech," which was added to his Pennsylvania Almanac in answer to the question of heavy taxes in America. In it, Franklin wrote: "Friends, says Father Abraham, and neighbours, the taxes are indeed very heavy, and if those laid on by the government were the only ones we had to pay, we might more easily discharge them; but we have many others, and much more grievous to some of us." See PBF 7:341, "Father Abraham's Speech," *Poor Richard's Almanac*, 1758. This essay became "The Way to Wealth," and was part of the twenty-sixth and last almanac prepared by Franklin himself. It is the most widely reprinted of Franklin's writings, including the *Autobiography*. See PBF 7:326–55.

A Mr. Thomson tender'd me a response, of which I gave an extract to a friend, who printed it in the *London Chronicle*. (I reprinted everything from America that I thought might help our common cause.) It said in part, "The Sun of Liberty is indeed fast setting, if not down already, in the American colonies: But I much fear instead of the candles you mentioned being lighted, you will hear of the works of darkness."

A MOB AT MY HOME IN PHILADELPHIA

In November 1765, I received letters from my wife, my daughter Sally, and our good neighbors relating to raising a mob at my home in Philadelphia in protest of the Stamp Act. I honoured much the spirit and courage my wife showed, and the prudent preparations she made in that time of danger. I wrote her, "The woman deserves a good house who is determined to defend it." The disturbances in the colonies gave me great concern, as I feared the event would be pernicious to America in general. The rashness of the Assembly in Virginia was amazing! I had hoped that ours would keep within the bounds of prudence and moderation; for that, I believed, was the only way to lighten or get clear of our burdens, and facilitate my endeavor to get the Stamp Act repeal'd. I assured my wife and friends that nothing could be falser than the reports that I had even the least hand in framing the Stamp Act, or procuring any other burden on our country. In truth, I never in my life labour'd any point more heartedly than I did that of obtaining the repeal. I shall long remember a pious Presbyterian countryman who set the people amadding, by telling them that I plann'd the Stamp Act. I thanked him that he did not charge me (as they do their God) with having plann'd Adam's Fall, and the damnation of mankind.

I had a long audience at this time with Lord Dartmouth. He had been highly recommended to me by Lords Grantham and Bessborough as a young man of excellent understanding and the most amiable disposition. I found him to be all they said of him. I gave him my opinion that the general execution of the Stamp Act was impracticable without occasioning more mischief than it was worth, by totally alienating the affections of the Americans from Britain, and thereby lessening its commerce. I strongly recommended either a thorough union with America, or that government in Britain would proceed in the old method of requisition, by which, I was confident, more would be obtained in the way of voluntary grant, than could probably be got by compulsory taxes laid by Parliament. Particular colonies might at times be backward, but at other times, when in better temper, they would make up for that backwardness, so that on the whole it would be nearly equal. To send armies and fleets to enforce the Act would not, in my opinion, answer any good end, except the danger, by mutual violences, excesses and severities, of creating a deep-rooted aversion between the two countries, and laying the foundation of a future total separation. A great deal more I said on our American affairs. His Lordship heard all with great attention and patience. He thank'd me politely for the visit, and desired to see me often.

I SPOKE MY MIND PRETTY PLAINLY

During the course of the debate on the Stamp Act, I appear'd on February 13, 1766 before the Committee of the Whole of the House of Commons, and spoke my mind pretty plainly. I enclose the imperfect account that was taken of that examination.

Q. What is your name, and place of abode?
A. Franklin, of Philadelphia.
Q. Do the Americans pay any considerable taxes among themselves?
A. Certainly many, and very heavy taxes.

Q. Are not the colonies, from their circumstances, very able to pay the stamp duty?

A. In my opinion there is not gold and silver enough in the colonies to pay the stamp duty for one year.

Q. Are you not concerned in the management of the post office in America?

A. Yes. I am Deputy Post-Master General of North America.

Q. Don't you think the distribution of stamps, by post, to all the inhabitants, very practicable, if there was no opposition?

A. The posts only go along the sea coasts; they do not, except in a few instances, go back into the country; and if they did, sending for stamps by post would occasion an expense of postage amounting, in many cases, to much more than that of the stamps themselves.

Q. Do you think it right that America should be protected by this country and pay no part of the expenses?

A. America has been greatly misrepresented and abused here, in papers and pamphlets and speeches, as ungrateful and unreasonable and unjust; and in having put this nation to immense expense for their defense and refusing to bear any part of that expense. But that is not the case. The colonies raised, clothed, and paid, during the last war, near 25,000 men and spent many millions.

Q. Were you not reimbursed by Parliament?

A. We were only reimbursed what, in your opinion, we had advanced beyond our proportion, or beyond what might have been reasonably expected from us; and it was a very small part of what we spent. Pennsylvania, in particular, disbursed about £500,000, and the reimbursements in the whole did not exceed £60,000. This is the strongest of all proofs that the colonies, far from being unwilling to bear a share of the burden, did exceed their proportion.

Q. Do you not think the people of America would submit to pay the stamp duty if it was moderated?

A. No, never, unless compelled by force of arms.

Q. What was the temper of America toward Great Britain before the year 1763?

A. The best in the world. They submitted willingly to the government of the Crown, and paid, in all their courts, obedience to acts of Parliament. Numerous as the people are in the several provinces, they cost you nothing in forts, citadels, garrisons, or armies to keep them in subjection. They were governed by this country at the expense only of a little pen, ink, and paper. They were led by a thread. They had not only a respect but an affection for Great Britain; for its laws, its customs and manners, and even a fondness for its fashions, that greatly increased the commerce. Natives of Britain were always treated with particular regard; to be an old England man was, of itself, a character of some respect and gave a kind of rank among them.

Q. And what is their temper now?

A. Oh, very much altered.

Q. In what light did the people of America use to consider the Parliament of Great Britain?

A. They considered the Parliament as the great bulwark and security of their liberties and veneration. Arbitrary ministers, they thought, might possibly at times attempt to oppress them; but they relied on it that Parliament on application would always give redress.

Q. And have they not still the same respect for Parliament?

A. No, it is greatly lessened.

Q. To what causes is that owing?

A. To a concurrence of causes: the restraints lately laid on their trade by which the bringing of foreign gold and silver into the colonies was prevented; the prohibition of making paper money among themselves, and then demanding a new and heavy tax by stamps; taking away, at the same time, trials by jury and refusing to receive and hear their humble petitions.

Q. Have you not heard of the resolutions of this House, and of the House of Lords, asserting the right of Parliament relating to America, including a power to tax the people there?

A. Yes, I have heard of such resolutions.

Q. What will be the opinion of the Americans on those resolutions?

A. They will think them unconstitutional and unjust.

Q. Was it an opinion in America before 1763 that the Parliament had no right to lay taxes and duties there?

A. I never heard any objection to the rights of laying duties to regulate commerce; but a right to lay internal taxes was never supposed to be in Parliament, as we are not represented there.

Q. If the Act is not repealed, what do you think will be the consequences?

A. The total loss of the respect and affection the people of America bear to this country, and of all the commerce that depends on that respect and affection.

Q. But if the legislature should think fit to ascertain its right to lay taxes, by an act laying a small tax contrary to their opinion, would they submit to pay the tax?

A. The proceedings of the assemblies have been very different from those of the mobs, and should be distinguished, as having no connection with each other. The assemblies have only peaceably resolved what they take to be their rights; they have taken no measures for opposition by force; they have not built a fort, raised a man, or provided a grain of

ammunition, in order to enforce such opposition. The ring-
leaders of riots they think ought to be punished. But as to
an internal tax, how small so ever, laid by the legislature
here on the people there: while they have no representatives
in this legislature, I think it will never be submitted to. They
will oppose it to the last. They do not consider it at all necessary for you to raise money on them by your taxes;
because they are, and always have been, ready to raise
money by taxes among themselves and to grant large sums,
equal to their abilities, upon requisition from the Crown.

Q. What used to be the pride of the Americans?
A. To indulge in the fashions and manufactures of Great Britain.
Q. What is now their pride?
A. To wear their own clothes over again till they can make new
ones.

I WAS NEVER PROUDER OF ANY DRESS IN MY LIFE

Two weeks after my examination before the government, I was made
very happy by a vote of the Commons on February 22, 1766, for the
repeal of the mother of mischiefs, the Stamp Act. The House of Commons, after a long debate, came to a resolution, 275 to 167. Great
honour and thanks was due to the British merchants trading to
America, all of them being our zealous and indefatigable friends. In
honour of its repeal, I sent my wife a new gown, informing her that
had the trade between the new countries totally ceas'd, it was a comfort to me to recollect that I had once been cloth'd from head to foot
in woolen and linen of my wife's manufacture; that I never was
prouder of any dress in my life; and that she and my daughter might
do it again if it was necessary. I learned from letters from home that
upon the news in America, bells rang, bonfires were set, fire works
illuminated, and cannon fired.

Enemies do a man some good

As to the reports that spread to my disadvantage during the Stamp Act affair, I gave myself as little concern about them as possible. I have often met with such treatment from people that I was all the while endeavouring to serve. At other times I have been extoll'd extravagantly when I have had little or no merit. These are the operations of nature. It sometimes is cloudy, it rains, it hails; again 'tis clear and pleasant, and the sun shines on us. Take one thing with another, and the world is a pretty good sort of world; and 'tis our duty to make the best of it and be thankful. One's true happiness depends more on one's own judgement of one's self, on a consciousness of rectitude in action and intention, and on the approbation of those few who judge impartially, than upon the applause of the unthinking, undiscerning multitude, who are apt to cry "hosanna" today, and tomorrow, "crucify him."

I thank God that I have enjoyed a greater share of health, strength and activity than is common with people of my years. As to the abuses I have met with, I number them among my honours. One cannot behave so as to obtain the esteem of the wise and good without drawing on one's self at the same time the envy and malice of the foolish and wicked, and the latter is testimony of the former. The best men have always had their share of this treatment, and the more of it in proportion to their different and greater degrees of merit. A man has therefore some reason to be asham'd of himself when he meets with none of it. And the world is not be condemn'd in the lump because some bad people live in it. Their number is not great, the hurt they do is but small, as real good characters always finally surmount and are established, notwithstanding attempts to keep them down. And in the mean time such enemies do a man some good, while they think they are doing him harm, by fortifying the character they would destroy; for when he sees how readily imaginary faults and crimes are laid to his charge, he must be more apprehensive of the danger of committing real ones. I call to mind what my friend good Mr. Whitefield said to me once on such an occasion: "I read the libels writ against you, when I was in a remote province, where I could not be inform'd of the truth of the facts; but they rather gave me this good opinion of you, that you continued to be useful to the public: for when I am on the road, and see boys in a field at a distance, pelting a tree, though I am too far off to know what tree it is, I conclude it has fruit on it."

Never ask, never refuse, never resign

My enemies were forc'd to content themselves with abusing me plentifully in the newspapers. 'Tis the fashion in the newspapers to abuse and roast one another, and I sometimes took a little of that diversion myself. In their endeavour to provoke me to resign from the Post Office, they were not likely to succeed, I being deficient in that Christian virtue of resignation. If they would have my office, they must take it—I have heard of some great man, whose rule it was with regard to offices, *never to ask for them*, and *never to refuse them*: To which I have always added in my own practice, *never to resign them*.*

I travelled a good deal for my health

During the course of the Stamp Act affair, I was extremely busy, attending members of both Houses, informing, explaining, consulting,

---

* It should be pointed out that Franklin did on occasion violate this personal principle. In 1751, Franklin applied to become Deputy Postmaster General of America (PBF 4:134–35); in 1781, he tried to resign his position as ambassador to France, but was turned down (PBF 34:447–48, 533, 35:59, 66, 84, 175, 365, 382, 474–75).

disputing, in a continual hurry from morning to night till the affair was happily ended. Following the affair, I became ill again. I had been us'd to making a journey once a year, the want of which the previous year had, I believed, hurt me, so that tho' I was not quite to say sick, I was often ailing that winter and thro' this spring. Once nearly well, but feeble, by summer I set out with my friend Sir John Pringle, the queen's physician, on a journey to Prymont, Germany, where we drank the waters some days. I travelled a good deal for my health in Germany that summer, which I found a very fine country, and seemingly not so much hurt by the late war as one might have expected, since it appeared every where fully cultivated, notwithstanding the great loss it sustained in people. As I was soon well, my hearty journey had perfectly answered its intention.

Refrain from all idle, useless amusements

In December 1766, I was asked to recommend two young sons of my friends in Philadelphia to the study of physic [medicine] in Edinburgh. Herein is a letter I sent to them.

To Benjamin Rush and Jonathan Potts
London, Dec. 20, 1766

Gentlemen,

With this I send you letters for several of my friends at Edinburgh. It will be a pleasure to me if they prove of use to you.

But you will be your own best friends, if you apply diligently to your studies, refraining from all idle, useless amusements that are apt to lessen or withdraw the attention from your main business. This, from the characters you bear in the letters you brought me, I am persuaded you will do. Letters of recommendation may serve a stranger for a day or two, but where he is to reside for years, he must depend on his own conduct, which will either increase or totally destroy the effect of such letters. I take the freedom therefore of counselling you to be very circumspect and regular in your behaviour at Edinburgh (where the people are very shrewd and observing), that doing so you may bring from thence as good a character as you carry thither, and in that respect not be inferior to any American in going to study at Edinburgh at this time, where there happens to be collected a set of as truly great professors of the several branches of knowledge, as have ever appeared in any age or country. I recommend one thing particularly to you, that besides the study of medicine, you endeavour to obtain a thorough knowledge of natural philosophy* in general. You will from thence draw great aids in judging well both of diseases and remedies, and avoid many errors. I mention this, because I have observed that a number of physicians, here as well as in America, are miserably deficient in it. I wish you all happiness and success in your undertakings, and remain, your friend and humble servant

B FRANKLIN

MY LONG PARTNERSHIP EXPIRES

In 1748, at the age of 42, I took the proper measures for obtaining leisure to enjoy life and my friends more than heretofore, and put my printing house under the care of my partner, Mr. David Hall, absolutely leaving off bookselling, &c. In 1767, my long partnership of the printing business with Mr. Hall expired, wherein a great source of my income was cut off. My family's subsistence was thereby reduced to our rent and interest of money, which meant by no means could I afford the chargeable housekeeping and entertaining I had

---

* In the eighteenth century, "natural philosophy" referred to the physical sciences.

been used to; for my own part I lived in London as frugally as possible not to be destitute of the comforts of life, making no dinners for any body, and contenting myself with a single dish when I dined at home; and yet such was the dearness of living in every article that my expenses amazed me. I saw, too, that in my absence my wife's expenses were very great. Her situation was very much sensible that naturally occasioned a great many visitors, which expense was not easily avoided, especially when one has been long in the practice and habit of it. But when people's incomes are lessened, if they cannot proportionately lessen their outgoings, they must come to poverty. If we were young enough to begin business again, it might have been another matter, but I doubt not we were passed it; and business not well managed ruins one faster than no business. In short, with frugality and prudent care we may subsist decently on what we have, and leave it entire to our children; but without such care, we shall not be able to keep it together; it will melt away like butter in the sunshine; and we may live long enough to feel the miserable consequences of our indiscretion. Therefore, I had to limit payments to my wife to the sum of thirty pounds per month, making 360 pounds a year, and receiving the rents of seven or eight houses besides, which might be sufficient for the maintenance of my family in Philadelphia. I judged such a limitation the more necessary, as my wife was not very attentive to money-matters in her best days, and I did not like her going about among my friends to borrow money.

An "unpromising" marriage
survives and prospers

At the same time, Deborah inform'd me that our daughter Sally had become engag'd to a gentleman, Richard Bache. I at first could say nothing agreeable about the marriage, writing him that I loved my daughter perhaps as well as ever a parent did a child; but being that my estate was small, scarce a sufficiency for the support of me and my wife, who were growing old and could not bustle for a living as we had done, that little could therefore be spared out of it while we lived. Moreover, I thought the step Mr. Bache had taken to engage himself in the charge of a family, while his affairs bore so unpromising an aspect with regard to the probable means of maintaining it, was a very rash and precipitate one. I could not therefore but be dissatisfy'd with it, and displeas'd with him whom I look'd upon as an instrument of bringing future unhappiness on my child, by involving her in the difficulty and distress that seem'd connected with his circumstances, his having not merely nothing beforehand, but being besides greatly in debt. Nevertheless, time and his better prospects in business made me easier, and I gave them my best wishes; that if he proved a good husband to her, and a good son to me, he would find me as an affectionate father. Soon they gave birth to a son, Benjamin Franklin Bache. All who saw my grandson Benny agreed of his being an uncommonly fine boy, which brought often afresh to my mind the idea of my son Franky, tho' dead many years ago, whom I have seldom since seen equal'd in every thing, and whom to this day I cannot think of without a sigh.

Any profession is preferable to an office held at pleasure

In December 1771, I found Mr. Bache at his mother and sister's house in Preston, England. I very much liked his behaviour. We spent two days in Preston and I brought him to London with me, where I introduced him to Mrs. Stevenson and her daughter Polly. Mr. Bache had some views of obtaining an office in America, but I dissuaded him from the application and advis'd him to settle down to business in Philadelphia where he would always be with Sally; that it would have been wrong for Sally to leave her mother. Industry and frugality would pay his debts and get him forward in the world. I am of the opinion that almost any profession a man has been educated in is preferable to an office held at pleasure, as rendering him more independent, more a freeman and less subject to the caprices of superiors. I advis'd Sally to learn accounts and keep a store, and thereby be serviceable to him as my wife was to me. Till my return, I offer'd them no expense for rent, so that they might attend my dear wife as she grew infirmed, and she could take delight in their company and the child's. I gave him £200 sterling as good luck.

I was happy to learn from my sister Jane Mecom that a good understanding continued between her and my folks upon her visit to Philadelphia. My father, a very wise man, us'd to say nothing was more common than for those who lov'd one another at a distance, to find many causes of dislike when they came together; and therefore he did not approve of visits to relations in distant places, which could not well be short enough for them to part good friends. I saw a proof of it, in the disgusts between him and his brother Benjamin; and tho' I was a child I still remember how affectionate their correspondence was while they were separated, and the disputes and misunderstandings they had when they came to live some time together in the same house.

Seeking a land grant

I often wish'd that I were employ'd by the Crown to settle a colony in Ohio, that we could do it effectually and without putting the nation to much expense. What a glorious thing it would have been to settle in that fine country a large strong body of religious and industrious people! What a security to the other colonies, and advantage to Britain by increasing her people, territory, strength and commerce. Might it not have greatly facilitated the introduction of pure religion among the heathen, if we could, by such a colony, show them a better sample of Christians than they commonly saw in our Indian traders, the most vicious and abandoned wretches of our nation? In such an enterprise I could have spent the remainder of my life with pleasure.

In 1769, I joined with Thomas Walpole, Richard Jackson, and others in the Grand Ohio Company to apply for a grant of 2,400,000 acres of land in the territory on the Ohio purchased of the Indians, which land was to be settled by people from the neighboring provinces, and that would be of great advantage in a few years to the undertakers [of the project], an opportunity of making a considerable addition to our fortunes, as the expense was a trifle. Each share was equal to 40,000 acres. The application was raised to twenty million acres in January 1770. We were daily amus'd with expectations that it would be compleated at this and t'other time, but I saw no progress made in it. And I think more and more that I was right in never placing any great dependence on it. The Ohio affair always seemed near a conclusion, but so difficult was it to get business forwarded in London, in which some party purpose was not to be served, that as to our prospect of success, many things slip between cup and lip. The affair of the grant dragged on but slowly, and I began to be a little of the sailor's mind when they were handing a cable out of a store into a ship, and one of them said, "'Tis a long heavy cable; I wish we could see the end of it." "D—n me," says another, "if I believe it has any end: Somebody has cut it off."

Years later, in 1774, I was told that some persons in administration had suggested that my conduct in affairs between England and North America had entitled me to a mark of favour in the granting of lands on the Ohio. I never considered the purchase of these lands as a favour from the government, nor a great bargain to the purchasers; the agreement for them was fair and public, at a price fully adequate to their value. I nevertheless wrote a letter to Thomas

Walpole desiring that my name be struck out of the list of associates, and wished them all success in their hazardous undertaking.*

SOME LATE INCIDENTS BETWEEN
PARLIAMENT AND THE COLONIES

In 1767, some incidents revived the contest between the two countries, creating great disorder in public affairs. In the same session with the Stamp Act, an act had been pass'd to regulate the quartering of soldiers in America, with a clause directing that empty houses, barns, &c. should be hired for them; and that the respective provinces where they were should pay the expense, and furnish the firing, bedding, drink, and some other articles to the soldiers, gratis. But the New York Assembly refus'd to do it, which caused great mischief and alienation of the affection of the people of America toward the British empire.

It was a common but mistaken notion in Britain that the colonies were planted at the expense of Parliament, and that therefore the Parliament had a right to tax them, &c. The truth is, they were planted at the expense of private adventurers, who went over to America to settle, with leave of the King given by charter. On receiving this leave and these charters, the adventurers voluntarily engag'd to remain the King's subjects, though in a foreign country, a country which had not been conquer'd by either King or Parliament, but was possess'd by a free people. When our planters arriv'd, they purchas'd the lands of the natives without putting King or Parliament to any expense. Parliament had no hand in their settlement, was never so much as consulted about their constitution, and took no kind of notice of them

---

* However, despite this letter of resignation, Franklin remained an active
  silent partner in the Ohio land grant scheme. Soon after his return to
  America, he was one of four principals who signed a power of attorney
  for the company. Ultimately, the Ohio land petition was never obtained.
  See PBF 21:32.

till many years after they were established; but nothing was more common at this time in England than to talk of the sovereignty of Parliament, and the sovereignty of that nation over the colonies.

AMERICA IS FAVOURED BY NATURE

Upon the whole, I had lived so much of my life in Britain, and formed so many friendships in it, that I said at the time that I loved it and wished its prosperity and its union secur'd and establish'd. But as to America, the advantages of such a union to her were not so apparent. Scotland and Ireland were differently circumstanc'd. Confin'd by sea, they could scarcely increase in numbers, wealth and strength so as to overbalance England. But America, an immense territory, favour'd by nature with all advantages of climate, soil, great navigable rivers and lakes, &c., was destined to become a great country, populous and mighty; and would in a less time than was generally conceiv'd be able to shake off any shackles that might be impos'd on her, and perhaps place them on the impostors. In the mean time, every act of oppression soured their tempers, lessened greatly if not annihilated the profits of British commerce with them, and hastened their final revolt: For the seeds of liberty are universally sown there, and nothing could eradicate them.

FRANCE: A PRESTIGIOUS MIXTURE OF MAGNIFICENCE AND NEGLIGENCE

I stayed too long in London, and made a trip with Sir John Pringle into France in August. At Dover we embark'd for Calais. Various impositions we suffer'd from boatmen, porters, &c on both sides the water. I knew not which were more rapacious, the English or the French; but the latter have with their knavery the most politeness. The roads we found equally good with the English, in some places pav'd for many miles together with smooth stone like the new streets in London, and rows of trees on each side, and yet there were no turnpikes. But then the poor peasants complain'd to us grievously, that they were oblig'd to work upon the roads full two months in the year without being paid for their labour; whether this is truth, or whether, like Englishmen, they grumble cause or no cause, I was not able fully to inform myself.

There were fair women in Paris who, I thought, were not whiten'd by art. As to rouge, they didn't pretend to imitate nature in laying it on. This was the mode, from the actresses on the stage upward thro' all ranks of ladies to the princesses of the blood, but it stopped there, the Queen not using it, having in the serenity, complacency and benignity that shone so eminently in or rather through her countenance, sufficient beauty, tho' then an old woman, to do extremely well without it. I speak of the Queen as if I had seen her, and so I had, at Court. We went to Versailles on a Sunday, and had the honour of being presented to the King [Louis XV], who spoke to both of us very graciously and cheerfully. He was a handsome man, had a very lively look, and appeared younger than he was. In the evening we were at the Grand Couvert, where the royal family supped in public. An officer of the Court brought us up thro' the crowd of spectators, and plac'd Sir John so as to stand between the King and Madame Adelaide, and me between the Queen and Madame Victoire. The King talk'd a good deal to Sir John, asking many questions about the Royal family; and did me too the honour of taking some notice of me.

Versailles had infinite sums laid out in building it and supplying it with water: Some say the expense exceeded 80 millions sterling. The range of building was immense, the garden front most magnificent, all of hewn stone; the number of statues, figures, urns, &c in marble and bronze of exquisite workmanship was beyond conception. But the waterworks were out of repair, when we were there, and so was a great part of the front next to the town, looking with its shabby half brick walls and broken windows not much better than the houses in Durham Yard. There was, in short, both at Versailles and Paris, a pres-

tigious mixture of magnificence and negligence, with every kind of elo-
quence except that of cleanliness, and what we call tidiness. Tho' I
must do Paris the justice to say that in two points of cleanliness they
exceeded us: The water they drank, tho' from the river, they rendered
as pure as that of the best spring, by filtering it thro' cisterns fill'd with
sand; and the streets by constant sweeping were fit to walk in tho' there
was no pav'd foot path. Accordingly many well dress'd people were
constantly seen walking in them. The crowds of coaches and chairs for
that reason were not so great; men as well as women carried umbrellas
in their hands, which they extended in case of rain or too much sun.

The civilities we every where received gave us the strongest impressions of the French politeness. It seemed to be a point settled universally that strangers were to be treated with respect, and one had just
the same deference shown one in France by being a stranger as in
England by being a lady. The custom house officers at Port St. Denis,
as we enter'd Paris, were about to seize 2 doz. of excellent bourdeaux
wine given us at Boulogne, and which we brought with us; but as soon
as they found we were strangers, it was immediately remitted on that
account. At the Church of Notre Dame, when we went to see a magnificent illumination with figures &c for the deceas'd Dauphiness, we
found an immense crowd who were kept out by guards; but the officer being told that we were strangers from England, he immediately
admitted us, accompanied and show'd us everything. Every night,
Sundays not excepted, were plays and operas; and tho' the weather
was hot, and the houses full, one is not incommoded by the heat so
much as with us in winter. They must have had some way of changing the air that we are not acquainted with.

Travelling is one way of lengthening life, at least in appearance. It
had been but a fortnight since we left London; but the variety of
scenes we had gone through made it seem equal to six months living
in one place. Perhaps I had suffered a greater change too in my own
person than I could have done in six years at home. I had not been

there six days before my tailor and peruquier had transform'd me into a Frenchman. Only think what a figure I made in a little bag wig and naked ears! They told me that I was become 20 years younger, and look'd very *galante*; so being in Paris where the mode was to be sacredly follow'd, I was once very near making love to my friend's wife, Mrs. Dalibard, which made a lasting impression on my memory. In our return home, we were detained a week at Calais by contrary winds and stormy weather, which was the more mortifying to me when I reflected that I might have enjoy'd Paris and my friends there all that time. I returned to London safe and well, having had an exceedingly pleasant journey, and quite recover'd my health. But the time I spent as a stranger in Paris, in the improving conversation and agreeable society of so many learned and ingenious men, seemed now to me like a pleasing dream, from which I was sorry to be awakened by finding myself again at London.

I often wished I could procure more attention to the British ministry. I had urged over and over the necessity of the change we desired; but as we entered the year 1768, England was in a situation very little better than ours, which weakened our argument that a royal government would be better managed and safer to live under than that of a proprietary. All respect to law and government seemed to be lost among the common people, who were, moreover, continually inflamed by seditious scribblers to trample on authority and everything that used to keep them in order.

So many instances of goodness by the rich!

I wrote a piece under the name "Medius"* in the *Gentleman's Magazine* for the month of April, 1768, intended to lessen the effect of

---

* Franklin used dozens of pennames in writing essays in newspapers in America and Europe, which sometimes makes it difficult to determine his authorship.

the numerous inflammatory papers on the minds of the labouring poor. I noted that for two years past much invective had been met in the papers against the hard-heartedness of the rich, and much complaint of the great oppressions suffered by the labouring poor, as if the rich in England had no compassion for the poor. I remarked that the condition of the poor in England was by far the best in Europe. Except in England and the American colonies, there is not in any country of the known world, not even in Scotland or Ireland, a provision by law to enforce a support for the poor. This law was not made by the poor. The legislators were men of fortune. By that act they voluntarily subjected their own estates, and the estates of others, to the payment of a tax for the maintenance of the poor. I wish they could be benefited by this generous provision in any degree equal to the good intention with which it was made. But I fear the giving mankind a dependence on any thing for support in age or sickness, besides industry and frugality during youth and health, tends to flatter our national indolence, to encourage idleness and prodigality, and thereby to promote and increase poverty, the very evil it was intended to cure; thus multiplying beggars, instead of diminishing them.

Besides this tax, which the rich in England subjected themselves to in behalf of the poor, amounting in some places to five or six shillings in the pound of the annual income, they had, by donation and subscriptions, erected numerous schools in various parts of the kingdom, for educating gratis the children of the poor in reading and writing, and in many of those schools the children were also fed and clothed. They erected hospitals at an immense expense for the reception and cure of the sick, the lame, the wounded, and the insane poor, for lying-in women, and deserted children. They also continually contributed toward making up losses occasioned by fire, by storms, or by floods, and to relieve the poor in severe seasons of frost, in times of scarcity, &c. Surely there should be some gratitude due for so many instances of goodness!

A LAW MIGHT BE MADE TO
RAISE THEIR WAGES, BUT...

Much malignant censure did some writers bestow upon the rich for their luxury and expensive living, while the poor starve, &c. However, they do not consider what the rich expend and what the labouring poor receive in payment for their labour. The rich do not work for one another. Their habitations, furniture, clothing, carriages, food, ornaments, and everything in short that they, or their families use and consume, is the work or produce of the labouring poor who are, and must be continually, paid for their labour in producing the same. In these payments the revenues of the private estates are expended, for most people live up to their incomes. So that finally *our labouring poor receive annually the whole of the clear revenues of the nation.*

If it be said that their wages are too low, I heartily wish any means could be fallen upon to raise them, consistent with their interest and happiness. How is this to be remedied? A law might be made to raise their wages; but if our manufactures are too dear, they will not vend abroad, and all that part of employment will fail, unless by fighting and conquering we compel other nations to buy our goods.

A law might be made to raise their wages; but I doubt much whether it could be executed to any purpose, unless another law, now indeed almost obsolete, could at the same time be revived and enforced; a law, I mean, that many have often heard and repeated, but few have ever duly considered. *Six days shalt thou labour.* This is as positive a part of the commandment as that which says, *the Seventh Day thou shalt rest.* But we remember well to observe the indulgent part, and never think of the other. Monday is generally as duly kept by our working people as Sunday; the only difference is that, instead of employing their time cheaply, at church, they are wasting it expensively at the alehouse.

My piece, along with one I wrote against smuggling in the *Chronicle* of November last, was shown to the Chancellor of the Exchequer, who expressed themselves much pleased with them.

John Wilkes and drunken mad mobs

The Parliament was sitting, but would not continue long together, nor undertake any material business. Nothing was talked or thought of in England but elections. There were amazing contests all over the kingdom, £20,000 or £30,000 of a side spent in several places, and inconceivable mischief done by debauching the people and making them idle, besides the immediate actual mischief done by drunken mad mobs to houses, windows, &c. The scenes were horrible. London was illuminated two nights running at the command of the mob for the success of John Wilkes* in the Middlesex election; the second night exceeded anything of the kind ever seen on the greatest occasions of rejoicing, as even the small cross streets, lanes, courts, and other out-of-the-way places were all ablaze with lights, and the principal streets all night long, as the mobs went around again after two o'clock, and obliged people who had extinguished their candles to light them again. Those who refused had all their windows destroyed. The damage done and the expense of candles had been computed at £50,000.

'Twas really an extraordinary event, to see this Wilkes, an outlaw and exile of bad personal character, not worth a farthing, come over

---

* Wilkes was a "notorious rake" involved in a variety of scandals as a member of the notorious Hell-Fire Club, yet was an early advocate of English rights and opposed the war against the American colonies. He published a "seditious libel" against the King and Parliament in No. 45 of the *North Britain*, for which he was eventually imprisoned. Nevertheless, in 1774 he was elected Lord Mayor of London.

John Wilkes: "Mobs were patrolling the streets at noon day, some knocking all down who would not roar for 'Wilkes and Liberty.'"

from France, set himself up as candidate for the capital of the king, miss his election only by being too late in his application, and immediately carry it for the principal county. The mob (spirited up by numbers of different ballads sung or roared in every street) required gentlemen and ladies of all ranks as they passed in their carriages to shout for "Wilkes and Liberty," marking the same words on all their coaches with chalk, and No. 45 on every door, which extended a vast way along the roads into the country. In April I went to Winchester, and observed that for fifteen miles out of town, there was scarce a door or window shutter next to the road unmarked; and this continued here and there quite to Winchester, which is 64 miles. I was sorry to see in the American papers that some people there were so indiscreet as to distinguish themselves in applauding his No. 45, which I suppose they did not know was a paper in which their King was personally affronted, whom they surely loved and honoured at the time. It hurts to see sober, sensible men so easily infected with the madness of English mobs.

The mobs roar for Wilkes and Liberty!

Even the capital, the residence of the King, became a daily scene of lawless riot and confusion. Mobs were patrolling the streets at noon day, some knocking all down who would not roar for "Wilkes and Liberty." Courts of justice were afraid to give judgment against him. Coalheavers and porters pulled down the houses of coal merchants who refused to give them more wages; sawyers destroyed the new sawmills; sailors unrigged all the outward-bound ships, and suffered none to sail till merchants agreed to raise their pay; watermen destroyed private boats and threatened bridges; weavers entered houses by force, and destroyed the work in the looms; soldiers fired among the mobs and killed men, women and children, which seemed only to have produc'd a universal sullenness that looked like a great black cloud coming on, ready to burst in a general tempest. What the event would be, God only knew; but some punishment seemed preparing for a people who were ungratefully abusing the best con- stitution any nation was ever blest with, intent on nothing but lux- ury, licentiousness, power, places, pensions and plunder. Meanwhile, the ministry, divided in their counsels, with little regard for each other, worried by perpetual oppositions, in continual apprehension of changes, intent on securing popularity in case they should lose favour, had for some years past had little time to attend to great national interests, much less to our small American affairs, whose remoteness made them appear still smaller.

The Court of King's Bench postponed giving sentence against Wilkes on his outlawry till the next term, intimidated as some say by his popularity, and willing to get rid of the affair for a time till it should be seen what the Parliament would conclude as to his membership. His friends complained of it as a delay of justice, saying the court knew the outlawry to be defective, and that they must finally pronounce it void, but would punish him by long confinement. Great mobs of his adher- ents assembled before the prison, and the guards fired on them: it is said five or six were killed and fifteen or sixteen wounded, and some circumstances attended this military execution, such as its being done by the Scotch regiment, the pursuing of a lad and killing him at his father's house &c. &c. that exasperated people exceedingly, and more mischief seemed brewing. Several of the soldiers were imprisoned. It was said that English soldiers could not be confided in to act against these mobs, being suspected as rather inclined to favour and join them.

By summer the tumults and disorders were pretty well subsided. Wilkes's outlawry was reversed, but he was sentenced to twenty-two months imprisonment, and £1000 fine, which his friends, who had feared he would be pilloried, seemed rather satisfied with.

THE KING OF DENMARK
SHOW'D AN INQUISITIVE MIND

Later in 1768 the visit of the King of Denmark engrossed all the conversation. That young monarch gained daily on the affections of England by his great affability and condescension, and the pleasure he appeared to take in everything he saw, and in every amusement and entertainment contrived for him. I had seen him at the ridotto* and had no expectation of seeing him again; but in early October 1768 I receiv'd a very polite card from Baron Diede, his minister, expressing that the Prince of Travendahl (the King's travelling name) desired much to make an acquaintance with me, and had ordered him to invite me to his table for Saturday at St. James's. I went accordingly, and was most graciously receiv'd. He was pleased to say he had long desired to see and converse with me. The questions he asked were such as show'd an inquisitive mind and a good understanding. I was placed near him at table, only Lord Moreton† being between us, who was so good as to be my interpreter, I choosing not to speak in French, a language that I did not speak well at the time.

---

* A public spectacle with dancing and music, often in masquerade, which was popular at the time. See PBF 15:225n.
† President of the Royal Society.

A MALICE AGAINST US IN SOME POWERFUL PEOPLE

On the one hand, there was a general disposition in the British nation to be upon good terms with the colonies, and to leave us in the enjoyment of all our rights, and that no future impositions on America would be attempted. And yet this disposition was not to be relied on. There was a malice against us in some powerful people, that discovered itself in all their expressions when they spoke to us, and thus prevented those healing measures that all good men wished to take place.

Lord Hillsborough, the new Secretary of State, mentioned the Farmer's Letters to me, said he had read them, that they were well written, and he believed he could guess who was the author, looking in my face at the same time as if he thought it was me.* He censured the doctrines as extremely wild, &c. The more I thought and read on the subject, however, the more I found myself confirmed in the opinion that no middle doctrine could be well maintained; that Parliament had a power to make all laws for us, or that it had a power to make no laws for us: and I thought the arguments for the latter more numerous and weighty than those of the former.

PERVERSE AND SENSELESS MANAGEMENT OF LORD HILLSBOROUGH

In January 1771, at the earnest request of Mr. Strahan, I went to wait on Lord Hillsborough. I was shown into the levee room, and his Lordship came toward me. I said that my business was not much, only to pay my respects to his Lordship and to acquaint him with my

---

Letters from a Farmer were written by John Dickinson of Pennsylvania between 1767 and 1768. He warned the British of the economic folly and unconstitutionality of new British revenue laws that ignored the rights of Englishmen living in the American Colonies.

appointment by the House of Representatives of the Province of Massachusetts Bay,* to be their agent there. But his Lordship, whose countenance chang'd at my naming that province, cut me short, by saying, with something of a smile and a sneer,

L.H. I must set you right there, Mr. Franklin; you are not agent.

B.F. Why, my Lord?

L.H. You are not appointed.

B.F. I do not understand your Lordship. I have the appointment in my pocket.

L.H. You are mistaken. I have a letter from Governor Hutchinson. He would not give his assent to the bill.

B.F. There was no bill, my Lord; it is a vote of the House.

L.H. The House of Representatives has no right to appoint an agent. We shall take no notice of agents but such as are appointed by acts of assembly to which the governor gives his assent.

B.F. I cannot conceive, my Lord, why the consent of the *Governor* should be thought necessary to the appointment of an agent for the *People.*

L.H. (*With a mix'd look of anger and contempt*) I shall not enter into a dispute with you, sir, upon this subject. When I came into the administration of American affairs, I found them in great disorder; by my firmness they are now something mended; and while I have the honour to hold the seals, I shall continue the same conduct.

B.F. I beg your Lordship's pardon for taking up so much of your time. It is, I believe, no great importance whether the appointment is acknowledged or not, for I have not the least

---

* Franklin was agent to Pennsylvania, Massachusetts, New Jersey, and Georgia.

conception that an agent can at present be any use to any of the colonies. I shall therefore give your Lordship no further trouble. *Withdrew.*

After this conference between the Secretary and me, I heard that Lord Hillsborough had taken great offense at some of my last words, which he called extremely rude and abusive. He assur'd a friend of mine they were equivalent to telling him to his face that the colonies could expect neither favour nor justice during his administration. I found he did not mistake me.

This conference was one of the many instances of the Secretary's behaviour and conduct that gave me the very mean opinion I entertained of his abilities and fitness for his station. His character was conceit, wrongheadedness, obstinacy and passion. I had hoped, however, that our affairs would not much longer be perplex'd and embarrass'd by his perverse and senseless management.

THE SEEDS ARE SOWN OF TOTAL DISUNION

I did not pretend the gift of prophecy, but I thought one could clearly see, in the system of customs exacted in America by act of Parliament,* the seeds sown of total disunion of the two countries. I wrote the following to the Massachusetts House of Representatives Committee of Correspondence in 1771:

---

* Franklin has particular reference to the Townsend Acts of 1767, named after the new chancellor of the exchequer, Charles Townsend, which imposed heavy duties on American imports (following Franklin's opinion that Americans would not oppose "external taxes"). Franklin misjudged America's reaction to the Townsend Acts, and Boston's refusal to submit to the Townsend duties, highlighted by the Boston Tea Party of December 1773. The uproar in New England caused Britain to send troops to Boston.

The course and natural progress in England seems to be, first, the appointment of needy men as officers, for others do not care to leave England; then, their necessities make them rapacious, their office makes them proud and insolent, their insolence and rapacity make them odious, and, being conscious that they are hated, they become malicious; their malice urges them to continual abuse of the inhabitants in their letters of administration, representing them as disaffected and rebellious, and (to encourage the use of severity) as weak, divided, timid, and cowardly. Government believes all; thinks it necessary to support and countenance its officers; their quarrelling with the people is deemed a mark and consequence of their fidelity; they are therefore more highly rewarded and this makes their conduct still more insolent and provoking.

The resentment of the people will, at times and on particular incidents, burst into outrages and violence upon such officers, and this naturally draws down severity and acts of further oppression from hence. The more the people are dissatisfied, the more rigor will be thought necessary; severe punishments will be inflicted to terrify; rights and privileges will be abolished; great force will then be required to secure execution and submission; the expenses will become enormous; it will then be thought proper, by fresh exactions, to make the people defray it; thence, the British nation and government will become odious, and the subjections to it will be deemed no longer tolerable; war ensues, and the bloody struggle will end in absolute slavery to America, or ruin to Britain by the loss of her colonies; the latter more probable, from America's growing strength and magnitude.

But, as the whole empire must, in either case, be greatly weakened, I cannot but wish to see much patience and the utmost discretion in our general conduct, that the fatal period may be postponed, and that, whenever this catastrophe shall happen, it may appear to all mankind, that the fault has not been ours. History shows that, by these steps, great empires have crumpled heretofore; and the late transactions we have so much cause to complain of show, that we are in the same train, and that, without a greater share of prudence and wisdom than we have seen both sides to be possessed of, we shall probably come to the same conclusion.

Visit to Northern England:
Their work was extremely hard

Temple came home to us during the Christmas vacation from school. He seemed to improve continually, and more and more engaged the regard of all that were acquainted with him, by his pleasing, sensible, manly behaviour. I had debates with myself whether or not I would continue in London any longer. I grew homesick, and being in my 67TH year, I began to apprehend some infirmity of age might attack me, and make my return impracticable. I had also some important affairs to settle before my death, a period I thought at the time could not be far distant. I had indeed so many good friends in England, that I could spend the remainder of my life among them with pleasure, if it were not for my American connections, and the incredible affection I retained for that dear country, from which I had so long been in a state of exile.

We had a severe and tedious winter in England in 1771. By late April, there had not been yet the smallest appearance of spring. Not a bud had push'd out, nor a blade of grass. The turnips that us'd to feed the cattle had been destroy'd by the frost. The hay in most parts of the country was gone, and the cattle were perishing for want, the lambs dying by thousands, thro' cold and scanty nourishment.

In May, I made with friends a journey of a fortnight to Manchester, Sheffield, Leeds, and Birmingham, and return'd in time to be at Court on the King's birthday. My journey was of use to my health, the air and exercise giving me fresh spirits. In Manchester, we visited a school for poor boys and admired its old and well stocked library, and then embarked in a luxurious horse-drawn boat on the Duke of Bridgewater's canal and followed it to its end in the Duke's coal mines. The last thousand yards to the first coal face were subterranean. We observed the miners at work in cramped quarters, and watched the coal being brought out and loaded into a forty-ton canal boat, which a single horse then pulled to Manchester. There the canal again tunneled under a hill to a large hole, running up to the surface, through which a water-driven crane unloaded the coal.

The next morning we left Manchester and reached Leeds by evening. We visited the cloth hall at Leeds, where each subscriber had a booth for selling his wares on market days; the hall was then almost empty because of the demands of the American trade, which had raised the price by sixpence a yard. We then called on Joseph Priestley, who made some very pretty electrical experiments and demonstrated some of the different properties of different kinds of air. The next day we arrived at Sheffield, where we went to see a factory making articles of silver-plated copper, and in the afternoon to inspect the iron-works and manufacture of tin plate at nearby Rotherham, and to visit an ironworks where we saw them melting the iron ore and casting pots, etc., which is perform'd as in America. The labourers received 14*d.* per day; their work was extremely hard, and in summer time must have been very disagreeable.

The next day we came to Birmingham. On the morning we visited Matthew Boulton's Soho ironworks*, which employed 700 people. Its products were extremely varied, from farthing buttons to hundred-guinea ornaments. We went through his works but there was

---

* Boulton manufactured the revolutionary steam engines of partner James Watt (1736–1819). "I sell here, Sir, what all the world desires to have— Power," he told James Boswell in 1776. See James Boswell, *Life of Johnson* (Oxford University Press, 1998), 704.

not much and we stayed so little that it was almost impossible for the strongest memory to retain it. The work of a button had 5 or 6 branches in it, each of which is performed in a second of time. He likewise worked plated goods—watch rings and all kinds of hardware, all of which was performed by machinery in such a manner that children and women performed the greatest part of it.

THE RECOLLECTION OF MY LIFE

In June of 1771, I went out of town and spent a few days among the pleasing society of Rev. Shipley, the Bishop of St. Asaph, and his family. I returned home, breathing with reluctance the smoke of London, and regretting my leaving the sweet air of Twyford. I promised myself the happiness of returning to that most agreeable retirement. In August, I spent three weeks of uninterrupted leisure in Hampshire at my friend's home, where I began writing the recollection of my life. The bishop's lady knew what children and grandchildren I had, their ages, &c. So when I was about to return to London, she insisted on my staying one day longer that we might together keep my grandson's birthday. At dinner, among other nice things, we had a floating island, which they always particularly had on the birthdays of any of their own six children, who were all but one at table, where there was also a clergyman's widow then above 100 years old. The chief toast of the day was Master Benjamin Bache, to which the bishop's lady added, "That he may be as good a man as his grandfather." I said I hope'd he would be much better!

My wife sent to the bishop's family a fine large gray squirrel from America, a favourite amusement that they called Mungo. Unfortunately, a year later, the squirrel got out of his cage and was rambling over a common three miles from home when he met a man with a dog. The dog pursuing him, the squirrel fled to the man for protection, running up to his shoulder, but the man shook him off and set the dog on him, thinking him to be, as he said afterwards, some varmint or other. So poor Mungo died and was buried in the garden. I lamented the loss of the squirrel with the Shipley children, and wrote the following epitaph (knowing that "skugg" is a common name by which all squirrels are called in England, as all cats are called "puss"):

> Here skugg
> Lies snug
> As a bug
> In a rug.

IRELAND AND SCOTLAND IN A MOST WRETCHED SITUATION

I set out for Ireland, where Mr. Jackson and I were invited to dine with Mr. Hillsborough. He was extremely civil, wonderfully so to me whom he had not long before abus'd to Mr. Strahan as a factious turbulent fellow, always in mischief, a Republican, enemy to the King's service, and what not. He drank my health and was otherwise particularly civil. I knew not what to make of it, unless that he foresaw a storm on account of his conduct to America, and was willing to lessen beforehand the acrimony with which the people and friends of that country might possibly pursue him. At length Lord Hillsborough, who was extremely disliked by all his brother ministers, resigned and Lord Dartmouth took his place in August, 1772, to the great satisfaction of all the friends of America.

In Ireland I had a good deal of conversation with the patriots; they were all on the American side of the question in which I endeavour'd to confirm them. The lower people in that unhappy country were in a most wretched situation, thro' the restraints on their trade and manufactures. Their houses were dirty hovels of mud and straw, their clothing rags, and their food little beside potatoes.

In Scotland, I spent 5 days with Lord Kames, Blair Drummond near Stirling, two or three days at Glasgow, two days at Carron Iron Works, and the rest of the month in and about Edinburgh, lodging at David Hume's, who entertain'd me with the greatest kindness and hospitality, as did Lord Kames and his lady.

So much general comfort and happiness in America

In Scotland things made a better appearance and seemed on the mending hand, yet half the people there wore neither shoes nor stockings, or wore them only in church. In both countries, a small part of society were landlords, great noblemen and gentlemen, extremely opulent, living in the highest affluence and magnificence, while the bulk of the people were tenants, extremely poor, living in the most wretchedness. In many parts of England, too, the working poor were miserably fed, clothed and lodged. I thought often of the happiness of New England, where every man was a freeholder, had a vote in public affairs, lived in a tidy warm house, and had plenty of good food and fuel, with whole clothes from head to foot, the manufactury perhaps of his own family. Long may they continue in this situation! Had I never been in the American colonies, but was to form my judgment of civil society by what I had seen in Ireland and Scotland, I should never have advised a nation of savages to admit of civilization: For in the possession and enjoyment of the various comforts of life, compar'd to these people, every American Indian is a gentleman: And the effect of this kind of civil society seemed only to be the depressing of multitudes below the savage state that a few may be rais'd above it. In short I saw no country of Europe where there was so much general comfort and happiness as in America, Holland perhaps excepted: tho' it may be, some parts of Germany or Switzerland which I had not seen are as well provided as Holland.

MY THEORY OF COLDS: I WOULD SIT IN MY CHAMBER WITHOUT ANY CLOTHES WHATEVER

I return'd again to London after my journey of some months in Ireland and Scotland with Mr. Jackson. My constitution, and too great confinement to business during the winter, seemed to require the air and exercise of a long journey once a year, which I have practiced for many years. I have long been satisfy'd from observation that besides the general colds now termed influenzas, which may possibly spread by contagion as well as by a particular quality of the air, people often catch colds from one another when shut up together in small closed rooms, coaches, &c. and when sitting near and conversing so as to breathe in each other's transpiration, the disorder being in a certain state. I think too that it is the frowzy corrupt air from animal substances, and the perspired matter from our bodies, which, being long confin'd in beds not lately used, and clothes not lately worn, and books long shut up in closed rooms, obtains that kind of putridity which infects us, and occasions the colds observed upon sleeping in, wearing, or turning over, such beds, clothes or books, and not their coldness or dampness. From these causes, but more from too full living with too little exercise, proceed, in my opinion, most of the disorders which, for 100 years past, the English have called colds. Travelling in our severe winters, I have suffered cold sometimes to an extremity only short of freezing, but this did not make me catch cold. And for moisture, I have been in the river every evening two or three hours for a fortnight together, when one would suppose I might imbibe enough of it to take cold if humidity could give it; but no such effect followed. Boys never catch cold by swimming.

The cold bath has long been in vogue in London as a tonic; but the shock of the cold water always appeared to me, generally speaking, as too violent: and I found it much more agreeable to my constitution, to bathe in another element, I mean cold air. With this view I would rise early almost every morning, and sit in my chamber, without any clothes whatever, half an hour or an hour, according to the season, either reading or writing. This practice was not in the least painful, but on the contrary, agreeable; and if I returned to bed afterwards, before I dressed myself, as sometimes happened, I made a supplement to my night's rest, of one or two hours of the most pleasing sleep that could be imagined. I found no ill consequences whatever resulting from it, and at least I did not injure my health, if it did not in fact contribute much to its preservation. If I can persuade people not to be afraid of their real friend *fresh air*, and can put them more upon their guard against those insidious enemies, *full living* and *indolence*, I imagine they may be somewhat happier and more healthy.

It is of the greatest importance to prevent diseases, since the cure of them by physic is so very precarious. In considering the different kinds of exercises, I have thought that the *quantum* of each is to be judged of, not by time or by distance, but by the degree of warmth it produces in the body: Thus I observe that if I am cold when I get into a carriage in a morning, I may ride all day without being warmed by it, and that if on horseback my feet are cold, I may ride some hours before they become warm; but if I am ever so cold on foot, I cannot walk an hour briskly, without glowing from head to foot by the quickened circulation; I have been ready to say that there is more exercise in one mile's riding on horseback, than in five in a coach; and more in one mile's walking on foot, than in five on horseback; to which I may add, that there is more in walking one mile up and down stairs, than in five on a level floor. The two latter exercises may be had within doors, when the weather discourages going abroad; and the last may be had when one is pinched for time, as containing a great quantity of exercise in a handful of minutes. The dumb bell is another exercise of the latter compendious kind; by the use of it I have in forty swings quickened my pulse from 60 to 100 beats in a minute, counted by a second watch.

I seldom dined at home in winter

As to my situation in London, nothing could have been more agreeable, especially as I had hoped for less embarrassment from the new minister. My company was so much desired that I seldom dined at home in winter, and could have spent the whole summer in the country houses of inviting friends if I chose it. Learned and ingenious foreigners who came to England almost all made a point of visiting me, for my reputation was still higher abroad than in England; several of the foreign ambassadors assiduously cultivated my acquaintance, treating me as one of their corps, partly, I believe, from the desire they had from time to time of hearing something of American affairs, an object of importance in foreign courts, who began to hope Britain's alarming power would be diminished by the defection of her colonies. The King, too, had lately been heard to speak of me with great regard. I received a letter from Paris, where I was chosen *Associe etranger* (foreign member) of the Royal Academy there. There were but eight of these *Associes etrangers* in all Europe, and those of the most distinguished names for science. These were flattering circumstances, but a violent longing for home sometimes seized me, which I could no other way subdue but by promising myself a return the next spring or next fall. I had some important affairs to settle at home, and considering my double expenses, I hardly thought my salaries fully compensated the disadvantages. The change in the government, however, being thrown into the balance determined me to stay another winter.

Out of debt... out of danger

I was fortunate enough not to suffer in the general wreck of credit in 1772. My two banking houses, Browns & Collinson, and Smith,

Wright & Grey, stood firm, and they were the only people in the City in debt to me, so I lost nothing by the failure of others; and being out of debt myself my credit could not be shaken by any run upon me: Out of debt, as the proverb says, was being out of danger. But I did hazard a little in using my credit with the bank to support that of a friend as far as £5000, for which I was secur'd by bills of the Bank of Douglas, Herod & Company, accepted by a good house; and therefore I call it only hazarding a little.

SECURING BUILDINGS FROM LIGHTNING

The philosophical transactions of the Royal Society were published containing the report of the means of securing an edifice against lightning. It reported that attaching pointed conductors to secure buildings from lightning had been in use near 20 years in America, and had become so common that numbers of them appeared on private houses in every street of the principal towns, besides those on churches, public buildings, magazines of powder, and gentlemen's seats in the country. Thunderstorms are much more frequent in America than in Europe, and hitherto there had been no instance of a house so guarded being damaged by lightning: for wherever it has broken over any of them, the point has always receiv'd it, and the conductor has convey'd it safely into the earth, of which we have now five authentic instances. In England the practice made a slower progress, damage by lightning being less frequent, and people of course less apprehensive of danger from it.

In late 1772, I settled into my new apartment on Craven Street, but removing and sorting my papers and placing my books and things was a troublesome job. I was amaz'd to see how many books had grown upon me since my return to England. I had brought none with me, yet had now a roomful, many collected in Germany,

Holland and France, and consisting chiefly of such as contain knowledge that might hereafter be useful to America.

A fifth edition of my book, *Experiments and Observations*, was printed in England, and a new translation of my book was printed in Paris, being the third edition in France. To the French edition they prefix'd a print of me, which, tho' a copy of that per Chamberlain, had such a French countenance that one might have taken me for one of that lively nation.*

An experiment to still the waters

I had, when a youth, read and smiled at an account of a practice among the seamen to still the waves in a storm by pouring oil into the sea. At length, being in Clapham, where there is, on the common, a large pond, which I observed to be one day very rough with the wind, I fetched out a cruet of oil, and dropt a little of it on the water. I saw it spread itself with surprising swiftness upon the surface, but the effect of smoothing the waves was not produced; for I had applied it first on the leeward side of the pond where the waves were the largest, and the wind drove my oil back upon the shore. I then went to the windward side, where they began to form; and there the oil, tho' not more than a teaspoon full, produced an instant calm, over a space several yards square, which spread amazingly, and extended itself gradually till it reached the lee side, making all that quarter of the pond, perhaps half an acre, as smooth as a looking glass. After this, I contrived to take with me, whenever I went into the country, a little oil in the upper hollow joint of my bamboo cane, with which I might repeat the experiment as opportunity should offer; and I found it constantly to succeed.

---

* The frontispiece was based on the Martinet engraving of the original painting in 1762 by Mason Chamberlain.

ALL THEIR SCHEMES OF LIFE WERE OVERTHROWN!

Two of the only descendants of my grandfather Thomas remained in England that retained that name of Franklin: Thomas, a widower and dyer working in Leicestershire, and Sally, his only child. Sally Franklin lived with me at Craven Street for six years, and married a farmer's son. I do miss her, as she was nimble-footed and willing to run errands and wait upon me. She was very serviceable to me for some years, so that I did not keep a man [servant].

Mrs. Stevenson's daughter Polly married a very worthy young man, Mr. Hewson. They bore two boys and a girl. The children lived in the same street as I did, the eldest calling on me sometimes to tell "God-Papa" little stories of what he had seen there; his pretty prattle made me the more long to see my own grandchildren, but alas, I found myself staying another winter absent from my family.

In 1774, Mrs. Hewson had the smallpox, the eldest child in the common way very full, the youngest by inoculation lightly, and all recovered. But Mr. Hewson came down with a terrible fever, which baffled the skill of our best physicians, and died suddenly, a great loss to the family. He was an excellent man, ingenious, industrious, useful, and belov'd by all that knew him. He was just established in a profitable growing business, with the best prospects of bringing up his young family advantageously. They were a happy couple! But now all their schemes of life were overthrown!

"I'LL BE HANGED IF THIS IS NOT ONE OF YOUR AMERICAN JOKES!"

In 1773, I wrote two pieces in England for the Public Advertiser on American Affairs, designed to expose the conduct of the country toward the colonies in a short, comprehensive, and striking view, and stated in out-of-the-way forms, as most likely to take the general attention. The first was called *Rules by which a great empire may be reduced to a small one;* the second, *An Edict of the King of Prussia.** In my mind, I preferred the first, but I found that others generally preferred the second. I was not suspected as the author, except by one or two friends; and heard the latter spoken of in the highest terms as the keenest and severest piece that had appeared in a long time. What made it the more noticed in Britain was that people in reading it were, as the phrase is, taken in, till they had got half through it, and imagined it a real edict, to which mistake I suppose the king of Prussia's character must have contributed. I was down at Lord Le Despencer's when the post brought the day's papers. Mr. Paul Whitehead (the author of *Manners*) was there too. He would always run early through all the papers, and tell the company what he found remarkable. He had them in another room, and we were chatting in the breakfast parlour when he came running in to us, out of breath, with the paper in his hand and said, "Here! Here's news for ye! Here's the king of Prussia claiming a right to this kingdom!" All stared, and I as much as any body; and he went on to read it. When he had read two or three paragraphs, a gentleman said, "Damn his impudence! I dare say, we shall hear by next post that he is upon his march with one hundred thousand men to back this." Whitehead, who was very shrewd, soon after began to smoke it out, and looking in my face said, "I'll be hanged if this is not some of your American jokes upon us." The reading went on, and ended with abundance of laughing, and a general verdict that it was a fair hit: and the piece was cut out of the paper and preserved in my lord's collection.

---

* A hoax purporting to be a declaration issued by King Frederick II, wherein the Germans imposed a 4.5% duties on all English trade to pay for a war between Prussia and France; sent felons in German jails to England; etc., ending that all these measures were "copied" from the rules imposed by the British on the American colonies.

The affair of the Hutchinson letters[*]

Having been from my youth more or less engag'd in public affairs, it has often happened to me in the course of my life to be censured sharply for the part I took in them. Such censures I have generally passed over in silence, conceiving, when they were just, that I ought not to defend myself against them; and when they were undeserved, that a little time would justify me. Spots of dirt thrown upon my character I suffered, while fresh, to remain; I did not choose to spread them by endeavouring to remove them, but rely'd on the vulgar adage, that they would all rub off when they were dry. Much experience has confirm'd my opinion of the propriety of this conduct, for notwithstanding the frequent and sometimes virulent attacks which the jostling of party interests have drawn upon me, I have had the felicity of bringing down to a good old age, as fair a reputation (may I be permitted to say it) as most public men that I have known, and have never had reason to repent my neglecting to defend it.

I should therefore have taken no notice of the invective of the Solicitor General, nor of the abundant abuse of the [Hutchinson] papers, were I not urged by my friends to furnish the public with a knowledge of the facts.

Herein is the background: It has long appeared to me that the only true British politics were those which aim'd at the good of the *whole British empire*, not those who sought the advantage of one part thro'

---

[*] The Hutchison letters refer to correspondence between Thomas Hutchinson, lieutenant governor of Massachusetts, and Andrew Oliver, Hutchinson's brother-in-law, and a British undersecretary, Thomas Whately in 1773. In these letters, Hutchinson urged strict measures against the Americans, including the abridgment of English liberties. Franklin's disclosure of these private letters to American patriots created an uproar, resulting in Franklin's dismissal as Postmaster General and his return to America as an advocate of independence.

the disadvantage of the others. Therefore all measures of procuring gain to the mother country arising from loss to her colonies, and all gain to the colonies arising from or occasioning loss to Britain; every abridgement of the power of the mother country where that power was not prejudicial to the liberties of the colonists; and ever diminution of the privileges of the colonists, where they were not prejudicial to the welfare of the mother country, I condemned as improper, partial, unjust, and mischievous, tending to create dissensions, and weakening that union, on which the strength, solidity, and duration of the empire greatly depended. And I opposed, as far as my little powers went, all measures either in Britain or in America, that had such tendency. Hence it often happened to me, that while I was thought in England to be too much of an American, I have in America been deemed too much of an Englishman.

Every affront is not worth a duel

At the same time, I am a mortal enemy to arbitrary government and unlimited power. I am naturally very jealous for the rights and liberties of my country, and the least encroachment of those invaluable privileges is apt to make my blood boil. In conformity with these principles, and as agent for the colonies, I opposed the Stamp Act, and endeavoured to obtain its repeal, as an infringement of the rights of the colonists, and of no real advantage to Britain, since she might ever be sure of greater aids from our voluntary grants than she could expect from arbitrary taxes. Moreover, by losing our respect and affection, on which much of her commerce with us had depended, she would lose more in that commerce than she could possibly gain by such taxes, as it was detrimental to the harmony which had till then so happily subsisted. To keep up a deference for the King, and a respect for the British nation, I industriously, on all occasions, in my letters to America, represented the measures that were grievous to the colonies as being neither Royal nor national measures, but the schemes of an administration which wished to recommend itself for its ingenuity in finance, or to avail itself of new revenues in creating, by places and pensions, new dependencies; I judged at the time that the King was a good and gracious prince, and the people of Britain our real friends. I represented the people of America as fond of Britain, concerned for its interest and glory, and without the least desire of a separation from it. I trusted the general prudence of our countrymen would realize that by our growing strength we advanced fast to a situation in which our claims must be allow'd; that by a premature struggle we might be crippled and kept down another age; that, as between friends every affront is not worth a duel, and between nations every injury is not worth a war, so between the governed and the governing, every mistake in government, every encroachment on rights, is not worth a rebellion.

Hutchinson: "There must be an abridgment of what are called English liberties."

In 1773, I opposed (without success) the tax on tea. The act passed in spite of me. The tea was burnt in Boston.* Parliament, incensed, closed the port, and by various acts took away privileges, forbid fishing, &c. I could not but see with concern the sending of troops to Boston; their behaviour to the people there gave me infinite uneasiness as I apprehended the worst of consequences, a breach between the two countries, till I was, to my great surprise, assured by a gentleman of character and distinction (whom I shall not name†) that the measure and all other grievances we complain'd of took their rise

---

* Actually, the tea was thrown into Massachusetts Bay.
† Franklin never disclosed who gave him the Hutchinson letters; historians do not know his source.

not from government in Britain, but were proposed, solicited and obtained by some of the most respectable among the Americans themselves! As I could not readily assent to the probability of this, he undertook to convince me, and he hoped thro' me (as their agent), my countrymen. Accordingly he call'd on me some days after, and produc'd to me these very letters, written by Lt. Govr. Hutchinson, Secry. Oliver, and others, which became since the subject of so much discussion, especially a letter by Govr. Hutchinson stating that the American crisis required "an abridgment of what are called English liberties."

I sent the original letters to my particular correspondents in America; fearing to be known as the person who sent them, I insisted on their keeping the circumstance a secret, and engag'd them not to print them. I wrote, "I must hope that great care will be taken to keep the people quiet, lest violence provide an excuse for increasing armed coercion." But my correspondent related to me how the Assembly having heard of them, oblig'd him to produce them, and that they afterwards did nevertheless print them. The effect of the governors' letters on the minds of the people in New England, when they came to be read there, was precisely what had been expected and proposed by sending them over. It was seen that the grievances which had been so deeply resented as measures of the mother country were in fact the measures of two or three of their own people.

I KEPT SILENT TILL I HEARD OF A SECOND DUEL

The news being arriv'd in England of the divulging those letters in America, great inquiry was made as to who had transmitted them. Mr. John Temple, a gentleman of customs, was accus'd of it in the papers, but he vindicated himself. A public altercation ensu'd upon it between him and a Mr. William Whately, brother and executor to the person to whom it was supposed the letters had been originally writ-

ten, and who was suspected of communicating them, on the supposition that by his brother's death they might have fallen into his
hands. I suffered that altercation to go on without interfering, supposing it would end, as other newspaper debates usually do, when
the parties and the public should tire of them. But this debate unexpectedly produced a duel. The gentlemen were parted; Mr. Whately
was hurt, but not dangerously. This, however, alarmed me, and made
me wish I had prevented it. But imagining all now over between
them, I still kept silence, till I heard that the duel was understood to
be unfinish'd, as having been interrupted by persons accidentally
near, and that it would probably be repeated as soon as Mr. Whately,
who was mending daily, had recover'd his strength. I then thought it
high time to interpose; and as the quarrel was for the public opinion,
I took what I thought the shortest way to settle the opinion with
regard to the parties, by publishing a letter to the printer. This declaration of mine was at first generally approv'd, except that some
blam'd me for not having made it sooner, so as to prevent the duel;
but I had not the gift of prophecy; I could not have foreseen that the
gentlemen would fight; I did not even foresee that either of them
could possibly take it ill of me. I imagin'd I was doing them a good
office, in clearing both of them from suspicion, and removing the
cause of their difference. I should have thought it natural for them
both to have thank'd me; but I was mistaken as to one of them. The
return this worthy gentleman made me was, without the smallest
previous notice, warning, complaint or request whatsoever, to clap
upon my back a chancery suit. His bill set forth that Whately was the
administrator of the goods and chattels of his late Brother Thomas
Whately; that some letters had been written to his said brother by the
governors Hutchinson and Oliver; that by carrying on the trade of a
printer I had by my agents printed and published the same letters in
America, and that he had applied to me to deliver up to him the said
letters and desist from printing and publishing the same, and account

with him for the profits thereof; that he was in hopes I would have complied with such a request, but so it was that I had refused, &c, contrary to equity and good conscience and to the manifest injury and oppression of him the complainant. The gentleman himself must have known that every circumstance of this accusation toward me was totally false. Those as little acquainted with law as I was (who indeed never before had a suit of any kind) may wonder at this as much as I did. But I learned that in Chancery, tho' the defendant must swear to the truth of every point in his answer, the plaintiff is not put to his oath, or obliged to have the least regard to truth in his bill, but was allowed to lie as much as he pleased. I did not understand this, unless it be for the encouragement of business.

My answer to the oath was that the letters in question had been given to my agents for the House of Representatives of the Province of Massachusetts Bay; that when given to me I did not know to whom they had been addressed, no address appearing upon them; nor did I know before that any such letters had existed; that I had not been for many years concern'd in printing; that I did not cause the letters to be printed, nor direct the doing it; that I did not erase any address that was on the letters, nor did I know that any other person had made such erasure; that I did as agent to the province transmit (as I apprehended it my duty to do) the said letters to one of the committee with whom I had been directed to correspond, inasmuch as in my judgment they related to matters of great public importance to that province, and were put into my hands for that purpose; that I had never been applied to by the complainant as asserted in that bill, and had made no profit of the letters, nor intended to make any, &c.

This they call Government!

It had about this time become evident that all thought of reconciliation with the colony of the Massachusetts Bay had been laid aside;

that severity was resolv'd; and that decrying and vilifying the people of that country, and me their agent among the rest, was quite a court measure. It was the tone with all the ministerial folks to abuse them and me in every company and in every newspaper; and it was intimated to me as a thing settled, long before it happened, that the Assembly's petition for removal of the governors was to be rejected, the Assembly censur'd, and myself, who had presented it, to be punished by the loss of my place in the post office. For all this I was therefore prepar'd: But the attack from Mr. Whately was, I own, a surprise to me. Without the slightest provocation, I could not have imagined any man base enough to commence of his own motion such a vexatious suit against me. My finances were not sufficient to cope at law with the Treasury, especially when administration had taken care to prevent my constituents of New England from paying me any salary, or reimbursing me any expenses, by a special instruction to their governor, nor to sign any warrant for that purpose on the Treasury there. The injustice of thus depriving the people in New England of the use of their money to pay an agent acting in their defense, while the governor with a large salary out of the money extorted from them by Act of Parliament was enabled to pay plentifully solicitors Mauduit and Wedderburn to abuse and defame them and their agent, is so evident as to need no comment. And this they call Government.

Meeting in the Cockpit

I heard from all quarters that the ministry and all the courtiers were highly enraged against me for transmitting those letters. I was called an incendiary, and the papers were filled with invectives against me. Hints were given me that there were some thoughts of apprehending me, seizing my papers, and sending me to Newgate prison. I was well informed that a resolution had been taken to deprive me of my place; it was only thought best to defer it till after the hearing. My situation was a little hazardous, for if by some accident the troops and people of New England had come to blows, I would probably have been taken up to prison. I was frequently caution'd to secure my papers, and, by some, advis'd to withdraw. But I ventured to stay in compliance with the wish of others; and I confided, in my innocence, that the worst which could happen to me would be an imprisonment on suspicion, tho' that was a thing I would much desire to avoid, as it would be expensive and vexatious, as well as dangerous to my health.

On the 29th of January 1774 a hearing on the matter began in the Cockpit.* The council for the petition opened the matter with great strength of argument as well as propriety and decency. The solicitor-general Mr. Wedderburn then went into what he called "a history of the province for the last ten years," and bestowed plenty of abuse upon it, mingled with encomium on the governors. But the favorite part of his discourse was leveled at me, and I stood the butt of his invective and ribaldry for near an hour. Not a single lord checked and recalled this orator to the business before them; but on the contrary (a very few excepted) they seemed to enjoy highly the entertainment, and frequently burst out into loud applause. This part of his speech was thought so good, that they later printed it in order to defame me everywhere, and particularly to destroy my reputation in America. But I did not find that I lost a single friend on the occasion. All visited me repeatedly with affectionate assurances of unaltered respect. The day following I received a written notice from the Secretary of the General Post Office, that his majesty's Postmaster General found it necessary to dismiss me from my office of Deputy Postmaster General in North America. Thus I was depriv'd in the post office of £300 sterling a year. I was obliged to resign as agent of the colonies of Pennsylvania, Massachusetts, New Jersey, and Georgia, in the whole £1500 sterling per

---

* The Privy Council of Plantation Affairs met in a room known as the Cockpit, famous for cockfights held there during the time of Henry VIII.

annum, and orders were sent to the King's governors not to sign any warrants on the Treasury for the arrears of my salaries.

My son saw everything with government eyes

I wrote my son William in New Jersey to acquaint him that my office of Deputy Postmaster had been taken from me, that there was no prospect of his being ever promoted to a better government, and that he would be better if he were well settled in his farm. I wrote, "'tis an honester and more honourable and more independent employment." However, he continued in office, which did no favour to me or him. I knew he would execute his office with fidelity, but I thought independence more honourable than any service, and that in the arbitrary state of American affairs, he would find himself in no comfortable situation, and would be better if he disengaged himself. But I knew his sentiments differed from mine on these subjects. He was a thorough courtier, a government man who saw everything with government eyes.

Journal of negotiations in London*

During the whole of my time in England I was otherwise much taken up by friends calling on me continually to inquire news from America; members of both houses of Parliament to inform me what passed in the houses, and discourse with me on the debates, and on motions made or to be made; merchants of London and of the manufacturing and port towns on their petitions; the Quakers upon theirs, &c. &c., so that I had no time to take notes of almost anything. I write this

---

* The remainder of this chapter is drawn from a condensed version of Franklin's "Journal of Negotiations in London," which he wrote while on board the Pennsylvania Packet Capt. Osborne, bound to Philadelphia, March 22, 1775.

account therefore chiefly from recollection, in which doubtless much must have been omitted, from deficiency of memory; but what there is, I believe to be pretty exact; except that discoursing with so many different persons about the same time on the same subject, I may possibly have put down some things as said by or to one person, which passed in conversation with another.

During the recess of the last Parliament, which had pass'd the severe acts* against the province of the Massachusetts Bay, the minority, having been quite sensible of their weakness as an effect of their want of union among themselves, began to think seriously of a coalition. They saw in the violence of these American measures, if persisted in, a hazard of dismembering, weakening, and perhaps ruining the British Empire. In conversations with several of the principals among the minority of both houses, I beseeched and conjured most earnestly not to suffer, by their little misunderstandings, so glorious a fabric to be demolished by these blunderers.

From the time of the affront given me at the Council Board in January 1774, I remained in London but never attended the levee of any minister. I made no justification of myself from the charges brought against me: I made no return of the injury by abusing my adversaries, but held a cool sullen silence, reserving myself to some future opportunity, for which conduct I had several reasons not necessary here to specify.

COUNTRIES REMOTE FROM THE EYE
OF GOVERNMENT ARE NOT WELL GOVERNED

When I first came to England in 1757, I made several attempts to be introduc'd to Lord Chatham (Mr. Pitt, at that time First Minister) on account of my Pennsylvania business, but without success. He was

---

* Commonly referred to as the Intolerable Acts in the colonies.

then too great a man, or too much occupy'd in affairs of great moment. I was therefore oblig'd to content myself with a kind of non-apparent and unacknowledg'd communication thro' Mr. Potter and Mr. Wood, his secretaries, who seem'd to cultivate an acquaintance with me by their civilities, and drew from me what information I could give relative to the American war, with my sentiments occasionally on measures that were proposed or advised by others. I afterwards considered Mr. Pitt as an inaccessible: I admired him at a

William Pitt: "I admired him at a distance, but made no more attempts for a nearer acquaintance."

distance, but made no more attempts for a nearer acquaintance. I had only once or twice the satisfaction of hearing thro' Lord Shelburne (and, I think, Lord Stanhope) that he did me the honour of mentioning me sometimes as a person of respectable character.

Toward the end of August 1774, returning from Brighthelmstone, I called to visit my friend Mr. Sargent at his seat, Halsted, in Kent, agreeable to a former engagement. He let me know that he had promised to conduct me to Lord Stanhope's at Chevening, who expected I would call on him when I came into the neighborhood. We accordingly waited on Lord Stanhope that evening, who told me Lord Chatham desired to see me. This was done accordingly. That truly great man, Lord Chatham, receiv'd me with abundance of civility, inquired particularly into the situation of affairs in America, spoke feelingly of the severity of the laws against Massachusetts, gave me some account of his speech in opposing them and express'd great regard and esteem for the people of that country, who he hop'd would continue firm and united in defending by all peaceable and legal means their constitutional rights. I assur'd him that I made no doubt they would do so. I then took occasion to remark to him that, in former cases, great empires had crumbled first at their extremities from this cause: that countries remote from the seat and eye of government which therefore could not well understand their affairs for want of full and true information, had never been well governed, but had been oppress'd by bad governors, on presumption that complaint was difficult to be made and supported against them at such a distance. Hence such governors have been encouraged to go on, till their oppressions became intolerable.

He mention'd an opinion, prevailing in Britain, that America aimed at setting up for itself as an independent state, or at least to get rid of the Navigation Acts. I assur'd him that having more than once travelled almost from one end of the continent to the other and kept a great variety of company, eating, drinking and conversing with them freely, I never had heard in any conversation from any person drunk or sober, the least expression of a wish for a separation, or hint that such a thing would be advantageous to America. In fine he express'd much satisfaction in my having call'd upon him, and particularly in the assurances I had given him that America did not aim at independence at that time.

A certain lady desiring to play with me at chess

The new Parliament was to meet the 29TH of November, 1774. About the beginning of that month, being at the Royal Society, Mr. Raper, one of our members, told me that there was a certain lady who had a desire of playing with me at chess, fancying she could beat me, and had requested him to bring me to her: it was, he said, a lady with whose acquaintance he was sure I should be pleas'd, a sister of Lord Howe's, and he hop'd I would not refuse the challenge. I said I had been long out of practice, but would wait upon the lady when he and she should think fit. I named the Friday following. He call'd accordingly. I went with him, play'd a few games with the lady, whom I found of very sensible conversation and pleasing behaviour, which induc'd me to agree most readily to an appointment for another meeting a few days after, tho' I had not the least apprehension that any political business could have any connection with this new acquaintance.

A time was appointed on which I was to have my second chess party with the agreeable Mrs. Howe. After playing as long as we lik'd,

Franklin and Mrs. Howe: "There was a certain lady who had a desire of playing with me at chess, fancying she could beat me."

we fell into a little chat, partly on a mathematical problem, and partly about the new Parliament that had just met when she said, "And what is to be done with this dispute between Britain and the colonies? I hope we are not to have a civil war."

"They should kiss and be friends," *said I.* "What can they do better? Quarrelling can be of service to neither but is ruin to both."

"I have often said," *said she,* "that I wish'd government would employ you to settle the dispute for 'em. I am sure nobody could do it so well."

Said I, "I thank you for the good opinion, but the ministers will never think of employing me in that good work; they choose rather to abuse me."

"Ay," *said she,* "they have behav'd shamefully to you."

The good character of Lord Howe

On Christmas day, I again visited Mrs. Howe. She told me as soon as I came in, that her brother, Lord Howe,* wish'd to be acquainted with me; that he was a very good man, and she was sure we should like each other. I said I had always heard a good character of Lord Howe, and should be proud of the honour of being known to him. "He is but just by," said she. "Will you give me leave to send for him?"

"By all means, Madam, if you think proper," said I.

She rang for a servant, wrote a note, and Lord Howe came in a few minutes later. After some extremely polite compliments, he said he had a particular desire at this time, viz., the alarming situation of our affairs with America, which no one, he was persuaded, understood better than myself; that it was the opinion of some friends of his, that

---

* Caroline Howe (c1721–1814), sister of Lord Richard Howe, was married to John Howe. Franklin and John Adams met with General Richard Howe in July 1776, in an unsuccessful attempt to reconcile the two nations.

no man could do more toward reconciling our differences than I could if I would undertake it; that I had been very ill treated by the Ministry, and that he had much disapproved of their conduct toward me.

Mrs. Howe offered to withdraw, but I begg'd she might stay, as I desired no secret in a business of this nature that I could not freely confide to her prudence. I had never conceiv'd a higher opinion of the discretion and excellent understanding of any woman on so short an acquaintance. I begg'd his lordship to give me credit for a sincere desire of healing the breach between the two countries; that I would cheerfully and heartily do everything in my power to accomplish it; but that I apprehended from the King's speech and from the measures talk'd of, that no intention or disposition of the kind existed in the present ministry. He wished me to draw up in writing some propositions containing the terms on which I conceived a good understanding might be obtained and established, which propositions, as soon as prepared, we might meet to consider. It was concluded to be best to meet at his sister's, who readily offered her house for the purpose. I undertook accordingly to draw up something, and so for that time we parted, agreeing to meet at the same place again on the Wednesday following.

I returned to town the next Wednesday in time to meet Lord Howe at the hour appointed. I apologiz'd for my not being ready with the paper I had promis'd, by my having been kept longer than I intended in the country. We had, however, a good deal of conversation on the subject, and his Lordship told me he could now assure me of a certainty that there was a disposition in Lord North and Lord Dartmouth to accommodate the differences with America and to listen favourably to any propositions that might have a probable tendency to answer that salutary purpose. He then ask'd me what I thought of sending person or persons over to America, commission'd to inquire into the grievances of America, converse with the leading people, and endeavor with them to agree upon some means of composing our differences. I said that a person of rank and dignity, who had a character of candor, integrity and wisdom, might possibly, if employed in that service, be of great use.

Mrs. Howe said, "I wish, brother, you were to be sent thither in such a service; I should like that much better than Lord Howe going to command the army there."

"I think, Madam," said I, "they ought to provide for Lord Howe some more honorable employment."*

What the French call *spitting in the soup*

Lord Howe then took out of his pocket a paper, and offered it to me said, smiling, "If it is not an unfair question, may I ask whether you know any thing of this paper?" Upon looking at it, I saw it was a copy in D. Barclay's hand of the *Hints*.[†] I said that I had seen it, that I had been consulted on the subject, and had drawn up that paper. He said he was rather sorry to find that the sentiments express'd in it were mine, as it gave him less hopes of promoting my assistance in the wish'd-for reconciliation, since he had reason to think there was no likelihood of the admission of these propositions. He hop'd however that I would reconsider the subject, and form some plan that would be acceptable in Britain. He expatiated on the infinite service it would be to the nation, and certainly I might with reason expect any reward in the power of government to bestow. This to me was what the French call *spitting in the soup*. However, I promis'd to draw some sketch of a plan at his request, tho' I much doubted, I said, whether it would be

---

* Lord Richard Howe had recently been named commander in chief of the British Navy in the American colonies and would soon travel to New York for that purpose.

[†] *Hints for Conversation*, a paper written by Franklin outlining seventeen specific points regarding the various differences between Britain and the colonies. See PBF 21:366-68 (Dec. 4–6, 1774).

thought preferable to that he had in his hand. He was willing to hope that it would, but that it might possibly propose something improper to be seen in my handwriting; therefore it would be best to send it to Mrs. Howe, who would copy it and send the copy to him to be communicated to the Ministry, and return me the original. This I agreed to.

In a day or two, I sent the paper in a cover directed to the Honorable Mrs. Howe, who transcrib'd and sent the paper to Lord Howe in the country, and she return'd me the original. In this paper, I stated that Britain would lose nothing by repealing the acts that the Congress asked to have repealed; that Britain should authorize the next Congress and send a royal representative of stature to preside over it; then, having thus strengthened the hands of Britain's American friends, ask for such reciprocal concessions as the government deemed necessary.

On the following Tuesday, Jan. 3, 1775, I receiv'd a note from her, enclosing a letter she had received from Lord Howe, which stated that the propositions of "our worthy friend" would make agreement much more difficult than he had anticipated, but he would forward them to the Ministry. Sometime after, perhaps a week, I received a note from Mrs. Howe desiring to see me. I waited upon her immediately, when she show'd me a letter from her brother, desiring to know from me whether the Assembly would approve of my payment of the tea as a preliminary redress of their grievances. As Mrs. Howe proposed sending [a packet] to her brother that evening, I wrote immediately the following answer, which she transcrib'd and forwarded: "The proposition remains unchanged, and my constituents would not agree to pay for the tea before redress of their grievances."

A VISIT FROM THIS GREAT MAN FLATTERED MY VANITY

On the Sunday being the 29ᵀᴴ of January his Lordship Chatham came to town and called upon me in Craven Street. He brought with him his plan [of reconciliation with the American colonies] transcrib'd in the form of an act of Parliament, which he put into my hands, requesting me to consider it carefully. He was pleas'd to say that he knew no man so thoroughly acquainted with the subject, or so capable of giving advice upon it; that he thought the errors of the ministers in American affairs had been often owing to their not obtaining the best information; that, therefore, though he had considered the business thoroughly in all its parts, he was not so confident of his own judgment, but that he came to set it right by mine, as men set their watches by a regulator. He stayed with me nearly two hours, his equipage waiting at the door, and being there while people were coming from church it was much taken notice and talk'd of, as was every little circumstance that men thought might possibly affect American affairs. Such a visit from so great a man, on so important a business, flattered not a little my vanity; and the honour of it gave me the more pleasure, as it happen'd on the very day 12 months earlier, that the Ministry had taken so much pains to disgrace me before the Privy Council.

"ONE OF THE MOST MISCHIEVOUS ENEMIES THIS COUNTRY HAS KNOWN"

On Wednesday Lord Stanhope, at Lord Chatham's request, call'd upon me and carry'd me down to the House of Lords, which was very soon full. Lord Chatham, in a most excellent speech, introduc'd, explain'd and supported his plan. When he sat down, Lord Sandwich* rose, and in a petulant vehement speech oppos'd its being receiv'd at all, and gave his opinion that it ought to be immediately rejected with the contempt it deserv'd; that he could never believe it

---

* Sandwich was also a member of the Hell-Fire Club, a secret society that held black masses and orgies (Franklin was an occasional guest). The sandwich is named after him, as are the Sandwich (Hawaiian) Islands.

to be the production of any British peer; that it appear'd to him rather the work of some American; and turning his face toward me, who was leaning on the bar, said that he fancied he had in his eye the person who drew it up, one of the bitterest and most mischievous enemies this country had ever known. This drew the eyes of many Lords upon me: but as I had no inducement to take it to myself, I kept my countenance as immovable as if my features had been made of wood. Then several other Lords of the administration gave their sentiments also for rejecting it, of which strong opinion was also the wise Lord Hillsborough. Lord Chatham, in his reply to Lord Sandwich, took notice of his illiberal insinuation that the plan was not the person's who had proposed it, and declar'd that it was entirely his own, a declaration he thought himself the more oblig'd to make, as many of their Lords appear'd to have so mean an opinion of it.

THE GREATEST OF ABSURDITIES

To hear so many of these *hereditary* legislators declaiming so vehemently against, not the adopting merely, but even the consideration of a proposal [of Lord Chatham's] so important in its nature, offered by a person of so weighty a character, one of the first statesmen of the age, who had taken up his country when in the lowest despondency, and conducted it to victory and glory thro' a war with two of the mightiest kingdoms in Europe; to hear them censuring a plan not only for their own misunderstandings of what was in it, but for their imaginations of what was not in it, which they would not give themselves an opportunity of rectifying by a second reading; to perceive the total ignorance of the subject in some, the prejudice and passion of others, and the willful perversion of plain truth in several of the ministers; and upon the whole to see it so ignominiously rejected by so great a majority, and so hastily too, in breach of all decency and prudent regard to the character and dignity of their body as a third part of the national legislature, gave me an exceeding mean opinion of their abilities, and made their claim of sovereignty over three millions of virtuous sensible people in America, seem the greatest of absurdities, since they appear'd to have scarce discretion enough to govern a herd of swine. Hereditary legislators, thought I. There would be more propriety, because less hazard of mischief, in having hereditary professors of mathematics! But this was a hasty reflection: for the *elected* House of Commons was no better, nor ever would be while the electors receive money for their votes, and pay money wherewith ministers may bribe their representatives when chosen.

WE DID NOT WISH FOR WAR...

After this proceeding I expected to hear no more of any negotiation for settling our differences amicably. Yet in a day or two I received a note from Mr. Barclay, requesting a meeting at Dr. Fothergill's the 4ᵀᴴ of February 1775 in the evening. I attended accordingly, and was surpris'd by being told that a very good disposition appear'd in the administration; that the *Hints* had been considered, and several of them thought reasonable, and that others might be admitted with small amendments. The good doctor, with his usual philanthropy, expatiated on the miseries of war, that even a bad peace was preferable to the most successful war; that America was growing in strength, and whatever she might be oblig'd to submit to at present, she would in a few years be in a condition to make her own terms. Mr. B. hinted how much it was in my power to promote an agreement; how much it would be to my honor to effect it; and that I might expect not only restoration of my old place [Postmaster General], but almost any other I could wish for, &c. I need not tell those who know me so well how improper and disgusting this language was to me. The doctor's was more suitable. Him I answered that we did not wish for war, and desir'd nothing but what was reasonable and necessary for our security and well being.

We had not at this time a great deal of conversation upon these points, for I shortened it by observing that while the Parliament claim'd and exercis'd a power of altering our constitutions at pleasure, there could be no agreement; for we were render'd unsafe in every privilege we had a right to, and were secure in nothing. And it being hinted by them how necessary an agreement was for America, since it was so easy for Britain to burn all our sea port towns, I grew warm, and said that the chief part of my little property consisted of houses in those towns; that they might make bonfires of them whenever they pleased; that the fear of losing them would never alter my resolution to resist to the last that claim of Parliament; and that it behoov'd this country to take care what mischief it did us, for sooner or later it would certainly be obliged to make good all damages with interest. The doctor smil'd, as I thought, with some approbation of my discourse, passionate as it was, and said he would certainly repeat it to Lord Dartmouth.

About this time, I was asked by a nobleman what would satisfy the Americans. I answered that it might easily be comprised in a few Re's:

	-call your forces,
	-store Castle William,
	-pair the Damage done to Boston,
	-peal your unconstitutional acts,
	-nounce your pretensions to tax us,
Re	-fund the duties you have extorted; after this
	-quire, and
	-ceive payment for the destroyed tea, with the
	voluntary grants of the colonies, and then
	-joice in a happy
	-conciliation.

On the morning of Feb. 20, it was currently and industriously reported all over the town that Lord North would that day make a motion in the House for healing all differences between Britain and

America. The House was accordingly very full and the members full
of expectation. At length a motion was made. My old proposition of
giving up the regulating duties to the colonies was in part to be found
in this motion, and many who knew nothing of that transaction, said
it was the best part of the motion. Lord North's motion stated in part,
"forbear in respect of such province or colony, to levy any duties, tax
or assessment, or to impose any further duty, tax or assessment,
except only such duties as it may be expedient to impose for the regulation of commerce." After a good deal of wild debate, they all
agreed at length in voting it by a large majority.*

BAD WEATHER DOES NOT LAST ALWAYS IN ANY COUNTRY

It was during this time I wrote the following letter to my sister Jane
Mecom of Boston:

> London, Feb. 26, 1775
>
> Dear Sister,
>
> I hope you continue well, as I do, thanks to God. Be of good
> courage. Bad weather does not last always in any country. Suppos-
> ing it may be agreeable to you, I send you a head they make here
> and sell at the china shops.† My love to your children, & to cousin
> Williams and family. I am ever
>
> Your affectionate brother,
>
> B FRANKLIN

---

* Lord North's motion ultimately did not satisfy either nation. As Franklin
  reports in the next few pages, the Americans objected, among other
  things, to Britain's right to tax the colonies.
† Probably the Wedgwood cameo of himself, made in 1775.

I heard of the death of my wife in Philadelphia

It was at this time in 1775 that I was inform'd of the loss of my old and faithful companion Debby. I received notice of her death from son William and Mr. Bache, who informed me that she was attacked by a paralytic stroke, and was released from a troublesome world three days later on the 17ᵀᴴ of December, without much pain. Everyday I become more sensible of the greatness of that loss, which cannot now be repair'd. Her death made it necessary for me to return home.

Hearing nothing from Lord Howe, I mention'd his silence occasionally to his sister, adding that I suppos'd it owing to his finding what he had propos'd to me [payment of the tea] was not likely to take place; and I wish'd her to desire him, if that was the case, to let me know it by a line, that I might be at liberty to take other measures. She did so as soon as he return'd from the country, where he had been for a day or two. I receiv'd from her a note from Lord Howe, who said he would like to see me as soon as possible. I met his Lordship at the hour appointed. He said that he had not seen me lately, as he expected daily to have something more material to say to me than had yet occurr'd, and hop'd that I would have call'd on Lord Hyde, as I had intimated I should do when I apprehended it might be useful, which he was sorry to find I had not done. I answer'd that since I had last seen his Lordship, I had heard of the death of my wife at Philadelphia, in whose hands I had left the care of my affairs there, and it was become necessary for me to return thither as soon as conveniently might be.

The next morning (March 1), I accordingly met early with Lord Hyde, who receiv'd me with his usual politeness. We talk'd over a great part of the dispute between the countries. I found him ready with all the newspaper and pamphlet topics, of the expense of settling our colonies, the protection afforded them, the heavy debt under which Britain labour'd, the equity of our contributing to its alleviation; that many people in England were no more represented than we were, yet all were tax'd and govern'd by Parliament, &c &c. I answer'd all, but with little effect. He had hop'd, he said, that Lord North's motion would have been satisfactory, and ask'd what could be objected to in it. I reply'd that the terms of it were that we should grant money till Parliament had agreed we had given enough, without having the least share in judging of the propriety of the measures for which it was to be granted; that these grants were also to be made under a threat of exercising a claimed right of taxing us at pleasure, and compelling such taxes by an armed force, if we did not give till it should be thought we had given enough; that the proposition was similar to a highwayman who presents his pistol and hat at a coach window, demanding no specific sum, but if you will give all your money or what he is pleas'd to think sufficient, he will civilly omit putting his own hand into your pockets. If not, there is his pistol. Besides, a new dispute had now been raised by the Parliament's pretending to a power of altering our charters and established laws, which was of still more importance to us than their claim of taxation, as it had set us all adrift, and left us without a privilege we could depend upon but at their pleasure. This was a situation we could not possibly be in. And thus ended this conversation.

WE WERE TREATED WITH THE UTMOST CONTEMPT

A little before I left London, being at the House of Lords to hear a debate in which Lord Camden was to speak, and who indeed spoke admirably on American affairs, I was much disgusted from the ministerial side by many base reflections on American courage, religion, understanding, &c. in which we were treated with the utmost contempt, as the lowest of mankind, and almost of a different species from the English of Britain; but particularly the American honesty was abused by some of the Lords, who asserted we were all knaves, and wanted only this dispute to avoid paying our debts; that if we had any sense of equity or justice, we should offer payment of the tea &c. I went home somewhat irritated and heated, and, partly to retort upon that nation, on the article of equity, I drew up a memorial to present to Lord Dartmouth before my departure to America; but when consulting my friend Mr. Walpole upon it, who was a member of the House of Commons, he looked at it and at me several times alternately, as if he apprehended me a little out of my senses. As I was in the hurry of packing up, I requested him to take the trouble of showing it to his neighbor Lord Camden, and asking his advice upon it, which he kindly undertook to do; and returned it to me, with a note, wherein Walpole stated his opinion that the memorial would endanger my life and exasperate the nation.

CONVERSATION EVERYWHERE TURNS UPON THE SUBJECT OF AMERICA

Mr. Walpole called at my house the next day, and hearing I was gone to the House of Lords, came there to me, and repeated more fully what was in his note, adding that it was thought my having no instructions directing me to deliver such a protest would make it appear still more unjustifiable, and be deemed a national affront. I had no desire to make matters worse, and being grown cooler, took the advice so kindly given me.

The day before I left London for America, I passed the time with Dr. Priestley in the London Coffee House, without any other company, and much of the time was employed reading American newspapers, especially accounts of the reception which the "Boston Port Bill"* met with

---

* The Boston Port Bill, passed in March 1774, closed the port of Boston and prohibited the landing or discharging of goods, wares, and merchandise.

in America. In some places they were printed with a black border, and were cried about the streets under the title "a barbarous, cruel, bloody and inhuman murder." The newspapers reported accounts of citizens shutting up their houses, and the obnoxious law being burned with great solemnity, similar to what was done in the time of the Stamp Act. Several newspapers were ornamented with a figure of a snake, exactly divided into thirteen parts, each inscribed with the initials of one of the colonies, and underneath the words *join or die*.* As I read the addresses to the inhabitants of Boston, I dreaded a war with the mother country that could last *ten years*. I attempted to take every measure in my power to prevent a rupture between the two countries, but it was not to be, and tears wet my cheeks.

That evening I received a note from Dr. Fothergill, with some letters to his friends in Philadelphia. In that note he desired me to get those friends and others together, and tell them of the negotiations, and assure them that the government's attitude offered no hope of real conciliation. The doctor, in the course of his daily visits among the great in the practice of his profession, had full opportunity of being acquainted with their sentiments, the conversation every where at this time turning upon the subject of America. "Farewell," he wrote, "and befriend this infant, growing empire with the utmost exertion of thy abilities, and no less philanthropy, both which are beyond my powers to express. A happy prosperous voyage!"

---

* Franklin was the first to publish a "join or die" political cartoon, on May 9, 1754, in *The Pennsylvania Gazette*. At the time there were eight colonies. See PBF 5:272, 275.

Chapter Four

Congress and the Declaration of Independence, 1775-76

I arrived at home on the evening of the 5ᵗʰ of May, 1775, after a pleasant passage of 6 weeks, the weather constantly so moderate that a London wherry* might have accompanied us all the way. I observed the warmth of the sea-water by Fahrenheit's thermometer in crossing the gulf stream. The gulf stream is little known by European navigators, and yet of great consequence, since in going to America they often get into that stream and unknowingly stem it, whereby the ship is much retarded and the voyage lengthened enormously. A vessel from Europe to North America may shorten her passage by avoiding the stream, in which the thermometer is very useful; and a vessel from America to Europe may do the same by the same means of keeping in it. Thus, passages are generally shorter from America to Europe than from Europe to America. I published a chart of the gulf stream in French and English to acquaint them with this fact.[†]

I brought over a grandson with me, William Temple, and his father took him to Amboy in New Jersey, but to be returned to me in

---

* Large boat.

[†] Franklin published a chart of the gulf stream in America and Europe to help sea captains reduce the time crossing the Atlantic ocean by a week or more. See PBF 15:246 and FPR 41:u384ff.

September to prosecute his studies in college. I found my daughter Sally and Mr. Bache well and in good health; my children affectionately dutiful and attentive to everything that might be agreeable to me; with three very promising grandsons, in whom I took great delight, the youngest boy, Will, like an infant Hercules, the strongest and stoutest child of his age I had ever seen. He had a little gun, marched with it, and whistled at the same time by way of fife. Were it not for our public troubles, my felicity would have been perfect.

Nothing thought of but arms

I found at my arrival all America, from one end of the 13 united provinces to the other, busily employed in learning the use of arms, all trade and business, building, improving, &c. being at a stand, and nothing thought of but arms. The attack upon the country people near Boston* by the army had rous'd everybody, and exasperated the whole continent; the tradesmen of Philadelphia were in the field twice a day, at five in the morning, and six in the afternoon, disciplining with the utmost diligence, all being volunteers. We had three battalions, a troop of light horse, and a company of artillery, who made surprising progress. The same spirit appeared everywhere and the unanimity was amazing.

The Massachusetts governor call'd an assembly to propose Lord North's pacific plan, but General Gage drew the sword, and the war commenced. It is said that he carried the sword in one hand, and the olive branch in the other; and it seemed he chose to give us a taste of the sword first. All America was exasperated by his conduct, and more firmly united than ever.

---

* The battle of Lexington and Concord on April 19, 1775, the beginning of war with Great Britain.

A delegate to Congress

The next morning I was unanimously chosen by the General Assembly of Pennsylvania as a delegate for the Continental Congress. I was a member of the first Congress in Albany in 1754, and had proposed the first plan of union of the colonies. The new Congress met the next week, and the delegates were directed to consult together on the critical and alarming situation in the colonies and recommend the further measures of obtaining redress of American grievances with Great Britain. The numerous visits of old friends and the public business devoured all my time: we met at nine in the morning, and often sat till four. I was also upon a Committee of Safety, appointed by the Pennsylvania Assembly to put the province in a state of defense, which met at six in the morning. The members attended closely without being bribed to it, by either salary, place or pension, or the hope of any; which I mention for reflection on the difference between a virtuous people who have public spirit and an old corrupt one, who have not so much as an idea that such a thing exists in nature. There was not a dissenting voice among us in any resolution for defense, and our Army which was already formed would soon consist of above 20,000 men.

They are a barbarous tyranny

The Congress met at a time when all minds were exasperated by the perfidy of General Gage, and his attack on the country people, the burning of houses, and our seaport towns, and other treacherous conduct. Without the least necessity, they barbarously plundered and burnt a fine, undefended town, opposite to Boston, called Charlestown, consisting of about 400 houses, many of them elegantly built; some sick, aged and decrepit poor persons, who could not be carried off in time, perish'd in the flames. In all our wars, from our first settlement in America to the present time, we never received so much damage from the Indian savages, as in this one day from these. In this ministerial war against us, all Europe was conjur'd not to sell us arms or ammunition, that we would be found defenseless, and more easily murdered. The humane Sir W. Draper, who had been hospitably entertain'd in every one of our colonies, proposed, in his papers call'd the *Traveller*, to excite the domestic slaves to cut their master's throats. Dr. Johnson, a court pensioner, in his *Taxation no Tyranny** adopted and recommended that measure, together with another of hiring the Indian savages to assassinate our planters in the back settlements. These are by no means acts of a legitimate government: they are acts of barbarous tyranny and dissolve all allegiance.

MAKE YOURSELF SHEEP
AND THE WOLVES WILL EAT YOU

Thus, propositions from Britain attempting an accommodation were not much relished; and it was with difficulty that we carried another humble petition to the crown, to give Britain one more chance, one opportunity of recovering the friendship of the colonies; which however she did not have sense enough to embrace, and thus had lost them forever. We were preparing and determined to run all risks rather than comply with her mad demands. As Britain began to use force, it seemed absolutely necessary that we should be prepared to repel force with force. It is a true old saying that *make yourself sheep and the wolves will eat you*: to which I may add another, *God helps them that help themselves*. The General was secure, I suppose, that we would never be able to return the outrage in kind; but the defeat of a great body of his troops by the country people at Lexington, and

---

* *Taxation no Tyranny: An Answer to the Resolutions and Address of the American Congress* was an anonymous pamphlet written in 1775 by the celebrated Dr. Samuel Johnson.

the action at Bunker's Hill, in which they were twice repulsed, and the third time gained a dear victory, was enough to convince the ministers that the Americans can fight, and that this was a harder nut to crack than they imagined. Britain, at the expense of three millions, killed 150 Yankees in this campaign, which is £20,000 a head; and at Bunker's Hill she gained a mile of ground, half of which she lost again by our taking post on Ploughed Hill. During the same time 60,000 children were born in America. From these data his mathematical head could easily calculate the time and expense necessary to kill us all, and conquer our whole territory.

YOU ARE NOW MY ENEMY, AND I AM...YOURS

I addressed (but never sent) the following letter to Mr. Strahan:

> Philada. July 5, 1775
>
> Mr. Strahan,
>
> You are a member of Parliament, and one of that majority which has doomed my country to destruction. You have begun to burn our towns, and murder our people. Look upon your hands! They are stained with the blood of your relations! You and I were long friends: You are now my enemy, and
>
> I am,
>
> Yours,
>
> B FRANKLIN

If a temperament naturally cool and phlegmatic can, in old age, be thus heated, you will judge by that of the general temper in America, which was little short of madness.

*Franklin's famous letter to William Strahan was
shown to friends in Philadelphia but never sent.*

Great frugality and great industry became fashionable: Gentlemen
who used to entertain with two or three courses began to pride themselves in treating with simple beef and pudding. By these means, and
the stoppage of our consumptive trade with Britain, we were better
able to pay our voluntary taxes for the support of our troops. Our
savings in the article of trade amounted to nearly five million sterling
per annum.

On July 21, 1775 my proposed sketch of the Articles of Confederation and perpetual union for the United Colonies of North America
was read before Congress, the purpose of which was to bind them-

selves for their common defense and the security of their liberties and properties, the safety of their persons and families, and their mutual and general welfare.*

The Congress adjourned on August 2ᴺᴰ to the 5ᵀᴴ of September, which allowed me to settle a new general post office, having been chosen Postmaster General of the United Colonies of North America, and a treaty to be held with the Indians on the Ohio, besides smaller businesses, all to be transacted by the time the Congress was to meet again. They voted me 1,000 dollars per annum as Postmaster General, and I devoted the whole sum to the assistance of the disabled in defense of their country, that I might not be suspected to have the least interested motive for keeping the breach open. I obtained from our Committee of Safety a permission to send to Boston what powder remain'd in our hands. I dispatched a wagon with 2,400 lb. weight, there being at this time an extreme scarcity of lead in Pennsylvania.

In addition to muskets, I suggested adding bows and arrows as good weapons, because a man may shoot as truly with a bow as with a common musket; he can discharge 4 arrows in the time of charging and discharging one bullet; his object is not taken from his view by the smoke of his own side; a flight of arrows seen coming upon them terrifies, and disturbs the enemy's attention to his business; an arrow sticking in any part of a man, puts him *hors du combat* till 'tis extracted; and bows and arrows are more easily provided everywhere than muskets and ammunition.

---

* Franklin's proposed articles formed the basis of the Articles of Confederation that were adopted by Congress on November 15, 1777, when Franklin was in France. The Articles took effect on March 1, 1781 after all 13 states approved the document, and served as the law of the land until May 1788, when the U.S. Constitution became law. Franklin's most controversial proposal was Article IX, which established an executive council of 12 persons to run the country. See PBF 22:120-25.

We gave up our commerce with Britain; our last ships, 34 sail, left port the 9ᵀᴴ of September. And in our minds we gave up our sea coast to the barbarous ravages of English ships of war; but the internal country we promised to defend. It was, with our liberties, worth defending, and would itself by its fertility enable us to defend it. By cutting off our trade, Britain had thrown us to the Earth, whence, like Antaeus, we would rise yearly with fresh strength and vigour. Agriculture is the great source of wealth and plenty. As part of our defense, I designed *chevaux de frise** to hinder the approach of warships, a new invention which served to close ports. It had great effect, and the English were held up by it for seven weeks.

The Rattlesnake as a symbol of America: "Don't tread on me"

I observed on one of the drums belonging to the Marines being raised that there was painted a rattlesnake, with this modest motto under it, "Don't tread on me." It occurred to me that the rattlesnake, being found in no other quarter of the world besides America, might therefore be chosen to represent her. Having frequently seen the rattlesnake, I ran over in my mind every property by which she was distinguished. I recollect that her eye excelled in brightness, that of any other animal, and that she has no eye-lids. She may therefore be esteemed an emblem of vigilance. She never begins an attack, nor, when once engaged, ever surrenders; she is therefore an emblem of magnanimity and true courage. As if anxious to prevent all pretensions of quarrelling with her, the weapons with which nature has furnished her she conceals in the roof of her mouth, so that, to those who are unacquainted with her, she appears to be a most defenseless

---

* A defensive structure used to obstruct cavalry, consisting of a movable obstacle composed of barbed wire or spikes attached to a wooden frame.

animal, and even when those weapons are shown and extended for her defense, they appear weak and contemptible; but their wounds however small, are decisive and fatal. Conscious of this, she never wounds till she has generously given notice, even to her enemy, and cautioned him against the danger of treading on her.

I confess I was wholly at a loss what to make of the rattles, till I went back and counted them and found them just thirteen, exact the number of the colonies united in America; and I recollected too that this was the only part of the snake that increases in numbers; perhaps it might be only fancy, but, I conceited the painter had shown a half formed additional rattle, which, I suppose, might have been intended to represent the province of Canada.

'Tis curious and amazing to observe how distinct and independent of each other the rattles of this animal are, and yet how firmly they are united together, so as never to be separated but by breaking them to pieces. One of those rattles singly is incapable of producing sound, but the ringing of thirteen together is sufficient to alarm the boldest man living. The rattlesnake is solitary and associates with her kind only when it is necessary for their preservation. In winter, the warmth of a number together will preserve their lives, while singly they would probably perish. The power of fascination attributed to her, by a generous construction, may be understood to mean that those who consider the liberty and blessing which America affords, and once come over to her, never afterwards leave her, but spend their lives with her. She strongly resembles America in this, that she is beautiful in youth and her beauty increaseth with her age, "her tongue also is blue and forked as the lightning, and her abode is among impenetrable rocks."

I communicated my sentiments to a neighbour of mine, who had a surprising readiness at guessing everything which related to public affairs. He instantly declared it as his sentiments that the Congress meant to allude to Lord North's declaration in the House of Commons that he never would relax his measures until he had brought America to his feet, and to intimate to his Lordship that were she brought to his feet, it would be dangerous treading on her.

This bustle is unsuitable to age

I was as happy as I could be under the fatigue of more business than was suitable for my age at 70. I was immers'd in so much business that I had scarce time to eat or sleep. The greatest part of the year 1775 I was almost every day 10 or 12 hours of the day employ'd in business or consultation with many other persons sitting in a closed room, and had no leisure for exercise. The winter I promised myself to bring with it some relaxation with my family. Such bustle is unsuitable to age. I wrote Rev. Shipley how happy I was in the sweet retirement of Twyford, where my only business was a little scribbling in the garden study, writing my memoirs, and my pleasure of conversation with the Reverend and his amiable family!

In October 1775, I travelled with two other delegates of the Congress to Cambridge, Massachusetts, to confer with General Washington* on sundry matters. The General requested that the committee would represent to the Congress the necessity of having money constantly and regularly sent. For my own part I was for the most prudent parsimony of the public treasury. I was not terrified by the expense of this war. A little more frugality, or a little more industry would with ease defray it, I said. Suppose it cost £100,000 a month or £1,200,000 a year: If 500,000 families would each spend a shilling a week less, or earn a shilling a week more, they would pay the whole sum without otherwise feeling it. Forbearing to drink tea would save three fourths of the money; and 500,000 in a week would pay the rest.

---

* Franklin and Washington were friends and corresponded frequently on war issues.

I learned that there were as many cheerful countenances among those who were driven from house and home at Boston or lost their all at Charlestown, as among other people. Not a murmur was heard, that if they had been less zealous in the cause of liberty they might still have enjoy'd their possessions. During the hostilities, my sister Jane Mecom left her house lock'd up with the furniture in it, and moved to Warwick with Mrs. Greene. I purchased a carriage and horses with the intent of taking my sister home with me to Philadelphia.

The real author of *Common Sense*

In early 1776, I received a letter from Gen. Charles Lee in New York regarding a now famous pamphlet that made a great impression in America called *Common Sense*, which Mr. Lee called a "masterly, irresistible performance" in making the case for independence. I told Mr. Lee that Mr. Thomas Paine, an ingenious honest man, was the real author of *Common Sense*, and that Mr. Paine had requested a line of introduction to him, which I did willingly, knowing his sentiments were not very different from the General's.

The ancient Roman and Greek orators could only speak to the number of citizens capable of being assembled within the reach of their voice: their writings had little effect because the bulk of the people could not read. Now, by the press, we can speak to nations; and good books and well written pamphlets have great and general influence. The facility with which the same truths may be repeatedly enforced by placing them daily in different lights in newspapers which are every where read, gives a great chance of establishing them. And we now found that it was not only right to strike while the iron was hot, but that it was very practicable to heat it by continually striking.

I always valu'd Mr. Paine's friendship. Instead of repenting that I was his introducer into America, I valued myself on the share I had in procuring for it the acquisition of so useful and valuable a citizen, by which the revolution was greatly forwarded.

From the Pennsylvania Assembly to Congress

It would be a happiness to me if I could serve the public duly in all stations; but aged as I was, I felt myself unequal to so much business, and on that account thought it my duty to decline part of it, and therefore requested that the Pennsylvania Assembly dispense my further attendance as one of the Committee of Safety, tho' remaining a delegate to Congress.

In Congress, I was made a member of the Committee of Secret Correspondence. We immediately appointed Mr. Silas Deane to go to France to transact business, commercial and political, on behalf of the thirteen united colonies, and to meet with individuals friendly to our cause. Mr. Deane would appear in the character of a merchant and make immediate application to Monsieur de Vergennes, *Minister des Affairs Etrangeres*, and then acquaint him that the Congress, finding

Silas Deane: "Finding that it was not practicable for the continent of America to furnish the arms and ammunition necessary for its defense, Mr. Deane was dispatched by our authority to apply to France for a supply."

that it was not practicable for the continent of America to furnish the arms and ammunition necessary for its defense, Mr. Deane was dispatched by our authority to apply to France for a supply.

A trip to Canada

The Committee then reported that they had conferr'd with a person just arriv'd from Canada. He said that when the Canadians first heard of the dispute they were generally on the American side; but that by the influence of the Clergy and the Noblesse, who had been continually preaching and persuading them against America, they were brought into a state of suspense or uncertainty as to which side to follow. He thought it would be a great service if some persons from the Congress were sent to Canada, and the Congress thereby appointed three commissioners to go to Canada, of which number I was honoured to be one, along with Charles Carroll and Samuel Chase. Our purpose was to convince them of the uprightness of our intentions, and that the people of Canada should set up such a form of government to produce their happiness, and that it was our earnest desire to adopt them into our union as a sister colony. We set out the week of March 11 to Canada by way of New York, a journey of 500 miles. We were detain'd in Saratoga by the lakes in which the unthaw'd ice obstructed navigation, which caused me to undertake a fatigue that at my time of life proved almost too much for me. We were in a small open boat, where I was kept sitting without exercise for many days.

We were in a critical and most irksome situation

After some difficulty and delay in getting thro' the ice of Lake George, we arrived in Montreal in late April, and were very politely received by General Arnold, who commanded the post. The smallpox was in the army, and General Thomas* had unfortunately never had it. It is impossible to give a just idea of the lowness of the Continental credit there from the want of hard money, and the prejudice it was to our affairs. Not the most trifling service could be procured without an assurance of instant pay in silver or gold. The inhabitants had experienced frequent breaches of promise and were determined to trust our people no farther. The general apprehension was that we would be driven out of the province as soon as the King's troops arrived. We urged the forwarding of a large sum to Canada (we believed twenty thousand pounds would be necessary); otherwise it would be impossible to continue the war in this country, or to expect the continuance of our interest with the people there, who began to consider the Congress as bankrupt as their cause was desperate. I advanced to General Arnold and others £353 in gold out of my own pocket on the credit of Congress, which was of great service in procuring provisions for our army, but we concluded that till the arrival of more money, it seemed improper to propose the federal union of this province with the others, as the few friends we had there would scarce venture to exert themselves in promoting it, till they saw our credit recover'd, and a sufficient army arrived to secure the possession of the country. We reported that without a speedy supply of money, our forces would suffer exceedingly from the want of many necessaries, particularly flour. It was very difficult to keep soldiers under proper discipline without paying them regularly. We recommended that if hard money could not be procured and forwarded with dispatch to Canada, it would be advisable to withdraw our army and fortify the passes on the lakes to prevent the enemy, and the

---

*John Thomas was promoted to Major General in March 1776, but died of smallpox in late May. See PBF 22:415n.

Canadians, if so inclined, from making irruptions into and depredations on our frontiers. We also learned that the army was entirely without surgeons. We had daily intimations of plots hatching and insurrections intended for expelling us, on the first news of the arrival of a British army. We were in a critical and most irksome situation, pestered hourly with demands great and small that we could not answer, in a place where our cause had the majority of enemies, the garrison weak, and a greater [demand] would, without money, increase our difficulties. Forwarding provisions was the absolute necessity, or the army must starve, plunder, or surrender.

On the 10ᵀᴴ of May, five ships of war arrived from Quebec, with an enemy of less than a thousand. Our forces were so dispersed that no more than two hundred could be collected at headquarters. In this situation a retreat was inevitable and made in the utmost confusion with the loss of our cannon on the batteries, provisions, five hundred stand of small arms, and a batteau load of powder. Two days later I took leave of the other two commissioners to return home, having grown daily more feeble, with symptoms of the gout. I was afflicted with a succession of boils, sometimes two or three together, each when heal'd left round about it spots of scurff, which obstinately continu'd. I could hardly have got along but for Mr. Carroll's friendly assistance and tender care of me. It was with the utmost difficulty I got a conveyance, the country being all afraid to be known to assist us with carriages, but I arrived in New York safe on the evening of May 26. I met two officers from Philadelphia with a letter from the Congress to the commissioners, and a sum of hard money. I opened the letter and seal'd it again, directing them to carry it forward to Boston and Canada.

We were obliged to quit Canada, being too much of a bold thing to block up Quebec a whole winter with an army much inferior in numbers to the garrison, and our troops sent too late to support them, or having had the smallpox, being much disabled by that distemper.

I arrived home in Philadelphia, recovering from a severe fit of the gout, which kept me from Congress and company for a month, so I knew little of what had passed there. The Committee of Secret Correspondence instructed William Bingham to repair aboard a sloop on a voyage to the West Indies and endeavour to procure ten thousand good muskets, well fitted with bayonets.

IT IS THE NATURAL RIGHT OF MEN TO QUITE THE STATE

In June, I was asked to assist in the preparing of a declaration of independence before the Congress for a final separation from Great Britain. It has always been my opinion that it is the natural right of men to quit, when they please, the society or state, and the country in which they were born, and either join with another or form a new one as they may think proper. The Saxons thought they had this right when they quitted Germany and established themselves in England. I had written a draft of a resolution to Congress along these lines in late 1775, viz.:

> Whereas, whenever kings, instead of protecting the lives and property of their subjects, as is their bounded duty, do endeavour to perpetrate the destruction of either, they thereby cease to be kings, become tyrants, and dissolve all ties of allegiance between themselves and their people; we hereby further solemnly declare, that whenever it shall appear clearly to us, that the King's troops and ships now in America, or hereafter to be brought there, do, *by his Majesty's orders*, destroy any town or the inhabitants of any town or place in America, or that the savages have been by the same orders hired to assassinate our poor out-settlers and their families, we will from that time renounce all allegiance to Great Britain, so long as that kingdom shall submit to him, or any of his descendants, as its sovereign.

The Declaration of Independence:
We hazard our lives and fortunes

While recovering from boils and the gout, I was asked by Mr. Thomas Jefferson, the author of the draft of the declaration, to peruse it and suggest such alterations as necessary. I made some small revisions, striking the words "sacred and undeniable" and replacing them with "self evident" so as to read "We hold these truths to be self-evident." However, when the Declaration of Independence was under the consideration of Congress, there were many more changes and depredations on the document, such as expressions on the Scotch and the importation of slaves, which gave offense to some members, and were disapproved. I was sitting by Mr. Jefferson and saw that he was not insensible to these mutilations. I told him that I had made it a rule, whenever in my power, to avoid becoming the draughtsman of papers to be reviewed by a public body. I took my lesson from an incident which I related to him.

When I was a journeyman printer, one of my companions, an apprentice hatter, having served out his time, was about to open shop for himself. His first concern was to have a handsome signboard, with a proper inscription. He composed it in these words, "John Thompson, *Hatter, makes* and *sells hats* for ready money," with a figure of a hat subjoined; but he thought he would submit it to his friends for their amendments. The first he showed it to thought the word *"Hatter"* tautologous, because followed by the words "makes hats," which show he was a hatter. It was struck out. The next observed that the word *"makes"* might as well be omitted, because his customers would not care who made the hats. If good and to their mind, they would buy, by whomsoever made. He struck it out. A third said he thought the words *"for ready money"* were useless, as it was not the custom of the place to sell on credit. Every one who purchased expected to pay. They were parted with, and the inscription now stood, "John Thompson sells hats." *"Sells hats!"* says his next friend. Why nobody will expect you to give them away, what then is the use of that word? It was stricken out, and *"hats"* followed it, the rather as there was one painted on the board. So the inscription was reduced ultimately to "John Thompson" with the figure of a hat subjoined.

The Congress, after mature deliberation, voted unanimously for final separation from Great Britain. It was the universal demand of the people, justly exasperated by the obstinate perseverance of the Crown in its tyrannical and destructive measures. We signed the Declaration of Independence, thereby hazarding our lives and fortunes, and then distributed the Declaration for public reading, and sent copies to France and other courts of Europe.

Breaking that fine and noble China vase, the British Empire

It was impossible to think of submission to a government that had, with the most wanton barbarity and cruelty, burnt our defenseless towns in the midst of winter, excited the savages to massacre our farmers, and our slaves to murder their masters, and brought foreign mercenaries to deluge our settlements with blood. These atrocious injuries extinguished every remaining spark of affection for that parent country we once held so dear. Long had I endeavoured with unfeigned and unwearied zeal, to preserve from breaking that fine and noble China vase, the British Empire: for I knew that once broken, the separate parts could not retain even their share of strength or value that existed in the whole, and that a perfect reunion of those parts could scarce even be hoped for. I remember the tears of joy that wet my cheek, when, at his good sister's in London, Lord Howe once gave me expectations that a reconciliation might take place. I had the misfortune to find those expectations disappointed, and to be treated as the cause of the mischief I was labouring to prevent. My consolation under that groundless and malevolent treatment was, that I retained the friendship of many wise and good men in that country.

MEETING WITH LORD HOWE ON STATEN ISLAND

Upon arrival in New York, Lord Howe contacted me to effect a lasting peace and reunion between the two countries. In obedience to the order of Congress, I, along with John Adams and Edward Rutledge, had a meeting with Lord Howe upon Staten Island. His lordship entered into a discourse of considerable length which contained no explicit proposition of peace except that the colonies should return to their allegiance and obedience to the government. Lord Howe informed us that he did not have powers to consider the colonies as independent states by their Declaration of Independency; that he could not confer with them as a Congress, their not being acknowledged by the King; and that his powers were generally to restore peace and grant pardons, and to attend to complaints and representations. I reply'd that America lamented that earlier petitions to the crown had not been accepted. But the contempt with which those petitions were treated, and the cruel measures since taken, had chang'd that temper; that to propose now to the colonies a submission to the Crown of Great Britain would be fruitless. The time was past. Lord Howe said that if the colonies would not give up the system of independency, it was impossible for him to enter into any negotiations.

I wrote the following letter to Lord Howe, which ends as follows:

To the Honorable Lord Howe

Philada. July 20ᵀᴴ, 1776.

My Lord,

The well founded esteem, and permit me to say affection, which I shall always have for your Lordship, makes it painful to me to see you engag'd in conducting a war against us. I consider this war against us both unjust and unwise; and I am persuaded cool dispassionate posterity will condemn to infamy those who advised it; and that even success will not save from some degree of dishonour, those who voluntarily engag'd to conduct it. I know your great motive in coming hither was the hope of being instrumental in a reconciliation; and I believe when you find that impossible on any terms given you to propose, you will relinquish so odious a command, and return to a more honourable private station. With the greatest and most sincere respect I have the honour to be, my Lord your Lordships most obedient humble servant

B FRANKLIN

REBELLION TO TYRANTS IS OBEDIENCE TO GOD

On July 4ᵀᴴ I had been appointed to a committee, along with Thomas Jefferson and John Adams, to design the great seal of the United States. I urg'd the following to be adopted: Moses standing on the shore, and extending his hand over the sea, thereby causing the same to overwhelm Pharaoh who is sitting in an open chariot, a crown on his head and a sword in his hand. Rays from a pillar of fire in the clouds reach to Moses, to express that he acts by command of the Diety. Motto, *Rebellion to tyrants is obedience to God.**

---

* The great seal was a collaborative project, but when finalized and adopted on June 20, 1782, Franklin's design was rejected in favor of the American bald eagle as the chief symbol of the United States. However, both Franklin and Jefferson did propose one of the Latin phrases, "E Pluribus Unum" (out of many, one).

LIKE CUTTING OFF THE SPRING FROM THE YEAR

At this time, Temple proposed to go to his father, William, then gover-nor of New Jersey. As my son William adhered to the party of the King, his people had taken him prisoner, and sent him under a guard to Con-necticut, where he continued but was allow'd a district of some miles to ride about, upon his parole of honour not to quit that country. How-ever, I could not approve of Temple taking such a journey, on account of the length of the journey, his youth and inexperience, and the num-ber of sick returning on that road with the infectious camp distemper,* which made the beds unsafe, together with the loss of time in his stud-ies. I told Billy that he should return to his studies at college; that this was the time of life in which he was to lay the foundations of his future improvement, and his importance among men, and that if this season was neglected, it would be like cutting off the spring from the year.

Nothing has ever hurt me so much and affected me with such keen sensations, as to find myself deserted in my old age by my only son, William; and not only deserted, but to find him taking up arms against me in a cause where my good fame, fortune and life were all at stake. William conceived, he said, that his duty to his king and regard for his country require'd this. I ought not to blame him for differing in senti-ment with me in public affairs. We are men, all subject to errors. Our opinions are not in our power; they are form'd and govern'd much by circumstances that are often as inexplicable as they are irresistible. His situation was such that few would have censured his remaining neu-tral, tho' there are natural duties which precede political ones, and can-not be extinguish'd by them. This is a disagreeable subject. I drop it.

The several colonies approv'd and confirm'd the Declaration of Independence, and form'd their separate constitutions as independent

---

* Smallpox.

states.* A general confederation was also plann'd by the Congress whereby, for general purposes and the common defense, the power of the whole was united in that body. In August, however, I drew up a paper as President of the Convention of Pennsylvania in protest of the 17ᵀᴴ article in the first draft of the Articles of Confederation, which gives one vote to the smallest state, and no more to the largest, when the difference between them may be as 10 to 1, or greater. On behalf of the representatives of the state of Pennsylvania, I declared dissent to this article, which we regarded as unjust and injurious to the larger states, since all of them are by other articles obliged to contribute in proportion to their respective abilities. Votes in Congress should be proportion'd to the importance of each state. However, I was dissuaded from endeavoring to carry through this protest, from some prudential considerations respecting the necessary union at that time of all the states in confederation.

IT WAS LONG FORESEEN THAT WE COULD NOT HOLD NEW YORK

The Declaration of Independence was met with universal approbation, and the people everywhere seemed more animated by it in defense of their country. In the different colonies we had nearly 80,000 men in the pay of the Congress. General Washington's army was in possession of New York, but by August 1776, General William Howe had posted on Staten Island, with the troops he carried to Halifax when he was

---

* From July 15 to September 28, 1776, Franklin was president of the Pennsylvania province and the Pennsylvania Constitutional Convention. Although he played only a minor role in drafting it, the Pennsylvania constitution was signed by Franklin, who defended its controversial unicameral assembly. He carried a copy of the Pennsylvania constitution to France. See PBF 22:512–15.

driven out of Boston. Lord Richard Howe arrived there with some reinforcements, including the Hessian mercenaries from Germany. The greater part of our militia were in New Jersey, and arms and ammunitions were arriving daily, the French government having resolv'd to wink at the supplying of us, as they heartily wished us success.

The fleet under Lord Howe was vastly superiour to anything we had in the Navy way; therefore it was long foreseen that we could not hold either Long Island or New York. They landed 20,000 men or upwards on Long Island, and we had our army consisting of not more than 20,000 effective men stationed at King's Bridge, New York, and on Long Island. They, however, out general'd us and got a body of 5,000 men between our people and the lines, so that we were surrounded and came off second best; but they purchased the victory dear and such would be their ruin. General Howe then laid a trap, with which he fully expected to have caught every man we had on that island; but General Washington saw and frustrated his design by an unexpected and well conducted retreat across the Sound. This retreat was spoken of on both sides as a master stroke.

It had been previously determined to abandon New York, and most of our cannon and military stores were removed from thence in time. The enemy took possession of the city and encamped on the plains of Harlem. Since then the City of New York was set on fire and one fifth or one sixth of it reduced to ashes. They endeavoured to throw the odium of such a measure on us, but in this they failed, for General Washington, previous to the evaluation of that city, desired to know the sense of Congress, which resolved that it should be evacuated and left unhurt as they no had no doubt of being able to take it back at a future date. This would convince all the world we had no desire to burn towns or destroy cities but that we left such meritorious works to grace the history of our enemies. Upon the whole our army near New York were not sufficiently strong to cope with General Howe in the open field; they therefore entrenched themselves and acted on the defensive.

Men cannot cheerfully enter a service where they have the prospect of facing a powerful enemy and encountering the inclemencies of a hard, cold winter, without covering at the same time. These were discouraging circumstances but we had to encounter them with double diligence.

The only source of uneasiness among us arose from the number of Tories found in every state. They were more numerous than formerly and spoke more openly, very many from fear of the British force, some because they were dissatisfied with the general measures of Congress, more because they disapproved of the men in power and the measures in their respective states; but these different passions, views and expectations were so combined in their consequences that if America had fallen it would have been owing to such divisions more than to the force of our enemies.

COMMISSIONER TO FRANCE

In September, the Congress appointed me, Silas Deane, and Arthur Lee* commissioners of the United States of America to the King of France, and to deliver a plan of a treaty. I told my friend and delegate Benjamin Rush that I had only a few years to live and I was resolved to devote them to the work that my fellow citizens deemed proper for me; or speaking as old-clothes dealers do of a remnant of good, *You shall have me for what you please.*

Our appointment on this business remained a profound secret, and we were instructed to take passage to France with all speed. The Congress ordered the Secret Committee to lodge ten thousand pounds sterling in France, subject to the drafts or orders of the commissioners for their support. We believ'd that if France were to join us, there would be no danger but America would soon be established an inde-

---

* At the time Arthur Lee was a confidential American correspondent in London.

pendent empire and France, drawing from her the principal part of those sources of wealth and power that formerly flowed into Great Britain, would immediately become the greatest power in Europe. We were instructed to obtain from the French a recognition of our independency and sovereignty; to conclude treaties of peace and commerce; to prevent their taking part with Great Britain in the war; and to procure from the Court of France an immediate supply of twenty or thirty thousand muskets and bayonets, a large supply of ammunition, and either by purchase or loan eight line of battle ships of 74 and 64 guns, well manned, and fitted in every respect for service.

Before my departure, I ordered all the money I could raise, upward of three thousand pounds, into the hands of Congress. It was the first or nearly the first loan they received, which encouraged others to lend their money in support of the cause.

Being once more order'd to Europe, and about to embark on the 25ᵀᴴ of October, 1776, I wrote Rev. Samuel Cooper of Boston that I

The arrest of William Franklin: "The only source of uneasiness among us arose from the number of Tories found in every state."

had no doubt of our finally succeeding in this war by the blessing of God. It was computed that we had already taken a million sterling from the enemy, and they must soon sicken of their piratical project. Nothing would give us greater weight and importance in the eyes of the commercial states than a conviction that we might annoy on occasion their trade and carry our prizes into safe harbors; and whatever expense we were at in fortifying would soon be repaid by the encouragement and success of privateering.

A MIRACLE IN HUMAN AFFAIRS

The manner in which the whole of this business had been conducted was such a miracle in human affairs, that if I had not been in the midst of it, and seen all the movements, I could not have comprehended how it was effected. To comprehend it we must view a whole people for some months without any laws or government at all. In this state their civil governments were to be formed and an army and navy were to be provided by those who had neither a ship of war, a company of soldiers, nor magazines, arms, artillery or ammunition. Alliances were to be formed, for we had none. All this was to be done, not at leisure nor in a time of tranquility and communication with other nations, but in the face of a most formidable invasion, by the most powerful nation, fully provided with armies, fleets, and all the instruments of destruction, powerfully allied and aided, the commerce with other nations in a great measure stopped up, and every power from whom they could expect to procure arms, artillery, and ammunition, having by the influence of their enemies forbade their subjects to supply them on any pretence whatever. Nor was this all; they had internal opposition to encounter, which alone would seem sufficient to have frustrated all their efforts. The Scotch, who in many places were numerous, were secret or open foes as opportunity offered. The Quakers, a powerful body in Pennsylvania, gave every opposition that their art, abilities and influence could suggest. To these were added all those who, through contrariety of opinion, Tory principles, personal animosities, fear of so dreadful and dubious an undertaking, joined with the artful promises and threats of the enemy or lukewarm friends to the proposed revolution.

It was, however, formed and established in spite of all these obstacles, with an expedition, energy, wisdom, and success of which most certainly the whole history of human affairs has not, hitherto, given an example. To account for it we must remember that the revolution was not directed by the leaders of factions, but by the opinion and voice of the majority of the people; and that the grounds and principles upon which it was formed were known, weighed and approved by every individual of that majority. It was not a tumultuous resolution, but a deliberate system. Consequently, the feebleness, irresolution, and inaction which generally—nay, almost invariably—attends and frustrates hasty popular proceedings, did not influence this. On the contrary, every man gave his assistance to execute what he had soberly determined, and the sense of the magnitude and danger of the undertaking served only to quicken their activity, arouse their resources, and animate their exertions. Those who acted in council bestowed their whole thoughts upon the public; those who took the field did so, with what weapons, ammunition and accommodation they could procure.

In commerce, such profits were offered as tempted the individuals of almost all nations, to break through the prohibition of their governments, and furnish arms and ammunition, for which they received from a people ready to sacrifice every thing to the common cause, a thousand fold. The effects of anarchy were prevented by the influence of public shame, pursuing the man who offered to take a dishonest advantage of the want of law. So little was the effects of this situation felt, that a gentleman, who thought their deliberations on the establishment of a form of government too slow, gave it as his opinion that the people were likely to find out that laws were not necessary, and might therefore be disposed to reject what they pro-posed, if it were delayed.

The greatest revolution the world has ever seen

The consequence was, that in a few months, the governments were established; codes of law were formed, which for wisdom and justice, were the admiration of all the wise and thinking men of Europe. Ships of war were built and a multitude of cruisers was fitted out, which did more injury to the British commerce than it ever suffered before. Armies of offense and defense were formed, and kept the field, through all the rigours of winter, in the most rigorous climate. Repeated losses, inevitable in a defensive war, quickly repaired them. The enemy was everywhere resisted, repulsed, or besieged. On the ocean, in the chan-nel, in their very ports, their ships were taken, and their commerce obstructed.

This is the greatest revolution the world has ever seen, and the power that has for centuries made all Europe tremble, assisted by 20,000 German mercenaries, and favoured by the universal concur-rence of Europe to prohibit the sale of warlike stores, the sale of prizes, or the admission of the armed vessels of America, have effectually been humbled by those whom she insulted and injured, because she con-ceived they had neither spirit nor power to resist or revenge it.

We may therefore with great propriety take leave of England

I wish'd much for the restoration of peace, but it now was to be a peace of a different kind. I was fond to a folly of our British connection, and it was with infinite regret that I saw the necessity of breaking it: But the extreme cruelty with which we were treated extinguish'd every thought of returning to it, and separated us forever. England thereby lost limbs that will never grow again. We too suffered greatly, but our losses would soon be repair'd by our good government, our industry, and the fertility of our country. We could see the mischievous consequences of such a connection, and the danger of their being repeated if we should be weak enough again to enter into it: We saw them too plainly ever to listen in the least to any such proposition. We may therefore with great propriety take leave of England in those beautiful lines of Dante to the late mistress of his affections:

> O lady in whom my hope takes its root
> Thou has brought me, a slave, to freedom's state
> Through all those roads, by use of every means
> Which thou didst have the power to employ.

Chapter Five

Minister to France, 1776–78

The Treaty of Alliance

ON MY ARRIVAL I COULD SCARCELY STAND

I arrived in France, safe after a passage of 30 days, somewhat fatigued and weakened by the voyage, which was a rough one; I was badly accommodated in a miserable vessel, a Man of War called the *Reprisal*, improper for those northern seas (and which actual foundered in her return). My disorder of a dry scurff* on my head increase'd, and the boils became more frequent. I was badly fed, so that on my arrival I had scarce strength to stand. But I recovered my strength fast after my landing, and in a few days undertook the journey to Paris of about 250 miles. If the *post chaise* were as easy as the English carriage, such a journey would be no difficulty. But the carriage was a miserable one, with tired horses, the evening dark, scarce a traveller but ourselves on the road; and to make it more comfortable, the driver stopped near a wood we were to pass through, to tell us that a gang of eighteen robbers infested that wood, who but two weeks previous had robbed and murdered some travellers on that very spot.

I brought with me two grandsons: Temple, about 16, a promising youth, whom I brought with me partly to finish his education, having

---

* Probably psoriasis. See PBF 22:442n, 25:77.

a great affection for him, and partly to have his assistance as my private secretary; the other, Benny Bache, a child of 7, whom I purposed to place in boarding school, that he might learn the French language. His parents esteem'd it a happy circumstance his going with me to France during the war, for they thought that had he remain'd in America, he would have lost a deal of precious time in his education.

I WAS MADE EXTREMELY WELCOME IN FRANCE

I was made extremely welcome in France, where America has many friends, and where I was known for the useful discoveries in electricity and application of the pointed rods to prevent the terrible effects of thunderstorms. But the people were a good deal dejected with the gazette accounts of advantages obtain'd against us by the British troops. I help'd them recover their spirits a little, by assuring them that we would face the enemy, and were under no apprehensions of their two armies being able to complete their junction. I acquainted no one in France with my commission, continuing incognito as to my public character,* but I found it generally suppos'd that I was sent to negotiate, and that opinion seemed to give great pleasure, if I could judge by the extreme civilities I met with from numbers of the principal people who did me the honour to visit me. I found vessels laden with military stores ready to sail for America:† On the whole there was the greatest prospect that we would be well provided for another campaign, and much stronger than we were the last.

---

* Franklin was instructed to keep his mission (to obtain military and
   financial aid from France) a secret until he met with the French court.
† Although Franklin had not yet met with the French court to seek aid,
   recall that commissioner Silas Deane had successfully obtained some
   assistance.

Knowing that all views of accommodation with Great Britain had been totally at end since the Declaration of Independence, Congress directed the raising of 94 battalions of infantry, with some cavalry. Since the neighborhood of Philadelphia had, by the enemy's movement, become the seat of war, it was judged proper that Congress adjourn to Baltimore, where the public business could be attended to with undisturbed deliberation. I was informed by letter that General Washington, having been reinforced by the troops lately commanded by General Charles Lee and by some corps of militia, crossed the Delaware with 2,500 men, and attacked a body of the enemy, posted at Trenton, with success.* Knowing how all important it was to the security of American independence, we were urged to make tenders to France and Spain, hoping that France would enter the war as soon as might be possible, and how necessary it was to procure from her a line of battle ships, the scarcity of ships being so great.

THE COURT VIEWED AN APPROACHING WAR WITH RELUCTANCE

I arrived in Paris in two weeks, where I found Mr. Deane. Mr. Arthur Lee join'd us from London. We had an audience with the Minister of Foreign Affairs, Count de Vergennes, and were respectfully receiv'd. We left for his consideration a sketch of the propos'd treaty, and an instruction to apply for eight ships of the line, compleatly mann'd, an immediate supply of twenty or thirty thousand muskets and bayonets, and a large quantity of ammunition and brass field pieces, to be sent under convoy, the expense of which we would undertake to pay. By his advice we had an interview with the Spanish ambassador,

---

* This is a reference to Washington's crossing the Delaware with his men on Christmas Day 1776, and achieving their first major victory against the Hessian troops at Trenton on December 26, 1776.

Count d'Aranda, who seemed well dispos'd toward us, and said he would forward copies of our memorials to his court. Their fleets were said to be in fine order, mann'd and fit for sea. The cry of this nation was for us; but the king, it was thought, viewed an approaching war with reluctance.

The state of America in 1776–77

In my opinion the surest way to obtain liberal aid from others is vigourously to help ourselves. People fear assisting the negligent, the indolent and the careless, lest the aids they afford should be lost. I knew we had done a great deal; but it is said we were apt to be supine after a little success, and too backward in furnishing our contingents. A small increase of industry in every American, male and female, with a small diminution of luxury, would produce a sum far superior to all we could hope to beg or borrow from all our friends in Europe.

Consequently, in my "Memoir concerning the present State of the late British Colonies in North America," I informed the French Court with regard to our union and strength. The number of souls in the 13 United States was commonly estimated at 3 million. Such was the rapid increase of people there, thro' early marriages, that it could not be long before that number was exceeded, the inhabitants having been generally found to double themselves by natural generation every 25 years,* and in a quicker proportion in those colonies that received an accession of strangers. And, thus, probably England would not be wanting to continue this war.

---

* Franklin had made this observation as early as 1751 in his important political tract, "Observations Concerning the Increase of Mankind." In this tract, he was even more optimistic: "Our people must at least be doubled every 20 years. . . . What an accession of power to the British Empire by sea as well as by land! What increase of trade and navigation!" See PBF 4:225–34.

I inform'd the French and Spanish that America had a squadron of small ships at sea, which had greatly annoy'd the English commerce. A number of American privateers were also out against the enemy, with an abundance of fishermen being put out of their employment by the war, entering in the frigates or engaging in the privateers.

As to agriculture and commerce, the agriculture had not hitherto been much lessen'd by the war, those who were not in arms working more diligently, so that the country was full of provisions and cheap. Some diminution had been made in planting of tobacco, from a prospect of less demand, but more cotton and flax had been raised, as being immediately wanted for clothing. The commerce was for the most part stopp'd from two causes: the fear of captures by the English, and the want of ships to export the produce. The merchants of the middle and more northern colonies, who used to export wheat, flour, fish, and other provisions, having sold most of their ships to Europe when they foresaw the stoppage, and our carpenters now employ'd in building frigates and privateers, very little trade could be carry'd on. This commerce before the war amounted to about five millions of pounds sterling, and employ'd between 800 and 900 sail of ships. England had lost this commerce. America might now, with all its future increase, gain by France and Spain if they would protect it; and they would thereby be as much strengthen'd, in the vending of manufactures and produce, increase of wealth and seamen, &c. as England would be weaken'd, whereby the difference would be doubled. The tobacco &c. which France and Spain could not consume, they might vend with profit, to the rest of Europe.

This generous and noble benefaction

The hearts of the French were universally for us, and the cry was strong for immediate war with Britain. Indeed everything tended that way, but the Court had its reasons for postponing it a little longer. So strong was the inclination of the wealthy in France to assist us that we were offered a loan of two millions livres,* without interest, and to be repaid when the United States would be settled in peace and prosperity; no conditions or securities were required, not even an engagement from us. We accepted this generous and noble benefaction.

In our first conversation with the minister, it was evident that this Court, while it treated us privately with all civility, was cautious of giving umbrage to England, and was therefore desirous of avoiding an open reception and acknowledgement of us, or entering into any formal negotiation with us, as ministers from the Congress. To make us easy, however, we were told that the ports of France were open to our ships, as friends; that our people might freely purchase and transport as merchandise whatever our states had occasion for, vending at the same time our own commodities; that in doing this we should receive all the facilities that a government disposed to favour us could, consistent with treaties, afford to the enemies of a friend. But tho' it was at that time no secret that 200 field pieces of brass and 30,000 fusils[†] with other munitions of war in great abundance had been taken out of the king's magazines for the purpose of exportation to America, the minister, in our presence, affected to know nothing of that operation, and claimed no merit to his Court on that account. But he intimated to us that it would be well taken if we communicated with no other person about the Court concerning our affairs but himself, who would be ready at all convenient times to confer with us.

Means were proposed of our obtaining a large sum of money for current use by an advance from the Farmers General to America to

---

* Livre was the French currency—officially livre tournoise (Tournoise pound), named after Tours, where it was minted. The British adopted a similar system with the British pound sterling, which was worth approximately 24 times the value of a French livre. The livre was abolished during the French Revolution and was replaced by the franc.

[†] A light flintlock musket used by infantrymen.

be repaid in tobacco, of which they wanted 20,000 hogsheads.* We entered accordingly into a treaty with that company, who lent us money in our distress after some difficulty in settling the terms. Afterwards we were informed that a grant was made of two million livres from the French Court, of which 500,000 was ready to be paid us down, and an equal sum should be paid the beginnings of April, July, and October; that such was the King's generosity, he exacted no conditions or promise of repayment; he only required that we should not speak to anyone of our having received this aid: We accordingly observed strictly this injunction.

OFFICERS OF ALL RANKS WORRY ME FROM MORNING TO NIGHT

The desire in France of military officers of all ranks to go into the service of the United States was so general and so strong as to be quite amazing. We were hourly fatigu'd with their applications and offers, which we were obliged to refuse, and with hundreds of letters which we could not possibly answer to satisfaction, having had no orders to engage any but engineers.

I apprehended that General Washington had already more foreign officers than he could possible employ. Nevertheless, contrary to my advice, a Monsr. Dorcet went over to America at his own expense and without the smallest expectation given him by me of his obtaining a place in our army. He was extremely desirous of entering into the American service. This at least showed a zeal for our cause that merited some regard.

Baron de Steuben, lately a lieutenant general in the King of Prussia's service, whom he attended in all his campaigns, being an aide de camp, quartermaster general, &c., went to America with a true zeal for

---

* A large cask measuring 54 gallons.

our cause. He was recommended to us by two of the best judges of
military merit, M. de Vergennes and M. de St. Germain, who had long
been personally acquainted with him from a full persuasion that the
knowledge and experience he acquired by 20 years' study and practice
in the Prussian School would be of great use in our armies. The French
Court encouraged and promoted the voyage of Count Pulawski of
Poland, an officer famous throughout Europe for his bravery and conduct in defense of the liberties of his country against the three great
invading powers of Russia, Austria and Prussia. I thought he might be
useful in our service. And the Marquis de Lafayette, a young nobleman
of great family connections and great wealth, went to America in a
ship of his own, accompanied by some officers of distinction, in order
to serve in our armies. He was exceedingly beloved, and everybody's
good wishes attended him to meet with an agreeable reception. Those
who censured it as imprudent in him did nevertheless applaud his
spirit; and we were satisfy'd that the civilities and respect that might
be shown him were serviceable to our affairs in France, as pleasing not
to his powerful relations and to the Court, but to the whole French
nation. He left a beautiful young wife big with child; and for her sake
particularly we hoped that his bravery and ardent desire to distinguish
himself would be a little restrain'd.

Most officers going to America for employment were probably disappointed. Our armies were full; there were a number of expectants
unemployed and starving for want of subsistence. My recommendation did not make vacancies, nor could it fill them to the prejudice of
those who had a better claim. Then the voyage was long, the passage
very expensive, and the hazard of being taken and imprison'd by the
English very considerable. If, after all, no place affording a livelihood
could be found for the gentleman, he would perhaps be distress'd in
a strange country, and ready to blaspheme his friends that by their
solicitations procur'd for him so unhappy a situation. In my opinion
the natural complacence of France often carried people too far in the

articles of recommendations. Frequently if a man had no useful talents, was good for nothing, and burdensome to his relations, or was indiscreet, profligate and extravagant, they were glad to get rid of him by sending him to the other end of the world. In consequence of my crediting such recommendations, my own would be out of credit, and I could not advise anybody to depend on them.

You have no conception how I was harass'd

Oh, how I was harass'd. These applications were my perpetual torment. People believed, notwithstanding my continually repeated declarations to the contrary, that I was sent hither to engage officers. In truth I never had any such orders. It was never so much as intimated to me that it would be agreeable to my constituents. Nevertheless, not a day passed in which I had not a number of soliciting visits besides letters. If I could have gratified them all, or any of them, it would have been a pleasure. I might indeed give them the recommendations and the promises they desired, and thereby pleased them for the present. But when the certain disappointment of the expectations with which they would so obstinately flatter themselves arrived, they must curse me for complying with their mad requests, and not undeceiving them, and would have become so many enemies to our cause and country. All my friends were sought out and teas'd to tease me; great officers of all ranks in all departments, ladies great and small, besides profess'd solicitors, worried me from morning to night. The noise of every coach that entered my court terrified me. I was afraid to accept an invitation to dine abroad, being almost sure of meeting with some officer, or officer's friend, who, as soon as I was put into good humour by a glass or two of champagne, began his attack on me. Luckily I did not often in my sleep dream myself in these vexatious situations, or I would have been afraid of what were then my only hours of comfort.

MODEL OF A LETTER OF RECOMMENDATION

In response to these persistent requests, I wrote the following model
of a letter of recommendation:

Paris, April 2, 1777

Sir,

The bearer of this who is going to America, presses me to give him
a Letter of Recommendation, tho' I know nothing of him, not even
his name. This may seem extraordinary, but I assure you it is not
uncommon here. Sometimes, indeed, one unknown person brings
me another equally unknown to recommend him; and sometimes
they recommend one another! As to this gentleman, I must refer
you to himself for his character and merits, with which he is certainly better acquainted than I can possibly be; I recommend him,
however, to those civilities which every stranger, of whom one
knows no harm, has a right to, and I request you will do him all the
good offices and show him all the favour that on further acquaintance you shall find him to deserve. I have the honour to be, &c.

B FRANKLIN

By 1779, the Congress had expressed extreme embarrassment and
was put to great expenses by the number of foreign officers who went
to America in expectation of employment, and who could not be
employed, our armies being already arranged and more than fully
officer'd. It signified to me their pleasure that I should give no encouragement or expectation for the future to any officer whatsoever.

OUR CAUSE WAS ESTEEM'D
THE CAUSE OF ALL MANKIND

All Europe was for us. Our Articles of Confederation being translated
and published in France gave us the appearance of consistence and

firmness to the American states and government. The separate constitutions of the several states were also translated and published in Europe. It was a very general opinion that if we succeeded in establishing our liberties, we would, as soon as peace was restored, receive an immense addition of numbers and wealth from Europe, by the families who would come over to participate in our privileges and bring their estates with them. Tyranny is so generally established in the rest of the world that the prospect of an asylum in America for those who love liberty gave general joy, and our cause was esteem'd the cause of all mankind. Those who are enslaved naturally become base as well as wretched; therefore, we were fighting for the dignity and happiness of human nature. Glorious is it for the Americans to be call'd by Providence to this post of honour. Cursed and detested will everyone be that deserts or betrays it.

The French fleet was nearly ready and would be much superior to the English when join'd with that of Spain, which was preparing with all diligence. The tone of the Court had accordingly risen. It was said that when the British ambassador Stormont intimated to the minister of France that if the Americans were permitted to continue drawing supplies of arms &c. from that kingdom, the peace could not last much longer, he was firmly answer'd, *Nous ne desirons pas la guerre, et nos ne le craignons pas.* "We neither desire war, nor fear it." It was the universal opinion that the peace could not continue another year. Every nation in Europe wished to see Britain humbled, having all in their turns been offended by her insolence, which in prosperity she was apt to discover on all occasions.

WE WILL MOST CHEERFULLY RISK OUR PERSONAL LIBERTY OR LIFE

In early 1777, we received general alarming accounts of successes of the English against our country, and authentic intelligence from England that eight thousand men, chiefly Germans, under the command of General Burgoyne, were to be sent early in the spring to America, and to be employed with some ships of war in the invasion of Virginia and Maryland. We therefore submitted this critical situation of our country to the courts of France and Spain, in hopes that they would conclude a treaty of amity and commerce with our states, and enter into a war with Great Britain. Having reason to believe that one of us might be useful in Madrid, and another in Holland, and some courts farther northward, we agreed that Mr. Lee would go to Spain, and Mr. Deane to the Hague. It was further considered that in the present peril of the liberties of our country, it was our duty to hazard everything in their support and defense. Therefore as American commissioners we resolv'd unanimously:

Resolution of the Commissioners

Paris, Feby. 5th 1777

If it should be necessary for the attainment of anything, in our best judgment, material to the defense and support of the public cause, we should pledge our persons, or hazard the censure of the Congress by exceeding our instructions; we will, for such purpose most cheerfully risk our personal liberty or life.

B Franklin
Silas Deane
Arthur Lee

All Europe was on our side of the question, as far as applause and good wishes could carry them; those who live under arbitrary power do nevertheless approve of liberty, and wish for it. They almost despaired of recovering it in Europe; they read the translations of our separate colony constitutions with rapture, and there were such numbers everywhere who talked of removing to America with their families and fortunes as soon as peace and our independence were established, that 'twas generally believed we should have a prodigious addition of strength, wealth and arts from the emigrations of Europe, and 'twas thought that to lessen or prevent such emigrations, the tyrannies established in Europe must relax and allow more liberty to their people.

COMMERCE WITH EVERY NATION; WAR WITH NONE

Mr. Hartley, a member of the British Parliament and an old acquaintance of mine, arrived from London in April, 1778. He was generally in the opposition, especially on American issues, but had some respect for Lord North. In conversation, he express'd the strongest anxiety for peace with America, and appear'd extremely desirous to know my sentiments of the terms which might probably be accept'd if offer'd; whether America would not, to obtain peace, grant some superior advantage in trade to Britain and enter into an alliance, offensive or defensive; and whether, if war were to be declared against France, we had oblig'd ourselves by treaty to join with her against England. My answers were that the United States was not fond of war, and with the advice of their friends would probably be easily prevailed with to make peace on equitable terms; but we had no terms committed to us to propose, and I did not choose to mention any; that Britain, having injur'd us heavily by making this unjust war upon us, might think herself well off if on reparation of those injuries we admitted her to equal advantages with other nations in commerce, but certainly she had no reason to expect superior; that her known fondness for war, and the many instances of her readiness to engage in wars on frivolous occasions, were probably sufficient to cause an immediate rejection of every proposition for an offensive alliance with her; and that, if she made war against France on our account, a peace with us, at the same time, was impossible; for that, having met with friendship from that generous nation when we were cruelly oppos'd by England, we were under

ties stronger than treaties could form, to make common cause, which
we would certainly do to the utmost of our power.

In sum: The system of America is universal commerce with every
nation; war with none.

OUR PRISONERS COMPLAIN'D
OF VERY SEVERE TREATMENT

I inform'd Mr. Hartley that our prisoners in English jails complain'd
of very severe treatment, contrary to every rule of war among civilized nations. Far from friends and families, and with winter coming
on, they suffered extremely, were fed scantily on bad provisions, and
were without warm lodging, clothes or fire; and not suffer'd to write
to or receive visits from their friends, or even from the humane and
charitable among their enemies. We received accounts from the mill
prison in Plymouth that our people were not allow'd the use of pen
and ink, nor the sight of newspapers, nor the conversation of friends.
I assur'd Mr. Hartley that prisoners in America were treated with
great kindness, and were serv'd with the same rations of wholesome
provisions with our troops; comfortable lodgings were provided for
them, and they were allowed large bounds of villages in a healthy air,
to walk and amuse themselves in upon their parole. I petition'd him,
and later Lord North, to find a trusty, humane, discreet person who
would undertake to distribute what relief we could afford to those
unhappy brave men, martyrs to the cause of liberty. I received reports
later from Mr. Hartley of his efforts to relieve our poor captives, and
a Rev. Wrens for his benevolent conduct.

Meanwhile, we had in France above two hundred prisoners, cap-
tur'd by John Paul Jones, who were confin'd in the Drake, where
they must be kept, as we did not have the use of prisons on shore.
Later we obtained permission to make use of French prisons for
British captives, and they were ordered on shore. I wrote to England

about the exchange of our prisoners with the 500 prisoners they held in England.

Our first applications for exchanging prisoners were haughtily rejected. The prisoners were at that time consider'd rebels, committed for high treason, who could only be delivered by course of law. We then did everything in our power to make their situation as comfortable as possible. Thanks to the indefatigable endeavours of Mr. Hartley, by long solicitation we obtain'd an agreement of the Lords of the Admiralty to an exchange of man for man, and the pass required for a cartel ship to bring over as many as we had in France to give in return, was sent to England. But the execution was long delay'd. Mr. Hartley mentioned "that the alliance between France and America is the great stumbling block in the way of making peace," and the affair was dropped, and many of those unfortunate people suffered greatly. Afterwards, I felt we had no kind of faith in the British government, which appeared to us as insidious and deceitful as it was unjust and cruel. Its character was that of the *Spider*, in Thomson,* *cunning and fierce; mixture abhorr'd!!*

It appeared that Mr. Hartley had been deceived as well as we. It became evident that the delays had been of design, to give more opportunity of seducing the men by promises and hardships, to seek their liberty in engaging against their country. We learned from those who had escaped that there were persons continually employed in cajoling and menacing them, representing to them that we had neglected them; that the British government was willing to exchange them, and that it was our fault it was not done; that all the news from America was bad on their side; that we would be conquer'd and they would be hang'd if they did not accept the gracious offer of being pardon'd on condition of serving the King, &c.

---

*James Thomson, "Summer," *The Seasons* (Oxford, 1981), 72, lines 269–70. PBF 28:588n.

The exchange of prisoners was finally begun in April 1779, when I was glad to hear of the arrival of the American prisoners from England. The ship employ'd brought us one cargo from the prison at Plymouth. The number was intended for an hundred, but proved 97. And she was returned with as many in exchange, to bring us a second number from the prison at Portsmouth. By agreement this was to continue 'till all were exchanged. The Americans were chiefly engaged with Capts. Jones and Landais. This exchange was all the more remarkable, as our people were all committed as for high treason.

I wished it had been in my power to relieve all the wants and even to gratify the wishes of prisoners, who suffered in the cause of their country. But there were limits to everything, and the frequent intercepting of our supplies from the Congress by the British cruisers very much narrow'd the limits in this case. As to those remaining in prison, who wrote for ten guineas a piece to be sent them to enable them to escape, the request, if it were reasonable, was not practicable; the number would make the sum enormous. The scantiness of our funds and the multitude of demands prevented it.

The English conduct with regard to the exchange of prisoners continued very unjust. After long suspense, and affected delays for the purpose of wearing out our poor people, they finally refused to deliver us a man in exchange for those set at liberty by our cruisers on parole. There was no gaining anything upon those barbarians by advances of civility or humanity.

To me it seemed all along that this war would end in our favour

I believe in my conscience that mankind are wicked enough to continue slaughtering one another as long as they can find money to pay the butchers. But of all the wars in my time, in this one the part of England appeared to me the wickedest, having no cause but malice against liberty, and the jealousy of commerce. And I think the crime seemed likely to meet with its proper punishment: a total loss of her own liberty and the destruction of her own commerce. As to the state of affairs in America, I was of the opinion that we would be much stronger the next campaign than we were in the last; better arm'd, better disciplin'd, and with more ammunition. When I was at the camp before Boston, the army had not 5 rounds of powder a man. This was kept a secret even from our people. The world wonder'd that we so seldom fir'd a cannon. We could not afford it. But we soon made powder in plenty.

I continued amazingly well and hearty for my age, although I occasionally suffered from the gout, and always hoped to live to see the end of these troubles, and our country establish'd in freedom, when it would become great and glorious, by being the asylum of all the oppress'd in Europe, and the resort of the wealthy who love liberty from all parts of the continent to establish themselves and their families among us. To me it seemed all along that this war would end in our favour, and in the ruin of Britain. An English gentleman, one day in company with some French, remark'd that it was folly in France not to make war immediately; *And in England,* reply'd one of them, *not to make peace.*

THE FLAG CONSISTS OF THIRTEEN STRIPES, ALTERNATELY RED, WHITE AND BLUE

It was with pleasure that we acquainted the European governments with the flag of the United States of America, which consists of thirteen stripes, alternately red, white and blue—a small square in the upper angle next to the flagstaff is a blue field, with thirteen white stars, denoting a new constellation. Some of the states had vessels of war carrying flags distinct from those of the United States. For example, the vessels of war of the state of Massachusetts Bay had sometimes a pine tree, and South Carolina a rattlesnake in the middle of the thirteen stripes. Merchant ships had often only thirteen stripes. But the flag of the United States ordained by Congress is the thirteen stripes and thirteen stars as first described.

About spies and safety

Before his leaving, Mr. Hartley warn'd me to take care of my own safety. Events are uncertain, and men may be capricious, said he; but, having nearly finish'd a long life, I set but little value on what remained of it. Like a draper, when one chaffers with him for a remnant, I am ready to say: "As it is only the fag-end, I will not differ with you about it; take it for what you please." Perhaps the best use such an odd fellow can be put to is to make a martyr of him.

Mr. Hartley also warn'd me of French spies, to which I responded that I did not care how many spies were placed around me by the French Court, having nothing to conceal from them. I have long observ'd one rule which prevents any inconvenience from pretended friends or spies; it is simply this: to be concern'd in no affairs that I should blush to have made public; and to do nothing but what spies may see and welcome. When a man's actions are just and honourable, the more they are known, the more his reputation is increase'd and establish'd. If I was sure, therefore, that my *valet de place* was a spy (as probably he was), I think I would not discharge him for that, if in other respects I lik'd him.

We were in imminent danger of bankruptcy

In financial matters, the total failure of remittances from the Congress for a long time embarrass'd us exceedingly; the contracts we enter'd into for clothing and arms in expectation of those remittances and which were now beginning to call for payment, distressed us much and we were in imminent danger of bankruptcy. We stated the difficulties of our situation to both the French and Spanish courts, and waited with patience the answer. In the mean time they gave us fresh assurances of their good will to our cause, and we received a fourth sum of 500,000 livres. We were continually charge'd to keep the aids a dead secret even from the Congress, where they supposed England had some intelligence; but we felt obliged to dispense with this injunction.

We were much troubled with complaints of our armed vessels taking the ships and merchandise of neutral nations. From Holland they complained of the taking of the sloop *Chester* by two privateers of Charlestown, called the *Fair American* and the *Experiment*; from Cadiz of the taking of the French ship *Fortune* by the *Civil Usage* privateer, having on board Spanish property; and in Paris of the taking of the *Empereur* of Germany. We requested that upon fair trials, speedy justice be done and restitution made to the reclaimers. It was of the utmost consequence to our affairs in Europe that we should wipe off the aspirations of our enemies who proclaimed us everywhere as pirates, and endeavoured to excite all the world against us.

A SURPRISE VICTORY AT SARATOGA

On December 4, 1777, a Mr. Austin arriv'd from Nantes with dispatches from Boston. I asked hastily, "Sir, is Philadelphia taken?"

"Yes sir," he replied.

I started to return to the hotel,* when he continu'd, "But, sir, I have greater news than that. General Burgoyne and his whole army are prisoners of war!"

We immediately issued a public announcement, and the effect was electrical thro' France. This exceedingly great news of General

---

* The first American embassy was located at the Hotel de Valentinois at
  Passy, a few miles outside Paris, which also served as Franklin's residence.
  The beginning of the next chapter discusses his residence at Passy.

Burgoyne's defeat occasion'd as much general joy in France as if it had been a victory of their own troops over their own enemies. I communicated immediately to M. Vergennes of the total reduction of the force under General Burgoyne, himself and his whole army having surrendered themselves prisoners; that Gen. Howe was in possession of Philadelphia, and that Washington's army was in huts to the westward of Schuylkill,* refreshing and recruiting during the winter in an attempt to expel Howe. We proposed the conclusion of the long-postponed treaty at this time would have the most happy effect in raising the credit of the United States at home, and discouraging their enemies.

Alliance with France in 1778

Within several weeks, we had succeed'd in our negotiations for the completion of two treaties with France: the one of amity and commerce, on the plan of that projected in Congress, with some good additions; and the other of alliance for mutual defense, in which the King of France agreed to make a common cause with the United States, if England attempted to obstruct the commerce of his subjects with them. The treaties guaranteed to the United States their liberties, sovereignty, and independence, absolute and unlimited, with the possessions they had, or might have at the conclusion of the war; and the States in return guaranteed to the King his perfect equality and reciprocity, with no advantage being demanded by France, or privileges in commerce, which the States might not grant to any and every other nation. There was a separate and secret clause by which Spain was to be received into the Alliance, tho' long delayed.

The treaties were signed by the plenipotentiaries on both sides on February 6, 1778, but were kept secret until published and forwarded

---

* At Valley Forge. See PBF 25:504.

to Congress. The King treated us generously and magnanimously, taking no advantage of our present difficulties to exact terms which we would not have willingly granted when established in prosperity and power. I might add that he acted wisely in wishing that the friendship contracted by these treaties might be durable. I advis'd our people in all parts of America to cultivate a friendship with the French people, and used every means to remove ancient prejudices.

On the occasion of the signing of the treaty, I put on the same coat I wore the day Wedderburn abused me at Whitehall. When Mr. Deane asked why, I responded: "To give it a little revenge."

Several of our American ships, laden with supplies for our armies, sailed under the convoy of a strong French squadron. England was in great consternation, and their minister Lord North, on the 17TH of that month, confessed in a long speech that all his measures had been wrong and that peace was necessary, and proposed two bills for quieting America; but they were full of artifice and deceit.

Chapter Six

Minister to France, 1778–79

An Ambassador's Life

I ENJOY'D A GOOD NEIGHBOURHOOD
OF VERY AGREEABLE PEOPLE

Several months after arriving in Paris, I took lodging at Hotel de Valentinois in Passy, where I found a little leisure, free from the perpetual interruption I suffered by the crowds continually coming in, some offering goods, others soliciting for offices in our army, &c. &c.

The extreme hurry we engaged in since my arrival prevented my writing to many of my correspondents. The difficulty, delay & interruption of correspondence with those I love was one of the great inconveniences I found in living so far from home. I pitied my poor old sister Jane to be so harass'd and driven about by the enemy in Pennsylvania, for I felt a little myself the inconvenience of being driven about by my friends. I lived in France in great respect and dined every day with great folks; but I still longed for home and for repose, and would have been happy to eat Indian pudding under the hospitable roof of my friends in Philadelphia.

Mr. de Chaumont, my landlord at Passy, was one of our most early friends in France, which he also manifested by crediting us with two thousand barrels of gun powder and other military stores in 1776, before we had provided any apparent means of payment. He proposed to leave the house rent till the end of the war, and then to

accept for it a price of American land from the Congress, or other settlement as they might find equivalent. This was most agreeable to
me, as I enjoyed no bargain in this appointment, having been promised by a note the salary of only £500 sterling per annum with my
expenses, and to be assisted by a secretary. When the Pennsylvania
Assembly sent me in 1764 on the same salary, they allow'd me one
year's advance for the passage in consideration of my private affairs
that must be occasion'd by my sudden departure and absence. But I
received no such allowance from Congress.

Valentinois was a fine airy house, situated in a neat well-built village on a hill, within two miles of Paris, with a large garden and
neighbouring woods to walk in. I had a bath in my house, besides the
river in view. I walked in the garden every day, had a good appetite
and slept well. I think the French cookery agreed with me better than
the English, I suppose because there is little or no butter in their
sauces: for I never once had the heartburn there, tho' I ate heartily,
which showed that my digestion was good. I enjoy'd a good neigh-
bourhood of very agreeable people who appeared very fond of me. I
had an abundance of acquaintances, and dined abroad six days in
seven. Sundays I reserved to dine at home, with such Americans as
passed that way; & I then had my grandson Benny with some other
American children from his school. If being treated with all the
politeness of France, & the apparent respect & esteem of all ranks,
from the highest to the lowest, can make a man happy, I ought to
have been so.

I GREW PERFECTLY SICK OF PORTRAITS

The clay medallion of me was the first of the kind made in France.
A variety of others have been made since of different sizes; some to
be set in lids of snuff boxes, and some so small as to be worn in
rings; and the number sold were incredible. These, with pictures,

busts, and prints (of which copies upon copies were spread everywhere) made my face as well known as that of the moon. It is said by learned etymologists that the name *Doll*, for the images children play with, is derived from the world IDOL; from the number of dolls now made of me, it may be truly said, in that sense, that I was *i-doll-ized* in that country.

I had, at the request of friends, sat so much and so often for painters and statuaries that I grew perfectly sick of it. I know of nothing so tedious as sitting hours in one fix'd posture. I courteously asked one friend to excuse me from another portrait. I would do it if it were necessary, but there were already so many good likenesses of my face that if the best of them were copied it would probably be better than a new draw from the life: any artist can add such a body to the face. Or, I told them, it might be taken from a Chamberlin's print.*

Think how I must have appeared among the powder'd heads of Paris! Jolly, strong and hearty, very plainly dress'd, wearing my thin gray straight hair that peeped out under my only coiffure, a fine fur cap, which came down my forehead almost to my spectacles. I wished every gentleman and lady in France would have been so obliging as to follow my fashion, comb their own heads as I did mine, dismissed their friseurs, and paid me half the money they paid to them.

Besides being harass'd with too much business, I was expos'd to numberless visits, some of kindness and civility, but many of mere idle curiosity, from strangers of America and of different parts of Europe, as well as the inhabitants of the provinces who came to Paris.

---

* Mason Chamberlin's 1762 painting shows Franklin with quill in hand and lightning flashing in the background. An engraving of the Chamberlin painting was made by Francois Martinet in 1773, which made Franklin look French.

These devoured my hours, and broke my attention, and at night I often found myself fatigu'd without having done anything. Celebrity may for a while flatter one's vanity, but its effects are troublesome.

As to the Latin verse that has been applied to me, *Eripuit coelo fulmen, sceptrumque tirannis,** translated as "He stole the thunder from heaven, and the scepter from tyrants," I am restrained from giving any opinion on that line, except that it ascribes too much to me, especially in what relates to the tyrant; the revolution having been the work of many able and brave men, wherein it is sufficient honour for me if I am allowed a small share.

I FOUND FRANCE A MOST
AMIABLE NATION TO LIVE IN

They told me that in writing to a lady from Paris, one should always say something about the fashions. Temple observed them more than I did. He took notice that at the ball in Nantes, there were no heads less than five, and a few were seven, lengths of the face, above the top of the forehead. Yet we din'd at the Duke de la Rochefoucauld, where there were three duchesses and a countess, and no head higher than a face and a half. So it seemed the farther from Court, the more extravagant the mode.

Nevertheless, I found them a most amiable nation to live with. The Spaniards are, by common opinion, supposed to be cruel, the English proud, the Scotch insolent, the Dutch avaricious, &c. But I think the French have no national vice ascribed to them. They have some frivolities, but they are harmless. To dress their heads so that a hat can-

---

* The famed epigram of Franklin was composed by finance minister Anne-Robert-Jacques Turgot. See Walter Isaacson, *Benjamin Franklin: An American Life* (New York: Simon & Schuster, 2003), 145.

not be put on them, & then wear their hats under their arms, and to fill their noses with tobacco, may be follies perhaps, but they are not vices. They are only the effects of the tyranny of custom. In short there is nothing wanting in the character of the Frenchman that belongs to that of an agreeable and worthy man.

Somebody gave it out that I lov'd ladies

The desire of pleasing by the perpetual use of compliments in this polite nation had so us'd up all the common expressions of approbation that they became flat and insipid, and to use them almost implied censure. Hence music, that formerly might be sufficiently prais'd when it was call'd *bonne*, to go a little farther they call'd it *excellente*, then *superbe, magnifique, exquise, celeste,* all which being in their turns worn out, there remains now only *divine*; and when that is grown as insignificant as its predecessors, I think they must return to common speech and common sense; as, from vying with one another in fine and costly paintings on their coaches, and not being able to go farther in that way, they return'd to plain carriages, painted without arms or figures, in one uniform colour.

In sum, France is the civilest nation upon the earth. Your first acquaintances endeavour to find out what you like, and they tell others. If 'tis understood that you like mutton, dine where you will find mutton. Somebody, it seemed, gave it out that I lov'd ladies; and then everybody presented me their ladies (or the ladies presented themselves) to be embrac'd, that is to have their necks kiss'd. For as to kissing of lips or cheeks it was not the mode there; the first was reckon'd rude, & the other might rub off the paint. The French ladies had, however, a thousand other ways of rendering themselves agreeable by their various attentions and civilities, & their sensible conversation. 'Tis a delightful people to live with.

THE PLEASING CONVERSATION OF MADAME BRILLON

Madame Brillon was one such friend, the mistress of an amiable family living in the neighborhood, with which I spent an evening twice in every week. She was a lady of the most respectable character and pleasing conversation. She had, among other elegant accomplishments, that of an excellent musician, and with her daughters who sang prettily, and some friends who played, she kindly entertained me and my grandson with little concerts, a dish of tea and a game of chess. Her good husband, M. Brillon, told me many stories and his conversation always cheered me. I called this my opera; for I rarely went to the opera at Paris.

Madame Brillon wished to divert me for a moment from my affairs with a little amusement. I adopted her as a good daughter, for by coming to this country I have lost the sweet company and respectful care of my own affectionate daughter. While in France, I never failed to visit her at least two evenings a week, if it was possible. I was always happy when I was with her, enjoying her sweet society, seeing her and hearing her speak. It is true that I sometimes suspected my heart of wanting to go further, but I tried to conceal it from myself. For if at my age it was not fitting to say that I was in love with a young woman, there was nothing to prevent me from confessing that I admired and loved an assemblage of all female virtues and of all admirable talents, and I loved my French daughter because she was truly worthy of love, and because she loved me. It was a form of madness to say so because it served no purpose: It earned me favors never obtained! But one must do mad things when one loves madly.*

---

* Thomas Jefferson observed that "in the company of women. . . . he [Franklin] loses all power over himself and becomes almost frenzied." See *Benjamin Franklin: The Autobiography and Other Writings*, ed. by Kenneth Silverman (New York: Penguin Books, 1986), 206.

Here below is an exchange of letters, translated into English (as I wrote a great deal of very bad French).

30 July 1777

To B. Franklin,

Madame Brillion has the honor of presenting a thousand compliments to Mr. Franklin and of sending him the little [Scottish] tune he seemed to enjoy yesterday.

It is a real source of joy for her to think that she can sometimes amuse Mr. Franklin, whom she loves and esteems as he deserves; still, she is a little miffed about the six games of chess he won so inhumanly and she warns him that she will spare nothing to get her revenge!

MADAME BRILLON

WE CAUSED GREAT INCONVENIENCE BY DETAINING YOU SO LONG IN THE BATH

Nov. 29, 1777

To Madame Brillon,

Upon returning home, I was astonished to find that it was almost eleven o'clock. I fear that because we were overly engrossed in the game of chess as to forget everything else, we caused great inconvenience to you, by detaining you so long in the bath.* Tell me,

---

* This refers to the famous bathtub scene. Franklin and his neighborhood friend Louis Le Veillard had become so engrossed in a game of chess that they forgot the time and stayed late while Madame Brillon was in the tub, soaking under her wooden plank. See Claude-Anne Lopez, *Mon Cher Papa: Franklin and the Ladies of Paris* (New Haven: Yale University Press, 1990), 59.

my dear friend, how you feel this morning. Never again will I consent to start a game in your bathing room. Can you forgive me for this indiscretion?

I am sending you Monsieur Bitaube's *Homer*. This lovable man is very desirous of making the acquaintance of Madame Brillon, and hearing some of her music. Might I be permitted to bring him with me next Wednesday?

B FRANKLIN

30 November 1777

To B. Franklin,

No, you did not do me any harm yesterday. I am so happy to see you that the good it does me more than balances the little fatigue of overstaying somewhat in the tub.

I will read Mr. Bitaube's *Homer*, and I thank you for it, my good friend.

Farewell until Wednesday, until Saturday, until all the Wednesdays and Saturdays of all the rest of our lives.

MADAME BRILLON

"ALL GREAT MEN ARE TAINTED WITH IT: IT IS CALLED THEIR WEAKNESS"

March 7, 1778

To B. Franklin,

You were kind enough yesterday, my dear brother, to entrust me with your conversation. A minister usually arranges matters with a few to his own glory and profit. As long as he loves God, America and me above all things, I absolve him of all his sins, present, past and future; and I promise him paradise where I shall lead him along a path strewn with roses.

It is well for my penitent to know that there are seven grave sins, and of the seven, my dear brother, you commit only one. To prove this to you is easy:

The first is pride—when a sage has always done good, solely for the love of goodness and the happiness of his fellowmen, and then if there happens to be glory at the outcome of this conduct, it is not its motivation; hence you are not proud.

The second is envy—mediocre men envy the reputation, the merits, the success of superior men: it is impossible for you to be envious.

The third is avarice—moderate desires, simplicity, tidiness place you above all suspicion.

The fourth is gluttony—it does seem to me that you are fond enough of good things, but that it would be no great sacrifice for you to live like a savage chief, so you are not a glutton.

The fifth is anger—your calm soul, ever guided by reason, is flawless on this point.

The sixth is sloth—America, nay the very thunderbolt, if one could summon it as a witness, will testify that if all men resembled you, sloth would be unknown.

The seventh—I shall not name it. All great men are tainted with it: it is called their weakness. I dare say this so-called weakness removes the roughness, the austerity that unalloyed philosophy might have left with them. You have loved, my dear brother; you have been kind and lovable; you have been loved in return! What is so damnable about that? Go on doing great things and loving pretty women; provided that, pretty and lovable though they may be, you never lose sight of my principle: always love God, America, and me above all.

MADAME BRILLON

I CONFESS I BREAK THIS COMMANDMENT CONSTANTLY

To Madame Brillon

Passy, March 10, 1778

I am charm'd with the goodness of my spiritual guide, and resign myself implicitly to her conduct, as she promises to lead me to heaven in a road so delicious, when I could be content to travel thither even in the roughest of all the ways with the pleasure of her company. How kindly partial to her penitent, in finding him, on examining his conscience, guilty of only one capital sin, and to call that by the gentle name of a foible! I lay fast hold of your promise to absolve me of all sins past, present, and future, on the easy and pleasing condition of loving God, America, and my guide above all things. I am in raptures when I think of being absolv'd of the FUTURE.

People commonly speak of the *Ten* Commandments; I have been taught that there are twelve. The first, *increase and multiply* and replenish the earth. The twelfth is, a new commandment I give unto you, *that ye love one another.* It seems to me that they are a little misplac'd, and that the last should have been the first. However, I never made any difficulty about that, but was always willing to obey them both whenever I had an opportunity. Pray tell me, my dear casuist, whether my keeping religiously these two commandments, tho' not in the Decalogue, may not be accepted in compensation for my breaking so often one of the ten, I mean that which forbids coveting my neighbour's wife, and which I confess I break constantly, God forgive me, as often as I see or think of my lovely confessor: And I am afraid I should never be able to repent of the sin, even if I had the full possession of her.

And now as I am consulting you upon a case of conscience, I will mention the opinion of a certain father of the church, which I find myself willing to adopt, tho' I am not sure it is orthodox. It is this, that the most effectual way to get rid of a certain temptation is, as often as it returns, to comply with and satisfy it. Pray instruct me how far I may venture to practice upon this principle?

But why should I be so scrupulous, when you have promised to absolve me of the future! Adieu, my charming conductress, and believe me ever, with the sincerest esteem and affection,

Your most obedient humble servant,

B FRANKLIN

"A WOMAN MAY HAVE DESIRES BUT SHE MUST NOT YIELD"

March 16, 1778

To B. Franklin,

You are a man, I am a woman, and while we might think along the same lines, we must speak and act differently. Perhaps there is no great harm in a man having desires and yielding to them; a woman may have desires, but she must not yield. You have kept two very pleasant commandments religiously; you have broken another, one easily violated. My friendship, and a touch of vanity, perhaps, prompted me strongly to pardon you; but I dare not decide the question without consulting that neighbor whose wife you covet, because he is a far better casuist than I am. And then, too, as Poor Richard would say, *In weighty matters, two heads are better than one.*

Farewell, my dear penitent; before closing, I want to confess to you in all humility that in the matter of desire, I am as great a sinner as yourself. I have desired to see you, desired to know you, desired your esteem, desired your friendship. I have even given you mine at the very outset, in the hope of receiving a little of yours. And now, I desire that you may love me forever; this desire grows day by day in my heart and it will last all my life. But such is the compassion of God, it is said, that I have not the slightest doubt that all our desires will eventually lead us to Paradise!

MADAME BRILLON

"I HAVE CHOSEN YOU FOR MY FATHER"

September 30, 1778

To B. Franklin,

You adopt me as your daughter, just as I have chosen you for my father. In America, you say, you had a daughter who respected you and cherished you; I make up for that loss! We love our American allies, but we revere and idolize their leader. The friendship which reigns between the two peoples will always endure, because it can only be extremely useful to both of them; but if the Americans leave you in France, this union of interests will be matched by a union of souls.

Yesterday, I forgot, *mon cher papa*, to remind you that you were so good as to promise to lend me a volume of your works, which will teach me what water spouts are. Captain Cook turns to the famous Doctor Franklin in order to instruct himself on the same subject.

When I go to paradise, if St. Peter asks me of what religion I am, I shall answer him: "Of the religion whereby people believe that the Eternal Being is perfectly good and indulgent; of the religion whereby people love all those who resemble him. I have loved and idolized Doctor Franklin." I am sure that St. Peter will say: "Come in and go promptly to take place next to Mr. Franklin. You shall find him seated next to the Eternal Being." I will go there and enjoy everlasting happiness.

D'HARDANCOURT BRILLON

December 10, 1778

To Madame Brillon,

Since you assure me that we would meet each other and recognize each other in paradise, I have been thinking constantly about the arrangement of our affairs in that country. More than 40 years will probably elapse from the time of my arrival there until you follow me. I shall have enough time during those 40 years to practice on the armonica, and perhaps I may be able to play well enough to accompany you on the piano-forte. From time to time, we shall have little concerts: good Pagin will be of the party; your neighbor and his dear friend; M. de Chaumont, M. B., M. Jourdain, M. Grammont, Mademoiselle Du Tartre, the *petite mere*, and other chosen friends will form our audience. We shall eat together apples of paradise roasted with butter and nutmeg, and we shall pity those who are not dead.

B FRANKLIN

"PEOPLE HAVE CRITICIZED MY SWEET HABIT OF SITTING ON YOUR LAP"

December 15, 1778

To B. Franklin,

I am thinking about our affairs in paradise. I was informed that certain criticisms have been uttered by persons whom I meet in society concerning the kind of familiarity that reigns between us. Do you know, my good papa, that people have criticized the sweet habit I have taken of sitting on your lap, and your habit of soliciting from me what I always refuse? People see evil everywhere in this miserable country, and as I have the easy-going nature of the Americans, that irks me; but the wise must tolerate the mad, the wicked and the foolish. Let us deprive them of ways to talk and do harm; let us love each other always, and delight in the happiness of being better that they are.

I despise the back-biters and am at peace with myself. But one must submit to what is called propriety. Though I may not sit upon your knee so often, it certainly will not be because I love you less. I fear publicity, and through discreet and modest conduct, we shall have shut the mouths of evil speakers, and that is no small feat, even for a sage.

Come to tea tomorrow, come every Wednesday and Saturday, and you would have music, chess and friendship as much as you like.

MADAME BRILLON

WE PASSED THE DAY TOGETHER AT MOULIN JOLI

In the summer of 1778, we pass'd the day together at the Moulin Joli, a little island in the Seine River about 2 leagues from thence. That day a swarm of those little flies known as Ephemeras, and by the people called Manna, hovered over the river. I studied them carefully and the next day sent Madame Brillon the letter of which this is a translation:

Passy. Sept. 20, 1778

To Madame Brillon

You may remember, my dear friend, that when we lately spent that happy day in a delightful garden and sweet society of the *Moulin*

Joli, I stopped a little in one of our walks, and stayed some time behind the company. We had been shown numberless skeletons of a kind of little fly, called an ephemera, whose successive generations, we were told, were bred and expired within the day. I happen'd to see a living company of them on a leaf, who appear'd to be engag'd in conversation. You know I understand all the inferior animal tongues: my too great application to the study of them is the best excuse I can give for the little progress I have made in your charming language. I listened thro' curiosity to the discourse of these little creatures, but as they in their national vivacity spoke three or four together, I could make but little of their discourse. I found, however, by some broken expressions that I caught now and then, they were disputing warmly the merit of two foreign musicians, one a cousin, the other a musketo; in which dispute they spent their time seemingly as regardless of the shortness of life, as if they had been sure of living a month. Happy people! thought I, you live certainly under a wise, just and mild government, since you have no public grievances to complain of, nor any subject of contention but the perfections or imperfections of foreign music. I turned my head from them to an old gray-headed one, who was single on another leaf, and talking to himself. Being amus'd with his soliloquy, I put it down in writing, in hopes it would likewise amuse her to whom I am so much indebted for the most pleasing of amusements, her delicious company and heavenly harmony.

It was, says he, the opinion of learned philosophers of our race, who lived and flourished long before my time, that this vast world, the *Moulin Joli*, could not itself subsist more than 18 hours; and I think there was some foundation for that opinion, since by the apparent motion of the great Luminary that gives life to all nature, and which in my time has evidently declin'd considerably toward the ocean at the end of our earth, it must then finish its course, be extinguish'd in the waters that surround us, and leave the world in cold and darkness, necessarily producing universal death and destruction. I have lived seven of those hours; a great age, being no less than 420 minutes of time. How very few of us continue so long! I have seen generations born, flourish, and expire. My present friends are the children and grandchildren of the friends of my youth, who are now, alas, no more! And I must soon follow them; for by the course of nature, tho' still in health, I cannot expect to live above 7 or 8 minutes longer. What now avails all my toil and labour in amassing honey-dew on this leaf, which I cannot live to enjoy! What the political struggles I have been engag'd in for the good of my compatriots, inhabitants of this bush; or my philosophical studies for the benefits of our race in general! For in politics, what can laws do without morals? Our present race of ephemeras will in a course of minutes become corrupt like those of other and older bushes, and consequently as wretched. And in philosophy how small our progress! Alas, *art is long, and life is short!* My friends would comfort me with the idea of a name they say I shall leave behind me; and they tell me I have lived long enough to nature and to glory: But what will fame be to an ephemera who no longer exists? And what will become of all history, in the 18th hour, when the world itself, even the whole *Moulin Joli*, shall come to its end, and be buried in universal ruin? To me, after all my eager pursuits, no solid pleasures now remain, but the reflection of a long life spent in meaning well, the sensible conversation of a few good lady-ephemeras, and now and then a kind smile, and a tune from the ever-amiable *Brillante*.

A proposal of marriage to Madame Helvétius

Another friend in France, whom Madame Brillon called "my kind and formidable rival," was Madame Helvétius, who lived in Auteuil and had so many friends of such various kinds drawn around her as straws about a fine piece of amber—statesmen, philosophers, historians, poets, and men of learning of all sorts.* I would not attempt to explain it but by the story of the ancient, who being asked why philosophers sought the acquaintance of kings, and kings not that of philosophers, replied that philosophers knew what they wanted, which was not always the case with kings. We found in her sweet society that charming benevolence, that amiable attention to oblige, that disposition to please and be pleased, which we did not always find in the society of one another.

I had often noticed, when reading the works of M. Helvétius [her late husband], that even though we had been born and brought up in the opposite parts of the world, we often met one another in the same thoughts; and it is very flattering to me to reflect we loved the same studies, the same friends,[†] and the same woman.

On September 19, 1779, I addressed the following proposal to Monsieur Cabanis,[‡] requesting him to deliver it to Our Lady of Auteuil: "Dr. Franklin is upset to have caused the least harm to that beautiful hair, that he always looks at with pleasure. If this lady likes to spend her days with him, he would like as much to spend his

---

* Following her late husband's custom of inviting distinguished French scientists and philosophers to their estate every Tuesday for dinner and discussions into the night, Madame Helvétius hosted what was informally called "l'Academie d'Auteuil" and included such guests as the French finance minister Turgot, the philosopher Diderot, the economist Condorcet, and the chemist Lavoisier. Turgot was especially close to Madame Helvétius, and proposed to her twice (and twice rejected). See Claude-Anne Lopez, *Mon Cher Papa* (New Haven: Yale University Press, 1990), 244–50.

† Franklin adds this footnote: Messieurs Voltaire, Hume, Turgot, Marmontel, Le Roy, Abbes Morellet, De la Roche, etc., etc.

‡ Pierre-Georges Cabanis, a young medical student staying at Madame Helvétius's house.

nights with her; & as he has already given her many of his days, although he has so few remaining to give, she seems ungrateful to never give him a single one of her nights, which flow by continually as a pure loss, without bringing anyone happiness, with the exception of Poupon. He nevertheless embraces her very tightly, because he loves her infinitely despite all her faults."

A dream in "The Elysian Fields"

Sadly, she resolved to remain single all her life, and I returned home to write the following tale, "The Elysian Fields,"* viz.:

Vexed by your barbarous resolution, announced so positively last evening, to remain single all your life in respect to your dear husband, I went home, fell on my bed, and, believing myself dead, found myself in the Elysian Fields.

There M. Helvétius received me with great courtesy, having known me for some time, he said, by the reputation I had there. He asked me a thousand things about the war, and about the present state of religion, liberty, and the government in France. "You ask nothing then of your dear friend Madame H—;" I said, "Nevertheless she still loves you excessively and I was at her place but an hour ago."

"Ah!" said he, "you make me remember my former felicity.—But it is necessary to forget it in order to be happy here. During several of the early years, I thought only of her. Finally I am consoled. I have taken another wife. The most like her that I could find. She is not, it is true, so completely beautiful, but she has as much good sense, a little more of Spirit, and she loves me infinitely. Her continual study is to please me; and she has actually gone to hunt the best nectar and

---

* From Elysium, which in Greek mythology means paradise, the abode of the blessed.

the best ambrosia in order to regale me this evening; remain with me and you will see her."

At these words the new Madame H———entered with the nectar: at which instant I recognized her to be Madame F———,* my old American friend. I reclaimed to her. But she told me coldly, "I have been your good wife forty-nine years and four months, nearly a half century; be content with that. Here I have formed a new connection, which will endure to eternity."

Offended by this refusal of my Eurydice, I suddenly decided to leave these ungrateful spirits, to return to the good earth, to see again the sunshine and you. "Here I am! Let us revenge ourselves."

I often think of the happiness I so long enjoy'd in the sweet company of Madame Helvétius and her family at Auteuil. When we meet in Paradise, the pleasures of that place will be augmented by our recollection of all the circumstances of our acquaintance on earth below.

My long continu'd friendship with Mrs. Stevenson

It was always with great pleasure to think of my long continu'd friendship, some of the happiest years of my life, that I spent with Mrs. Stevenson and her daughter Polly under her room and her company in London. I wrote to her as often as I could do. If circumstances had permitted, nothing would have afforded me so much satisfaction as to have been with her in the same house & to experience again her faithful tender care and attention to my interests, health and comfortable living, which so long & steadily attach'd me to her, & which I shall ever remember with gratitude. I wrote her the following:

---

* That is, Deborah Franklin, Ben Franklin's wife, who had passed away in 1775.

To Margaret Stevenson

Jan. 25, 1779

I rejoice to learn that your health is establish'd, & that you live pleasantly in a country town with agreeable neighbours, & have your dear children about you. My love to every one of them. I long to see them and you; but the times do not permit me the hope of it.

Why do you never write to me? I us'd to love to read your letters, & I regret your long silence. They were season'd with good sense and friendship, & even your spelling pleas'd me: Polly knows I think the worst spelling the best. I do not write to her by this conveyance: You will let her know that I acknowledge the receipt of her pleasing letter dated the 11ᵀᴴ instant.

I have nothing to complain of but a little too much business, & the want of that order and economy in my family that reign'd in it when under your prudent direction. My paper gives me only room to add, that I am ever

Yours most affectionately,

B Franklin

Good health for nearly 20 years

I had enjoy'd continu'd health for nearly 20 years, except once in two or three years a slight fit of the gout,* which generally terminated in a week or ten days; and once an intermitting fever, got from making experiments over stagnant waters. I was sometimes vex'd with an itching on the back, which I observed particularly after eating freely of beef. And sometimes after long confinement at writing, with little

---

* A painful form of arthritis, usually caused by eating rich foods. Gout was known as the disease of kings.

exercise, I felt sudden pungent pains in the flesh of different parts of the body, which I was told was scorbutic. A journey used to free me of them. I continued in health, notwithstanding the omission of my yearly journeys, which I was never able to take while in France, being confined necessarily by business. I was accustomed to what is called good living, used but little exercise, being, from the nature of my employment as well as from love of books, much in my chamber writing and reading. But I had a large garden to walk in, and I took some advantage from that.

A PERPETUAL MOTION MACHINE

I had not much time to consider philosophical matters, but did receive an account of M. Volta's electrical machine, called by the discoverer *Electrophorus perpetuus*, which speculated that the electric force once excited might be kept alive years together. From what I could tell from his description, it must be a mistake. I had known an electric force to be continued many months in a phial hermetically sealed, and supposed it might be so preserved for ages; but though one may, by repeatedly touching the knob of a charg'd bottle with a small insulated plate (like the upper one of the electrophore) draw successively an incredible number of sparks, one after each touch, and those for a while not apparently different in magnitude, yet at length they will become small, and the charge be finally exhausted. But I had not seen the experiment, and would be wrong to give an opinion.

I HAVE NEVER MADE THE LEAST PROFIT BY ANY OF MY INVENTIONS

I have never entered into any controversy in defense of my philosophical opinions; I leave them to take their chance in the world. If they are right, truth and experience will support them. If wrong, they ought to be refuted and rejected. Disputes are apt to sour one's temper and disturb one's quiet. I have no private interest in the reception of my inventions by the world, having never made nor proposed to make the least profit by any of them. The English King's changing his pointed conductors for blunt ones was therefore a matter of small importance to me. If I had had a wish about it, it would have been that he had rejected them altogether as ineffectual, for it is only since he thought himself and family safe from the thunder of heaven that he dared to use his own thunder in destroying his innocent subjects.

ADVENTURES OF ONE DAY'S ANNOYANCE

Adventures of all descriptions came my way in Paris. The following account records only one day's annoyance:

First, a man came to tell me he had invented a machine which would go of itself, without the help of a spring, weight, air, water, or any of the elements, or the labour of man or beast; and with force sufficient to work four machines for cutting tobacco; that he had experience'd it; would show it me if I would come to his house; and would sell the secret of it for two hundred louis.* I doubted it, but promis'd to go to him in order to see it.

Next, a Mons. Coder came with a proposition, in writing, to levy 600 men to be employ'd in landing on the coast of England and Scotland, to burn and ransom towns and villages in order to put a stop to the English proceedings in that way in America. I thanked him and told him I would not approve it, nor had I any money at hand for such a purpose. Moreover, it would not be permitted by the French government.

---

* The gold louis coin was equivalent to approximately one British pound sterling, or 24 livres.

Then, a man came with a request that I would patronize & recommend to the government an invention he had by which means a considerable body might be admitted into a town, one at a time, unsuspected, and after assembling, surprise it. I told him I was not a military man, of course no judge of such matters, and advised him to apply to the Bureau de la Guerre. He said he had no friends and so could procure no attention. The number of wild schemes propos'd to me was so great, and they had heretofore taken so much of my time, that I began to reject all, tho' possibly *some* of them may have been worth notice.

Finally, I received a parcel from an unknown philosopher, who submitted to my consideration a memoir on the subject of elementary fire, containing experiments in a dark chamber. It seemed to be well written, and was in English, with a little tincture of French idiom. I wished to see the experiments, however, without which I could not well judge of it.

An anonymous letter was delivered to me at 9 in the evening, May 20, 1778. It seemed intended to draw me out into the gardens for some bad purpose, as the person who pretended to have such urgent business with me never appeared, though (refusing to go out at that time of night) I appointed the next day at 11 o'clock.

I had a great deal of pleasure in Temple and Ben

My grandson Temple was well and served as my right hand in France, but I was surprised to hear from Mr. Bache in Philadelphia that there was a cabal for removing him from me. Methinks it was rather some merit that I rescu'd a valuable young man from the danger of being a Tory, and fix'd him in honest republican Whig principles; as I think, from the integrity of his disposition, his industry, his early sagacity, and uncommon abilities for business, he might in time become of great service to his country. Was it not enough that I had lost my son; would they add my grandson? An old man of seventy, I undertook a winter voyage at the command of the Congress, and for the public service, with no other attendant to take care of me. Who would comfort me and, if I died, close my eyes and take care of my remains? His dutiful behaviour towards me and his diligence and fidelity in business were both pleasing and useful to me. His conduct, as my private secretary, was exceptional, and I was confident the Congress would never think of separating us.

I had a great deal of pleasure in Ben too. He was a good, honest lad, and would in time make a valuable man. He dined with me every Sunday and some holidays. He had made as much proficiency in his learning as the boarding-school he was at could well afford him; and after some consideration where to find a better school for him, I at length fixed on sending him to Geneva, which had schools as good as in Paris. There he would be educated a Republican and a Protestant, which could not be so conveniently done at the schools in France. I had a good opportunity by a gentleman of that city, who had a place for him in his chaise, and had a son about the same age at the same school. He went very cheerfully, tho' I miss'd his company on Sundays at dinner. Soon he began to speak and read French readily, and he gained a prize by having made the best translation from Latin into French.

I LOST ALL MY CORRESPONDENCE
FOR NEARLY TWENTY YEARS

About this time, I received a report from James Lovell of Congress that the enemy had evacuated the City of Philadelphia in June 1778, which was then occupied by our troops from Valley Forge. My daughter Sally and Mr. Bache wrote me that after Gen. Howe's departure, my family had been brought back to my house at Philadelphia, and found that the English enemies who had been in possession of my house carried off with them my portrait,* leaving that of its companion, my wife, by itself a kind of widow. I also learned that my son William was exchanged for an American prisoner and would shortly go for England, and that the chest of my papers, which included all the books of my letters containing my public and private correspondence during my residence in England, had been broken open, and emptied, the papers scattered, some in the house and some out of doors, many of the latter suffered from the weather. Some of the papers from the top were found scattered about the floor and gathered up, but the manuscript books were missing, and perhaps other valuable papers. Among my papers in the trunk were eight books of rough drafts of my letters, containing all my correspondence when in England, for nearly twenty years. I have been able to recover only two. I would not have left my papers in the care of Mr. Galloway, if he had not deceived me, by saying that, since the King had declared us out of his protection, and the Parliament by an act had made our properties plunder, he would go as far in defense of his country as any man; and accordingly he had, with pleasure, given colours to a regiment of militia, and an entertainment of 400 of them before his house. I therefore thought he had become a stanch friend to the glorious cause. I was mistaken. As he was a friend of my son's, I made him one of my executors, and put the trunk of papers into his hands, imagining them safer in his house (which was out of the way of any probable march of the enemy's troops) than in my own. It was very unlucky.

For of all things, I hate altercation

With the addition of Mr. Izard and Mr. William Lee, we were five of us commissioners in the City of Paris, all honest and capable men (if

---

* Portrait of Franklin by Benjamin Wilson, now located in the White House.

I may include myself in that description) and all meaning well for the public, but our tempers did not suit, and we got into disputes and contentions that were not to our credit, and which sometimes went to extremes.

I had always resolved to have no quarrel, and have therefore made it a constant rule to answer no angry, affronting or abusive letter, of which I have received many and long ones from Mr. Lee and Mr. Izard, who wrote liberally, or rather ill-lib-erally against me, to prevent any impressions my writing against them might occasion to their prejudice.

Arthur Lee: "Mr. Lee was the most unpleasant man I ever knew."

I frequently received letters from Mr. Arthur Lee with angry charges and artful and unjust insinuations about me and Mr. Deane; that he resented the court's sending a minister without advising with him; that we did not settle the public accounts before us; and that I acted inconsistent with my duty to the public. Mr. Lee was the most unpleasant man I ever knew, full of little arts, and constantly on the watch to take advantage, with a suspicion of everybody that is exceedingly troublesome, and would make one think that he never knew an honest man in his life except himself.

Herein a correspondence between myself and Mr. Lee, amended:

To the Honorable Benjamin Franklin Esqr:

Chaillot April 2d, 1778

Sir,

It was with the utmost surprise that I learn'd yesterday that Mr. Girard was to set out in the evening for America, in a public character; and that Mr. Deane was to accompany him, without either you or he having condescended to answer my letter of the preceding day.

That a measure of such moment as Mr. Girard's mission should have been taken without any communication with the commissioners is hardly credible.* I do not live but ten minutes distance from you. The communication therefore could not be attended with delay or difficulty. Within these few days, as usual, I have seen you frequently. During all this time and with these circumstances you have been totally silent to me about the present opportunity of writing to Congress, about the important public measure in agitation, and about Mr. Deane's departure. Nay more, what you have said and the manner in which you acted, tended to mislead me from imagining that you knew of any such thing. Had you studied to deceive the most distrusted and dangerous enemy of the public, you could not have done it more effectually.

I trust, sir, you will think with me that I have a right to know your reasons for treating me thus. If you have anything to accuse me of, avow it; and I will answer you. If you have not, why do you act so inconsistent with your duty to the public, and injurious to me? Is the

---

* This concealment was not of Deane's or Franklin's choosing, but was requested by the French court. Girald told members of Congress a year later that Vergennes feared Lee and those around him, and wished to keep the sailing a secret from him. See PBF 26:222n.

present state of Europe of so little moment to our constituents as not to require our joint consideration, and information to them?

I trust too, sir, that you will not treat this letter as you have done many others, with the indignity of not answering it. Tho' I have been silent, I have not felt the less, the many affronts of this kind which you have thought proper to offer me. I have the honor to be with great respect

ARTHUR LEE

I WROTE THIS LETTER TO ARTHUR LEE. . . .

This is the draft of a letter I wrote but did not send:

To Arthur Lee

Passy, April 3, 1778

Sir

It is true I have omitted answering some of your letters. I do not like to answer angry letters. I hate disputes. I am old, cannot have long to live, have much to do and no time for altercation. If I have often received and borne your magisterial snubbing and rebukes without reply, ascribe it to the right causes: my concern for the honour and success of our mission, which would be hurt by our quarrelling; my love of peace, my respect for your good qualities, and my pity for your sick mind, which is forever tormenting itself, with its jealousies, suspicions and fancies that others mean you ill, wrong you, or fail in respect for you. If you do not cure your self of this temper, it will end in insanity, of which it is the symptomatic forerunner, as I have seen in several instances. God preserve you from so terrible an evil: and for his sake pray suffer me to live in quiet. I have the honour to be very respectfully, sir, your most humble servant

B FRANKLIN

But sent this one.....

This is the letter I actually sent (in part):

To Arthur Lee

Passy, April 4, 1778

Sir,

Mr. Deane communicated to me his intention of setting out for America immediately as a secret, which he desired I would mention to nobody. I comply'd with his request. If he did not think fit to communicate it to you also, it is from him you should demand his reasons.

You ask me why I act so inconsistent with my duty to the public. This is a heavy charge, sir, which I have not deserved. But it is to the public I am accountable and not to you. I have been a servant to many publics thro' a long life, having served them with fidelity, and having been honoured by their approbation. There is not a single instance of my ever being accus'd before of acting contrary to their interest or my duty. I shall account to the Congress, when call'd upon for this, my terrible offense of being silent to you about Mr. Deane's and M. Girald's departure. And I have no doubt of their equity in acquitting me.

It is true that I have omitted answering some of your letters, particularly your angry ones, in which you with very magisterial airs school'd and documented me, as if I had been one of your domestics. I saw in the strongest light the importance of our living in decent civility toward each other while our great affairs were depending here. I saw your jealous, suspicious, malignant, and quarrelsome temper, which has daily manifested itself against Mr. Deane and almost every other person you had any concern with. I, therefore, pass'd your affronts in silence, did not answer but burnt your angry letters, and received you when I next saw you with the same civility as if you had never written them. For of all things I hate altercation. I bore all your rebukes with patience, for the sake of the service, but it went a little hard with me.

One more word about the accounts. The infinity of business we have had is the true and only reason that I know of why they have not been settled; that is, why we did not meet, sit down and compare the vouchers with the articles in the banker's account, in order to see that his charges were supported, and that he had given us due credit for the moneys we had put into his hands. This I apprehend is all we have to do here. It is to the Congress we are separately to account for the separate drafts we have made on him. This Mr. Deane can do when he arrives, having taken a copy of the account with him. If you think we should account to one another for our expenses, I have no objection, tho' I never expected it. I believe they will be found very moderate. I am sure mine will, having had only the necessaries of life, and purchas'd nothing besides except the *Encyclopedia*, nor sent a sixpence' worth of anything to my friends or family in America.

B Franklin

They wrote me long abusive letters, which I never answered

I was very easy about the efforts of Messrs. Lee and Izard to injure me on that side of the water and cause so much dissensions in Congress. We had Wedderburnes in France as well as in England. They quarreled at me, rather than with me, for I would not quarrel with them. They wrote me long abusive letters which I never answered, but treated the gentlemen with the same civility when we met as if no such letters existed. This I think most prudent for public character, but I suspect myself of being a little malicious in it, for I imagined they were more vex'd by such neglect than they would have been by a tart reply. Such malignant natures cannot long agree together even in mischief. No revenge was necessary for me; I need only leave them to hiss, bite, sting and poison one another.

I trusted in the justice of the Congress that they would listen to no accusations against me. I knew those gentlemen had plenty of ill will to me, tho' I had never done to either of them the smallest injury, or given the least just cause of offense. But my too great reputation and the general good-will this people have had for me, the respect they showed me and even the compliments they made me, all grieved those unhappy gentlemen; unhappy indeed in their tempers, and in their dark uncomfortable passions of jealousy, anger, suspicion, envy, and malice. It is enough for good minds to be affected at other people's misfortunes; but they that are vexed at everybody's good luck can never be happy: I take no other revenge of such enemies, than to let them remain in their miserable situation in which their malignant natures have placed them, by endeavouring to support an estimable character; and thus by continuing the reputation the world has hitherto indulged me with, I shall continue them in the present state of damnation; I am not disposed to reverse my conduct for the alleviation of their torments.

THE DEFORMED AND THE HANDSOME LEG

My experiences with Lee and Izard reminded me at times of a bagatelle I wrote later called "La Belle et la Mauvaise Jambe." It has been translated as follows:

There are two sorts of people in the world, who with equal degrees of health and wealth and the other comforts of life, become the one happy, the other unhappy. Those who are to be happy fix their attention on the pleasant parts of conversation, and enjoy all with cheerfulness. Those who are to be unhappy think and speak only of the contraries. Hence they are continually discontented themselves, and by their remarks sour the pleasures of society, offend personally many people, and make themselves everywhere disagreeable. If these people will not change this bad habit, and condescend to be pleas'd with what is pleasing, it is good for others to avoid an acquaintance with them, which is always disagreeable, and sometimes very inconvenient, particularly when one finds one's self entangled in their quarrels.

An old philosophical friend of mine, grown from experience very cautious in this, carefully shun'd any intimacy with such people. He had, like other philosophers, a thermometer to show the heat of the weather, and a barometer to mark when it was likely to prove good or bad; but there being no instrument yet invented to discover at first sight this unpleasing disposition in a person, he for that purpose made use of his legs. One was remarkably handsome, the other by some accident crooked and deform'd. If a stranger at the first interview regarded his ugly leg more than his handsome one, he doubted him. If he spoke of it, and took no notice of the handsome leg, that was sufficient to determine my philosopher to have no farther acquaintance with him.

I therefore advise these critical, querulous, discontented, unhappy people that if they wish to be loved and respected by others and happy in themselves, they should *leave off looking at the ugly leg*.

America may be cheaply governed

The body of our people are not merchants but humble husbandmen who delight in the cultivation of their lands, which from their fertility and variety of our climates are capable of furnishing all the necessaries and conveniences of life without external commerce: And we have too much land to have the least temptation to extend our territories by conquest from peaceable neighbours, as well as too much justice to think of it. Our militias are sufficient to defend our lands from invasion, and the commerce with us will be defended by all the

nations who find an advantage in it. We therefore have not the occasion of fleets or standing armies, but may well leave those expensive
machines to be maintain'd for the pomp of princes and by the wealth
of ancient states.

We purpose, if possible, to live in peace with all mankind; we
have hope that no other power will judge it prudent to quarrel with
us, lest they divert us from our own quiet industry, and turn us into
corsairs preying upon others. The weight therefore of an independent empire will not be so great: The expense of our civil government
we have always borne, and can easily bear because it is small. A virtuous and labourious people may be cheaply govern'd. Determined
as we are to have no offices of profit, nor any sinecures or useless
appointments, so common in ancient and corrupted states, we can
govern overselves a year for the sums England pays in a single
department.

On free trade

I received notice from Congress proposing to abrogate articles eleven
and twelve of the Treaty of Commerce with France regarding duties
on molasses from the West Indies.* Vergennes agreed to drop these
articles. In my opinion proposing to abrogate them had an unpleasing appearance, as it looked like a desire of making that commercial
kind of war, which no honest state can begin with. It might be consider'd an act of hostility that provoked as well as justify'd reprisals,
and render'd the first project as unprofitable as it was unjust. Commerce among nations as well as between private persons should be
fair and equitable, by equivalent exchanges and mutual supplies. The
taking unfair advantage of a neighbour's necessities, tho' attended

---

* Articles eleven and twelve of the Treaty of Commerce with France called
  for the abolition of the duties on molasses imported from the West Indies.

with a temporary success, always breeds ill blood. To lay duties on a commodity exported which our friends want is a knavish attempt to get something for nothing. The statesman who first invented it had the genius of a pickpocket; and would have been a pickpocket if fortune had suitably plac'd him. The nations who have practis'd it have suffer'd for it fourfold, as pickpockets ought to suffer. Savoy by a duty on exported wines lost the supplying of Switzerland, which thenceforth raised it own wine; and (to wave other instances) Britain by her duty on exported tea lost the trade of her colonies. But as we produce no commodity that is peculiar to our country, and which may not be obtained elsewhere, the discouraging the consumption of ours by duties on exportation, and thereby encouraging a rivalship from other nations in the ports we trade to, is absolute folly, which is indeed mixed more or less with all knavery. For my part, if my protest were of any consequence, I should protest against our ever doing it even by way of reprisal. It is a meanness with which I would not dirty the conscience or character of my country.

I asked Congress to separate us

My colleague Mr. Deane had been recall'd by Congress, to be replaced by Mr. John Adams, who arrived on a continental frigate, the *Boston* (which took a prize with a cargo valued at £70,000). I believe Mr. Deane's recall was the effect of some misrepresentations from an enemy or two at Paris and at Nantes. Having lived intimately with him for fifteen months, the greatest part of the time in the same house, and been a constant witness of his public conduct, I esteem'd him a faithful, active and able minister, who to my knowledge had done in various ways great and important services to his country, whose interests I wished might always, by everyone in her employ, be as much and as effectually promoted. However, Congress accused Mr. Deane of embezzling public money, or trading with it on his private account and employing it in stock-jobbing. I thought him a man of integrity, and innocent, but gave him up.

To Mr. Lovell of Congress, I inquired into the intention of Congress whether to keep *three* ambassadors at the French court; indeed we had *four* with Mr. Izard, who continued in Paris and was very angry that he was not consulted in making the Treaty. We would have a *fifth* soon, for the envoy to Vienna, Mr. William Lee, was not received there and was returning. I assured Mr. Lovell that the necessary expense of maintaining us all was enormously great. But as to our number, whatever advantage there might be in the joint counsels of three for framing and adjusting the articles of the Treaty, there could be none in managing the common business of a resident there. And where everyone must be consulted on every particular of common business, in answering every letter, &c., and one of them is offended if the smallest thing is done without his consent, the difficulty of being often and long enough together, the different opinions, and the time consumed in debating them, the interruption by new applications in the time of meeting, &c. &c. occasion so much postponing and delay, that correspondence languished, occasions were lost, and the business was always behind hand. In consideration of the whole I asked Congress to separate us.

We had no news from America but what came thro' England. We learned that the English army was well worried in its march, and that their whole fleet and forces were block'd up in New York by Washington and Gates on the land side, and by Count D'Estaign by sea, and they would soon be in want of provisions.

Chapter Seven

Minister to France, 1779–81

The War Continues

MY APPOINTMENT AS
MINISTER PLENIPOTENTIARY

On the 11th of February, 1779, the Marquis de Lafayette arrived in Paris, covered with laurels, and brought me the news from the Congress of my appointment to be their minister plenipotentiary at the French Court, together with a letter to be present'd to his Majesty. This mark of public confidence was most agreeable to me as it was not obtained by any solicitation or intrigue on my part, nor did I ever write a syllable to any person in or out of Congress magnifying my own services or diminishing those of others. The commission of three persons was dissolv'd, my former colleagues having destinations to other courts in Europe. Mr. Adams took his passage to America to return immediately to Congress in Philadelphia. I wrote M. De Vergennes excusing my not going to Versailles on account of a severe access of the gout, but on Tuesday the 23RD of March, I thought myself able to go through the ceremony, and accordingly went to Court at Versailles, had my audience with the King in the new character, presented my letter of credence, and was received very graciously, after which I went the rounds with the other foreign ministers, in visiting all the royal family. The fatigue, however, was a little too much for my feet, and disabled me for near another week.

After that I constantly attended the levee every Tuesday with the other foreign ministers, and took every proper occasion of repeating the assurances I was instructed to give, of the grateful sentiments of Congress, and their determined resolution to fulfill religiously their engagements. Much pain was constantly taken by the enemy to weaken the confidence of this court in their new allies, by representing our people as weary of the war and of the government of Congress, which they represented as distracted by dissensions &c. But all this had little effect. Notwithstanding the great losses suffer'd by the commerce of the kingdom of France, since the commencement of the war, the disposition of the Court to continue it (till its purpose of establishing our independence was compleated) had not in the least changed, nor their regard for us diminished.

LAFAYETTE, HIS BRAVERY AND GOOD CONDUCT

All our letters from different persons in Congress, the Army, and the government of separate states were full of Lafayette's praises. By his bravery and good conduct he appeared to have gain'd the esteem and the affection of the whole continent of America. Gen. Washington sent me a letter of recommendation of the Marquis de Lafayette, tho' his modesty detain'd it long in his own hands. We became acquainted, however, from the time of his arrival at Paris; and his zeal for the honour of our country, his activity in our affairs in France, and his firm attachment to our cause and to Gen. Washington impress'd me.

WAR NEWS FROM HOME

The Marquis de Lafayette spoke of the taking of Savannah by British troops, which made a noise in England and helped to keep up their spirits, but I apprehended that before the summer was over, they would find the possession of that capital of Georgia of as little consequence as their former possessions of Boston and Philadelphia; and that the distempers of that unwholesome part of the country would very much weaken, if not ruin that army. I was glad to see in news from home the American spirit rous'd again and I was much pleased with the subscriptions of the ladies and merchants. They confuted the assertion of the Scotch writer, who says that women have not the *amor patrie* and that merchants are attach'd to no country.* I saw by the Virginia papers that the 6ᵀᴴ of February 1779, being the anniversary of the signing of the Treaty with France, was observed with great festivity by the Congress & at Philadelphia.

SOMETIMES I REGRET I WAS BORN TOO SOON

At this time I did not totally neglect philosophy, though I had little time for it. I wrote a paper on the Aurora Borealis, *One of the late Northern Lights*. The paper, translated into French, was read in the Academy of Sciences and well received.

I rejoiced to hear that Mr. Priestley was still employ'd in experimental researches into nature. The rapid progress true science now makes occasions my regretting sometimes that I was born so soon. It is impossible to imagine the heights to which the power of man may be carried over matter in a thousand years. We may perhaps learn to deprive large masses of their gravity and give them absolute levity for the sake of easy transport. Agriculture may diminish its labour and double it produce. All diseases may by sure means be prevented or

---

* Lord Kames wrote that women "have less patriotism than men" in *Sketches of the History of Man* (2nd ed., 4 vols., Edinburgh, 1778), II, 4–5. And Adam Smith wrote, "A merchant, it has been said very properly, is not necessarily the citizen of any particular country" in *The Wealth of Nations* (2 vol., London, 1776), I, 509 (Book III, chapter 4).

cured, not excepting even that of old age, and our lives lengthened at pleasure even beyond the antediluvian standard. O that moral science were as fair a way of improvement, that men would cease to be wolves to one another, and that human beings would at length learn what they now improperly call humanity!

We make great improvements in nature daily. There is one I wish to see in moral philosophy: the discovery of a plan that would induce and oblige nations to settle their disputes without first cutting one another's throats. When will human reason be sufficiently improv'd to see the advantage of this! When will men be convinc'd that even successful wars do at length become misfortunes to those who unjustly commenc'd them, and who triumph'd blindly in their success, not seeing all its consequences.

An American passport for Captain James Cook

In March 1779, I sent letters to all the American cruisers then in the ports of France and Spain, with orders to our agents to communicate them to others, forbidding our American cruisers to intercept or molest Captain Cook, the celebrated navigator and discoverer, in case they should meet with him on his return.* Capt. Cook had set out from England in 1776, before the commencement of the war, to make discoveries of new countries in unknown seas, an undertaking truly laudable, as the increase of geographical knowledge would facilitate the communication between distant nations, the exchange of useful products and manufactures, and the extension of arts, whereby the

---

* It turned out that the Franklin's granting of a passport to Captain James Cook was unnecessary, as the famed discoverer had been killed by Sandwich Islanders on February 14, 1779. The news of Cook's death did not reach Europe until January, 1780. PBF 29:86.

common enjoyments of human life would be multiplied, and science of other kinds increased to the benefit of mankind in general. I also sent the letter to Holland, to be printed in the Dutch papers, as a means of making it more generally known to our cruisers at sea not to suffer any plunder, nor detain his ship, but that they should treat Capt. Cook and his people with all civility and assistance.

It was to be Cook's last voyage. In 1784, the Council of Royal Society voted me a gold medal on account of my letter in favor of Capt. Cook, and the Admiralty made me a present of his last voyage, which Lord Howe sent to me in France.

WASTING OUR WEALTH ON PRODIGALITY

My apprehensions of approaching distress regarding money matters grew stronger, and gave me a great deal of anxiety. We were under the necessity of supplies from Europe and the difficulty in making returns. The interest bills would do a good deal toward purchasing arms, ammunition, clothing, sailcloth and other necessaries for defense. Upon inquiring of those who presented those bills to me for acceptance, what the money was to be laid out in, I found that most of it was for superfluities, and more than half of it for tea! How unhappily, in this instance, the folly of our people and the avidity of our merchants concurred to weaken & impoverish our country! I formerly computed that we had consumed before the war, in that single article, the value of £500,000 sterling annually. Much of this was saved by stopping the use of it. I honoured the virtuous resolution of our women in foregoing that little gratification, and I lament that such virtue was of so short duration. Five hundred thousand pounds sterling annually laid out in defending ourselves or annoying our enemies would have had great effects. With what face could we ask aids and subsidies from our friends while we were wasting our own wealth on such prodigality?

CORRESPONDENCE WITH MY DAUGHTER, SALLY

With this in mind, I wrote the following letter to my daughter Sally, viz:

Passy, June 3, 1779

Dear Sally,

I have before me your letters of Oct. 22, and Jan. 17ᵀᴴ: They are the only ones I received from you in the course of eighteen months. If you knew how happy your letters make me, and considered how many miscarry, I think you would write oftener.

When I began to read your account of the high prices of goods, "a pair of gloves seven dollars, a yard of common gauze twenty-four dollars, and that it now requires a fortune to maintain a family in a very plain way," I expected you would conclude with telling me, that everybody as well as yourself was grown frugal and industrious; and I could scarce believe my eyes in reading forward, that "there never was so much dressing and pleasure going on," and that you yourself wanted black pins and feathers from France, to appear, I suppose, in the mode! This leads me to imagine that perhaps it is not so much that the goods are grown dear, as that the money is grown cheap, as everything else will do when excessively plenty; and that people are still as easy nearly in their circumstances as when a pair of gloves might be had for half a crown. The war indeed may in some degree raise the price of goods, and the high taxes which are necessary to support the war may make our frugality necessary; and as I am always preaching that doctrine, I cannot in conscience or in decency encourage the contrary, by my example, in furnishing my children with foolish modes and luxuries. I therefore send all the articles you desire that are useful and necessary, and omit the rest; for as you can say you should "have great pride in wearing anything I send, and showing it as your father's taste," I must avoid giving you an opportunity of doing that with either lace or feathers. If you wear your cambric ruffles as I do, and take care not to mend the holes, they will come in time to be lace; and feathers, my dear girl, may be had in America from every cock's tail.

If you happen again to see General Washington, assure him of my very great and sincere respect, and tell him that all the old generals here amuse themselves in studying the accounts of his operations, and approve highly of his conduct.

Present my affectionate regards to all friends that enquire after me, particularly Mr. Duffield and family, and write often, my dear child, to

Your loving father,

B FRANKLIN

PITY MY SITUATION

A merchant of Amsterdam had undertaken to procure a loan to us of 1,500,000 Florins at 6 per cent. But by what I learned and judged of that person, I thought there was little dependence to be had upon his success; especially as the English borrowed there at a higher rate, and the House of Hornica Fizeaux & Co. already engaged more than 6 per cent. After months of endeavouring to obtain such a loan, I had succeeded only to the amount of 51,000 Florins.

I had in various ways and thro' various channels laid before the French ministry the distressed state of our finances in America. There seemed a great willingness in all of them to help us, except in the controller, M. Necker, who was said to be not well disposed toward us, and was embarrassed by every measure proposed to relieve us by grants of money. Under the resolution, perhaps too hastily declared, of the King's imposing no new taxes on his subjects for that year [1779], the Court had great difficulties in defraying expenses, the vast exertions to put the navy in a condition to equal that of England having cost immense sums. However, the King, to encourage our loan in Holland, engaged under his hand to be security for our payment of the interest of three millions of livres; but that loan amounted to no more than 80,000 Florins.

As to our finances in France, I suffer'd anxiety and distress of mind lest I should not be able to pay our disbursements: Great quantities of clothing, arms, ammunition and naval stores sent from time to time; to our prisoners in England, and after their escape to help some home, and to other Americans in distress in France, a great sum, I cannot at present say how much; to commissioners Mr. William Lee and Mr. Izard £5,500 sterling; for the fitting of the frigates *Raleigh, Alfred, Boston, Providence, Alliance, Ranger* &c., I imagine not less than 60,000 or 70,000 livres each, taken one with another; for maintenance of the English prisoners I found 100,000 livres not sufficient, having already paid above 65,000 for that article; and then, the drafts on the treasury of the loans coming very fast upon me. To apply again to this Court for money was extremely awkward. I therefore repeated the general applications which we had made when together for aids of money, and received the general answers, that the expense of government for the navy was so great that it was exceedingly difficult to furnish the necessary supplies. Thanks to God, I did get over the difficulty as related to the bills, which were all punctually paid; but I warned the Congress that if the navy boards were to send more ships to France to be fitted, or the Congress continued to draw for the payment of other debts, I would probably be made a bankrupt.

The Committee of Commerce sent me over an invoice of goods amounting, I guess, to more than twelve million livres. I was obliged to abridge it greatly, the sums granted me not sufficing. If Mr. Jay could have obtained a sum from Spain it would have helped to supply the deficiency. Pity my situation. Too much was expected of me, and not only the Congress drew upon me, often unexpectedly, for large sums, but all the agents of the Committee of Commerce in

Europe and America thought they might do the same when pinch'd, alleging that it was necessary to the credit of the Congress, that their particular credit ought to be supported. The little success that attended the late applications of money mortified me exceedingly; and the storm of bills which I found coming upon me and John Jay in Madrid terrified and vexed me to such a degree that I was deprived of sleep, and so much indisposed by continual anxiety as to be render'd almost incapable of writing.

I HAD LONG BEEN HUMILIATED
BEGGING FOR MONEY AND FRIENDSHIP

Our credit and weight in Europe depended more on what we did than on what we said. I had long been humiliated with the idea of our running about from court to court begging for money and friendship, which were the more withheld the more eagerly they were solicited, yet would perhaps have been offer'd if they had not been asked. The supposed necessity was our only excuse. The proverb says *God helps them that help themselves*, and the world too in this sense is very godly.

At length I got over a reluctance that was almost invincible and made another application to the government in France for more money. I drew up and presented a state of debts and newly expected demands, and requested its aid to extricate me. Judging from the letters from Mr. Jay that he was not likely to obtain anything from the court of Spain, I put down in my estimate the 25,000 dollars drawn upon him with the same sum drawn upon me, as what would probably come to me for payment. I had the pleasure of acquainting Mr. Jay that my memorial was well received in the kindest and most friendly manner; and tho' the court was not without its embarrassments on account of money, I was told to make myself easy, for that I would be assisted with what was necessary. I ended my letter to Mr. Jay with the comment, "If you find any inclination to hug me for the good news of this letter, I constitute and appoint Mrs. Jay my attorney to receive in my behalf your embraces."

THIS CURRENCY AS WE MANAGED IT
WAS A WONDERFUL MACHINE

The principal difficulty at the time in America consisted in the depreciation of our currency, owing to the over-quantities issued, and the diminished demand for it in commerce. The depreciation of our money greatly affected salaried men, widows and orphans. I received a report from the Congress how the manners of the country were much affected by the depreciation, so that almost every officer, civil or military, felt a desire to engage in speculation, finding that his salary was inadequate to the harping demands which are made upon him for the necessaries of life.

I took all the pains I could in Congress to prevent the depreciation by proposing first that the bills should bear interest; this was rejected, and they were struck accordingly. Secondly, after the first emission, I proposed that we should stop, strike no more, but borrow on interest those which had issued. This was not approved and more bills were issued. When, from the too great quantity, these began to depreciate, they agreed to borrow on interest, and I propos'd that in order to fix the value of the principal, the interest should be promis'd in hard dollars. This was objected to as impracticable. When the whole mass of the currency was under way in depreciation, the momentum of its descent was too great to be stopped. The only remedy then seemed to be a diminution of the quantity by a vigorous taxation, of great nominal sums, which the people were more able to pay in proportion to the quantity and diminished value. The only consolation under the evil is that the public debt was proportionably diminish'd with the depreciation, by an imperceptible tax everyone paid as the value fell between his receiving and paying such sums as pass'd thro' his hands. For it should always be remembered that the original intention was to sink the bills by taxes, which as effectually extinguish the debt as an actual redemption.

This effect of paper currency is not understood in Europe. And indeed the whole is a mystery even to the politicians; how we were able to continue a war four years without money; and how we could pay with paper that had no previously fix'd fund appropriated specifically to redeem it. This currency as we managed it was a wonderful machine. It performed its office when we issued it; it paid and clothed the troops, and provided victuals and ammunition; and when we were oblig'd to issue a quantity excessive, it paid itself off by depreciation.

An expedition to Canada was deferred for want of a sufficient quantity of hard money. The Canadians were afraid of paper and would not take the Congress's money. To enter a country which you mean to make a friend of, with an army that must have occasion every day for fresh provision in horses, carriages, and labour of every kind; having no acceptable money to pay those that serve you; and to be obliged therefore to take that service by force, is the sure way to disgust, offend, and by degrees make enemies of the whole people, after which all operations will be more difficult, all motions discovered, and every endeavour used to have us driven back out of their country.

THOSE WHO LOVE TO RECEIVE LETTERS SHOULD WRITE LETTERS

Correspondence between friends in America and Europe were miserably cut to pieces by the capture of vessels, and the sinking of dispatches. It was sometimes long, very long, before I had the great pleasure of hearing from my friends. But it was my fault. I had long omitted my part of the correspondence. Those who love to receive letters should write letters. I wished I could safely promise an amendment of that fault. But besides the indolence attending age, and growing upon us with it, my time was engross'd by too much business, and I had too many inducements to postpone doing what I felt I ought to do for my own sake, and what I could never resolve to omit entirely.

I did take time to write my old friend Thomas Viny of Kent, England, viz:

To Thomas Viny

Passy, May 4, 1779

Dear Sir,

When all the bustle is over, if my short remainder of life will permit my return thither, what a pleasure it will be to me to see my old friend and his children settled there. I hope he will find vines and fig trees there under which we may sit and converse, enjoying peace and plenty, a good government, good laws and liberty, without which men lose half their value. I am, with much esteem, my dear friend

Yours most affectionately

B Franklin

I thought every day of my grandson Benny, who was in school in Geneva. There was nothing I desired more than to see him furnish'd with good learning, that I might return him to his father and mother so accomplish'd, with such knowledge and virtue as to give them pleasure, and enable him to become an honourable man in his own country. I learned that the smallpox was in that school, and four of the scholars were dead of it. How happy it was for Benny that his parents took care to have him inoculated when he was an infant.

Intrigue and treachery at Madame Brillon's

At this time, I received a letter from Madame Brillon announcing that her heart had been cruelly wounded by her husband, and asking to see me at ten in the morning on Wednesday [May 5, 1779] in a closed meeting to receive comfort and advice. She confided to me that her husband had fallen under the spell of their maid, Mademoiselle J (a woman my landlord had proposed I hire!). "My life is torn by grief through her intrigue and treachery!" she said.

After our private meeting, I wrote her this letter:

May 11, 1779

To Madame Brillon,

You told me, my dear daughter, that your heart is too sensitive. I see by your letters that this is true. A keen awareness of our own faults is good because it leads us to avoid them in the future. But to be very sensitive to, and afflicted by, the faults of other people—that is not good. They are the ones who should be sensitive and afflicted by what they have done. As for us, we should preserve that tranquility that is the just portion of innocence and virtue. If you exact a vengeance by punishing them, you restore them to the state of equality that they had lost. But if you were to forgive them, without any punishment, you would fix them in the low state into which they have fallen, and from which they can never emerge without true repentance and full reparation. Follow then, my very dear and always amiable daughter, the good resolution that you have so wisely taken, to continue to fulfill all your duties as good mother, good wife, good friend, good neighbor, good Christian, etc. (without forgetting to be a good daughter to your papa), and to neglect and forget, if you can, the wrongs you may be suffering at present. And be sure that, given time, the rectitude of your conduct will win over the minds of even the worst people. Time will turn everything to good. Then all of them will ask with compunction for the return of your friendship and they will become in the future your most zealous friends.

I am aware that I have written a great deal of very bad French here; perhaps that will repulse you, you who write this charming language with so much purity and elegance.

B Franklin

Do not pay too much for your whistle

I followed up with this letter in November:

November 10, 1779

To Madame Brillon,

Instead of spending this Wednesday evening, as I have long done, in your delightful company, I sit down to spend it in thinking of you, in writing to you, & in reading over & over again your letters.

I am charm'd with your description of paradise & with your plan of living there. And I approved much of your conclusion that in the mean time we should draw all the good we can from this world. In my opinion we might all draw more good from it than we do and suffer less evil, if we would but take care *not to give too much for our whistles.* For to me it seems that most of the unhappy people we meet with are becoming so by neglect of that caution.

You ask what I mean? You love stories, and will excuse my telling you one of myself. When I was a child of seven years old, my friends on a holiday fill'd my little pocket with halfpence. I went directly to a shop where they sold toys for children; and being charm'd with the sound of a whistle that I met by the way in the hands of another boy, I voluntarily offer'd and gave all my money for it. When I came home, whistling all over the house, much pleas'd with my whistle (but disturbing all the family), my brothers, sisters and cousins, understanding the bargain I had made, told me I had given four times as much for it as it was worth, and then put me in mind what good things I might have bought with the rest of the money, and laughed at me so much for my folly that I cry'd with vexation; and the reflection gave me more chagrin than the whistle gave me pleasure.

This, however, was afterwards of use to me, the impression continuing on my mind; so that often when I was tempted to buy some unnecessary thing, I said to myself, Do not give too much for the whistle; and I sav'd my money.

As I grew up, came into the world, and observed the actions of men, I thought I met many who gave too much for their whistle. When I saw one ambitious of court favour, sacrificing his time in attendance at levees, his repose, his liberty, his virtue and perhaps his friend, to obtain it; I have said to myself, This man gives too much for his whistle. When I saw another fond of popularity, constantly employing himself in political bustles, neglecting his own affairs, and ruining them by that neglect; He pays, says I, too much for his whistle. If I knew a miser, who gave up every kind of comfortable living, all the pleasure of doing good to others, all the esteem of his fellow citizens, and the joys of benevolent friendship, for the sake of accumulating wealth; Poor man, says I, he pays too much for his whistle. When I met with a man of pleasure, sacrificing every laudable improvement of his mind or of his fortune, to mere corporeal satisfactions, and ruining his health in their pursuit; Mistaken man, says I, he pays too much for his whistle. If I see one fond of appearance, of fine clothes, fine houses, fine furniture, fine equipages, all above his fortune, for which he contracts debts, and ends his career in a prison; Alas, says I, he has paid too much for his whistle. When I see a beautiful sweet-temper'd girl marry'd to an ill-natured brute of a husband; What a pity, says I, that she should pay so much for a whistle! In short, I conceiv'd that a great part of the miseries of mankind are brought upon them by the false estimates they have made of the value of things, and by their giving too much for their whistle.

Yet I ought to have charity for these unhappy people, when I consider that, with all this wisdom of which I am boasting, there are certain things in the world so tempting; for example the apples of King John, which happily are not to be bought, for if they were put on sale by auction, I might very easily be led to ruin myself in the purchase, and find that I had once more given too much for my whistle.

B Franklin

"I have often paid a high price for bad whistles"

Madame Brillon wrote the following reply:

November 16, 1779

To B. Franklin,

I assure you, my kind papa, that I shall be very careful not to give too much for the whistles. I have often paid a high price for bad whistles. I believed, for instance, that when I loved, one was bound to love me back, since I judged others by the standards of my own soul. I have seldom gotten back the worth of what I gave, which is called paying too much for the whistle.

M. Brillon laughed heartily at the whistles. We find that what you call your bad French often adds piquancy to your narration, due to the construction of certain sentences, and the words that you invent.

A week from Saturday, my good papa, I will give you a little music, some games of chess, and tea. Should I tell you how much pleasure it will give me to see you again? No! I would rather let you guess.

Madame Brillon

New copper coins might make an impression on young persons

In America, there was an intention to strike a copper coin that might not only be useful as small change, but serve other purposes. Instead of repeating continually upon every half-penny the dull story that everybody knows (and what it would have been no loss to mankind if nobody had ever known), that George III is King of Great Britain, France and Ireland &c. &c. I proposed to put on one side some important proverb of Solomon, some pious moral, prudential or economical precept, the frequent inoculation of which, by seeing it every time one receives a piece of money, might make an impression upon the mind, especially of young persons, and tend to regulate the conduct; such as on some, *The fear of the Lord is the begin-*

Franklin book shop next to Christ Church, Philadelphia: "Keep thy shop & thy shop will keep thee."

ning of wisdom; on others, *Honesty is the best policy*; on others, *He that by the plow would thrive; himself must either lead or drive.* On others, *keep thy shop & thy shop will keep thee.* On others, *a penny sav'd is a penny got.* On others, *He that buys what he has no need of, will soon be forced to sell his necessaries.* On others, *Early to bed & early to rise, will make a man healthy, wealthy & wise*, and so on to a great variety.

The other side I proposed to fill with good designs, drawn and engraved by the best artists in France, of all the different species of barbarity with which the English carry'd on the war in America, expressing every abominable circumstance of their cruelty and inhumanity, that figures can express, to make an impression on the minds of posterity as strong and durable as that on the copper. This resolution was a long time forborn, but the burning of defenseless towns in Connecticut, on the flimsy pretense that the people fired from behind their houses, when the burning was known to have been premeditated and ordered from England, might have given the finishing provocation, and might have occasioned a vast demand for the metal.

THIS PUT THE ENEMY TO MUCH EXPENSE

We gave the English a little taste of this disturbance upon their own coasts in the summer of 1779. And tho' we burned none of their towns, we occasioned a good deal of terror and bustle in many of them. One little privateer of Dunkirk, the *Black Prince*, with a Congress commission and a few Americans mixed with Irish and English smugglers, went round their islands and took 37 prizes in less than 3 months. The cruise of our little American squadron under Commodore John Paul Jones, under the same commissions and colours, alarm'd those coasts exceedingly, had occasion'd a good deal of internal expense and done great damage to their trade. The *Alliance* and the *Bonhomme Richard*, which was mann'd chiefly by Americans, took two frigates with 500 English prisoners. Had not contrary winds and accidents prevented it, the intended invasion of England with the combined fleet and a great army might have taken place, and might have made the English feel a little more of that kind of distress they so wantonly caused in America. The coasts of Britain and Ireland were greatly alarmed, being supposed that Jones had landed forces. This put the enemy to much expense in marching troops from place to place. Several valuable prizes were made of merchant ships, particularly two, one from London, 300 tons and 84 men, with 22 guns laden with naval stores for Quebec; the other from Liverpool bound to New York and Jamaica of 22 guns and 87 men, laden with provisions and bale goods. Our commodore's ship the *Bonhomme Richard* was so shatter'd that she could not be kept afloat, and the people being all taken out of her, she sank the second day after the engagement. The rest of the squadron were refitted in the *Texel,* from which neutral place they departed with their prizes and prisoners near 400. (So now we had more English prisoners than they had American.) Few actions at sea have demonstrated such steady, cool, determined bravery, as that of Jones in taking the *Serapis.* Jones's bravery and conduct in the action gain'd him great honour.

THEIR DEVILISHNESS WEAKENED THAT RESOLUTION

Accounts upon oath were taken in America by order of Congress, of the British barbarities committed there, among which was the covering with pease straw of 15 American soldiers wounded and disabled in a fight near a barn in New Jersey, and setting fire to the straw, whereby they were burnt to death. I was expected to make a school book of them, 35 in all. Prints were designed and engraved in Paris by good artists, each expressing one or more of the different horrid facts to be inserted in the book in order to impress the minds of children and posterity with a deep sense of our enemy's bloody and insatiable malice and wickedness. Every kindness I heard of done by an Englishman to an American prisoner made me resolve not to proceed in the work, hoping a reconciliation would take place. But every fresh instance of their devilishness weakened that resolution, and made me abominate the thought of reunion with such a people.

Meanwhile, the French Court issued a royal edict for abolishing the remains of slavery in that kingdom. Who would have thought a few years earlier, that we should have lived to see a king of France giving freedom to slaves, while a king of England endeavoured to make slaves of freemen!

ONE OF THE GREATEST CAPTAINS OF THE AGE

I frequently heard the old generals of this martial country (who study the maps of America, and mark upon them all his operations) speak with sincere approbation and great applause of Gen. Washington and his conduct, and join in giving him the character of one of the greatest captains of the age. I must soon quit the scene, but General Washington (and others) will live to see our country flourish, as it amazingly and rapidly did after the war was over. Like a field of young Indian corn, which long fair weather and sunshine has enfeebled and discolour'd, and which in that weak state, by a thunder gust of violent wind, hail and rain seem'd to be threatened with absolute destruction; yet the storm being past, it recovers fresh verdure, shoots up with double vigor, and delights the eye not of its owner only, but of every observing traveller.

MUTINY ON THE *ALLIANCE*

Mr. Jay was in Madrid, and Mr. Adams had returned to Paris in March, 1780. We lived upon good terms with each other, but Adams never communicated anything of his business to me at first, and I made no inquiries of him, nor did I receive any letter from Congress explaining it, so that I was in utter ignorance of his purpose.

Messrs. Lee and Izard together went to L'orient in order to embark on the *Alliance*. No souls regretted their departure. We parted civilly, for I never acquainted them that I knew of their writing against me to Congress. The *Alliance* was expected to sail immediately to America. But the men refusing to go till paid their shares of prize money, and sundry difficulties arising with regard to the sale and division, she had been detained thus long to my mortification, and I was yet uncertain when I would be able to get her out. I advanced 24,000 livres to supply the most urgent of their necessities, till the prize-money could be obtained. With regard to their wages, I thought the expectation of having them paid in France was wrong. Nobody in Europe was empower'd to pay them. (I believe it is a rule with all maritime states to pay their ships only at home by an office where the accounts are kept.) Later I received a letter signed by about 115 of the sailors of the *Alliance*, declaring that they would not raise the anchor nor depart from L'orient till they had six months wages paid them, and the utmost farthing of their prize money, including the ships sent to Norway, and until their Captain, P. Landais, was restored to them. This mutiny was undoubtedly excited by that captain. I went immediately to Versailles to demand the assistance of government, and on showing the letter by which his guilt plainly appear'd, an order was immediately granted and sent away the same evening, for apprehending and imprisoning him, and orders were promis'd to afford Capt. Jones all kind assistance to facilitate his departure. Mr. Arthur Lee had long been at L'Orient waiting for a passage on board the *Alliance*. He was supposed to have instigated the mutiny on board. I obtained and sent down orders to apprehend and imprison some of the chiefs. That restless genius, wherever he was, must either find or make a quarrel. The trouble and vexation these maritime affairs gave me was inconceivable. I often express'd to Congress my wish to be relieved from them, but was never able to do so.

I learned later that the Landais affair was over, that the *Alliance* had gone out of port (without taking any clothing and stores for the army), and that Capt. Jones had relinquished the command of her.

I MUST HAVE A LITTLE REPOSE

My time was more taken up with matters extraneous to the function of a minister than could possibly be imagined. I wrote often to the Congress to establish consuls in the ports and ease me of what related to maritime and mercantile affairs; but no notice was taken of my request. Bills of exchange and other money matters also gave me a good deal of trouble. And being kept in constant expectation of a secretary to be sent me, I did not furnish myself with the help I should otherwise have endeavoured to obtain. But I rubbed on, finding my grandson Temple daily more and more able to assist and ease me by supplying that deficiency. Without him I could not possibly have gone through with it. I had been too long in hot water, plagu'd almost to death with the passions, vagaries and ill humours and madnesses of other people. I retained my health *a merveille*, but what with bills of exchange, cruising ships, supplies &c., besides the proper business of my station, I found I had too much to do. I must have a little repose.

THE BEST MEN HAVE THE MOST ENEMIES

I received a kind letter of March 31, 1780, from Mr. Robert Morris of the Congress supporting Mr. Deane as a martyr in the cause of America. I had said before that enemies do a man some good, and the best men have always had their share of this treatment, to which Mr. Morris wrote, "I have been reviled and traduced for a long time by whispers and insinuations which at length were fortunately wrought up to public charges, which gave me an opportunity to show how groundless, and how malicious these things were, how innocent and honest my transactions. My enemies, ashamed of their prosecution, have quitted the pursuit and I am in the peaceable possession of the most honourable station my ambition aspires to, that of a private citizen in a free state. Yourself, my good sir, have had a share of these calamities, but the malice which gave them vent was so evident as to destroy its own poison. They could not cast even a cloud over your justly and much revered character. These things have taught me a lesson of philosophy that may be of service. I find the most useful members of society have the most enemies because there are a number of envious beings in the human shape; and if my opinion of mankind in general is grown worse from my experience of them, that very circumstance raises my veneration for those characters that justly merit the applause of virtuous men. In this light I view Doctor Franklin and Mr. Deane."

APPOINTMENT OF ROBERT MORRIS AS FINANCE SECRETARY

A year later, in July 1781, I received a letter from Congress announcing the appointment of Mr. Robert Morris as Superintendent of the

On Robert Morris: "I offered him every assistance that my situation might enable me to afford him; for besides my affection for the glorious cause we were both engag'd in, I valued his friendship."

Finances of the United States. But I warned him, "the business you have undertaken is of so complex a nature, and must engross so much of your time and attention, as necessarily to hurt your private interests; and the public is often niggardly even of its thanks, while you are sure of being censured by malevolent critics and bug-writers, who will abuse you while you are serving them, and wound your character in nameless pamphlets, thereby resembling those little dirty stinking insects that attract us only in the dark and disturb our repose, molesting and wounding us while our sweat and blood is contributing to their subsistence." I offered him every assistance that my situation might enable me to afford him; for besides my affection for the glorious cause we were both engag'd in, I valued his friendship.

RIOTS IN LONDON

London was in the utmost confusion for 7 or 8 days the beginning of June, 1780. The Protestant mob of fanatics, join'd by a mob of rogues, burnt and destroy'd property to the amount of a million sterling. Chapels of foreign ambassadors, houses of members of Parliament who had promoted an act favouring Catholicsm, and the houses of many private persons of that religion, were pillaged and consumed, or pulled down, to the number of fifty. Among the rest, Lord Mansfield's was burnt with all his furniture, pictures, books and papers, and himself almost frighten'd out of his wits. Thus he who approved the burning of American houses had fire brought home to him. He himself was horribly scar'd, and Govr. Hutchinson, it was said, died outright of the fright. They turn'd all the thieves and robbers out of Newgate prison to the number of three hundred, and instead of replacing them with an equal number of other plunderers of the public (which they might easily have found among the members of Parliament), they burnt the building. It is said they also attempted to plunder the Bank of England. The troops fired on them, and kill'd 33. They were not finally suppress'd till 9 at night. The next day Lord George Gordon was committed to the Tower.

The privateers *Black Prince* and *Black Princess*, with Congress commissions issued by me and mann'd partly with Americans, greatly harassed the English coasting trade, having taken, in 18 months, nearly 120 sail. The *Prince* was wreck'd on the coast, but the men saved. The *Princess* still reigned, and in a late cruise of 20 days between June 20 and July 10, 1780, took 28 prizes, some very valuable.

In truth England brought itself madly into the greatest distress, and did not have a friend in the world. No other nation wished it success in its present war, but rather desired to see it effectually humbled. No one, even their old friends the Dutch, afforded them any assistance. Such was the mischievous effect of pride, insolence and injustice, on the affairs of nations, as well as on those of private persons! The English Party in Holland was daily diminishing, and the states were arming vigorously to maintain the freedom of their navigation.

LETTERS FROM HOME

I received several pleasing letters from my daughter Sally and her husband Mr. Bache, and was glad to hear that William, Betsy and Louis, tho' the two latter were yet strangers to me, were all well and lively. I was informed that Sally did a great deal of good by promoting a subscription among the American women to send good things to the army for the comfort and encouragement of the soldiers. There was a great sum collected.

I told Sally that her son Ben wrote me often and recently obtained the prize of his school in Geneva for a best translation from the Latin into French, which was presented to him in the Cathedral Church by the first magistrate of the city. If I had more leisure, I would with pleasure have attended more nearly to his education. But he was in good hands in Geneva.

Two sorts of people in life

I sent the following letter to my grandson, which may have value to other young readers, viz:

Passy, Sept. 25, 1780

My dear boy,

It always gives me pleasure to hear from you, to be inform'd of your welfare, and that you mind your learning. It is now the season for you to acquire, at the expense of your friends, that which may be of use to you when they are dead and gone, and will qualify you to fill some station in life, that will afford you a decent subsistence.

You see everywhere two sorts of people. One sort are those who are well dress'd and live comfortably in good houses, whose conversation is sensible and instructive, and who are respected for their virtue. The other sort are poor, and dirty, and ragged and ignorant, and vicious, and live in miserable cabins or garrets on coarse provisions, which they must work hard to obtain, or which, if they are idle, they must go without or starve. The first had a good education given them by their friends, and they took pains when at school to improve their time and increase their knowledge. The others either had no friend to pay for their schooling, and so never were taught; or else when they were at school, they neglected their studies, were idle, and wicked, and disobedient to their masters, and would not be instructed; and now they suffer.

Take care therefore, my dear child, to make a good use of every moment of the present opportunity that is afforded you, and bring away with you from Geneva such a stock of good learning and good morals as may recommend you to your friends and country when you return home, make glad the hearts of your father and mother, and be a credit to the place where you receiv'd your education, and to the masters who have been so good to take the pains of instructing you.

I am ever, my dear child, your affectionate grandfather,

B Franklin

My dialogue with the gout

Soon after October, I was laid up with a long and severe fit of the gout, which confined me for nearly 8 weeks. My feet were still tender and my knees feeble, so that going up and down stairs was exceedingly difficult and inconvenient to me. This prevented my going out much, and put my writing business a good deal behind.

Madame Brillon sent me a pretty fable, *Le Sage et la Goutte*, in which one of the characters, Madame la Goutte, supposes that mistresses have a share in producing this painful malady. I replied that I, for one, believed the exact opposite. When I was a young man and enjoyed more of the favors of the sex than I do at present, I had no gout. Hence, if the ladies of Paris had shown more of that Christian charity that I have so often recommended to Madame Brillon in vain, I should not have suffered from the gout.

Nevertheless, Madame Brillon differed on this subject. "Pain sometimes becomes reason's mistress," said she, "and only patience can put an end to this quibbling. When wintry weather has saddened the earth, beautiful sunshine makes us forget it." I replied that human reason must be an uncertain thing, since two sensible persons, like Madame Brillon and me, can draw diametrically opposed conclusions from the same premises. I think reason is a blind guide;

true and sure instinct would be worth much more. All inferior animals, put together, do not commit as many mistakes in the course of a year as a single man within a month, even though this man claims to be guided by reason. This is why, as long as I was fortunate enough to have a wife, I had adopted the habit of letting myself be guided by her opinion on difficult matters, for women, I believe, have a certain feel, which is more reliable than our reasonings.

"Wrapped in this wretched game of chess, you destroy your constitution"

Madame Brillon encouraged me to write my *Dialogue entre la Goutte et M. Franklin*, in the hopes that it could bring her a few moments of pleasure. Herein is a translation of a part in English:

Franklin: Eh! oh! eh! What have I done to merit these cruel sufferings?

Gout: Many things; you have ate and drank too freely, and too much indulged those legs of yours in their indolence.

Franklin: Who is it that accuses me?

Gout: It is I, even I, the Gout.

Franklin: I take—eh! oh!—as much exercise—eh!—as I can, Madame Gout. You know my sedentary state, and on that account, it would seem, Madame Gout, as if you might spare me a little, seeing it is not altogether my fault.

Gout: Not a jot; your rhetoric and your politeness are thrown away; your apology avails nothing. If your situation in life is a sedentary one, your amusements, your recreation, at least, should be active. You ought to walk or ride; or, if the weather prevents that, play at billiards. But let us examine your course of life. While the mornings are long, and you have leisure to go abroad, what do you do? Why, instead of gaining an appetite for breakfast by salutary exercise, you amuse yourself with books, pamphlets, or newspapers, which commonly are not worth the reading. Yet you eat an inordinate breakfast, four dishes of tea with cream, and one or two buttered toasts, with slices of hung beef, which I fancy are not things the most easily digested. Immediately afterwards you sit down to write at your desk, or converse with persons who apply to you on business. Thus the time passes till one, without any kind of bodily exercise. But all this I could pardon, in regard, as you say, to your sedentary condition. But what is your practice after dinner? Walking in the beautiful gardens of those friends with whom you have dined would be the choice of men of sense; yours is to be fixed down to chess, where you are found engaged for two or three hours! This is your perpetual recreation, which is the least eligible of any for a sedentary man, because, instead of accelerating the motion of the fluids, the rigid attention it requires helps to retard the circulation and obstruct internal secretions. Wrapt in the speculations of this wretched game, you destroy your constitution. What can be expected from such a course of living but a body replete with stagnant humours, ready to fall prey to all kinds of dangerous maladies, if I, the Gout, did not occasionally bring your relief by agitating those humours, and so purifying or dissipating them? If it was in some nook or alley in Paris, deprived of walks, that you played a while at chess after dinner, this might be excusable; but the same taste prevails with you in Passy, Auteuil, Montmartre, or Sanoy, places where there are the finest gardens and walks, a pure air, beautiful women, and most agreeable and instructive conversation, all which you might enjoy by frequenting the walks. But these are rejected for this abominable game of chess. Fie, then, Mr. Franklin! But amidst my instructions, I had almost forgot to administer my wholesome corrections; so take that twinge—and that.

Franklin: Oh! oh!—for heaven's sake leave me! And I promise faithfully never more to play at chess, but to take exercise daily, and live temperately.

Gout: I know you too well. You promise fair; but, after a few months of good health, you will return to your old habits; your fine promises will be forgotten like the forms of last year's clouds. Let us then finish the account, and I will go. But I leave you with an assurance of visiting you again at a proper time and place; for my object is your good, and you are sensible now that I am your *real friend.*

Benedict Arnold's treason

In news from America, I received a large and particular account of Gen. Benedict Arnold's plot. We discover'd his motive by intercepted letters from London. One was sent from the army agent there to the traitor Arnold, by which it appeared that his bribe was £5,000 sterling. He tried to draw others after him, but in vain; not a man followed him. Judas sold only one man, Arnold three millions; Judas got for his one man 30 pieces of silver, Arnold not a halfpenny a head. A miserable bargainer, especially when one considers the quantity of infamy he acquir'd to himself and entail'd on his family. I found his baseness and treachery astonishing! He was despised even by those who expected to be serv'd by his treachery. His character was, in the sight of all Europe, already on the gibbet, and will hang there in chains for ages.

Long delays with Spain

Mr. Henry Laurens,* voted envoy extraordinaire to the Court of Versailles, was taken and confin'd in the Tower. Certain papers were found on him, relating to the drafts of a treaty propos'd in Holland, so the English declared war on Holland. Surely there never was a

---

* Laurens was captured in 1780 by the British on his way to negotiate a treaty with the Netherlands and was confined to prison. In July 1781, Congress commissioned Franklin to exchange him for General Burgoyne, and secured his release on bail in late 1781. Laurens came to Paris and served as one of the peace negotiators.

more unjust war. The British qualified poor Capt. Jones with the title of pirate, who was only at war with England: but if it be a good definition of a pirate, that he is *hostis humani generis*; they were much more pirates than he, having already made great progress towards being at war with all the world. If God governs, as I firmly believe, it was impossible such wickedness should prosper.

Regarding Spain, their long delay in entering into a treaty with us, in pursuance of the secret article, was to me a mark of their not being very fond of a connection with us, in which I thought they much mistake their interest, and neglect securing great and permanent advantages to their country. This was precisely their time to obtain and secure a firm and lasting friendship with a near neighbor, and not a time to obtain little advantages with a risk of laying foundations for future quarrels.

I have long imagined that we let ourselves down in offering our alliance before it was desired; and that it would have been better if we had never issued commissions for ministers to the courts of Spain, Vienna, Prussia, Tuscany, or Holland, till we had first privately learnt whether they would be received, since a refusal from one is an actual slight that lessens our reputation, and makes others less willing to form a connection with us.

LEE'S PAMPHLET AGAINST ME

I heard that a motion was made in Congress by a Carolina member for recalling me, but without success, and that Arthur Lee printed a pamphlet against me.* If my enemies would have a little patience, they would soon see me remov'd without their giving themselves any trouble, as I was then 75. I knew not what they meant by saying that

---

* Arthur Lee, *Observations on Certain Commercial Transactions in France, Laid before Congress* (Philadelphia, 1780).

I oppos'd the settling of Mr. Dean's account. I had no interest to induce such opposition; and no opposition was made.

By several letters to me from intelligent persons, it appeared that the great and expensive exertions of the last year were render'd ineffectual by the superiority of the enemy at sea. Their success in Carolina was chiefly owing to that superiority, and to our want of the necessary means for furnishing, marching, and paying the expense of troops sufficient to defend that province. The Marquis de Lafayette, who was back in America, wrote me of the distress of the troops and how they'd suffer'd for want of clothing. But the misfortunes of the last campaign, instead of repressing, had redoubled their ardour, and Congress was resolved to employ every recourse in their power to expel the enemy from every part of the United States by the most vigorous and decisive cooperation with the marine and other forces of their illustrious ally, France.

A FRESH APPLICATION FOR MORE MONEY

I was thus charged by Congress to write to the King of France requesting the most vigorous aid of our allies, and to make a fresh and strong application for more money. America had great expectations that a considerable supply of money would be obtained from Spain, but that expectation failed: The force of that nation had been employed to reduce small forts in Florida without rendering any direct assistance to the United States. Thus, we could rely on France alone, and therefore I wrote the following to his excellency, viz:

Passy, Feb. 13, 1781

To His Excellency the Ct. de Vergennes:

I am grown old. I feel myself much enfeebled by my late long illness; and it is probable I shall not long have any more concern in these affairs. I therefore take this occasion to express my opinion to your Excellency, that the present conjuncture is critical; that there is some danger lest the Congress should lose its influence over the people, if it is found unable to procure the aids that are wanted; and that the whole system of the new government in America may thereby be shaken. If the English are suffer'd once to recover that country, such an opportunity of effectual separation as the present may not occur again in the course of ages; and the possession of those fertile and extensive regions and that vast sea coast will afford them so broad a basis for future greatness, by the rapid growth of their commerce, and breed of seamen and soldier, as will enable them to become the terror of Europe and to exercise with impunity that insolence which is natural to their nation, and which will increase enormously with the increase of their power.

I am with great respect, your excellency's most obedient and most humble servant,

B Franklin

This request was well received: But the ministry being extremely occupied with other weighty affairs, and I obtaining for some time only general answers, that something would be done for us, &c., and Mr. Henry Laurens, the new envoy to this Court having not arrived, I wrote again and press'd strongly for a decision on the subject. Upon this I received a note appointing a meeting with the minister, which I attended punctually. He assured me of the King's goodwill to the United States, remarking however that, being on the spot, I must be sensible of the great expense France was actually engaged in, and the difficulty of lending us 25 millions at present impracticable; and that the depreciation of our paper had hurt our credit on that side of the water, adding that the King could not possibly favour a loan for us in his dominions, because it would interfere with and be a prejudice to those under a necessity of supporting the war. But to give the States a signal proof of his friendship, his majesty had resolv'd to grant them the sum of six millions, not as a loan, but as a free gift.

I PASSED MY 75TH YEAR AND SOUGHT TO RESIGN

In January 1781, I passed my 75TH year. The long and severe fit of the gout which I had suffered the previous winter had shaken me exceedingly, and I was unable to recover the bodily strength I had before enjoy'd, and thus suffer'd a great diminution of my activity. I found also that the business was too heavy for me and too confining. The constant attendance at home which was necessary for receiving and accepting bills of exchange (a matter foreign to my ministerial functions), to answer letters and perform other parts of my employment, prevented my taking the air and exercise which my annual journeys formerly used to afford me, and which contributed much to the preservation of my health. I had been engag'd in public affairs and enjoy'd public confidence in some shape or another during the long term of fifty years, an honour sufficient to satisfy any reasonable ambition.

Having long tired of the trade of minister, and wishing for a little repose to spend the evening of life more agreeably in philosophic leisure, I grew impatient and therefore troubled Congress to send somebody to supply my place (I suggested John Jay to succeed me), and permit me to retire, being oblig'd to perform all the functions of consul, judge of admiralty, merchant, banker, &c. &c. besides that of minister. I found the various employments too multifarious and too heavy for my old shoulders. For in this point I agreed even with my enemies, that another might easily be found who could better execute them. Yet it was not my purpose to return immediately home, unless ordered; hoping rather to remain in France till the peace, among a people that loved me and whom I loved, than to hazard an English prison. My proper situation indeed would have been in my own house, with my daughter to take care of me and nurse me in case of illness, and with her children to amuse me; but as this could not well be at the time, we had to manage as we could. I begged them to be assur'd that I had not the least doubt of our success in the glorious cause, nor had received any disgust in their service that induced me to decline it, but purely and simply the reasons mentioned above.

Congress refuses my resignation

However, I received dispatches from Congress dated the 19TH of June refusing to accept my resignation, and insisting on my continuing in their service till the peace, and ordering me upon an additional service, that of being join'd with Mr. Adams and Messrs. Jay, H. Laurens, and T. Jefferson in directing us to negotiate for peace. Also Congress empowered us to accept in their behalf the mediation of the emperor of Germany and empress of Russia. I was the more encourag'd by this resolution and honour, and I really esteemed it to be a greater one than my first appointment, when I considered that all the interest of my enemies, united with my own request, were not sufficient to prevent it. But these sorts of considerations should never influence our conduct. We ought always to do what appears best to be done, without much regard to what others may think of it. I therefore buckled again to business, and thanked God that my health and spirits were improved. I immediately went to Versailles and presented the letter address'd to the King, which was graciously received.

One more request for my grandson

I had one request more to make which, if I had serv'd the Congress to their satisfaction, I hoped they would not refuse me. It was that they would take my grandson William Temple Franklin under their protection. I had educated him from his infancy, and had brought him over with an intention of placing him where he might be qualified for the profession of the law; but the constant occasion I had for his service as a private secretary during the time of the commissioners, and more extensively since their departure, had induced me to keep him always with me; and indeed being continually disappointed by the secretary Congress had at different times intended me, it would have been impossible for me without this young gentleman's assistance, to have gone thro' the business incumbent on me! He thereby lost so much of the time necessary for law studies that I thought it rather advisable for him to continue in the line of public foreign affairs, for which he seemed qualified by a sagacity and judgment above his years, great diligence and activity, exact probity, a genteel address, a facility in speaking well the French tongue, and all the knowledge of business to be obtain'd by four years' constant employment in the secretary's office, where he might be said to have served a kind of apprenticeship. After all the allowance I was capable of making for the partiality of a parent to his offspring, I could not but think he might in time make a very able foreign minister for the Congress, or employed as a secretary to their minister at any European court. Unfortunately, it was not to be.

A PROPOSED MARRIAGE FOR MY GRANDSON

At this time I also spoke to Monsieur and Madame Brillon about my proposal of a marriage between their oldest daughter and my grandson Temple. I loved their whole family with no exceptions, and wanted to strengthen the tender ties of our friendship in this manner. Having almost lost my own daughter because of the wide distance between us, I hoped to find another one in Madame Brillon, and still

Deborah Read Franklin

Sarah Franklin Bache

William Temple Franklin

Benjamin Franklin Bache

Franklin by Mason Chamberlin

To William Strahan: "You and I were long friends: You are now my enemy."

Franklin before the Lords of the Privy Council: "The Ministry had taken so much pains to disgrace me before the Privy Council."

On Thomas Hutchinson: "Govr. Hutchinson stating that the American crisis required that 'there must be an abridgment of what are called English liberties.'"

On Lord North: "Their minister Lord North on the 17th of that month, confessed in a long speech that all his measures had been wrong and that peace was necessary, and proposed two bills for quieting America; but they were full of artifice and deceit."

English cartoon of the Repeal of the Stamp Act.

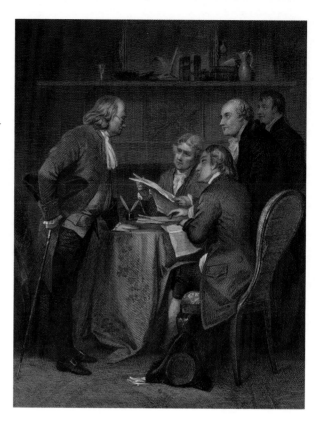

Drafting Declaration of Independence: "I made some small revisions, striking the words 'sacred and undeniable' and replacing them with 'self evident' so as to read 'We hold these truths to be self-evident.'"

On Benedict Arnold: "Judas sold only one man, Arnold three millions; Judas got for his one man 30 pieces of silver, Arnold not a half-penny a head."

On John Adams: "I am persuaded, however, that Mr. Adams meant well for his country, was always an honest man, often a wise one, but sometimes and in some things, absolutely out of his senses."

On Lafayette: "Gen. Washington sent me a letter of recommendation of the Marquis de Lafayette, tho' his modesty detain'd it long in his own hands."

To John Jay: "If you find any inclination to hug me for the good news of this letter, I constitute and appoint Mrs. Jay my attorney to receive in my behalf your embraces."

To his daughter on George Washington: "If you happen again to see General Washington, assure him of my very great and sincere respect, and tell him that all the old generals here amuse themselves in studying the accounts of his operations, and approve highly of his conduct."

Franklin at Court of Louis XVI.

An unfinished portrait of Treaty of Paris. Franklin with William Temple Franklin, John Jay, John Adams, and Henry Laurens.

On Madame Brillon (as played
by Elaine Comparone): "One must do
mad things when one loves madly."

Ladies' headdress during
Franklin's time in France.

Hotel de Valentinois at Passy, court and garden: "I lived in France in
great respect and dined every day with great folks; but I still longed
for home and for repose, and would be happy to eat Indian pudding
under the hospitable roof of my friends in Philadelphia."

Signing the U.S. Constitution: "It therefore astonished me to find this system so near perfection as it does."

Franklin in old age.

another in their daughter, to take care of my old age if I stayed in France, and to close my eyes after I die. I had a very good opinion of that amiable young lady, and having observed her for the four years of our acquaintance, I believed that she would make a good wife. I also believed that my grandson, who had no vices, would make a good husband. I noticed that they felt friendly toward one another, and when I talked to Temple about my plans for getting him married in France, he told me that he had only this objection, that his marriage in France would occasion a separation for us, should I go back to America. But when I told him that if he married Mademoiselle Brillon I would remain in France till the end of my days, he was very pleased, and agreed to the marriage.

Monsieur Brillon raised two objections with me. First was that his daughter could be taken away to America by my grandson, and second, the difference in religions. I myself had thought of those two things. For the first one, it was my intention to try to establish him in France in hopes that he would succeed me. For the second question, my thought was that in every religion, besides the essential things, there are others which are only forms and fashions, as a loaf of sugar may be wrapped in brown or white or blue paper, and tied with a string of flax or wool, red or yellow; but the sugar is always the essential thing. Now the essential principles of a good religion consist, it seems to me, of the following 5 articles, viz.:

1) That there is one God who created the universe, and who governs it by his providence.
2) That He ought to be worshipped and served.
3) That the best service to God is doing good to men.
4) That the soul of man is immortal, and
5) That in a future life, if not in the present one, vice will be punished and virtue rewarded.

These essential principles appeared both in their religion and mine, and divergencies were only the paper and the string.

However, Monsieur Brillon had other objections, and the matter was thus concluded.*

A RETURN TO PHILOSOPHICAL AFFAIRS

I was so engag'd in public affairs that I could not give the attention I wished to philosophical subjects, which used to afford so much pleasure. I was very sensible to the honour done me by the American Academy of Arts and Sciences in choosing me one of their members, and often wished I could be of some utility in promoting the noble design of their instruction.

It had been a long time since I had had the pleasure of writing to Mr. Ingenhousz on various subjects: his experiments on the conducting of heat; the finishing of my remarks on the stroke of lightning in Italy, &c. I wished him continued success in industry, sagacity and exactness in making experiments, adding: "You will have much pleasure immediately by that success, and in time great reputation. But for the present, the reputation will be given grudgingly and in as small a quantity as possible, mix'd too with some mortification. One would think that a man so labouring disinterestedly for the good of his fellow-creatures could not possibly by such means make himself enemies; but there are minds who cannot bear that another should

---

* Claude-Anne Lopez and Eugenia W. Herbert write, "Franklin was a total failure when it came to matchmaking. Sally did not marry young Strahan. William did not marry his father's choice for him, Polly Stevenson. One generation later, grandson Temple did not marry Cunegonde Brillon, the daughter of Franklin's closest friends in Paris. Neither did Benny Bache, his other grandson, marry Elizabeth Hewson, daughter of the same Polly Stevenson." See *The Private Franklin: The Man and His Family* (New York: W. W. Norton, 1975), 83.

distinguish himself even by greater usefulness; and tho' he demands no profit, nor anything in return but the good will of those he is serving, they will endeavour to deprive him of that, first by disputing the truth of his experiments, then their utility, and being defeated there, they will finally dispute his right to them, and would give the credit of them to a man that liv'd 3,000 years ago, or at 3,000 leagues distance, rather than to a neighbour or even a friend. Go on, however, and never be discouraged. Others have met with the same treatment before you, and will after you. And whatever some may think and say, it is worthwhile to do men good for the satisfaction one has in the reflection.

"Go on with your excellent experiments, therefore; produce facts, improve science and do good to mankind. Reputation will follow, and the little injustices of contemporary labourers will be forgotten. My example may encourage you, or else I should not mention it. You know that when my papers were first published, the Abbe Nollet, then high in repute, attack'd them in a book of letters. An answer was expected from me, but I made none, to that book nor to any other. They are now all neglected, and the truth seems to be established. You can always employ your time better than in polemics."

Those whom I had heard speak of Dr. Ingenhousz's book spoke well of it. But it was not so much talked of as might have been expected. This however is a matter that is subject to accidents. The death of a prince, a battle, or any other important event happening just on the publication of a new book, tho' a very good one, occasion it to be little spoken of, and for sometime almost forgotten. We printers and booksellers are well acquainted with this.

THE LOSS AT SEA WAS A HEAVY ONE

The ship having the honour of bearing the name *Marquis de Lafayette* sail'd the 29ᵀᴴ of March [1781] under the convoy of the *Alliance*, with a fair wind, and a large cargo of clothing for near 20,000 men, with arms, ammunition &c., valued at 1 million livres, sufficient to put the army into comfortable and respectable circumstances. Unfortunately the *Marquis de Lafayette* was lost at sea to the enemy, and the loss was a heavy one. I succeeded in having the goods replac'd, having received a letter from M. de Vergennes in favour of my solicitation of additional supplies of clothing, arms, ammunition, &c., but observing how badly our shipping and transporting our supplies were being managed, the French took that business entirely into its own hands in the case of replacing the cargo of the *Marquis de Lafayette*.

The *Indiana*, as she had been formerly call'd, then the *South Carolina*, was at last sail'd for Philadelphia from Amsterdam. She was a fine ship, well arm'd and well mann'd, and convoyed two others with clothing, &c. for our army. We received from America news that the Carolinas and Georgia were recovered by General Green, except the capitals of each province. The Marquis de Lafayette had receiv'd reinforcements, and Cornwallis was retiring after having burnt a great deal of tobacco.

Hazard no more drafts from Congress!

I begged Mr. Adams to concur with me in writing earnestly to Congress to hazard no more drafts where they had no funds. I believed there was hardly another instance in the world of a people risking their credit so much who unfortunately had so little and who must, by this proceeding, soon have none at all. The necessity of their affairs was the only excuse for it. The French Court was our firm friend, but even the best friends were wearied and worn out by too frequent and unexpected demands. We had obtained the promise of 20 millions in aid for the year, but as this sum was swallow'd in the bills already drawn by Congress, including drafts for interest money in favour of M. Beaumarchais and those drawn on Mr. Jay in Spain and Mr. Adams, who was in Holland, and the supplies going out, it was still necessary to entreat them not to continue that distressing practice. I was really afraid that by these proceedings, we would, as the saying is, *ride a free horse to death.*

Mr. Ferdinand Grand, our banker at Paris, and his brother Sir George Grand, our banker in Holland, had been our zealous and firm friends ever since our arrival in France. They aided us greatly by their personal interest and solicitations and often had 600,000 or 700,000 livres in advance for us, and were houses of unquestionable solidity. The commission charg'd to us by Mr. Grand for receiving and paying our money was a half per cent, which, considering the trouble given by the vast number of small drafts for interest of the loans, appeared to me a modest consideration.

How to pay off the war debts

I had no doubt that America would easily pay off not only the interest but the principal of all the debts she had contracted during the war. But whether duties upon her exports would be the best method of doing it, was a question I was not so clear in. England raised indeed a great revenue by duties on tobacco. But it was by virtue of a prohibition of foreign tobaccos, thereby obliging the internal consumer to pay those duties. If America were to lay a like duty of 5 pence sterling per pound on the exportation of her tobacco, would any European nation buy it? Would not the colonies of Spain and Portugal and the Ukraine of Russia furnish it much cheaper? Was not England herself obliged for such reasons to drop the duty on tobacco she furnish'd to France? Would it not cost an immense sum in officers &c to guard our long coast against the smuggling of tobacco, and running it out to avoid the duty? And would not many even of those officers become corrupted and connive at it? It is possibly an erroneous opinion, but I find myself rather inclined to adopt that modern one, which supposes it best for every country to leave its trade entirely free from all encumbrances.* Perhaps no country does this at present: Holland comes the nearest to it; and her commercial wealth seems to have increased in proportion.

Blessed are the peacemakers

I have never known a peace made, even the most advantageous, that was not censured as inadequate, and the makers condemn'd as injudicious or corrupt. Blessed are the peacemakers, as I supposed it to be understood, in the other world: for in this they are more frequently *cursed*. Being as yet rather too much attached to this world, I had therefore no ambition to be concerned in fabricating this peace: and know not how I came to be put into the commission. I esteemed it, however, an honour to be joined with Mr. Adams in so important a business.

The English played a desperate game. Fortune may have favoured them as it sometimes does a drunken dicer. But by their tyranny in the East they had at length rous'd the powers there against them, and I do not know that they had in the West a single friend. Thus empires, by pride & folly & extravagancy, ruin themselves like individuals.

My dispute with M. Beaumarchais

There arose a good deal of misunderstanding and dispute between Mr. Deane and Mr. Lee relating to the aids received thro' the hands of M. de Beaumarchais.† In 1776, being then in Congress, I received a letter from Mr. Lee acquainting me that M. Beaumarchais had applied to him in London, that 200,000 guineas had been put into his hands and was at the disposition of the Congress. Mr. Lee added that it was

---

* Here Franklin demonstrates the influence of Adam Smith, author of *The Wealth of Nations* (1776), an advocate of free trade.

† Watchmaker, courtier, dramatist, and international adventurer—one of the more colorful Frenchmen during the second half of the 18th century.

agreed between them that he (M. Beaumarchais) should remit the same in arms, ammunition &c. under the name of Hortalez & Co. Several cargoes were accordingly sent. Mr. Lee understood this to be a private aid from the government of France. But M. Beaumarchais later demanded from the Congress payment of a gross sum as due to him. I had, by order of Congress, desired him to produce his account that we might know exactly what we owed and for what: and he had several times promised it, but had not yet done it. In his conversations he often mentioned, as I was told, that we were greatly in his debt. Indeed, I imagine our country was really much obliged to M. Beaumarchais: and it is probable that Mr. Deane concerted with him for several large operations, for which he was not paid. These accounts in the air were unpleasant, and one was neither safe nor easy under them. It has been said that Mr. Deane, unknown to his colleagues, had written to Congress in favour of M. Beaumarchais's demand, in which Mr. Lee accused him of having, to the prejudice of his constituents, negotiated a gift into a debt. The transaction was a darkness; and we knew not whether the whole, or a part, or no part of the supplies he furnish'd were at the expense of government, the reports we had being so inconsistent and contradictory; nor if we were in debt for them, or any part of them: whether it was the King or M. Beaumarchais who was our creditor. Perhaps we must make allowance for M. Beaumarchais's not having been bred a merchant.

To many letters I never received any answer

Thanks to God I still enjoyed health and good spirits, tho' the English news writers had thought fit to kill me several times in their prints. It must at last have been true that I was dead; but the article reporting it was, as their papers phrased it, *premature.*

I received a letter from Mr. Jay in Spain complaining of the want of regular intelligence. I sympathized, because I suffered with him. I received indeed a number of letters from Mr. Lovell, but they were very short, and mostly to acquaint me that he could not write fully because the Committee of Correspondence were not easily got together. To many of my letters I never received any answer. The Congress had wisely put their finances into the hands of one intelligent person [Mr. Morris]; I wished they had done the same with their correspondence, by appointing a single secretary for foreign affairs.* I answered Mr. Jay that I could not pay the bills that had arrived. This Court being fatigued and displeased by my repeated applications for more money to pay new and unexpected demands of bills drawn not only on me but on Mr. Jay, and Mr. Laurens, and Mr. Adams &c., had ordered their minister at Philadelphia to remonstrate against this irregular proceeding.

I WAS SORRY FOR HIS MISFORTUNES, BUT...

By this time, there were still remaining in the English prisons nearly 500 of our unhappy countrymen, some of whom had languish'd there for many years under commitments of high treason. A great number of other prisoners in America, instead of being exchanged, were cruelly and unnecessarily sent by Admiral Rodney to England in irons, and pack'd together in the unwholesome holds of the ships, which kill'd many.†

I received a letter signed by 280 American soldiers, stating in part:

Feb. 3 1780 Forton Prison

May it please Your Excellency,

We the American prisoners residing at Forton Prison take the liberty of informing you by a couple of gentlemen from this place the

---

* Congress did so in August, 1781, appointing former New York delegate Robert R. Livingston to the post.
† In 1780, Admiral Rodney labeled American prisoners as unprincipled pirates and assigned them to the hospital ship Jersey, on which thousands died. See PBF 37:228n.

situation of the prisoners on this side of the Atlantic and the bad consequences that attends of neglect of them.

The season being cold and blustering, our donation has now almost exhausted. We are kept in prisons, situated in the midst of their marine hospitals where rage all kinds of distempers. Their corpses are brought through the midst of us sometimes nine or ten of a day, contrary to all humanity. We are growing very sickly amongst us.

We are very discontented among us, being informed that it is entirely owing to your neglect that we have not been exchanged. For certainly we should have gone long ago were it not that Dr. Franklin's age has rendered him incapable of that office. We earnestly hope, therefore, Your Excellency will condescend to answer this and let us know what is the reason for our being kept here so long when Britain would exchange us. Respectfully obedient humble servants and countrymen,

280 AMERICAN PRISONERS

The prisoners did not sign their above mentioned letter with any names, but I assured them in answer to their letter that these delays had not been owing to any neglect of mine.

I received a letter from Silas Talbot, a prisoner in Plymouth, who, Mr. Jay assured me, was a brave and enterprising officer, who desired some payment for his debts. I was sorry for his misfortunes, but I did not think it would be right for me to furnish him with the sum he desired. There were hundreds in the same situation, and if I were to comply with his request, how could I refuse the others? And even if I were willing to gratify them all, where would I find the money? It was easy for any man to write me a letter and tell me that Congress was indebted to him: I could not deny his assertion because I knew nothing to the contrary; but my ignorance of the facts, and my want of orders, if I knew it, made it improper for me to pay such debts. No one had any conception of the sums that were drawn from me by these applications: and I came to a resolution to make no difference on account of rank among the prisoners, because I knew nothing of their rank, but to consider them all as men, and relieve them equally as far as it lay in my power.

Nevertheless, I ordered another sum into the hands of Mr. William Hodgson, who was chairman of the committee that collected and dispens'd the charitable subscriptions for the American prisoners, a constant supply of a shilling each per week, and to make their winter allowance 18 pence. I wished it had been in my power to supply those honest, brave, patient fellows more liberally. I was infinitely oblig'd to him and his friends at Plymouth and Portsmouth for their kind care of our poor people.

WE HAVE NO NAME IN OUR LANGUAGE FOR SUCH VILLAINY

Mr. Thomas Digges, an American merchant residing in London, who pretended to be a zealous American and to have much concern for our poor people in the English prisons, drew upon me for their relief, at different times that winter, to the amount of £495 sterling, which he said had been drawn for upon him by the gentlemen at Portsmouth and Plymouth, who had the care of the distribution. To my utter astonishment, I learned that the villain had not apply'd above £30 of the money to that use, and that he had absconded with the funds. He who robs the rich of even a single guinea is a villian, but what is he who can break his sacred trust by robbing a poor man and a prisoner of eighteen pence given charitably for his relief, and repeat that crime as often as there are weeks in a winter, and multiply it by robbing as many poor men every week as make up the number of near 600! We have no name in our language for such atrocious wickedness and villainy as Digges. If such a fellow is not damn'd, 'tis not worth while to keep a devil.

That very great villian Digges later wrote me a letter in which he pretended he was coming to settle with me and to convince me that I had been mistaken with regard to his conduct; but he never appear'd, and I heard every day of new rogueries committed by him in England.

CRUEL CAPTIVITY OVER FOUR YEARS

The practice of sending prisoners taken in America to England greatly augmented the number of those unfortunate men, and proportionably increased the expense of relieving them. The subscriptions for that purpose in England had ceas'd. The allowance I made them of 6 pence each per week during the summer, tho' small, amounted to a considerable sum; and during the winter I was obliged to double, if not treble it. They complained that the food given them was insufficient. Their petition to the English government to have an equal allowance with the French and Spanish prisoners was rejected; this made the small pecuniary assistance I sent them more necessary. The Englishmen promised either to send our people in exchange, or to surrender themselves to me in France, not one of which was regarded, so little faith and honor remained in that corrupted nation. (Our privateers when in the European seas rarely brought in their prisoners when they could get rid of them at sea.) By my last accounts the number in the several prisons amounted to upward of 800. Some of our poor brave countrymen had been in that cruel captivity over four years.

I received a letter from Francis Coffyn recommending the case of Thomas Beer and Samuel Stevens, rope makers, who had been obliged to flee from England on account of their having assisted our prisoners to escape, and who desired to go to America. I knew nothing of Beer but from Mr. Coffyn's recommendation. Apparently he was one of those poor helpless bodies that God throws into the world to try its charity. It was very expensive and difficult to transport families in time of war, as they may be taken and carried back to England. I should therefore have thought it advisable for them to get into work at Dunkirk or Ostend, and maintain themselves there till a peace: Or if they could not find employment at those places, to go to Holland where there was a great demand for all kinds of workmen who were useful in fitting out ships. As there was now a considerable commerce carried on between America and Holland, and many American vessels were continually going from Amsterdam, where also the United States had a minister residing in Mr. Adams, I requested that Mr. Coffyn send the prisoners that way, recommending them to the care of John Adams Esq., Minister of the United States of America at Amsterdam.

I found that there were no people so improvident as seamen. We had several instances, when they had been furnished with money to bear their expenses to a seaport, that they stayed in Paris till it was spent, and then demanded more. Others riotously spent the whole sum given them for the journey in a few of the first days, and begged their way for the rest.

A gentleman arrived from America pressing me to accept immediately some bills he presented to me. I excus'd myself on account of the necessity I found of carefully examining all bills by the book we kept of acceptances, to see that none of a set had already been presented, and that it might take two or three days before we could get thro' the examination so as to come at his bills in their turn. He agreed in the propriety of this, because he said he had heard at Nantes that two bills of the same set had been presented to Mr. Jay at different times, and that he had accepted both of them. Not a week passed in which some such impositions were not attempted to be put upon me: but our accounts were kept in so good a method that it was scarcely possible those attempts should succeed.

HE *BRUSQUED* THE MINISTERS TOO MUCH

Col. Laurens, son of Henry Laurens, came to France on business to solicit a large aid in money for the army. It was thought that, as he was a witness of their wants, he would be able to represent their situation and necessities more forcibly than I could do. He was indefatigable, while he stayed, and took true pains, but he *brusqu'd* the ministers too much, and I found after he was gone that he had thereby given more offence than I could have imagin'd. He obtain'd a promise of a loan of 10 million livres to be borrowed in Holland; but as that borrowing did not succeed, he in fact obtained nothing. Fortunately, good humour and a kind disposition towards us seemed again to prevail. I had before his arrival got the grant of 6 million, and had since obtained more, or I could not have paid Mr. Jay's bills.

Holland did not seem to feel for us, or to have the least inclination to help us at first. No loan could be obtained there for our use, while so much was lent freely to our enemies. Some writer, I forget who, said that Holland was no longer a nation, but *a great shop*; and I began to think it had no other principles or sentiments but those of a shopkeeper.

I was exceedingly embarrass'd and distress'd by this business; and being obliged to apply repeatedly to the French court for aids, with one unexpected demand after another, I had given trouble and vexation to the ministers, by obliging them to find new funds for me, and thereby deranging their plans. They had, by their minister at Philadelphia, complain'd of these irregular unfunded drafts to Congress; and I was told that he had receiv'd a promise about the end of March 1781, that no more would be issued, until funds were in my hands to pay them.

The sentiment expressed by Mr. Robert Morris, "No country is truly independent until with her own credit and resources she is able to defend herself and correct her enemies," appeared to me perfectly just. If Europe had been in peace, and its governments therefore under no necessity of borrowing, much of the spare money of private persons might then have been collectible in a loan to our states. But four of the principal nations* being at war, all borrowing what they could, and bidding from time to time higher interest, money'd men would rather risk lending their cash to their own governments, then to those of their neighbors, than hazard it over the Atlantic with a new state, which to them hardly appeared to be yet firmly establish'd. Hence all our attempts to procure private loans had hitherto miscarried; and our only chance of pecuniary aids was from the governments of France or Spain, who being at war with our enemy were somewhat interested in assisting us. These two governments had indeed great revenues. But when it is considered that the ability of nations to assist one another is not in proportion to their incomes, but in proportion to their economy; and that saving and treasuring-up in time of peace is rarely thought of by ministers, when the expenses of the peace equal, if they do not exceed, the incomes; therefore when a war came on, they were, with regard to the means of carrying it on, almost as poor as we, being equally oblig'd to borrow; the difference only was that they had a credit which we wanted; which we had indeed with our own people, but lost by abusing it. Our credit, however, could only procure from the monies that were to spare, and those in so general a demand were few. Hence it was, and because her treasuries had been long detain'd in America, that Spain was able to help us very little; and tho' France did for us much more, it was not equal to our wants, altho' I sincerely believed it equal to her abilities, the war being otherwise exceedingly expensive

---

*Britain, France, Spain, and the Netherlands.

to her, and her commerce much obstructed. And thus I said to Mr. Morris, "You see, my dear friend, I have not endeavoured to flatter you with pleasing expectations of aids that may never be obtained; and thereby betray you into plans that might miscarry and disgrace you. Truth is best for you and for us all. When you know what you cannot depend on, you will better know what you can undertake. I shall certainly do what may lie in my power to help you; but do not expect too much of me."

I had received a very friendly letter from Mr. Edmund Burke, who was anxious for the liberty of his friend, General Burgoyne. Mr. Burke had always stood high in my esteem; his affectionate concern for his friend rendered him still more amiable. I was sure the restoring another worthy man to his family and friends was an addition to his pleasure. Having no direct communications with the British ministers, and Mr. Burke appearing by a letter to be warmly interested in favour of his friend General Burgoyne to prevent his being recalled, I requested and empower'd him to negotiate that exchange. Congress had no wish to prosecute General Burgoyne, so it offered to exchange him for Mr. Laurens, who was being held prisoner in the Tower of London.

There was now a great void for me in Passy

Captain Folger, a relation of mine, represented to me that he and some other inhabitants of Nantucket (friendly to the British) had property in England which they desired to withdraw from thence in goods useful to the States, and requested a passport. Having never refused it in any other instance of the kind, I could not refuse him. If under cover of this passport he carried goods to the enemy, I said, let our people catch him and hang him with all my heart, tho' it be true that he was a relation of mine; for I always think that a rogue hang'd out of a family does it more honour than ten that live in it. As to my being concerned with him or anybody else in trade licit or illicit, if they find it out, they are welcome to hang me into the bargain.

In the summer of 1781, Madame Brillon went to her apartment in Nice, leaving a great void for me in Passy. I often passed in front of her house. It seemed desolate. None of her amicable and laughing welcomes, none of her charming music, none of her lovable children running out to embrace me! In olden days, I broke a commandment, by coveting my neighbor's house, together with my neighbor's wife. Today, I don't covet it anymore, so that I am less of a sinner. But as far as the wife is concerned, I still think those commandments very bothersome, and I am sorry that they were ever devised.

Her good neighbors tried to fill the void as much as they could, but they simply could not. Mme. Le Veillard claimed me every Wednesday, and Mme. Helvétius for Saturdays, and Abbe Morellet played the cello for me at her home. He also wrote pretty songs and sang them sweetly while playing the bass, which I truly enjoyed. But it was not my sweet friend's music, nor the incomparable violin which had charmed us so often at her home. I wrote her letters, but so disliked writing in French that I would have completely given up doing so if she had understood the American language. She encouraged me by the positive reception she graciously granted my badly written epistles, but I didn't finish one because I didn't have the time to check the dictionary in order to correct the masculine and feminine nor a grammar book for the moods and tenses. Sixty years ago, masculine and feminine things (unrelated to moods and tenses) caused me much embarrassment. I used to hope that at the age of eighty, one could be liberated from such things. But there I was, seventy-six years old, and still those French feminines bothered me. This should make me happier to go to heaven where they say that all such distinctions will be abolished.

Fire at the Opera House!

Being without my good friend and neighbour Madame Brillon, I was deprived of her entertainment, and my grandson Temple and I resorted to an evening at the opera in Paris.* At the end of the opera, the building suddenly caught fire. We were among the last ones to leave the building. Smoke followed us and by the time we got in the carriage, the entire place was ablaze. Had it happened 15 minutes earlier, I believe pandemonium would have set in, with people hurrying about, and many people from the audience would have been unable to get out. My grandson and I would have died in the flames, as we were sitting high up in the balcony. Had it been so, I would have told my friends in Heaven, "I have died while Madame B was away," for had she not left Passy, I would not have gone to the opera. It was not known how many people from the house died.

Later that year, I received a letter from Mr. David Hartley of London suggesting a plan of preventing fire in opera and play-houses, such as the opera hall at the Palais Royal. I wrote the following reply:

Passy, Dec. 15, 1781

My dear friend,

I received your favour of September 26, containing your very judicious proposition of securing the spectators in the opera and play-houses from the danger of fire. I communicated it where it might be useful. Your concern for the security of life, even the lives of your enemies, does honour to your heart and your humanity. But what are the lives of a few idle haunters of play-houses compared with the many thousands of worthy men and honest industrious

---

* June 8, 1781, for a production of Gluck's Orpheus. See Stacy Schiff, *A Great Improvisation* (New York: Henry Holt, 2005), 279.

families butchered and destroyed by this devilish war! O! that would we could find some happy invention to stop the spreading of the flames, and put an end to so horrid a conflagration! Adieu, I am ever, yours most affectionately,

B FRANKLIN

NO SAFETY BUT OUR INDEPENDENCE

I wished most heartily that the cursed war were at an end, and I despaired of seeing it finish'd in my time, that thirsty nation having not yet drunk enough of our blood.

We had no safety but in our independence. With that we shall be respected, and become great and happy. Without it we shall be despised, lose all our friends, and then either be cruelly oppressed by a King who hates us and is incapable of forgiving us, or, having all that nation's enemies for ours, shall sink with it.

Chapter Eight

Minister to France, 1781–83

Peace Treaty with England

THE GLORIOUS NEWS...
GEN. CORNWALLIS CAPITULATES!

Glorious news! The Duke de Lauzun arrived at Versailles from Virginia with the happy news of the combined force of America and France having forced General Cornwallis to capitulate. The English garrison under Cornwallis marched out of Yorktown on the 19TH of October [1781] and laid down their arms: the troops consisted of about six thousand soldiers and 1,800 Negroes, 22 pair of coulours, and 170 vessels of 150 guns; and a considerable number of transports were burnt. A great and important event!* Most heartily did I congratulate Mr. Adams and the other commissioners on this glorious news, which could not possibly have made me more happy; it gave infinite pleasure. The infant Hercules in his cradle had now strangled his second

---

* The Battle at Yorktown on October 19, 1781, was the last great battle and marked the turning point in the American Revolutionary War, forcing the British to engage in peace negotiations. But it would be another 15 months before a treaty was signed and the war officially ended in 1783. As this chapter indicates, Franklin continued to seek aid from the French, exchange prisoners with the British, and work with the British to terminate the war.

serpent, and given hopes that his future history would be answerable. It brought to mind the possible creation of a medal commemorating the ending of the great war: representing the United States by the figure of an infant Hercules in his cradle, strangling two serpents, and representing France by that of Minerva, sitting by as his nurse with her spear and helmet, and her robe speck'd with a few Fleurs-de-lis.

I received a packet from General Washington, which contained the articles of capitulation. It is a rare circumstance, and scarce to be met with in history, that in one war an army should have been taken prisoners completely and not a man escaping. It is another singular circumstance that an expedition so complex, form'd of armies of different nations and of land and sea forces, should with such perfect concord be assembled from different places by land and water, and form their junction punctually, without the least being retarded by cross accidents of wind or weather, or interruption from the enemy; and that the army which was their object should in the meantime have the goodness to quit a situation from whence it might have escaped, and place itself in another from whence an escape was impossible. No expedition was ever better plann'd or better executed. It made a great addition to the military reputation Gen. Washington had already acquired, and brightened the glory that surrounds his name and that must accompany it to our latest posterity.

Madame Brillon complained because I had not sent her at once the story of our great victory. "I am sulking," said she. "What! You capture entire armies in America, you *Burgoynize* Cornwallis,* you capture guns, ships, ammunition, men, horses, &c., &c., you take

---

* "The great irony of the date [of the victory at Yorktown] was not lost on the allies. Exactly four years before—on October 17, 1777—at Sarasota, New York, Gentleman Johnny Burgoyne had also surrendered an entire British army." William H. Hallahan, *The Day the Revolution Ended* (New York: John Wiley & Sons, 2004), 193.

everything from everywhere, and your friends have to learn it from the gazettes. They get drunk on toasts to you, to Washington, to independence, to the King of France, to the Marquis de Lafayette, Rochambault, Chastellux &c., &c., but from you, not a peep!" I wrote to her that I was well aware of the magnitude of our advantage and of its possible good consequences [toward ending the war], but I did not wish to exult over it. Knowing that war is full of changes and uncertainty, in bad fortune I hope for good, and in good I fear bad. I play this game with almost the same equanimity as when I play chess. I never give up a game before it is finished, always hoping to win, or at least get a stalemate; and when I have a good game, I guard against presumption, which is often very damaging and always very dangerous; and when I am presumptuous, I try to conceal it to spare myself shame if my luck changes.*

MISFORTUNES MAKE PEOPLE WISE

From the English papers, I learned that the sense of England was fully against the continuation of the American war after Yorktown. They began to weary of the war, and with good reason, having suffered many losses, having four nations of enemies upon their hands, few men to spare, little money left, and very bad heads. The petitions of the cities of London and Bristol were unanimous against it; Lord North muster'd all his force in continuing the war, yet had a majority against him by a margin of 19. It was said there were but two who voted with him, that were not placemen or pensioners; and that even these in their private correspondence condemned the prosecution of the war, and lay it all upon the King's obstinacy. Misfortunes make people wise, and at present they seemed to be in the way of learning

---

* See Franklin's essay, "The Morals of Chess," PBF 29:750, written before June 28, 1779.

wisdom. We could not, however, be lull'd by these appearances. That nation was changeable. And tho' somewhat humbled, a little success would make them as insolent as ever. I remembered that when I was a boxing boy, it was allow'd after an adversary said he'd had enough, to give him a rising blow. Let ours be a douser.

DEMANDS AFTER DEMANDS

The French Court was highly disposed toward our great victory, and continued friendly toward us. The constant harmony subsisting between the armies of the two nations in America was a circumstance that afforded me infinite pleasure. The French officers who had return'd to France spoke of our people in the handsomest and kindest manner; and there was a strong desire in many of the young nobility to go over to fight for us: there was no restraining some of them; and several changes among the officers of their army took place in consequence. France is really a generous nation, fond of glory and particularly that of protecting the oppress'd.

However, I long feared that by our continually worrying the ministry with successive demands for more and more money, we would at length tire out their patience. The "cursed bills," as Mr. Jay justly termed them, were still coming in quantities drawn on Mr. Jay, Mr. Laurens, and Mr. Adams, and did us infinite prejudice. It was impossible for me to go on with demands after demands. I was never advis'd of the amount of the drafts either upon myself or upon any of the other ministers. The drafts themselves that were directed to me were indeed a justification of my paying them; but I never had any orders to pay those drawn on others, nor did I ever receive a syllable of approbation for having done so. Thus I stood charg'd with vast sums which I disburs'd for the public service without authority. I could not encourage Mr. Jay to accept any more bills. All things considered, if some of them had to go back protested, it was better to refuse Spain than either France or Holland.

I drew a bill on Congress for a considerable sum to be advanced me in France and paid thereby in provisions for the French troops. My bill was not honour'd! I was in hopes the loan in Holland, being for 10 million Florins, would have made us all easy. It had been long uncertain, but lately compleated: But unfortunately most of it was eaten up by advances in France.

I had much vexation and perplexity with the affair of our goods in Holland. I had great payments to make for the extravagant and very inconvenient purchases [of goods and shipments] in Holland, together with large acceptances by Mr. Adams of bills drawn on Mr. Laurens and himself; and I had no certainty of providing the money. I had also a quarrel upon my hands with Messr. de Neufville and others, owners of two vessels hired to carry the goods a Mr. Gillon had contracted to carry in his own ship. We at length recover'd those purchas'd by Messr. de Neufville; but those purchas'd of Gillon himself were stopp'd for his debts; and tho' I accepted and paid the bills for the purchase, according to the agreement with him and Col. Laurens, I learned that they were not to be had without paying for them over again. That man [Gillon] should have been immediately call'd to account for his conduct upon arrival in America, but I feared he had gone elsewhere. I had wearied the friendly and generous court with often repeated after-clap demands, occasioned by these un-advis'd (as well as ill-advised) and therefore unexpected drafts, and was asham'd to show my face to the minister. This, among other things, made me quite sick of my Gibeonite office, like that of drawing water for the whole congregation of Israel. But I was happy to learn from our Minister of Finance, Robert Morris, that after the following March no further drafts were to be made on me, or trouble given me by drafts on others.

LAFAYETTE, A GREAT MAN IN FRANCE

The Marquis de Lafayette was very serviceable to me in my applications for additional assistance. After the American victory, he had arriv'd back in Paris again, to my great joy, and was received by all ranks with all possible distinction.* He daily gained in the general esteem and affection, and promised to be a great man. He remained warmly attached to our cause; we were on the most friendly and confidential footing with each other.

The affair to seek additional aid was sometimes in suspense. The House of Fizeaux & Grand were appointed banker for France by a special commission from the King. At length the minister Vergennes told me we would be aided, but we could not expect it to be in the same proportion as the previous year. He was good enough to inform me we would have six million livres for the year 1782, paid quarterly, of which 1,500,000 livres would be ready for us at the end of March, thus allowing me enough to pay M. Beaumarchais, the interest bills, &c.

Mr. Deane's resentments and passions overcame his reason and judgment

I received a very long political letter from Mr. Deane on the 30ᵀᴴ of March 1782, but the multiplicity of business on my hands made it impossible for me to enter into the voluminous discussions that would have been necessary to answer it fully. My former friend had apparently lost himself entirely after writing a very indiscreet and mischievous letter,† which was intercepted and printed in New York, and then in the English papers. He and his letters were universally con-

---

* Lafayette was with Gen. Washington at the battle of Yorktown and returned home in triumph.

† Deane's private letters, written in late 1781, were written to friends in America urging the U.S. to quit the war and negotiate an immediate peace with Great Britain. His letters were viewed as highly partisan toward the British. Deane denied the charges (see PBF 36:u554), including rumors of embezzlement, and was finally vindicated after his death, in 1842, when Congress reimbursed his heirs.

demned and must ruin him forever in America and France. I thought we should soon hear of his retiring to England, and joining his friend Arnold. He continued, however, to sit croaking at Ghent, chagrin'd, discontented, and dispirited.

I was not convinced by Mr. Deane's letter. To me it appeared that his resentments and passions had overcome his reason and judgment; and tho' my ancient esteem and affection for him induced me to make all the allowances possible since he left France, yet the lengths he went to in endeavouring to discourage and diminish the number of friends of our country and cause in Europe and America, and to encourage our enemies, by those letters, made it impossible for me to say with the same truth and cordiality as formerly that I was his most affectionately.

ADVICE TO MY GRANDSON BENNY: "LOSS OF TIME IS A LOSS OF LEARNING"

I also received a letter from my grandson Benny, and was pleased that he had started keeping an account of his expenses. I told him that he would hereafter find it a great advantage if he acquired the habit of doing so, and continued the practice thro' life. He asked me for a gold watch, but I wrote back, "I cannot afford to give gold watches to children. When you are more of a man, perhaps, if you have behaved well, I may give you one, or something that is better. You should remember that I am at a great expense for your education, to pay for your board and clothing and instruction in learning that may be useful to you when you are grown up, and you should not tease me for expensive things that can be of little service to you." I also instructed him to learn to write a fair round hand, noting what a progress his brother had made in such writing, considering his age. I sent to London for some copy books of that hand for him, which he could try to imitate. Fair, legible writing is of great importance, and I am always much pleas'd to see my grandchildren improve in it.

A gentleman of Lyons repeatedly wrote to me proposing to remove a young man by the name of Samuel Cooper Johonnot to a school in his neighborhood. I told him that the proverb says wisely, *A rolling stone gathers no moss.* In frequent changing of schools much time is lost, before the scholar can be well acquainted with new rules and get into the use of them: And loss of time will be a loss of learning. It was time to think of establishing a character for manly steadiness, which a young man will find of great use in his life.

IT'S BAD TO HAVE A REPUTATION OF BEING CHARITABLE

In early 1782, I received the supplication of a certain family, written in grand style: big, beautiful paper, beautiful letters, flattering titles, &c. After having read the first two or three lines of it, "begging the kindness of his Highness," I threw it on the table, proclaiming, "Always supplications! Always demands of money! It is bad to have the reputation of being charitable. We expose ourselves to a thousand importunities and a good deal of expense as punishment for our pride, nay our vanity, which lets our small benefactions be known, whereas Our Lord has given us the good and political advice to keep our right hand from knowing what our left hand has done." But when I read the charming epistle of a friend, which I received at the same time, and which mentioned a supplication, I picked it up again, and read it until the end where I found the dear names of the whole family, which I kissed with sincere affection, since the supplication, instead of wanting money, only wanted my friendship.

EXCHANGING PRISONERS ONCE AGAIN

Despite the victory at Yorktown, there were still nearly a thousand of our brave fellows prisoners in England, and 200 in Ireland, who were destitute of every necessity, and died daily in numbers. All were committed and charged with high treason. Many had patiently endur'd the hardships of that confinement several years, resisting every temptation to serve our enemies. The slender supply I was able to afford of a shilling a week to each, for their greater comfort during the winter, amounted weekly to near £50 sterling. An exchange would have made so many of our countrymen happy, adding to our strength and diminishing our expense. But our privateers who cruised in Europe would not be troubled with bringing in their prisoners, so I had none to exchange for them.

I wrote the following letter to Mr. David Hartley in England, proposing an exchange:

> I am pleased to see in the votes and parliamentary speeches, and in your public papers, that in mentioning America the word *reconciliation* is often used. It is a sweet expression. It certainly means more than a mere peace. Will not some voluntary acts of justice and even of kindness on your part have excellent effects toward producing such a reconciliation? You have in England and Ireland twelve hundred of our people prisoners, who have for years bravely suffered all the hardships of that confinement rather than enter into your service to fight against their country. What if you were to begin your measures of reconciliation by setting them at liberty? I know it would procure for you the liberty of an equal number of your people.

The Peace Commission: A total change had taken place in the ministry

Soon after this we heard from England that a total change had taken place in the ministry. The military victories of Gen. Washington had so strengthened the hands of opposition in Parliament that they had become the majority, and all of them declared strongly against the American war as unjust. They compelled the King to dismiss all his old ministers and their adherents. Lord Shelburne became Secretary of State. His intended kindness to the American prisoners, so as to render their voyage comfortable, gave me great pleasure, not so much on account of an expense to be saved by that means, but because I knew it would have an excellent effect in America, by its tendency to *conciliate*.

Capt. Barry told me there was abundance of arms and ammunition in Boston, and the victory over Cornwallis furnished more. I was also informed that the cargo of clothing sent by the ship *Marquis de Lafayette* had arrived at Philadelphia from St. Thomas's and was laid upon the hands of the importers. In sum, our American affairs wore a better aspect now than at any time heretofore. Our councils were perfectly united, our people all arm'd and disciplined. Much and frequent service as militia had indeed made them all soldiers. Our enemies were much diminish'd and reduc'd to two or three garrisons. Our commerce and agriculture flourished.

England at length saw the difficulty of conquering us, and no longer demanded submission, but asked for peace. She endeavoured to obtain a federal union with us, but it was the interest of all Europe to prevent it. Having a change of sentiment, the British nation expressed an interest in making a separate peace with us exclusive of France, Spain and Holland, which, so far as it related to France, would be impossible. But Holland was stepping toward us, tho' Spain did not yet think our friendship worth cultivating.

I was one of five in the peace commission. The five persons were Messrs. Adams, Jay, Laurens, Jefferson and myself. I had hoped for the immediate assistance of Mr. Adams and Mr. Laurens, but the first was too engag'd in Holland to come to Paris, Mr. Laurens was still a prisoner in England, and Mr. Jefferson was not in Europe. Mr. Jay's residence at Madrid was no longer so necessary, so I pressed Mr. Jay to come to France as soon as possible, and leave Mr. Carmichael there, that it might not seem as if we abandon'd that court. The Marquis de Lafayette was of great use in our affairs, and as the campaign was not very active in North America, I prevailed with him to stay and assist us in the negotiations.

JOURNAL OF THE PEACE NEGOTIATIONS

I kept a very particular journal of what passed every day in the affairs of the peace negotiations, and prayed God that there would be wisdom enough assembled to make it possible a peace that would be perpetual, and that the idea of any nations being natural enemies to each other might be abolished, for the honour of human nature. I wished only for wise and honest men. With such, a peace might be speedily concluded, whereas with contentious wranglers the negotiation might be drawn into length and finally frustrated. Thus, we the commissioners of Congress were ready to meet those of Britain at such place as would be agreed to by all the powers of war, in order to form a treaty.

Great affairs sometimes take their rise from small circumstances. My good friend and neighbour Madame Brillon, being at Nice all that winter [1781–82] for her health, with her very amiable family, wrote to me that they had met with some English gentry there, whose acquaintance prov'd agreeable; among them she nam'd Lord Cholmondely, who she said had promis'd to call in on his return to England, and drink tea with us at Passy. He left Nice sooner than she suppos'd, and came to Paris long before her. On the 21st of March [1782] I receiv'd a note from him wishing to see me. I wrote for answer that I should be at home all the next morning, and he came accordingly. I had before no knowledge of this nobleman. We talk'd of our friends whom he had left at Nice and then of affairs in England. He told me that he knew Lord Shelburne held a great regard for me, and that he was sure his Lordship would be pleas'd to hear from me, so I wrote him a letter.

Soon after this we heard that Lord Shelburne had been made the new Secretary of State. An old friend and near neighbour of mine many years in London appeared at Passy and introduc'd a Mr. Richard Oswald, who gave me letters from Lord Shelburne and Mr. Laurens. Mr. Oswald was represented in the letter as fully appriz'd of Lord Shelburne's mind, that the new ministry sincerely wish'd for peace, and that if the independence of the United States was agreed to, there was no other point in dispute; that they were ready to treat of peace, but intimated that if France should insist upon terms too humiliating to England, they could still continue the war, having yet great strength and many resources left. I let him know that America would not treat but in concert with France, and that my colleagues not being there, I could do nothing of importance in the affair, but that if he pleas'd I would present him to M. de Vergennes, Secretary of State for Foreign Affairs.

Mr. Oswald came accordingly, and we arriv'd at Versailles punctually. M. de Vergennes receiv'd him with much civility. Mr. Oswald not being ready in speaking French, Mr. de Raynevall interpreted. The conversation continued nearly an hour. He seem'd to wish to obtain some propositions to carry back with him, but Mr. de Vergennes said to him very properly, "There are four nations engag'd in the war against you, who cannot, till they have consulted and know each other's minds, be ready to make propositions. Your court being without allies, and alone, knowing its own mind, can express it immediately. It is therefore more natural to expect the first propositions from you."

THEY WHO THREATEN ARE AFRAID

On our return from Versailles, Mr. Oswald took occasion to impress me with ideas that the weakness of the government in England with regard to continuing the war was owing chiefly to the division of sentiments about it, and that in case France should make demands too humiliating for England to submit to, the spirit of the nation would be rous'd, unanimity would prevail, and resources would not be wanting. He said there was no want of money in the nation; that the chief difficulty lay in the finding new taxes to raise it: and perhaps those difficulties might be avoided by shutting up the Exchequer, stopping the payment of the interest on the public funds, and applying that money to the support of the war. I made no reply to this, for I did not desire to discourage their stopping payment, which I considered as cutting the throat of their public credit, and a means of adding fresh exasperation against them with the neighbouring nations: Such menaces were besides an encouragement with me, remembering the adage, that *they who threaten are afraid.*

CANADA SHOULD BE GIVEN UP TO US

The next morning, when I had written a letter to Lord Shelburne, I went with it to Mr. Oswald's lodgings, and gave it him to read before I seal'd it, and he express'd himself much pleas'd. In going to him, I had also in view the entering into a conversation, which might draw out some of the mind of his court on the subject of Canada and Nova Scotia. I learned that there was a disposition in England to give us Canada and Nova Scotia. I had thrown some loose thoughts on paper, which I intended to serve as memorandums for my discourse, but without a fix'd intention of showing them to him. I remark'd that his nation seem'd to desire reconciliation with America; that I heartily wish'd the same thing: that a mere peace would not produce half its advantages if not attended with a sincere reconciliation; that to obtain this the party which had been the aggressor and had cruelly treated the other should show some mark of concern for what was past, and some disposition to make reparation; that perhaps there were things which America might demand by way of reparation and which England might yield; but that the effect would be vastly greater if they appeared to be voluntary, and to spring from returning goodwill; that I therefore wish'd England would think of offering something to relieve those who had suffer'd by its scalping and burning parties; lives indeed could not be restor'd nor compensated, but the villages and houses wantonly destroy'd might be rebuilt, &c.

I then touch'd upon the affair of Canada, and I spoke of the occasions of future quarrels that might be produc'd by England continuing to hold it, hinting at the same time but not expressing too plainly that such a situation so dangerous to us would necessarily oblige us to cultivate and strengthen our union with France. He appear'd much struck with my discourse; and as I frequently look'd at my paper, he desired to see it.

He then told me that nothing in his judgment could be clearer, more satisfactory and convincing than the reasonings in that paper; that he would do his utmost to impress Lord Shelburne with them; that as his memory might not do them justice, and it would be impossible for him to express them so well or state them so clearly as I had written them, he begg'd I would let him take the paper with him, assuring me that he would return it safely into my hands. I at length comply'd with this request also. We parted exceedingly good friends, and he set out for London.

I WAS ASHAMED TO LET THE
PAPER GO OUT OF MY HANDS

By the first opportunity after his departure, I wrote a letter to Mr. Adams and sent the papers mentioned, that he might be fully appriz'd of the proceedings. I omitted only the paper of notes for conversation with Mr. Oswald, but gave the substance of it. The reason for my omitting it was that on reflection, I was not pleas'd with my having hinted a reparation to the Tories for their forfeited estates; and I was a little asham'd of my weakness in permitting the paper to go out of my hands.

On the 4ᵀᴴ of May, 1782, Mr. Oswald return'd and brought me a letter from Lord Shelburne. He told me that they were very sincerely dispos'd to peace; that the whole ministry concurr'd in the same dispositions; that a good deal of confidence was plac'd in my character for open honest dealing; that it was also generally believ'd I had still remaining some part of my ancient affection and regard for old England; and it was hoped it might appear on this occasion.

Mr. Oswald then show'd me an extract from the minutes of council, where "it was propos'd to represent to His Majesty that it would be well for Mr. Oswald to return to Dr. Franklin and acquaint him that it is agreed to treat for a general peace at Paris; and that the principal points in contemplation are, the allowing of American independence on condition that England be put into the same situation that she was left in by the peace of 1763."

Mr. Oswald also inform'd me that he had convers'd with Lord Shelburne on the subject of my paper of notes relating to reconciliation. He had shown him the paper, and had been prevail'd on to leave it with him a night, but it was on his Lordship's solemn promise of returning it, which had been comply'd with, and he then return'd it to me. It seem'd to have made an impression, and he had reason to believe the matter might be settled to our satisfaction toward the end of the treaty; but in his own mind he wish'd it might not have been mention'd at the beginning, that his Lordship indeed said, he had not imagin'd reparation would be expected; and he wonder'd I should not know whether it was intended to demand it.

Finally Mr. Oswald acquainted me that, as the business now likely to be brought forward more particularly appertain'd to the department of the other secretary, Mr. Charles James Fox, he was directed to announce another agent coming from that department who might be expected any day, viz. the honorable Mr. Thomas Grenville, brother of Lord Temple, and son of the famous Mr. George Grenville, formerly Chancellor of the Exchequer, and author of the Stamp Act.

Mr. Oswald repeated to me his opinion that the affair of Canada would be settled to our satisfaction, and his wish that it might not be mention'd till toward the end of the treaty. He intimated too that the greatest obstructions in the treaty might come from Spain; but said, if she was unreasonable, there were means of bringing her to reason; that Russia, a friend to England, had lately made great discoveries on the back of North America, had made establishments there, and might easily transport an army from Kamchatka to the coast of Mexico and conquer all those countries. This appear'd to me a little visionary, but I did not dispute it.

Several days later, I had but just sent away a letter to Mr. Adams, when Mr. Oswald came in bringing with him Mr. Grenville, who had just arrived. I then entered into conversation with him on the subject of his mission, Mr. Fox having refer'd me to him as being fully acquainted with his sentiments. The gentlemen did me the honour of staying dinner with me, and this gave me an opportunity of a good deal of general conversation with Mr. Grenville, who appear'd to me a sensible, judicious, intelligent, good temper'd and well instructed young man, answering well the character Mr. Fox had given me of him.

Vergennes was glad to hear of Mr. Grenville's arrival, and said he would receive us the next day at half past 10 or 11 o'clock. We set out accordingly the next morning in my coach from Passy and arriv'd punctually at M. de Vergennes's, who receiv'd Mr. Grenville in the most cordial and friendly manner, on account of the acquaintance and friendship that had formerly subsisted between his uncle and M. de Vergennes, when they were ambassadors together at Constantinople. After some little agreeable conversation, Mr. Grenville presented his letter from Mr. Secretary Fox and another I think from the

Duke of Richmond. When these had been read, the subject of peace was entered on. What my memory retains of the discourse amounts to little more than this: that after mutual declarations of the good dispositions of the two courts, Mr. Grenville intimated that in case England gave America independence, it was expected that France would return the conquests she had made of British islands, and in return would receive back the islands of Miquelon and St. Pierre; and that the original object of the war being obtained, it was supposed that France would be contented with that.

"Mr. Franklin knows the truth"

The French minister seem'd to smile at the propos'd exchange and remark'd that the offer of giving independence to America amounted to little: "America," said he, "does not ask it of you: There is Mr. Franklin, he will answer you as to that point."

"To be sure," I said, "we do not consider ourselves as under any necessity of bargaining for a thing that is our own, and which we have bought at the expense of so much blood and treasure, and which we are in full possession of."

"As to our being satisfied with the original object of the war," continued Vergennes, "look back to the conduct of your nation in former wars. In the last war* [Seven Years War], for example, what was the object? It was the disputed right to some waste lands on the Ohio and the frontiers of Nova Scotia. Did you content yourselves with the recovery of those lands? No, you retain'd at the peace all Canada, all Louisiana, all Florida, Grenada and other West-India islands, the greatest part of the northern fisheries, with all your conquests in Africa, and the East Indies." Something being mention'd of its not being reasonable that a nation, after making an unprovoked, unsuccessful war upon its neighbours, should expect to sit down whole and have everything restor'd which she had lost in such a war, I think

Mr. Grenville remark'd that the war had been provok'd by the encouragement given by France to the Americans to revolt. On this M. de Vergennes grew a little warm and declar'd firmly that the breach had been made and our independence declar'd long before we receiv'd the least encouragement from France; and he defy'd the world to give the smallest proof of the contrary. "There sits," said he, "Mr. Franklin, who knows the facts and will contradict me if I do not speak the truth." He repeated to Mr. Grenville what he had said before to Mr. Oswald respecting the King's intention of treating fairly, and keeping faithfully the convention he should enter into; and added that the points which the King had chiefly in view were *justice* and *dignity*, and these he could not depart from. He acquainted Mr. Grenville that he should immediately write Spain and Holland, communicate to those courts what had passed, and request their answers.

The coming and going of these gentlemen was observ'd, and made much talk at Paris. The Marquis de Lafayette, having learned something of their business from the ministers, discoursed with me about it. He said that this Court might, thro' him, state what was from time to time transacted, to prevent misrepresentations and misunderstandings. Such an employ would be extremely agreeable to him on many accounts; that as he was now an American citizen, spoke both languages and was well acquainted with our interests, he believ'd he might be useful in it; and that as peace was likely from appearances to take place, his return to America was perhaps not so immediately necessary. I lik'd the idea and encourag'd his proposing it to the ministry. He then wish'd I would make him acquainted with Messrs. Oswald and Grenville, and for that end propos'd meeting them at breakfast with me if I could, and endeavoured to engage them for Saturday. Accordingly, I told Mr. Oswald that the Marquis de Lafayette would breakfast with me tomorrow, and as he (Mr. Oswald) might have some curiosity to see a person who had in this war render'd himself so remarkable, I propos'd his doing me the same honour. The gentlemen all met, had a good deal of conversation at and after breakfast, stayed till after one o'clock, and parted much pleas'd with each other.

The release of all American prisoners

On May 13, 1782, I received the good news from David Hartley of London that an order had been issued by his government for the release of all the American prisoners everywhere, an order not partial or conditional, but general and absolute. I rejoiced with him in this step, not only on account of the unhappy captives who by it were set at liberty and restor'd to their friends and families, but as it tended greater towards a reconciliation and a durable peace.

On May 26, Mr. Grenville visited me again. He acquainted me that his courier had return'd, and had brought him full powers to form a treaty for a peace *with France and her allies*; that he had been to Versailles and had shown his power to M. de Vergennes, and left a copy with him; that he had also a letter of credence, which he was not to deliver till France should think fit to send a minister of the same kind to London; that M. de Vergennes had told him he would lay it before the King; that Mr. Oswald had arrived in London about an hour before the courier came away; that Mr. Fox in his letter had charg'd him to thank me for that which I had written, and to tell me he hop'd I would never forget that he and I were of the same country. I answer'd that I should always esteem it an honour to be owned as a countryman by Mr. Fox. Mr. Grenville lent me a London *Gazette*, containing Admiral Rodney's account of his victory over M. de Grasse, and the accounts of other successes in the East Indies, assuring me, however, that these events made not the least change in the sincere desires of his court to treat for peace.

Mr. Jay wrote me from time to time of the unaccountable delays he had met with since his residence at the court of Spain, and that he was now no nearer in the business he had been charg'd with than when he had first arriv'd. Upon the first coming of Mr. Oswald, and the apparent prospect of a treaty, I had written to press Mr. Jay's coming to Paris; and being a little out of humour with the Spanish court, I said as they had already taken four years to consider whether they should treat with us, give them forty, and let us mind our own business.

It seemed to me that we had, in most instances, hurt our credit and importance by sending all over Europe begging alliances, and soliciting declarations of our independence. From this action the nations perhaps seemed to think that our independence was something which they had to sell, and that we didn't offer enough [in exchange] for it. Mr. Adams had succeeded in Holland, owing to their war with England, and a good deal to the late votes in the Commons toward a reconciliation; but the ministers of the other powers refus'd to return their visits, because our independence was not yet acknowledg'd by their courts.

The northern princes were not asham'd of a little civility committed toward an American, however. The King of Denmark, travelling in England under an assumed name, sent me a card expressing in strong terms his esteem for me, and inviting me to dinner with him at St. James's. The ambassador from Sweden applied to me about making a treaty with his master in behalf of the United States. I answer'd in the affirmative. He seem'd much pleased, and said the King had directed him to ask the question, and had charged him to tell me that he had so great an esteem for me that it would be a particular satisfaction to him to have such a transaction with me. The ambassador added that it was a pleasure to him to think, and he hop'd it would be remember'd, that Sweden was the first power in Europe which had voluntarily offer'd its friendship to the United States without being solicited. The King had charg'd him to tell me that it would flatter him greatly to make it with a person whose character he so much esteem'd &c &c. Such compliments probably would have made me a little proud, if we Americans were not naturally like the porter, who being told he had with his brethren jostled the great Czar Peter* (then in London walking the street) said *Poh, We are all czars here.*

IN THE MULTITUDE OF COUNSELORS THERE IS SAFETY

I have never yet known of a peace made that did not occasion a great deal of popular discontent, clamour and censure on both sides. This is perhaps owing to the usual management of the ministers and leaders of the contending nations, who, to keep up the spirits of their people for continuing the war, generally represent the state of their own affairs in a better light, and that of the enemy in a worse, than is consistent with the truth. Hence the populace on each side expect better terms than really can be obtained, and are apt to ascribe their disappointment to treachery. Thus the peace of Utrecht, and that of Aix la Chapelle, were said in England to have been influence'd by French gold, and in France by English guineas. Even the last peace [Seven Years War], the most advantageous and glorious for England that ever she made, was violently decry'd, and its makers as violently abus'd. So the blessing promis'd to peacemakers, I fancy, relates to the next world, for in this they seem to have a greater chance of being cursed. Another text observes, *in the multitude of counsellors there is safety.* For all these reasons, but especially for the support against the attack of my enemies, I wished for the presence of as many of the commissioners as possible.

During the negotiations, the Comte du Nord came to Mr. Vergennes while we were drinking coffee after dinner. He appeared lively

---

* Peter the Great (1672–1725), the Russian czar, visited London in 1697–98.

and active, with a sensible, spirited countenance. There was an opera at night for his entertainment. The house being richly furnish'd with abundance of carving and gilding, well illuminated with wax tapers, and the company all superbly dressed, many of the men in cloth of tissue, and the ladies sparkling with diamonds, form'd altogether the most splendid spectacle my eyes ever beheld.

Such flattering language might have made me vainer

Mr. Grenville came again with instructions to acknowledge the independence of America prior to the commencement of the treaty. He then spoke much of the great esteem the present ministry had for me, their desire of a perfect reconciliation between the two countries, and the firm and general belief in England that perhaps no single man had ever in his hands an opportunity of doing so much good as I had at this present of bringing about such a reconciliation, adding that if the old ministers had formerly been too little attentive to my counsels, the present were very differently disposed, and he hop'd that in treating with them I would totally forget their predecessors. There was a time when such flattering language from great men might have made me vainer and had more effect on my conduct than it could then, when I found myself so near the end of life, as to esteem lightly all personal interests and concerns, except that of maintaining to the last and leaving behind me the tolerably good character I have hitherto supported.

The true loyalists were the Americans

As to the loyalists, I repeated to Mr. Grenville what I had said to him when he first arrived, that their estates had been confiscated by laws made in the particular states where the delinquents had resided, and not by any law of Congress, who indeed had no power either to make such laws, or repeal them, and therefore could give no power to their commissioners to treat of a restoration of those people: that it was an affair appertaining to each state; that if there were justice in compensating them, it must be due from England rather than from America; but in my opinion England was not under any very great obligation to them, since it was by their misrepresentations and bad counsels that she had been drawn into this miserable war. And if an account were to be brought against us for their losses, we should more than balance it by an account of the ravages they had committed all along the coasts of America. The true loyalists were the Americans. The world had never seen a more universally loyal people than the Americans, who were forc'd by the mad measures of the ministry to take up arms in defense of their rights. They did it with reluctance. Very few if any of the pretended loyalists had any such principle, or any principle but that of taking care of themselves by securing safety with a chance of emolument and plunder. Mr. Oswald agreed to the reasonableness of all this, and said he had, before he had come away, told the ministers that he thought no recompense to those people was to be expected from us.

He had also, in consequence of our former conversation on the subject, given it as his opinion that Canada should be given up to the United States, as it would prevent the occasions of future difference, and as the government of such a country was worth nothing, and of no importance if they could have there a free commerce; that both the Marquis of Rockingham and Lord Shelburne, tho' they spoke reservedly, did not seem very averse to it; but that Mr. Fox appear'd to be startled at the proposition. He was, however, not without hopes that it would be agreed to.*

---

* Canada and Nova Scotia were not included in the final agreement, and remained members of the British commonwealth.

On Tuesday June 11, 1782, I was at Versailles and had a good deal of conversation with M. de Rayneval, secretary to the Council. I show'd him the letters I had receiv'd by Mr. Oswald from Lord Shelburne. We spoke of all its attempts to separate us, and of the prudence of our holding together, and treating in concert.

Mr. Jay finally arrives

In the afternoon of Sunday the 23d of June, Mr. Jay arriv'd, to my great satisfaction. I propos'd going with him the next morning to Versailles, and presenting him to Mr. Vergennes, which we did the next day. Mr. Jay inform'd me that the Spanish ministers had been much struck with the news from England respecting the resolutions of Parliament to discontinue the war in America, &c., and that they had since been extremely civil to him, and, he understood, intended to send instructions to their ambassador at the French court to make the long talk'd of treaty with him in Paris. We went together to see the Spanish ambassador, who receiv'd us with great civility and politeness. I had never made any visit to Count d'Aranda before. He spoke with Mr. Jay on the subject of the treaty they were to make together. I supposed he had in view something relating to boundaries or territories, because he added, "We will sit down together with maps in our hands, and by that means shall see our way more clearly." At our going out he took the pains himself to open the folding-doors for us, which is a high compliment here: And he told us he would return our visit (*rendre son devoir*) and fix a day with us for dining with him.

I find men to be a sort of being very badly constructed

During these negotiations, I received two kind letters from Sir Joseph Priestley, to which I replied the following:

Passy, near Paris, June 7, 1782

Dear Sir,

I have always great pleasure in hearing from you, in learning that you are well, and that you continue your experiments. I should rejoice much if I could once more recover the leisure to search with you into the works of nature; I mean the inanimate, not the animate or moral part of them. The more I discover'd the former, the more I admir'd them; the more I know of the latter, the more I am disgusted with them. Men I find to be a sort of being very badly constructed, as they are generally more easily provok'd than reconcil'd, more dispos'd to do mischief to each other than to make reparation, much more easily deceiv'd than undeceived, and having more pride and even pleasure in killing than in begetting one another, for without a blush they assemble in great armies at noon day to destroy, and when they have kill'd as many as they can, they exaggerate the number to augment the fancied glory; but they creep into corners or cover themselves with the darkness of night, when they mean to beget, as being asham'd of a virtuous action. A virtuous action it would be, and a vicious one the killing of them, if the species were really worth producing or preserving; but of this I begin to doubt. I know you have no such doubts, because in your zeal for their welfare, you are taking a great deal of pains to save their souls. Perhaps as you grow older you may look upon this as a hopeless project, or an idle amusement, repent of having murdered in mephitic air so many honest harmless mice, and wish that, to prevent mischief, you had used boys and girls instead of them.

In what light we are view'd by superior beings may be gather'd from a piece of the late West India News, which possibly has not yet reach'd you. A young angel of distinction, being sent down to this world on some business for the first time, had an old courier-spirit assign'd him as a guide. They arriv'd over the seas of Martinico in the middle of the long day of obstinate fights between the fleets of Rodney and DeGrasse. When, thro' the clouds of smoke, he saw the fire of the guns, the decks cover'd with mangled limbs, and bodies dead or dying, the ships sinking, burning, or blown into the air, and the quantity of pain, misery, and destruction to the crews those yet alive were, with so much eagerness, dealing round to one another, he turn'd angrily to his guide and said, "You blundering blockhead, you are ignorant of your business; you undertook to conduct me to the earth, and you have brought me into hell!"—"No, sir," says the guide, "I have made no mistake; this is really the earth, and these are men. Devils never treat one another in this cruel manner; they have more sense, and more of what men (vainly) call *Humanity!*"

But to be serious, my dear old friend, I love you as much as ever, and I love all the honest souls that meet at the London coffee-house.* I only wonder how it happen'd that they and my other friends in England came to be such good creatures in the midst of so perverse a generation. I long to see them and you once more, and I labour for peace with more earnestness, that I may again be happy in your sweet society.

I show'd your letter to the Duke de Rochefoucault, who thinks, with me, that the new experiments you have made are extremely curious. Yesterday the Count du Nord was at the Academy of Sciences, when sundry experiments were exhibited for his entertainment; among them one by M. Lavoisier to show that the strongest fire we yet know is made in a charcoal blown upon with dephlogisticated air. In a heat so produc'd he melted plastina presently, the fire being so much more powerful than that of the strongest burning mirror.

Adieu, and believe me ever, yours most affectionately,

B FRANKLIN

---

* The Club of Honest Whigs. PBF 37:445n.

Exchange of Cornwallis and Mr. Laurens

By resolution of the 14ᵀᴴ of June 1782, the Congress had empower'd me to offer an exchange of General Burgoyne for the honourable Mr. Laurens, then a prisoner of the Tower of London, which exchange had not been accepted. Then advice was received that General Burgoyne had been exchang'd in virtue of another agreement. Mr. Laurens thereupon had proposed Lord Cornwallis as an exchange for him. Mr. Laurens was soon after discharged and having since urged me earnestly in several letters to join with him in absolving the parole of General Cornwallis, I did absolve and discharge the parole of Lord Cornwallis given him in Virginia, setting him at entire liberty to act in his civil or military capacity. My authority for doing this appear'd questionable to myself, but Mr. Laurens judg'd it deducible from that respecting General Burgoyne, and by his letters to me seem'd so unhappy till it was done, that I ventur'd it, with a clause however reserving to Congress the approbation or disallowance of it. I saw by the English papers that on the receipt of it, Lord Cornwallis immediately appear'd at court and took his seat in the house of peers, which he did not before think warrantable.

My landlord was forever renewing demands

M. Le Ray de Chaumont, our landlord, had originally proposed to leave the rent until the end of the war, and then to accept for it a price of American land from the Congress, such as they might judge equivalent. But I was never able to settle my account with Mr. Chaumont. One was never sure of having finish'd anything with Mr. C. He was forever renewing old demands or inventing new ones. He refused to allow me interest on the 50,000 livres he kept so long in his hands, or on any other article of my account, and yet charged it on every one of his. And then he said that if I charged interest, he would charge me for I know not how many 100 tons of freight in the ship *Marquis de Lafayette* more than he was paid for. Mr. Chaumont, who was chosen by the captains of all the vessels in the expedition as their agent, had long been in a state little short of bankruptcy, and some of the delays were occasioned by the distress of his affairs. And thus the bad situation of his affairs forced him upon the use of all sorts of chicanery to evade a settlement and doing justice to his creditors. When a man naturally honest is thus driven into knavery by the effects of imprudent speculations, let it be a warning not to venture out of one's depth, in hope of gain, to the hazard of one's virtue, which ought to be dearer than any fortune, as being in itself more valuable and affording more comfort. My banker, Mr. Grand, gave it up as impracticable, but agreed to be the arbitrator. Mr. Grand considered all of Chaumont's pleas, even a private memoir which M. Chaumont desired might not be shown me (I suppose lest I should answer it) wherein he made a sort of account of all his losses in American transactions, and even of all his civilities to me or any of my friends. Finally, we came to an agreement. However, Mr. Chaumont's son, Mr. Le Ray de Chaumont, came to me in America after the war seeking additional sums that were impracticable, and I refused him because of lowness of funds. He spent four years in America seeking his father's claim upon the Congress, but was unable to obtain it.

I CANNOT COMPREHEND CRUEL MEN

A letter written by James Hutton containing an account of the abominable murders committed by some of the frontier people on the poor Moravian Indians gave me infinite pain and vexation. I wrote to the government of America urging that effectual care be taken to protect and save the remainder of those unhappy people. The dispensations of Providence in this world puzzles my weak reason. I cannot comprehend why cruel men should be permitted thus to destroy their fellow creatures. Some of the Indians may be suppos'd to have committed sins, but one cannot think the little children had committed any worthy of death. Why had a single man in England,* who happened to love blood and to hate Americans, been permitted to gratify that bad temper by hiring German murderers and joining them with his own to destroy, in a continued course of bloody years, nearly 100,000 human creatures, many of them possessed of useful talents, virtues and abilities to which he has no pretention! It was he who had furnished the savages with hatchets and scalping knives, and engaged them to fall upon our defenseless farmers, and murder them with their wives and children, paying for their scalps, of which the account kept already amounts, as I have heard, to near *two thousand*. Perhaps the people of the frontier, exasperated by the cruelties of the Indians, have been induced to kill all Indians that fall into their hands, without distinction, so that even those horrid murders of our poor Moravians could be laid at his charge. And yet this man lives, enjoys all the good things this world can afford, and is surrounded by flatterers, who keep even his conscience quiet by telling him he is the best of princes!

I wonder at this, but I cannot therefore part with the comfortable belief of a divine Providence; and the more I see the impossibility, from the numbers and extent of his crimes, of giving equivalent punishment to a wicked man in this life, the more I am convinc'd of a future state in which all that here appears to be wrong shall be set right, all that is crooked made straight. In this faith let us comfort ourselves. It is the only comfort in the present dark scene of things that is allow'd us.

---

* Here Franklin has reference to King George III.

A PLAN FOR A UNIVERSAL AND PERPETUAL PEACE

In the course of the summer a man very shabbily dressed—all his dress together was not worth five shillings—came and desired to see me. He was admitted and, on being asked his business, he told me that he had walked from one of the mountains of Provence for the purpose of seeing me and showing me a plan which he had formed for a universal and perpetual peace. I took his manuscript and read it, and found it to contain much good sense. I desired him to print it. He said he had no money: so I printed it for him. He took as many copies as he wished for, and gave several away; but no notice whatever was taken of it.

The accounts of America's rejoicing on the news of the Dauphin's birth gave pleasure in France.* Before he was even twenty-four hours old, I went as one of the wise men from the West rather than the East to show my adoration, which he received graciously. It was a happy event for France and for the queen, who was loved by France, and for me as I loved both and was always merry when I saw my friends happy. All ranks of that nation appeared to be in good humour with us, and our reputation had risen thro' out Europe.

PRESSING ME FOR MORE MONEY

Congress continued to press my obtaining more money. The losses suffer'd in the West Indies, and the unforeseen necessary expenses for the reparation there and in France, rendered it more difficult, nigh impossible, tho' the good disposition of the court toward us continued perfectly. Mr. Morris mentioned that ministers' salaries were to be hereafter paid in America. I empowered him to remit mine

---

* This refers to the birth in late 1781 of a son to King Louis XVI and Queen Marie Antoinette.

and to do it regularly and timely; for a minister without money makes a ridiculous figure, tho' secure from arrests. I took a quarter's advance of salary from the 4TH of July, supposing it not intended to *muzzle the mouth of the ox that treadeth out the corn.**

The English draw out
the negotiations at length

Tho' the English a few months earlier had seem'd desirous of peace, yet following their success in the West Indies, they desired rather to draw out the negotiations. They had at first some hopes of getting the belligerent powers to treat separately one after another; but finding that impracticable, they had, after several messengers sent to and fro, come to a resolution of treating with all together for a general peace, and at length agreed that the place would be Paris.

Mr. Grenville returned from Versailles, and told me that Lord Rockingham had died. He was at length recall'd. Mr. Fox also resigned, and Lord Shelburne was made first Lord of the Treasury; but no change was thereby made in the dispositions of that court for peace, &c. Mr. Fitz-Herbert arriv'd to replace him, with a commission in due form to treat with France, Spain and Holland. There were so many interests to be consider'd and settled in a peace between 5 different countries that it was well not to flatter ourselves with a very speedy conclusion.

A treaty with Madame Brillon

During the peace negotiations, I fancied the opportunity to draw upon the following articles of a Peace Treaty proposed to Madame Brillon de Jouy:

---

* Deuteronomy 24:4

Passy, July 27, 1782

What a difference, my dear friend, between you and me! You find my faults so many as to be innumerable, while I can see but one in you; and perhaps that is the fault of my spectacles. The fault I mean is that kind of covetousness, by which you would engross all my affections, and permit me none for the other amiable ladies of your country. You seem to imagine that it cannot be divided without being diminish'd: In which you mistake the nature of the thing and forget the situation in which you have plac'd and hold me. You renounce and exclude arbitrarily everything corporal from our amour, except such a merely civil embrace now and then as you would permit to a country cousin; what is there then remaining that I may not afford to others without a diminution of what belongs to you? The operations of the mind: esteem, admiration, respect, and even affection for one object, may be multiply'd as more objects that merit them present themselves, and yet remain the same to the first, which therefore has no room to complain of injury. They are in their nature as divisible as the sweet sounds of the piano forte produc'd by your exquisite skill: twenty people may receive the same pleasure from them, without lessening that which you kindly intend for me; and I might as reasonably require of your friendship that they should reach and delight no ears but mine.

You see by this time how unjust you are in your demands, and in the open war you declare against me if I do not comply with them. Indeed it is I that have the most reason to complain. My poor little boy, whom you ought methinks to have cherish'd, instead of being fat and jolly like those in your elegant drawings, is meager and starv'd almost to death for want of the substantial nourishment which you his mother inhumanly deny him, and yet would now clip his little wings to prevent his seeking it elsewhere!

I fancy we shall neither of us get anything by this war, and therefore as feeling myself the weakest, I will do what indeed ought always to be done by the wisest: be first in making the propositions of peace. That a peace may be lasting, the articles of the treaty should be regulated upon the principles of the most perfect equity and reciprocity. In this view I have drawn up and offer the following, viz.

Article 1.

There shall be eternal peace, friendship and love between Madame B and Mr. F.

Article 2.

In order to maintain the same inviolability, Madame B on her part stipulates and agrees that Mr. F shall come to her whenever she sends for him.

Article 3.

That he shall stay with her as long as she pleases.

Article 4.

That when he is with her, he shall be obliged to drink tea, play chess, hear music, or do any other thing that she requires of him.

Article 5.

That he shall love no other woman but herself.

Article 6.

The said Mr. F in his part stipulates and agrees that he will go away from Madame B's whenever he pleases.

Article 7.

That he will stay away as long as he pleases.

Article 8.

That when he is with her he will do what he pleases.

Article 9.

And that he will love any other woman as far as he finds her amiable.

Let me know what you think of these preliminaries. To me they seem to express the true meaning and intention of each party more plainly than most treaties. I shall insist pretty strongly on the eighth article, tho' without much hope of your consent to it; and on the ninth also, tho' I despair of ever finding any other woman that I could love with equal tenderness: being ever, my dear, dear friend,

Yours most sincerely,

B FRANKLIN

THERE WERE FEW PRIVATE HANDS WE COULD TRUST...

Accidents and a long severe illness interrupted my negotiations, but the arrival of Mr. Jay, Mr. Adams and Mr. Laurens relieved me from much anxiety, which must have continued if I had been left to finish the treaty alone; and it gave me the more satisfaction, as I was sure the business profited by their assistance. I also appointed my grandson Temple to perform and fulfill the duties of secretary to the commission.

My illness, the cruel gout, prevented my corresponding with Congress and Mr. Adams. The complaints of my not writing to Congress were also due to the difficulties in keeping up a regular and punctual correspondence. We were far from the seaports, not well informed, and often misinformed about the sailing of vessels. Frequently we were told they were to sail in a week or two, yet often they lay in port for months after, with our letters on board, either waiting for convoy, or for other reasons. The post office in France was an unsafe conveyance, many of the letters we received by it having evidently been opened, and doubtless the same happened to those we sent. At that time particularly there was so violent a curiosity in all trading people to know something relating to the negotiations, and whether peace may be expected or a continuation of the war, that there were few private hands or travelers that we could trust with carrying our dispatches to the sea coast; and I imagined they might have been opened sometimes, and destroy'd because they could not be well sealed again.

THE TREATY OF PARIS SIGNED

Much of the summer was taken up in objecting to the powers given to Great Britain, and in removing those objections. Using any expressions that might imply an acknowledgement of our independence seem'd at first industriously to be avoided. But our refusing otherwise to treat at length induced them to get over that difficulty. I received a letter from Mr. Secretary Townshend* acquainting me that the King had consented to declare the independence of America as the first article in the treaty. By the first of these articles the King of Great Britain renounced for himself and successors all claim and pretension to dominion or territory within the thirteen United States.

And then we came to the point of making propositions. After some weeks, an undersecretary, Mr. Strachey, arriv'd with whom we had much contestation about the boundaries and other articles which he proposed. We spent many days in disputing, and at length agreed on and signed the preliminaries. The British ministers struggled hard for two points: that the favours granted to the Royalists should be extended, and our fishery contracted. We silenc'd them on the first, by threatening to produce an account of the mischiefs done by those people; and as to the second, when they told us they could not possibly agree to it as we required, and must refer it to the ministry in London, we produced a new article to be referr'd at the same time,

---

* Thomas Townshend, whose cousin Charles Townshend authored the Townshend Acts of 1765, which imposed the notorious import duties on the American colonies.

with a note of facts in support of it. Apparently it seem'd that, to avoid the discussion of this, they suddenly changed their minds, dropped the design of recurring to London, and agreed to allow the fishery as demanded. By this article, fishery in the American seas was to be freely exercised by the Americans wherever they might have formerly exercised it while united with Great Britain, and that both peoples might continue to take fish of every kind in Newfoundland, the Gulf of St. Lawrence, and all other places where the inhabitants of both countries used to fish.

Everyone of the British ministry present, while in the minority, declared the war against us unjust, and nothing was clearer in reason than that those who have injured others by an unjust war should make full reparation. They stipulated too in these preliminaries, that in evacuating our towns they should carry off no plunder, which was a kind of acknowledgement that they ought not to have done it before.

In sum, our independence was acknowledged, our boundaries were good and extensive as we demanded, and our fishery more so than the Congress expected. Immediately after the conclusion of the proposed treaty, we agreed to a firm and perpetual peace between the two nations; that all hostilities, both by sea and land, would immediately cease; that all prisoners on both sides would be set at liberty; and that the British would, without causing any destruction, withdraw all their armies, garrisons and fleets from the United States.

We communicated all the articles as soon as they were signed to Mr. Le Comte de Vergennes, who justly observed that we did not consult him before they were signed and therefore were guilty of neglecting a point of *bienséance*. I informed the minister that this single indiscretion of ours was not from want of respect for the King, whom we all loved and honored, and hoped it would be excused. I told him that nothing was agreed in the preliminaries contrary to the interests of France, and that no peace was to take place between us and England till he had concluded theirs. He said that we had manag'd well, and told me that we had settled what was most apprehended as a difficulty in the work of a general peace by obtaining the declaration of our independency.

I was soon after taken ill with the gravel and sciatica, which together harass'd and confin'd me for some time. But thanks to God I was freed from both, tho' the sciatica left me weak on the left side, so that I went up and down stairs with difficulty.

The preliminaries of peace between France, Spain and England were signed on January 20, 1783, and a cessation of arms agreed to by the ministers of those powers, and by us in behalf of the United States. I informed the Congress of this act, which was very advantageous to France and Spain. I congratulated our country on the happy prospects afforded us by the finishing so speedily this glorious revolution.

Chapter Nine

Minister to France, 1783–85

My Last Years in Paris

At length we were at peace, God be praised; and long, very long may it continue! Having entered my 78TH year, with public business having engrossed fifty of them, I wished to be, for the little time I had left, my own master. I longed earnestly for a return to those peaceful times when I could sit down in sweet society with my philosophical friends, communicating to each other new discoveries, and proposing improvements of old ones, all tending to extend the power of man over matter, and avert or diminish the evils he is subject to, or augment the number of his enjoyments. Much more happy should I be, thus employ'd, than in that of all the grandees of the earth projecting plans of mischief, however necessary they may be supposed for obtaining greater good. I once reminded the Congress of their promise to dismiss me, happy to sing with old Simeon, *Now lettest thou thy servant depart in peace, for mine eyes have seen thy salvation.*

MR. ADAMS FANCIED THAT WE WERE CONTINUALLY PLOTTING AGAINST HIM

It was our firm connection with France that had given us weight with England, and respect throughout Europe. Mr. Adams, however, was of a very different opinion in these matters. He thought the French minister one of the greatest enemies of our country; that he would have straitened our boundaries to prevent the growth of our people, contracted our fishery to obstruct the increase of our seamen, and retained the Royalists among us to keep us divided; that he privately opposed all our negotiations with foreign courts, and afforded us during the war the assistance we received, only to keep it alive, that we might be so much the more weaken'd by it; that to think of gratitude to France was the greatest of follies, and that to be influenc'd by it would ruin us. He made no secret of his having these opinions; expressed them publicly, sometimes in the presence of the English ministers; and spoke of hundreds of instances which he could produce in proof of them. None, however, yet appear'd to me, unless the conversations and letters were reckoned such. I think they did not go further than to occasion a suspicion, but we had a considerable part of anti-gallicans in America who were not Tories, which consequently produced some doubts of the continuance of our friendship. As such doubts might have a bad effect, I think we could not take too much care to remove them.

I heard frequently of Mr. Adams's ravings against M. de Vergennes and me, whom he suspected of plots against him which had no existence but in his own troubled imaginations. I took no notice, and we were civil when we met. He supposed that the Count de Vergennes and myself were continually plotting against him and employing the news writings of Europe to depreciate his character, &c. but as Shakespeare says, "Trifles light as air," &c. I am persuaded, however, that Mr. Adams meant well for his country, was always an honest man, often a wise one, but sometimes and in some things, absolutely out of his senses.

I have observed some enemies in England, but they are my enemies as an American; I have also two or three in America, who are my enemies as a minister: but I thank God there are not in the whole world any who are my enemies as a man; for by his grace, thro' a long life I have been enabled so to conduct myself that there does not exist a human being who can justly say, Ben Franklin has wrong'd me. This is, in old age, a comfortable reflection. All of us have enemies. But let not that render us unhappy. If we make the right use of them, they will do us more good than harm. They point out to us our faults; they put us upon our guard; and help us to live more correctly.

This monstrous pride and insolence

The revolutionary war terminated quite contrary to the expectations of my friend and printer in London Mr. William Strahan. I still have a regard for him in remembrance of our ancient friendship, tho' he had, as a member of the Parliament, dipped his hands in our blood. He did not believe me when I told him repeatedly that England would lose her colonies, as Epictetus warn'd in vain his master that he would break his leg. He believ'd, rather, the tales he had heard of our poltroonery and impotence of body and mind. I then reply'd, "Do you not remember the story you told me of the Scotch sergeant who met with a party of forty American soldiers and tho' alone, disarm'd them all and brought them in prisoners?" He appear'd to believe this story. He also believ'd, apparently, the lie of the French troops and our army having killed each other. His believing such falsehoods would have been of less consequence if he had not propagated them by his chronicle, in the last of which I saw two lying letters said to be from New York but actually fabricated in London.

I am reminded of British General Clarke, who had the folly to say in my hearing at Sir John Pringle's that, with a thousand British grenadiers, he would undertake to go from one end of America to the other and geld all the males, partly by force and partly by a little coaxing. It is plain he took us for a species of animals very little superior to brutes. The Parliament, too, had believ'd the stories of another foolish general, I forget his name, who said that the Yankees never felt bold. A Yankee was understood to be a sort of yahoo, and the

Parliament did not think the petitions of such creatures were fit to be received and read in so wise an assembly.

What was the consequence of this monstrous pride and insolence? They first sent us small armies to subdue us, believing them more than sufficient, but soon found themselves obliged to send greater; these, whenever they ventured to penetrate our country beyond the protection of their ships, were either repulsed and obliged to scamper out, or were surrounded, beaten, and taken prisoners. An American planter who had never seen Europe was chosen by us to command our troops and continu'd during the whole war. This man sent home to England, one after another, five of their best generals, baffled, their heads bare of laurels, disgraced even in the opinion of their employers.

But I am not vain enough to ascribe our success to superiority in any of those points. I am too well acquainted with all the springs and levers of our machine, not to see that our human means were unequal to our undertaking, and that if it had not been for the justice of our cause, and the consequent interposition of Providence in which we had faith, we must have been ruined. If I had ever before been an atheist, I should now have been convinced of the being and government of a Deity. It is He who abases the proud and favours the humble! May we never forget his goodness to us, and may our future conduct manifest our gratitude.

England had lost by this mad war, but what is more, it had lost the esteem, respect, friendship and affection of all that great and growing people, who considered it at present as the worst and wickedest nation upon earth.

To those travelling to America

A multitude of people were continually applying to me, personally and by letters, for information respecting the means of transporting themselves, families and fortunes to America. To answer this, I wrote a little essay called *Information to those who would remove to America*. For a man to expatriate himself is a serious business, and should be well considered, especially where the distance is so great, and the expense of removing thither with his family, and of returning if the country should not suit him, will be so heavy. Our country is open, and strangers may establish themselves in America, where they soon become citizens and are respected according to their conduct. The only encouragements we hold out to strangers are a good climate, fertile soil, good pay for labour, kind neighbours, good laws, liberty, and a hearty welcome. The rest depends on a man's own industry and virtue. Lands are cheap, but they must be bought. All settlements are undertaken at private expense: the public contributes nothing but defense and justice.

Mr. Strahan argued that the emigration of Englishmen to America should be discouraged. In my essay on population,* I have proved, I think, that immigration does not diminish but multiplies a nation. Every man who comes among us and takes up a piece of land becomes a citizen, and by our Constitution has a voice in elections and a share in the government of the country. It is a fact that the Irish immigrants and their children are now in possession of the government of Pennsylvania, by their majority in the Assembly, as well as a great part of the territory; and I remember well the first ship that brought them over.

Our country affords a good climate, good laws, and cheap government

There is no doubt but that a body of sober, industrious and ingenious artisans, men of honest and religious principles, would be a valuable

---

* See "Observations Concerning the Increase of Mankind," published in 1751. PBF 4:225–34.

acquisition to any country; and I am certain they would meet with a kind and friendly reception in Pennsylvania and be put into possession of all rights and privileges of free citizens: But neither that government, nor any other in America that I know of, has ever been at any public expense to augment the number of its inhabitants. All who are establish'd there have come at their own charge. The country affords to strangers a good climate, fine wholesome air, plenty of provisions, good laws, just and *cheap* government, with all the liberties, civil and religious, that reasonable men can wish for. These inducements are so great and the number of people in all the nations of Europe who wish to partake of them is so considerable that if the States were to undertake transporting people at the expense of the public, no revenues that they have would be sufficient. Men are not forc'd there into the public service.

Mr. Ingenhousz wrote me about possible employments by commercial people and artists in America. I replied that I had been so little in America in 25 years that I was unqualified to answer. A new set of merchants had grown up into business, of whom I knew little; and the circumstances of the old ones whom I formerly knew had been much altered by time or by the war. My best advice to these commercial people was to send over a discreet, intelligent person with instructions to travel thro' the country, observe the nature of commerce, and in what quantities and proportions; and what of the produce of the country could be purchased to make advantageous returns.

I was asked about employment in statuary, which I hardly thought worthwhile at the present. The public, burden'd by its war-debts, would certainly think of paying those before going to the expense of marble monuments. A sculptor might indeed be easily paid in land, but land will produce him nothing without labour; and he and his workmen must subsist while they fashion their figures. Private persons are not rich enough to encourage sufficiently the fine arts; and therefore, our geniuses all go to Europe. In England at present the best history-painter is West; the best portrait-painter is Copley; and the best landscape-painter is Taylor at Bath. All are Americans. After a few years, such an artist may find employment in America, and possibly we may discover a white marble a little easier to work than that we have at present, which tho' it bears a fine polish, is reckon'd too hard.

The cultivators of land are made up of a respectable part of our people in Pennsylvania, being generally proprietors of the land they cultivate, out of whom are chosen the majority of our magistrates, legislators, &c. A year's residence gives a stranger all the rights of a citizen. I am not much acquainted with country affairs, having been always an inhabitant of cities; but I imagine a good plantation of two or three hundred acres in the hands of a man who understands agriculture and will attend to it, is capable of furnishing subsistence to his family. The law is also an honourable profession with us, and more profitable than agriculture; and if acquainted with English common law, which is the basis of ours, a man might be admitted to practice immediately, and would find but little difficulty in acquiring a knowledge of our few additions to, or variations of that law. I have known in my time several considerable estates made by that profession. But the study is dry and labourious and long, that is requisite to arrive at eminence; and a man must consider whether he has the habits of application, industry and perseverance that are necessary.

THE BOOK OF STATE CONSTITUTIONS IN FRENCH

The extravagant misrepresentations of our political state in foreign countries made it appear necessary to give our foreign friends better information, which I thought could not be more effectually and authentically done than by publishing a translation into French, now the most general language in Europe, of the book of constitutions of individual states which had been printed by order of Congress. This I accordingly did and presented two copies, handsomely bound, to every foreign minister in Paris, one for himself, the other more elegant for his sovereign. It was well taken, and afforded a matter of surprise to many who had conceived mean ideas of the state of civilization in America, and could not have expected so much political knowledge and sagacity had existed in our wilderness. From all parts I had the satisfaction to hear that our constitutions in general were much admired. I believe that the disbursement of these numerous copies would promote the emigration to our country of substantial people from all parts of Europe and facilitate treaties with foreign courts.

In America, people do not inquire What is he? but What can he do?

I wrote my daughter and Mr. Bache about the letters of recommendation I troubled them with from time to time. I was frequently solicited for letters of recommendations by friends whom I could not refuse, tho' I believe they did not always know well the persons they solicited for. I warned them, "When I recommend a person simply to your civilities and counsels, I mean no more than that you should give him a dinner or two, and your best advice if he asks it; but by no means that you should lend him money." For many I believe went to America with very little, and with such romantic schemes and expectations as must end in disappointment and poverty. I dissuaded all I could who had not some useful trade or art by which they might get a living; but there were many in Europe who hoped for offices and public employments, who valued themselves and expected to be valued by us for their birth or quality, tho' I told them those bear no price in our markets. In America, people do not inquire concerning a stranger, *What is he?* but *What can he do?*

It is incredible the quantity of good that may be done in a country by a single man who will *make a business* of it, and not suffer himself to be diverted from that purpose by different avocations, studies or amusements. There are two opinions prevalent in Europe, which have mischievous effects in diminishing national felicity; the one, that useful labour is dishonourable; the other that families may be perpetuated with estates. In America we have neither of these prejudices, which is a great advantage to us. It is mathematically demonstrable to be an impossibility under the present rules of law and religion to perpetuate an estate, since, tho' the estate may remain entire, the family is continually dividing. A man's son is but half of his family, his grandson but a fourth, his great grandson but an eighth, the next but a sixteenth of his family and, by the same progression, in only nine generations the present proprietor's part in the then possession of the estate will be but a 512TH, supposing the fidelity of all the succeeding wives equally certain with that of those now existing: Too small a portion to be anxious about, or to oppose a legal liberty of breaking entails and dividing estates, which would continue so much to the prosperity of the country.

THE MARRIED STATE IS, AFTER ALL OUR JOKES, THE HAPPIEST. . . .

I received an account of the family of my friend John Sargent, which I found pleasing except that his eldest son had continu'd so long unmarried. I told him that I hoped he did not intent to live and die in celibacy. The wheel of life that has roll'd down to him from Adam without interruption should not stop with him. I would not have one dead unbearing branch in the genealogical tree of the Sargents. The married state is, after all our jokes, the happiest, being comfortable to our natures. Man and woman have each of them qualities and tempers in which the other is deficient, and which in union contribute to the common felicity. Single and separate they are not the compleat human being; they are like the odd halves of scissors; they cannot answer the end of their formation.*

THE DEATH OF MRS. STEVENSON

The departure of my dearest friend Mrs. Margaret Stevenson, which I learned from a letter from her daughter Polly, greatly affected me. To meet with her once more in this life was one of the principal motives of my proposing to visit England again before my return to America. It had been a full quarter of a century, since 1757, that I was first acquainted with Mrs. Stevenson and her daughter. Twenty five years seems like a long period; but in looking back, how short! During the greatest part of the time I lived in the same house with my dear deceased friend, I saw and convers'd with her and Polly much and often. It is all to honours that in all that time we never had

---

* In 1745, Franklin wrote a notorious essay, "Old Mistresses Apologue,"
better known as "Advice to a Young Man on the Choice of a Mistress,"
in which Franklin recommends that if a young man insists on having a
mistress, he should "prefer old women to young ones." No nineteenth
century editor dared to publish the essay. However, the first part of the
essay is usually ignored; its views are similar to the ones Franklin makes
above: "Marriage is the most natural state of man, and therefore the state
in which one is most likely to find solid happiness. It is the man and
woman united that make the compleat human being. Separate, she
wants his force of body and strength of reason; he, her softness, sensibil-
ity and acute discernment. Together they are more likely to succeed in
the world. A single man has not nearly the value he would have in that
state of union. He is an incomplete animal. He resembles the odd half of
a pair of scissors. If you get a prudent healthy wife, your industry in
your profession, with her good economy, will be a fortune sufficient."
See PBF 3:27–31, "Old Mistresses Apologue," June 25, 1745.

among us the smallest misunderstanding. Our friendship was all clear sunshine, without any the least cloud in its hemisphere.

I received a kind letter of thanks from Polly on her visit to Passy following her mother's death. Because of her visit, I pass'd a long winter in a manner that made it appear the shortest of any I ever pass'd. Such is the effect of pleasing society with friends one loves. M. le Veillard in particular told me at different times what indeed I have known long since, *C'est une bien digne femme, cette Madame Hewson; une tres aimable femme.*

That year also carried off my friends Dr. Pringle and Dr. Fothergill, and Lord Kames and Lord le Despencer. Thus the ties I once had to that country, and indeed to the world in general, loosened one by one, and as time passes I shall have no attachment left to make me unwilling to follow. To those remaining old friends, I say, *the fewer we become, the more let us love one another.*

I DETERMINED TO GIVE HIM A TRADE

Then, being inform'd that my grandons, Benny, had been ill of a fever, and that he was dejected and pin'd at being so long absent from his relations, his having been four years at school at Geneva, I sent for him to come to me during the vacation of the schools. He accordingly came to Passy, where I found him well grown, and much improv'd in his learning and behaviour. He could translate common Latin readily into French; but his English had suffer'd for want of use, tho' he readily recovered it. I had intended to send him to England to continue his education, and engag'd Mr. Jay to take him over in his company: But when it came to be propos'd to him, he show'd such an unwillingness to leave me, and Temple such a fondness for retaining him, that I concluded to keep him till I should go over myself. He behaved very well and we loved him very much.

Benny being a very sensible and good lad, I had thoughts of bringing him up under his cousin, Jonathan Williams, and fitting him for public business, thinking he might be of service hereafter to his country; but being now convinc'd that *service is no inheritance*, as the proverb says, I determin'd to give him a trade that he may have something to depend on, and not be oblig'd to ask favours of offices of anybody. And I flattered myself that Benny would make his good in the world with God's blessing. He had already begun to learn his business, a printer and a letter-founder, from masters who came to my house, and was very diligent in working and quick to learn.

THE TREATIES WERE MET WITH GREAT DELAYS

The definitive treaties were met with great delays, partly by the tardiness of the Dutch, but principally by the distractions in the court of England, where for some time there was no proper ministry nor any business effected. In March, the English court was in confusion by another change of ministry; Lord Shelburne and his friends resigned, and Lord North and Mr. Fox were being reconcil'd!! It was said that Mr. Oswald, who signed the preliminaries, would not return, but that Mr. David Hartley would come to France in his stead, to settle the definitive treaty. As Mr. Hartley was an old friend of mine and a strong lover of peace, I did not expect much difficulty with him. Mr. Laurens left for Bath to mend his health, while Messrs. Jay and Adams continued in Paris.

We were also totally in the dark, having not had a line from Congress in six months, as to their opinion of the preliminary articles of the peace, which we sent by Capt. Barney in the *Washington*, which sail'd from L'Orient the 17ᵀᴴ of January 1783, and carried with our dispatches a large sum of money. These occasional interruptions of correspondence were the inevitable consequences of a state of war and of such remote situations. At length, Capt. Barney returned to

France and brought dispatches for us, with the preliminary articles ratified by the Congress.

Seeking further aid from France

I also received the resolutions of Congress empowering me to borrow another twenty million livres from France. Considering the enormous expense this extensive war had occasion'd France, I had hoped to avoid the necessity of repeating the original request of Congress for a large sum; with this view I had many consultations and considered various schemes with our banker Mr. Grand for procuring money elsewhere. As none of those schemes proved practicable, I was constrained to request at least six millions more to be added.

The finances in France were an embarrassment, and a new loan was proposed by way of lottery, which, by some calculators, the King paid at the rate of 7 percent. The government was obliged to stop payment for a year of its own bills of exchange drawn in America and the East Indies; yet it advanced six millions to save the credit of ours. The contract showed fresh marks of the King's kindness toward us in giving us so long a term for payment, and for giving the first year's interest. It was impossible for me to obtain more.

The late failure of payment in the Caisse d'Escompte, an institution similar to the Bank of England, occasioned partly by its having gone too far in assisting the French government, and the inability of the government to support their credit, tho' extremely desirous of doing it, was fresh proof that our not obtaining another loan was not by want of good will to assist us, as some unjustly supposed, but by a real want of the means. Money was at the time unaccountably scarce in France. The government proposed a second lottery to borrow 24 millions, and the Caisse d'Escompte continued on again with its operation, but it paid interest by the lottery plan of nearly 7 percent.

Events at length should have convinced our people of the truth of what I long since wrote to them, that *the foundation of credit abroad must be laid at home*. Nothing could recover our credit in Europe and our reputation in its courts but an immediate proof of our honesty and prudence by a general provision in all the states for the punctual payment of the interest and the final regular discharge of the principal. I saw that some states opposed a measure in Congress to discharge the national debt, which had very mischievous effects in France; it discouraged a loan going on in Holland, and thereby occasioned a protest of some of Mr. Morris's bills. Mr. Grand, however, advanc'd funds for me and the other commissioners, tho' at his own risk, being without orders.

If our people who neither paid rents nor tithes would only pay honestly in taxes half what other nations paid in those articles, our whole debt might have been discharged in twelve months. But I conceived the difficulty lay in the collection of our taxes, thro' the dispersed situation of our inhabitants, and the excessive trouble of going from house to house many miles to collect a few shillings from each, often obliged to repeat the calls.

ALL PROPERTY IS THE CREATURE OF SOCIETY

The problem is that our people in America were unwilling to pay taxes. I saw in some resolutions of town meetings, a remonstrance against giving Congress a power to take, as they call it, *the people's money* out of their pockets, tho' only to pay the interest and principal of debts duly contracted. They seemed to mistake the point. Money justly due from the people is their *creditor's* money, and no longer the money of the people, who, if they withhold it, should be compelled to pay by some law. Private property is a creature of society and is subject to the calls of that society whenever its necessities shall require it, even to its last farthing. All property indeed, except the savage's temporary cabin, his bow, his match coat, and other little acquisitions absolutely necessary for his subsistence, seems to me to be the creature of public convention. Hence the public has the right of regulating inheritances and all other conveyances of property, and even of limiting the quantity and the uses of it. All the property that is necessary for a man for the conservation of the individual and the propagation of the species is his natural right, which none can justly deprive him of. But of all properties of the public, who by their laws have created it, and who may therefore by other laws dispose of it, the welfare of the public shall demand their disposition. He that does not like civil society on these terms, let him retire and live among savages. He can have no right to the benefits of society who will not pay his club dues towards the support of it.

TRADE WITH FRANCE: THE MORE
UNRESTRAINED, THE MORE IT FLOURISHES

Our merchants complained in general of the embarrassments suffered by the numerous internal demands of duties, searches, &c. that they were subjected to in France. In general I would only observe that commerce, consisting in a mutual exchange of the necessaries and conveniences of life, the more free and unrestrained it is, the more it flourishes; and the happier are all the nations concerned in it. Most of the restraints put upon it in different countries seem to have been the projects of particulars for their private interests, under pretence of good.

We saw much in parliamentary proceedings, and in papers and pamphlets, of the injury the concessions to Ireland had done to the manufacturers of England, while the people of England seemed to have forgotten, as if quite out of the question. If the Irish could manufacture cottons, and stuffs, and silks, and clothes, and linens, and cutlery, and toys and books, &c &c &c, so as to sell them cheaper in England than the manufacturers of England sell them, was not this good for the people of England who are not themselves manufacturers? And will not even the manufacturers themselves share the benefit? If cottons are cheaper, all the other manufacturers who wear cottons will save in that article; and so of the rest. If books can be had much cheaper from Ireland (which I believe, for I bought Blackstone there for 24s. when it was sold in England at 4 guineas) is not this an advantage, not to English booksellers indeed, but to English readers, and to learning?

In transactions of trade, it is not to be suppos'd that like gaming, what one party gains the other must necessarily lose. The gain to each may be equal. If A had more corn than he can consume, but wants cattle, and B has more cattle but wants corn, an exchange is a gain to each; hereby the common stock of comforts in life is increas'd. If restrictive laws were everywhere abandoned, trade would thrive in those countries. When princes make war by prohibiting commerce, each may hurt himself as much as his enemy. Traders, farmers and fishermen should never be interrupted or molested in their business, but should enjoy the protection of all in the time of war and peace. The source of wealth is land and industry, and the state must nourish both.

No nation was ever ruined by trade

It would be better if government meddled no further with trade and let it take its course. Most of the statutes, acts, edicts, arets and placards of Parliaments, princes, and states, for regulating, directing, and restraining of trade have either political blunders or jobs obtain'd by artful men for private advantage under the pretence of public good. When Colbert assembled some wise old merchants of France and desir'd their advice and opinion how he could best serve and promote commerce, their answer was in three words only, *Laissez nous faire*. Let us alone. It is said by a very solid writer of the same nation, well advanced in the science of politics, who knows the full force of that maxim *Pas trop gouverner*: Not to govern too strictly, which perhaps would be of more use when applied to trade than in any other public concern. It is therefore wish'd that all commerce were as free between all the nations of the world as it is between the several counties of England: so would all, by mutual communication, obtain more enjoyments. Those counties do not ruin one another by trade; neither would the nations. No nation was ever ruin'd by trade; even, seemingly, the most disadvantageous.

Let us now forgive and forget. Let each country seek its advancement in its own internal advantages of arts and agriculture, not in retarding or preventing the prosperity of the other. America will, with God's blessing, become a great and happy country; and England, if she has at length gain'd wisdom, will have gain'd something more valuable, and more essential to her prosperity, than all she has lost, and will still be a great and respectable nation. Her great disease at present is the number and enormous salaries and emoluments of office. Avarice and ambition are strong passions, and separately act with great force on the human mind; but when both are united and may be gratified in the same object, their violence is almost irresistible, and they hurry men headlong into factions and contentions destructive to all good government.

THERE NEVER WAS A GOOD WAR, OR A BAD PEACE

It was certainly disagreeable to the English ministers that all their treaties for peace were carried on under the eye of the French court at Versailles. This began to appear especially toward the conclusion, when Mr. Hartley refused going to Versailles to sign our definite treaty with the other powers, and insisted on its being done at Paris, which we in good humour complied with. After a continued course of treating for nine months, the English ministry had at length come to a resolution to lay aside all the new propositions that they had made, and offered to sign again as a definitive treaty the articles of

November 30, 1782. We agreed to this, and the Treaty between England and the United States was signed on Wednesday, the 3ᴿᴰ of September, 1783, and a general peace was at last establish'd.

I rejoiced at the return of peace. We are now friends with England and with all mankind. I hope it will be lasting, and that mankind will at length, as they call themselves reasonable creatures, have reason and sense enough to settle their differences without cutting their throats. May we never see another war! For in my opinion *there never was a good war, or a bad peace.* What vast additions to the conveniences and comforts of living might mankind have acquired if the money spent in wars had been employ'd in works of public utility! What an extension of agriculture even to the tops of our mountains; what rivers render'd navigable, or join'd by canals; what bridges, aqueducts, new roads and other public works, edifices and improvements rendering England a compleat paradise, might not have been obtain'd by spending those millions in doing good, which in the great war were spent in doing mischief, and in bringing misery into thousands of families, and destroying the lives of so many thousands of working people who might have perform'd useful labour!

Nevertheless, it is a pleasing reflection arising from the contemplation of our successful struggle and the manly, spirited, and unanimous resolves at Dungannon, that liberty, which had appeared in danger of extinction, is regaining the ground she had lost; that arbitrary governments are likely to become more mild, and reasonable, and to expire by degrees, giving place to more equitable forms; and that despotism and priestcraft cannot keep the light from growing.

AN ACCUSATION THAT FALLS LITTLE SHORT OF TREASON

After the signing of the definitive treaty, I received a letter from a very respectable person in America that some heavy charges, written from

Paris and propagated among people at home, had been made against me respecting my conduct in the treaty, viz.,

"It is confidently reported, propagated and believed by some among us, that the court of France was at bottom against our obtaining the fishery and territory in that great extent in which both are secured to us by the treaty; that our minister at that court favoured, or did not oppose this design against us; and that it was entirely owing to the firmness, sagacity and disinterestedness of Mr. Adams, with whom Mr. Jay united, that we have obtained these important advantages."

It was not my purpose to dispute any share of the honour of that treaty which the friends of my colleagues might be dispos'd to give them; but having spent fifty years of my life in public offices and trust, and having still one ambition left, that of carrying the character of fidelity at least to the grave with me, I could not allow that I was behind any of them in zeal and faithfulness. I therefore thought that I ought not to suffer an accusation, which falls little short of treason to my country, to pass without notice, when the means of effectual vindication were at hand. Since Mr. Laurens and Mr. Jay had been witnesses of my conduct in that affair, I appealed to them as brother commissioners to send a letter that would do me justice and entirely destroy the effect of that accusation.

William Penn was a wise and good man, but Thomas was a miserable churl

Lady Dowager Penn, widow of Thomas Penn, was in France about the time of the treaty and made application to me with great complaints, begging my assistance in recovering her rights and possessions in Pennsylvania. But I found she was not well inform'd of the state of her affairs, and could not clearly show that she had suffer'd any injury by the public of Pennsylvania during the war. I understood

that her husband's lands had not been confiscated as represented; but
the proprietary government having fallen with that of the crown, the
colonial Assembly had taken the opportunity of insisting upon justice
in some points, which they could never obtain under the proprietary
government. A kind of compromise had then been made between the
Assembly and the family, whereby all the vacant lots and inappropriate wilderness lands were to be thenceforth in the disposition of the
Assembly, who were to pay £130,000 sterling to the family within 3
years after the peace, all other demands on both sides being thus
abolish'd. I was told this arrangement had been satisfactory to most
of them. But as the lady intended to send her son over to solicit her
interests, I gave him a letter of recommendation to the governor, proposing it for consideration, whether it might not be advisable to
reconsider the matter, and if the sum of £130,000 should be found
insufficient, to make a proper addition.

In my judgment, when I consider that for near 80 years, viz. from
the year 1700, William Penn and his sons had receiv'd the quitrents
which were originally granted for the support of government, and yet
refus'd to support the government, obliging the people to make a
fresh provision for its support all that time, which cost them vast
sums; when I consider the meanness and cruel avarice of the late proprietor, in refusing for several years of war to consent to any defense
of the frontiers, ravaged all the while by the enemy, unless his estate
should be exempted from paying any part of the expense; not to
mention other atrocities too long to list; I cannot but think the family well off, and that it would be prudent in them to take the money
and be quiet. William Penn, the first proprietor, father of Thomas,
the husband of the present Dowager, was a wise and good man, and
as honest to the people as the extreme distress of his circumstances
would permit him to be. But Thomas was a miserable churl, always
intent upon griping and saving; and whatever good the father may

have done for the province, was amply undone by the mischief receiv'd from the son, who never did anything that had the appearance of generosity and public spirit, but what was extorted from him by solicitation and the shame of backwardness in benefits evidently incumbent on him to promote, and which was done at last in the most ungracious manner possible.

The lady's complaints of not duly receiving her revenues from America became habitual; they had been the same during all the time of my long residence in London, being then made by her husband [before he died] as excuses for the meanness of his housekeeping and his deficiency in hospitality; tho' I knew at the time that he was then in full receipt of vast sums annually by the sale of lands, interest of money, and quitrents. But probably he might have concealed this from his lady, to induce greater economy: as it is known that he ordered no more of his income home than was absolutely necessary for his subsistence, but plac'd it at interest in Pennsylvania and the Jerseys, where he could have 6 and 7 per cent, while money bore no more than 5 per cent in England. I us'd often to hear of these complaints and laughed at them, perceiving clearly their motive.

Our rector of St. Martin's Parish in London, Dr. Saunders, once went about during a long and severe frost, soliciting charitable contributions to purchase coals for poor families. He came among others to me, and I gave him something. It was but little, very little; and yet it occasion'd him to remark, "You are more bountiful on this occasion than your wealthy proprietor Mr. Penn; but he tells me he is distress'd by not receiving his incomes from America"! The incomes of the family must still be great, for they have a number of manors consisting of the best lands, which are preserv'd to them, and vast sums as interest well secur'd by mortgages; so that if the Dowager did not receive her proportion, there must have been some fault in her agents.

AIR BALLOONS: WE THINK
OF NOTHING BUT OF FLYING

After the war, in 1783, all the conversation in France turned upon the balloons fill'd with light inflammable air, and the means of managing them so as to give man the advantage of flying.* This is one of the most extraordinary discoveries that this age has produced, by which men are enabled to rise in the air and travel with the wind. Having been an eye witness twice of this amazing experiment, I communicated it to the Royal Society.

The first balloon, invented by Messrs. Mongolfier of Annonay, was raised in Versailles. I was not present, but had been told it was filled in about ten minutes by means of burning straw. It was supposed to have risen about 200 toises:† It was carried horizontally by the wind and descended gently as the air within grew cooler. So vast a bulk, when it began to rise so majestically in the air, struck the spectators with surprise and admiration. The basket contained a sheep, a duck, and a cock, who, except the cock, received no hurt by the fall.

The next balloon was larger than that which went up from Versailles. Persons were plac'd in the gallery, which was made of wicker and attached to the outside near the bottom, where each had a port thro' which they could pass sheaves of straw into the grate to keep up the flame, and thereby keep the balloon full. As it went over our

---

* Franklin added this footnote: "Inflammable air puts me in mind of a
  little jocular paper I wrote some years since in ridicule of a prize question given out by a certain academy on this side of the water." The paper
  was a bagatelle on "farting" that Franklin wrote around 1780 "To the
  Royal Academy of Brussels." It ends "And I cannot but conclude
  that.... the figures inscrib'd in it, are, all together, scarcely worth a
  F A R T - H I N G." See PBF 32:396–400.
† A height measurement: a toise is approximately equal to 6.4 feet.

heads, we could see the fire, which was very considerable. When they were as high as they chose to be, they made less flame and suffered the machine to drive horizontally with the wind, of which however they felt very little, as they went with it, and as fast. They said that they had a charming view of Paris and its environs, the course of the river, &c. Multitudes in Paris saw the balloon passing, but did not know there were men with it, it being then so high that they could not see them.

THERE WAS A GOOD DEAL
OF ANXIETY FOR THEIR SAFETY

One of the courageous philosophers, the Marquis d'Arlandes, did me the honour to call upon me in the evening after the experiment with Mr. Montgolfier, the very ingenious inventor. I was happy to see him safe. He informed me that they lit gently without the least shock, and the balloon was very little damaged. As the flames slacken, the rarefied air cools and condenses, with the result that the bulk of the balloon diminishes and begins to descend. If those in the basket see it likely to descend in an improper place, they can throw on more straw, and renew the flame, making it rise again, and the wind carries it farther.

This method of filling the balloon with hot air is cheap and expeditious, and, it is supposed, may be sufficient for certain purposes, such as to give people an extensive view of the country, or elevating an engineer to take a view of an enemy's army, works, &c, conveying intelligence into, or out of, a besieged town, giving signals to distant places, or the like.

On several occasions, the new aerostatic experiment was repeated. In November, I intended to be present to witness the experiment of Mr. Charles and Mr. Robert, one of the very ingenious constructors of the machine. I declin'd going into the garden of the

Tuilleries where the balloon was plac'd, not knowing how long I might be oblig'd to wait there before it was ready to depart, and chose to stay in my carriage near the statue of Louis XV, from whence I could well see it rise. The morning was foggy, but about one o'clock, the air became tolerably clear. Some guns were fired to give notice that the departure of the great balloon was near, and a small one was discharg'd which went to an amazing height. Means were used to prevent the great balloon's rising so high as might endanger its bursting. Several bags of sand were taken on board before the cord that held it down was cut; and the whole weight then being too much to be lifted, such a quantity was discharg'd as to permit its rising slowly. Between one and two o'clock, all eyes were gratified with seeing it rise majestically from among the trees, and ascend gradually above the buildings a most beautiful spectacle! When it was about 200 feet high, the brave adventurers held out and wav'd a little white pennant to salute the spectators, who return'd loud claps of applause. When it arrived at its height, which I supposed might be 3 or 400 toises, it appear'd to have only horizontal motion. I had a pocket glass, with which I follow'd it, till I lost sight, first of the men, then of the car, and when I last saw the balloon, it appear'd no bigger than a walnut.

All Paris was out to see it. . . .
HALF A MILLION SPECTATORS

Messrs. Charles and Robert made a trip thro' the air to a place farther distant than Dover is from Calais, and would have gone farther if there had been more wind and daylight. They had perfect command of the machine, descending and rising again at pleasure. Never, surely, was a philosophical experiment so magnificently attended. All Paris was out to see it and all the inhabitants of the neighbouring towns, so that there could be hardly less than half a million spectators. The progress made in the management of balloon travel has been rapid, yet I fear it will hardly become a common carriage in my time, tho' it would be extremely convenient to me, given that my malady forbids the use of the old ones over a pavement.

It was said by some of those with experience that as yet they have not found means to keep up a balloon more than two hours; for that by now and then losing air to prevent rising too high and bursting, and now and then discharging ballast to avoid descending too low, these means of regulation are exhausted. In June 1785 M. Pilatre de Rosier, who had studied the subject as much as any man, lost his support in the air, by bursting of his balloon, or by some other means we are yet unacquainted with, and fell with his companion from the height of one thousand toises, onto the rocky coast, and was found dashed to pieces.

BEING NOW DISABLED BY THE STONE

I wrote M. de Vergennes that I could not pay my *devoirs* personally at Versailles, sending my grandson to supply my place, and urged Congress again to answer my request of being recalled. I was too much harassed by a variety of correspondence, together with gout and gravel, which induced me to postpone doing what I often fully intended to do. Being at that point in my 80TH year, and engag'd in much business that must not be neglected, writing had become more and more irksome to me, and I grew more indolent. Philosophic discussions, not being urgent as business, were postponed till they were forgotten.

My sitting too much at the desk had already almost killed me. The stone gave me much pain, wounded my bladder and occasioned me to make bloody urine, even when traveling in the easiest of carriage. I sought to prevent the stone from growing larger by abstemious living and gentle exercise, and was able to go pretty comfortably with it, but when I attempted to write, the pain would interrupt my train of thinking, so that I laid down my pen and sought some light amusement.

The relish for reading poetry had left me long ago, but I received a book of poetry from Mr. John Thornton, and there was something so new in the manner, so easy, and yet so correct in the language, so clear in the expression, yet concise, and so just in the sentiments, that I read the whole thing with pleasure, and some of the pieces more than once.

Madame Brillon did me the honor of asking for a copy of my writings, so through Mr. Le Roy I sent her the *Information to Those Who Would Remove to America,* and I added the *Remarks Concerning the Savages of North America.* I also sent several other little things printed in my house at Passy solely for our friends. If she had not lost *The Handsome and the Deformed Leg,* and *The Morals of Chess,* she should have had a complete collection of all my bagatelles which had been printed at Passy.

I had promised my dear friend Countess d'Houdetot* to spend a few days at her home and gardens in Sannois, and there was nothing I would have liked better than to do; but the more I thought about it, the less feasible it seemed, for I was less able to walk. Going no further than Madame Brillion's caused me to be in pain for several days. I was thus obliged to inform the Countess that I had to give up the pleasure of her charming Sannois retreat.

We had a terrible winter in France that year [1783–84], such another as had not been remembered by any man living. The snow lay thick upon the ground ever since Christmas, and the frost was constant. The severity of the winter in America as well hindered travelling and occasion'd a delay in the assembling of the states. Yet I was

---

* Countess d'Houdetot helped orchestrate a celebration in honor of Franklin in April 1781, at Sannois, her husband's country estate.

still alive, the sun started to return, the days to lengthen, the Spring to come, the trees and the gardens at Passy to regain their verdure, all nature to laugh, and to me, happiness.

THE ORDER OF CINCINNATI: DESCENDING HONOUR IS GROUNDLESS, ABSURD, AND HURTFUL TO POSTERITY

I received by Capt. Barney some newspaper reports relating to the Order of Cincinnati, wherein a number of private persons thought it proper to distinguish themselves and their posterity from their fellow citizens, and form an order of hereditary knights, in direct opposition to the solemnly declared sense of their country in the Articles of Confederation. Perhaps I should not myself object to their wearing their ribbons and badges according to their fancy, tho' I certainly should object to the entailing it as an honour of their posterity. For honour worthily obtain'd, is in nature a personal thing, and incommunicable to any but those who had some share in obtaining it. Thus among the Chinese, the most ancient, and from long experience the wisest of nations, honour does not *descend* but *ascends*. If a man from his learning, his wisdom or his valour is promoted by the emperor to the rank of Mandarin, his parents are immediately entitled to all the same ceremonies of respect from the people that are establish'd as due to the Mandarin himself, on this supposition: that it must have been owing to the education, instruction, and good example afforded him by his parents that he was rendered capable of serving the public. This *ascending honour* is therefore useful to the state as it encourages parents to give their children a good and virtuous education. But the *descending honour* to posterity who could have had no share in obtaining it, is not only groundless and absurd, but often hurtful to that posterity, since it is apt to make them proud, disdaining to be employed in useful arts, and thence falling into poverty and all the meannesses, servility and wretchedness attending it, which is the present case with much of what is called the *Noblesse* in Europe. Or if, to keep up the dignity of the family, estates are entailed entirely on the eldest male heir, another pest to industry and improvement of the country is introduced, which will be follow'd by all the odious mixture of pride and beggary and idleness that have half depopulated Spain, occasioning continual extinction of families by the discouragements of marriage and improvement of estates. I wish therefore that the Cincinnati, if they must go on with their project, would direct the badges of their order to be worn by their parents instead of handing them down to their children. It would be a good precedent, and might have good effects. It would also be a kind of obedience to the fourth commandment, in which God enjoins us to honour our father and mother, but has no where directed us to honour our children.

I hoped therefore that the Order would drop this part of their project and content themselves as the Knights of the Garter, Bath, Thistle, St. Louis and other orders of Europe do, with a life enjoyment of their little badge and ribbon, and let the distinction die with those who have merited it. At length, the Cincinnati institution was so universally dislik'd by the people that it was dropped.

I WISH THE BALD EAGLE HAD NOT BEEN CHOSEN

As to the figure to represent the order, I was not displeased that the figure looks more like a turkey than a bald eagle. For my own part I wish the bald eagle had not been chosen as the representative of our country. He does not get his living honestly. He perches on some dead tree near the river, where, too lazy to fish for himself, he watches the labour of the fishing hawk; and when that diligent bird has at length taken a fish, and is bearing it to his nest for the support of his mate and young ones, the bald eagle pursues him and takes it from him.

With all this injustice, he is like those among men who live by sharp-ing and robbing. Besides, he is a rank coward: the little king bird not bigger than a sparrow attacks him boldly and drives him out of the district. He is therefore by no means a proper emblem for the brave and honest Cincinnati of America, who have driven all the king birds from our country, tho' exactly fit for that order of knights which the French call *Chevaliers d'Industrie*.

In truth, the turkey is in comparison a much more respectable bird, and withal a true original native of America. Eagles have been found in all countries, but the turkey was peculiar to ours, the first of the species seen in Europe having been brought to France by the Jesuits from Canada, and serv'd up at the wedding table of Charles the ninth. He is besides, tho' a little vain and silly, a bird of courage, and would not hesitate to attack a grenadier of the British guards who should presume to invade his farm yard with a red coat on.

THIS HAS BEEN A TRICK OF MINE FOR DOING A DEAL OF GOOD WITH A LITTLE MONEY

I sent Benjamin Webb, at his solicitation, a bill for ten louis d'ors. I told him, "I do not pretend to *give* such a sum. I only *lend* it to you. When you shall return to your country with a good character, you cannot fail of getting into some business that will in time enable you to pay all your debts: In that case, when you meet with another hon-est man in similar distress, you must pay *me* by lending this sum to *him*; enjoining him to discharge the debt by a like operation when he shall be able and shall meet with such another opportunity. I hope it may thus go thro' many hands before it meets with a knave that will stop its progress." This has been a trick of mine for doing a deal of good with a little money. I have not been rich enough to afford *much* in good works and so I have been obliged to be cunning and make the most of a *little*.

A SATIRE ON DAYLIGHT SAVING

In the same spirit, I flattered myself to bring forward a scheme of finance. As we may be frequently disposed in this nation to engage in wars, and are sometimes embarrassed in what manner to raise money by taxes, it is hoped that, by the help of savings that must occur from adopting this economical project, we shall easily become the terror of nations. In any event, it may allow us to abolish various taxes that are a burden upon the public, and above all upon the poor. The payment of our national debt is another object that may readily be accomplished by it. A translation of it appeared in one of the daily papers of Paris about the year 1784, herein printed below:

To the authors of the journal:

Messieurs,

You often entertain us with accounts of new discoveries. Permit me to communicate to the public through your paper, one that has been late made by myself, and which I conceive may be of great utility.

I was the other evening in a grand company, where the new lamp of Messrs. Quinquet and Lange was introduced, and much admired for its splendor: but a general inquiry was made whether the oil consumed was in proportion to the light it afforded, in which case there would be no saving in the use of it. I was much pleased to see this general concern for economy; for I love economy exceedingly.

I went home and to bed, three or four hours after midnight, with my head full of the subject. An accidental sudden noise waked me about six in the morning, when I was surprised to find my room filled with light; and I imagined at first that a number of those lamps had been brought into it; but rubbing my eyes I perceived the light came in at the windows. I got up and looked out to see what might be the occasion of it, when I saw the sun just rising above the horizon, from whence he poured his rays plentifully into my chamber, my domestic having negligently omitted the preceding night to close the shutters.

I looked at my watch, which goes very well, and found that it was six o'clock; and still thinking it something extraordinary that the sun should rise so early, I looked into the almanac, where I found it to be the hour given for his rising on that day. I looked forward too and found he was to rise still earlier every day till toward the end of June, and that at no time in the year he retarded his rising so long as till eight o'clock. Your readers who, with me, have never seen any signs of sunshine before noon, will be as much astonished as I was, when they hear of his rising so early. I am convinced of this. I am certain of my fact. One cannot be more certain of any fact. I saw it with my own eyes. And having repeated this observation the three following mornings, I found always precisely the same result.

This event has given rise in my mind to several serious and important reflections. I considered that if I had not been awakened so early that morning, I should have slept six hours longer by the light of the sun, and in exchange have lived six hours the following night by candle light; and the latter being a much more expensive light than the former, my love of economy induced me to muster up what little arithmetic I was master of, and to make some calculations.

I took for the basis of my calculations the supposition that there are 100,000 families in Paris, and that these families consume in the night half a pound of candles per hour. Then estimating seven hours per day, and there being seven hours per night which we burn candles, the account gives us 128,100,000 hours spent at Paris by candle-light, which at half a pound of wax and tallow per hour, gives the weight of 64,075,000 pounds, which estimating the whole at the medium price of thirty sols the pound, makes the sum of ninety-six millions and seventy-five thousand livres. An immense sum that the city of Paris might save every year, only by the economy of using sunshine instead of candles!

If it should be said that people are apt to be obstinately attached to old customs, and that it will be difficult to induce them to rise before noon, consequently my discovery can be of but little use; I answer, *nil desperandum*. I believe all who have common sense, as soon as they have learned from this paper that it is daylight when the sun rises, will contrive to rise with him; and to compel the rest, I would propose the following regulations:

First. Let a tax be laid of a louis per window, on every window that is provided with shutters to keep out the light of the sun.

Second. Let the same salutary operation of police be made use of to prevent our burning candles that inclined us last winter to be more economical in burning wood; that is, let guards be placed in the shops of all the wax and tallow chandlers, and no family permitted to be supplied with more than one pound of candles per week.

Third. Let guards also be posted to stop all the coaches, &c. that would pass the streets after sunset, except those of physicians, surgeons, and midwives.

Fourth. Every morning, as soon as the sun rises, let all the bells in every church be set ringing; and if that is not sufficient, let cannon be fired in every street, to wake the sluggards effectually, and make them open their eyes to see their true interest.

All the difficulty will be in the first two or three days, after which the reformation will be as natural and easy as the present irregularity; for *ce n'est que le premier pas qui coute*. Oblige a man to rise at four in the morning, and it is more than probable he shall go willingly to bed at eight in the evening; and having had eight hours sleep, he will rise more willingly at four the morning following.

But this sum of 96,075,000 livres is not the whole of what may be saved by my economical project. You may observe that I have calculated upon only one half of the year, and much may be saved in the other, though the days are shorter. Besides, the immense flock of wax and tallow left unconsumed during the summer, will probably make candles much cheaper for the ensuing winter, and continue cheaper as long as the proposed reformation shall be supported.

For the great benefit of this discovery, thus freely communicated and bestowed by me on the public, I demand neither place, pension, exclusive privilege, nor any other reward whatever. I expect only to have the honour of it. And yet I know there are little envious minds who will, as usual, deny me this, and say that my invention was known to the ancients, and perhaps they may bring passages out of old books in proof of it. I will not dispute with these people that the ancients might have known the sun would rise at certain hours; they possibly had, as we have, almanacs that predicted it; but it does not follow from thence that they knew *he gave light as soon as he rose*. This is what I claim as my discovery. If the ancients knew it, it must have been long since forgotten, for it certainly was unknown to the moderns, at least to the Parisians, which to prove, I need use but one plain simple argument. They are as well-instructed, judicious, and prudent a people as exist any where in the world, all professing like myself to be lovers of economy; and from the many heavy taxes required from them by the necessities of the state, have surely an abundant reason to be economical. I say it is impossible that so sensible a people under such circumstances should have lived so long by the unwholesome and enormously expensive light of candles, if they had really known that they might have had as much pure light of the sun for nothing. I am &c.

An Abonne.

Stoop as you go through life

I received a kind letter from Samuel Mather, so I wrote him in return, and told him the following instance. When I was a boy, I met with a book entitled *Essays to Do Good*, which was written by his father. It had been so little regarded by a former possessor, that several leaves of it were torn out. But the remainder gave me such a turn of thinking as to have no [small] influence on my conduct thro' life; for I have always set a greater value on the character of a doer of good, than on any other kind of reputation; and if I have been a useful citizen, the public owes the advantage of it to that book.

It had been more than 60 years since I left Boston, but I remembered well both his father and grandfather,* having heard them both in the pulpit, and seen them in their houses. The last time I had seen his father was in the beginning of 1724 when I visited him after my first trip to Pennsylvania. He receiv'd me in his library, and on my taking leave, show'd me a shorter way out of the house thro' a narrow passage which was cross'd by a beam overhead. We were still talking as I withdrew, he accompanying me behind, and I turning partly toward him, when he said hastily *stoop, stoop!* I did not understand him till I felt my head hit against the beam. He was a man that never miss'd an occasion of giving instruction, and upon this he said to me, *You are young and have the world before you; stoop as you go through it and you will miss many hard thumps.* This advice, thus beat into my head, has frequently been of use to me, and I often think of it when I see pride mortified, and misfortunate brought upon people by their carrying their heads too high.

Hoping to return to Boston

I longed much to see again my native place, and hoped to lay my bones there. I left it in 1723; I visited it in 1733, 1743, 1753, and 1763. In 1773 I was in England; in 1775 I had a sight of the city, but could not enter, it being in possession of the enemy. I did hope to

---

* The famous Puritan minister, Cotton Mather.

have been there in 1783, but could not obtain my dismissal from France, and I fear I will never have that happiness. My best wishes, however, attended my dear country, *esto perpetua*: It is now blest with an excellent constitution. May it last forever.

A NEW COMMISSION

Mr. Jay sail'd for America from Dover the first of June 1784 to become Secretary of Foreign Affairs, and Mr. Laurens left London the 6ᵀᴴ to go home by way of the Falmouth packet. I had intended to return to America as well, but the Congress, instead of giving me leave to do so, sent me another commission, which kept me in Paris another year. I also received advice that Mr. Jefferson, late governor of Virginia, was commissioned with Mr. Adams our minister in Holland, and myself for the service of treaties of commerce with the powers of Europe. Mr. Adams arrived, and took house near me at Auteuil. Mr. Jefferson also arrived in August, after a journey thro' all the states from Virginia to Boston, assuring me that all was quiet, a general tranquility reigned, and the people were well satisfy'd with their present forms of government, a few insignificant persons only excepted. Congress had become parsimonious, and curtail'd the salaries of all their servants, no less than 500 louis a year for that of each minister plenipotenary at foreign courts. As money is not my object, being near my journey's end, and having enough to pay the remaining turnpikes and post chaises, I stuck to the service as long as the Congress required it of me, tho' they were to give me nothing. I continued, thanks to God, in very good health, being only troubled with the stone, which sometimes gave me more than a little pain, and prevented my going in a carriage where there are pavements, but did not otherwise make me very unhappy; I ate, drank, slept, read, took the exercise of walking, and enjoyed the conversation of my friends as usual.

The gout was bad, but the stone was worse, and I was happy in not having them both together. My disorder of the stone had its bad and good days, and I was tolerably affected by it; but sometimes the pain was hard to bear. I took a remedy, mentioned by Mr. Ingenhousz, for the stone, which is called Blackrie's Solvent. It is soap lye with lime water, which promis'd to have some effect in diminishing the symptoms and preventing the growth of the stone. It did not hurt my appetite. I slept well, and enjoyed my friends in cheerful conversation as usual. But as I could not use much exercise, I ate more sparingly than formerly, and I drank no wine.

INVENTION OF DOUBLE SPECTACLES

In a letter, George Whatley noted how his eyes must continue very good since he could write so small a hand without spectacles. I myself cannot distinguish a letter even of large print, but was happy in the invention of double spectacles, which serving for distant objects as well as near ones, makes my eyes as useful to me as ever they were. I imagined it used to be found pretty generally true that the same convexity of glass through which a man can see clearest and best at the distance proper for reading, is not the best for great distances. I therefore had formerly two pair of spectacles, which I shifted occasionally, as in traveling I sometimes read, yet often wanted to regard the surrounding prospects. Finding this change troublesome and not always sufficiently ready, I had the glasses cut, and half of each kind associated in the same circle. Thus by this means, as I wear my spectacles constantly, I have only to move my eyes up or down as I want to see distinctly far or near, the proper glasses being always ready. This I found more particularly convenient while being in France, as the glasses that served me best at table to see what I ate, not being the best to see the faces of those on the other side of the table who spoke to me; and when one's ears are not well accustomed to the sounds of a language, a sight of the movements in the features of him that speaks helps to explain, so that I understood French better by the help of my spectacles.

MR. MESMER AND ANIMAL MAGNETISM

We were much amiss'd in France for the past two years with the pretended new art of healing by what was called *Magnetisme Animale*. The professor of this art, Mr. Mesmer, had in a short time made nearly twenty thousand louis d'ors by teaching and practicing it. He proposed the presence of a universal animal magnetic fluid that could heal the sick and prevent illness through a simple laying of hands, gestures, and signs. Subjects who believed themselves magnetized felt pain, heat, and then a very intense heat, and in some more excitable patients, produced convulsions and what were called crises. The remedy met with enough success to encourage the hopes of the ill; and even educated people, including doctors and surgeons, admitted to the school of magnetism.

But one must not be indifferent to the ill-founded reign of false opinion: the sciences, which grow larger with the truth, have even more to gain by the suppression of an error. An error is always a spoiled yeast which ferments and eventually corrupts the substance in which it is introduced. But when this error leaves the empire of the sciences to spread among the multitude, and to divide and agitate minds when it presents a misleading way to heal the sick whom it discourages from looking elsewhere for help, a good government has an interest in destroying it.

The distribution of enlightenment is an excellent use of authority! Thus the King appointed a number of commissaries to inquire into this magnetism, and was pleased to request my joining them as one of the Academy of Science. In our investigation, we tried to detect the presence of the magnetic fluid; but this fluid was imperceptible to all the senses. The experiments we conducted on ourselves, including blindfolded subjects, caused us to reject it absolutely as a cure of illness. We concluded that the system of magnetism did not cure anything; that both magnetism and his brilliant theory exist only in the imagination; and that a spectacle such as this seemed to transport us to the age and the reign of the fairies.

Mr. Mesmer complain'd about our report* to the Parliament, and requested that they would appoint commissaries, to whom he might submit the examination of—not his theory and practice, but—*un Plan qui renfermera les seuls moyens possible, de constater infailliblement l'existence et l'utlité de sa décourverte*. The petition was printed. Many thought the Parliament would do nothing about it. But they laid hold of it to clinch Mesmer, and obliged him to expose all directly.

Mesmer still has some adherents and continues to practice his art. It is surprising how much credulity still subsists in the world. I suppose all the physicians in France put together did not make so much money during the time he was in France, as he alone had done. And we had another fresh folly afterwards. A magnetizer pretended that he could establish what is called a rapport between any person and a somnambular by a simple strong volition only, without speaking or making any signs; and many people daily flocked to see this strange operation!

ELECTRIC EXPERIMENTS WITH A PARALYTIC PATIENT

In 1750, I made an experiment in electricity that I desired never to repeat. Being about to kill a turkey by the shock from two large glass jars containing as much electrical fire as forty common phials, I

---

* *Rapport Secret sur le Mesmerisme* (Secret Report on Mesmerism), dated August 11, 1784, was signed by Franklin, Lavoisier, Guillotin, Le Roy, and five others. See FPR 42:t115.

inadvertently took the whole thro' my own arms and body, by receiving the fire from the united top wires with one hand, while the other held a chain connected with the outsides of both jars. I was about to try whether the jars were fully charged when I felt a universal blow thro'out my whole body from head to foot, and parts of my hand and fingers which held the chain were left white as tho' the blood had been driven out, and remained so 8 or 10 minutes after, feeling like dead flesh. The whole was over in less than a minute, but I had a numbness in my arms and back of my neck, which continued till the next morning. You will find an account of the first great electric stroke I received in pages 161 and 162 of my book, 5TH edition, 1774.

On a more recent occasion, I had a paralytic patient in my chamber, whose friends had brought him to receive some electric shocks. I made them join hands so as to receive the shock at the same time, and I charg'd two large jars to give it. By the number of these people I was oblig'd to quit my usual standing, and plac'd myself inadvertently under an iron hook which hung from the ceiling down to within two inches of my head, and communicated by wire with the outside of the jars. I attempted to discharge them, and in fact did so, but I did not perceive it, tho' the charge went thro' me, and not thro' the persons I intended it for. I neither saw the flash, heard the report, nor felt the stroke. When my senses return'd, I found myself on the floor. I got up not knowing how that had happened. I then again attempted to discharge the jars; but one of the company told me they were already discharg'd, which I could not at first believe, but on trial found it true. They told me they had not felt it, but they saw I was knock'd down by it, which had greatly surpris'd them. On recollecting myself and examining my situation, I found the case clear. A small swelling rose on the top of my head, which continued sore for some days; but I do not remember any other effect good or bad.

"AMERICANS WERE VERY HAPPY"

My letters from America informed me that everything went well there following the war; the newly elected Congress met, and consisted of very respectable characters with excellent dispositions, and the people in general were very happy under the new governments. The last year was a prosperous one for the country, the crops plentiful and sold at high prices for exportation, while all imported goods, from the great plenty, sold low. Since the peace, too many goods were sent there from all parts of Europe, which overstock'd the market, and made the prices so low as to afford but little profit and sometimes none to the adventurers. This was the happy consequence of our commerce being open to all the world, and no longer a monopoly to Britain.

The circumstances of the Royalists in the United States were mending, as the minds of the people irritated by the burning of their towns and massacre of their friends began to cool. A stop was put to all persecutions against them, and in time their offenses will be forgotten. Our people were happy in the change, and have not the least inclination to return to the domination of Britain.

PROPORTIONING PUNISHMENTS
ACCORDING TO OFFENSES

Two pamphlets were published at this time regarding the punishment to offenses. Both were address'd to the judges, but written in a very different spirit. An English author favoured hanging all thieves; a Frenchman was for proportioning punishments according to offenses.

If we really believe, as we profess we believe, that the Law of Moses is the Law of God, the dictate of divine wisdom infinitely superior to human, then on what principles do we ordain death as the punishment of an offense, which according to the Law of Moses was to be punish'd by a restitution of fourfold? To put a man to death for an offense which does not deserve death, is it not murder? And as the French writer says, *Doit-on punir un délit contre société, par un crime contre la nature?* I read in a newspaper from London that a woman is capitally convicted at the Old Bailey for privately stealing of a shop some gauze valued at 14 shillings three pence. Is there any proportion between the injury done by a theft valued at 14s. 3d., and the punishment of that human creature by death on a gibbet? Might not that woman by her labour have made the reparation ordain'd by God in paying four fold? Is not all punishment inflicted beyond the merit of the offense, so much punishment of innocence? In this light, how vast is the annual quantity of not only *injured* but *suffering* innocence, in almost all the civilized states of Europe!

MORE THAN 700 PRIVATEERS COMMISSIONED

By contrast, privateering has been the universal bent of the English nation at home and abroad, wherever settled. No less than 700 privateers were, it is said, commission'd in the last war! These were fitted out by merchants to prey upon other merchants who had never done them any injury. How then can a nation, which among the most honest of its people has so many thieves by inclination, and whose government encourag'd and commission'd no less than 700 gangs of robbers; how can such a nation have the face to condemn the crime in individuals, and hang 20 of them in a morning? Methinks it well behooves merchants, men enlightened by their education and perfectly free from any force or obligation, to consider well of the justice of a war, before they voluntarily engage a gang of ruffians to attack their fellow merchants of a neighbouring nation, to plunder them of their property, and perhaps ruin them and their families. Yet these things are done by Christian merchants, whether a war be just or unjust; and it can hardly be just on both sides. They are done by English and American merchants, who nevertheless complain of private thefts, and hang by dozens the thieves they have taught by their own example. For the sake of humanity, it is high time that a stop be put to this enormity. The United States of America, tho' better situated than any European nation to make profit by privateering (most of the trade of Europe with the West Indies passing before their doors), are endeavouring to abolish the practice, by offering in all their treaties with other powers, an article engaging solemnly that in case of future war no privateers shall be commission'd on either side, and that unarm'd merchant ships on both sides shall pursue their voyages unmolested. This will be a happy improvement of the laws of nations. The humane and the just cannot but wish general success to the proposition.

The desire to go home to my family in America was strong

At length I received from Congress my long-expected permission to return to America. The last act I did as minister plenipotentiary for making treaties was to sign with Mr. Jefferson, two days before I came away, the Treaty of Friendship and Commerce that had been agreed on with Prussia, and which was to be carried to the Hague by Mr. Short, there to be signed by Baron Thulemier on the part of his king, who, without the least hesitation, had approved and conceded to the new humane articles proposed by Congress. Mr. Short was also to call at London for the signature of Mr. Adams, who, I learned when at Southampton, was well received at the British court. I left the court of France in the same friendly disposition toward the United States that we had all along experienced, though concerned to find that ours was not better supported in the payment of interest money due on our loans. Mr. Jefferson was much esteemed and respected there. I received from the King at my departure the present of his picture set round with diamonds, usually given to ministers plenipotentiary who have signed any treaties with that court, and it is at the disposition of Congress.*

My friends in France were so apprehensive about my trip that they pressed me much to remain in France, and three of them offer'd me an asylum in their habitations. They protested that they universally esteemed and loved me; that my friends in America were diminish'd by death in my absence; that I might there meet with envy and its consequent enmity. The desire, however, of spending the little remainder of life with my family was so strong as to determine me to try at least, whether I could bear the motion of a ship.

Having stayed in France about eight and a half years, I took leave of the court and my friends, and set out on my return home July 12, 1785, leaving Passy with my two grandsons at 4 pm and arriving about 8 at St. Germains. M. de Chaumont, with his daughter Sophia, accompanied us to Nantere. M. Le Veillard continued with us to Havre de Grace, the seaport. I bore very well the journey in one of the King's litters (lent me by the Duke de Coigny) carried by large mules who walked very easy. I arrived extremely well, not at all hurt or fatigued by the carriage I used, which I found generally very gentle. We waited there a few days for baggage and for our traveling companion, statuary M. Houdon. On their arrival, we left France, the country that I loved best in the world; and there I left my dear friends. It seemed to me that things are badly managed in this world, when beings so made to be happy together are obliged to separate.

---

* This gift, a picture of Louis XVI surrounded by 408 diamonds, was so outlandish that it eventually led Congress to pass a law prohibiting American officials from taking gifts for personal use. In his last will, Franklin bequeathed the diamond miniature to his daughter, Sally, on condition that she not remove the diamonds under any circumstances. However, she and her husband soon sold the diamonds to pay for a trip to Europe. See Claude-Anne Lopez and Eugenia W. Herbert, *The Private Franklin* (New York: Norton, 1975), 306–07.

The voyage from thence to Southampton took forty-five hours, though the wind was a great part of the time contrary, arriving on Sunday, July 24. There I met my son, William, who had arrived from London the evening before, with Mr. Williams and Mr. J. Alexander. I wrote a letter to the good bishop of St. Asaph, acquainting him with my arrival, and he came with his lady and his daughter, Miss Kitty. On Monday, the bishop and his family lodging in the same inn, the Star, we all breakfasted and dined together. I went at noon to bathe in Martin's salt water hot-bath, and fell asleep while floating on my back. I slept nearly an hour by my watch without sinking or turning, a thing I never did before, and should hardly have thought possible. Water is the easiest bed that can be.

I read over the writings of conveyance, &c. of my son's lands in New Jersey and New York to my grandson. Deeds were signed between W. Franklin and W. T. Franklin, and I gave a power to my son to recover what might be due to me from the British government.

Capt. Jennings carried down our baggage that he brought from Havre, and my dear friend M. Le Veillard took leave to go with him. The ship had a large convenient cabin with good lodging places; the whole was at my disposition, and there was plenty of room. Mr. Vaughan arrived from London to see me, and we all dined once more with the bishop and family, who kindly accepted our invitation to board with us. The company stayed all night, and when I woke in the morning of Thursday, July 28, I found the company gone, and ship under sail to America.

Chapter Ten

The Creation of a
New Nation, 1785–87

We had a pleasant and not a long passage to America, in which there was but one day of violent storm. I purposed on my voyage to write the remaining notes of my life, but made no progress, for want of the documents that could only be had in Philadelphia. But I was not idle, writing three philosophical pieces, each of some length: one on nautical matters; another on chimneys (in France I was press'd by M. le Noir and M. Cadet to give a description of my stove for burning smoke, they conceiving that it might be useful to the citizens of Paris); and a third a description of my vase for consuming smoke, with directions for using it. The following year all were read to the Philosophical Society in Philadelphia and were printed in their journal.

GOD BE PRAISED....
I ARRIVE IN DEAR PHILADELPHIA!

On September 14, 1785, with the flood in the morning came a light breeze, which brought us above Gloucester Point, in full view of dear Philadelphia! We cast anchor to wait for the health officer, who, having made his visit and finding no sickness, gave us leave to land. I arrived with my two grandsons and cousin Jonathan Williams, thanks to God, after a pleasant passage of 5 weeks and 5 days from land to land. My son-in-law, Mr. Bache, came with a boat for us. We landed at Market Street wharf, where we were received by a crowd of people with huzzas, and accompanied with acclamations quite to my door, where I found my family well. God be praised and thanked for all his mercies!

I was continually surrounded by congratulating friends, and the affectionate welcome I met with from my fellow-citizens was far beyond my expectations. To find it in the full enjoyment of peace and liberty makes me esteem the day of my arrival among the happiest of my life. I was now in the bosom of my family, and found four new little prattlers, who clung about the knees of their grand papa, and afforded me great pleasure.

The vessel from Havre, after a long passage of about 12 weeks, arrived at last with all my things in pretty good order, and sundry parcels of books, &c., when I had almost given over all hopes of seeing them ever again; and with great satisfaction I was again drinking every day *les eaux epurees de Passy*, as they kept well, and seemed to be rendered more agreeable by the long voyage. I found myself happily situated in my own house, surrounded by my offspring, with all my playthings and amusements about me, and my malady not augmented, but still continuing tolerable.

Statuary Mr. Houdon, whom Mr. Jefferson and myself arranged with to come over for the purpose of taking a bust of Gen. Washington, arrived with us in Philadelphia. But he was much perplex'd by the accident of leaving his materials and instruments in France, which he sent down the Seine from Paris; but they did not arrive at Havre before we sail'd, and he was oblig'd to leave them. However, he found in Philadelphia the tools and materials he wanted, and set out for General Washington's. The bust of me, made by Houdon, was return'd perfectly safe, and continues to be the admiration of all that see it.

I WROTE A TRUER STATE OF AFFAIRS IN OUR COUNTRY

Upon my return, I found that the English newspapers, to please honest John Bull, had painted our situation in America in frightful colours, as if we were very miserable since we broke our connection with him. I wrote a piece on the internal state of America to convince the world that none of us are discontent with the revolution. I found all property in lands and houses augmented vastly in value since I left; that of houses and towns at least four-fold. The crops were plentiful, and yet the produce sold high in ready hard money, to the great profit of the farmer. At the same time all imported goods sold at low rates, some cheaper than the first cost. Working people had plenty of employ and high pay for their labour. Everybody was well cloth'd and well lodg'd, the poor provided for or assisted. And our commerce being no longer the monopoly of British merchants, we were well furnished with all the foreign commodities we needed, at much more reasonable rates than heretofore. These appeared to me as certain signs of public prosperity. Some traders indeed complained that trade was dead; but this pretended evil was not an effect of inability in the people to buy, pay for, and consume the usual articles of commerce, as far as they had occasion for them; it was owing merely to there being too many traders who had crowded hither from all parts of Europe with more goods than the natural demand of the country required. And what in Europe was called the debt of America is chiefly the debt of these adventurers and supercargoes to their principals, with which the settled inhabitants of America, who never paid better for what they want and buy, had nothing to do.

INSTEAD OF A FAST THEY PROCLAIMED A THANKSGIVING

There is a tradition that in the planting of New England, the first settlers met with many difficulties and hardships, as is generally the case when a civiliz'd people attempt to establish themselves in a wilderness country. Being so piously dispos'd, they sought relief from heaven by laying their wants and distresses before the Lord in frequent set days of fasting and prayer. Constant meditation and discourse on these subjects kept their minds gloomy and discontented, and like the children of Israel there were many dispos'd to return to the Egypt which persecution had induc'd them to abandon. At length, when it was proposed in the Assembly to proclaim another fast, a farmer of plain sense rose and remark'd that the inconveniences they suffer'd, and concerning which they had so often weary'd heaven with their complaints, were not so great as they might have expected, and were diminishing every day as the colony strengthen'd; that the earth began to reward their labour and furnish liberally for their subsistence; that their seas and rivers were full of fish, the air sweet, the climate healthy, and above all, they were in the full enjoyment of liberty, civil and religious. He therefore thought that reflecting and conversing on these subjects would be more comfortable and lead more to make them contented with their situation; and that it would be more becoming the gratitude they ow'd to the divine being, *if instead of a fast they should proclaim a thanksgiving.* His advice was taken, and from that day to this, they have in every year observ'd circumstances of public felicity sufficient to furnish employment for a *Thanksgiving Day*, which is therefore constantly ordered and religiously observed.

I saw in the public papers of different states frequent complaints of hard times, deadness of trade, scarcity of money, &c. &c. It was not my intention to assert or maintain that these complaints are entirely without foundation; there can be no country or nation existing in which there will not be some people so circumstanc'd as to find it hard to gain a livelihood, people who are not in the way of any profitable trade, and with whom money is scarce because they have nothing to give in exchange for it. And it is always in the power of a small number to make a great clamour. But let us take a cool view of the general state of our affairs, and perhaps the prospect will appear less gloomy than has been imagined.

No part are so well fed, well cloth'd, well lodg'd and well paid

The great business of the continent is agriculture. For one artisan or merchant we have at least 100 farmers, by far the greatest part cultivators of their own fertile lands, from whence many of them draw not only the food necessary for their subsistence, but the materials of their clothing, so as to have little occasion for foreign supplies, while they have a surplus of production to dispose of, whereby wealth is gradually accumulated. Such has been the goodness of divine providence to these regions, and so favourable the climate, that since the three or four years of hardship in the first settlement of our fathers here, a famine or scarcity has never been heard of among us; on the contrary, tho' some years may have been more, and others less plentiful, there has always been provision enough for ourselves, and a quantity to spare for exportation. And altho' the crops of 1784 were generally good, never was the farmer better paid for the part he could spare to commerce, as the published prices abundantly testified. The lands he possesses are also continually rising in value with the increase of population. And on the whole he is enabled to give such good wages to those who work for him, that all who are acquainted with the old world must agree that in no part of it are the labouring poor so well fed, so well cloth'd, well lodg'd and well paid as in the United States of America.

If we enter the cities, we find there too that since the revolution the owners of houses and lots of ground have had their interest vastly augmented in value; rents have risen to an astonishing height, and thence encouragement to increase building, which gives employment to an abundance of workmen, as does also the increas'd luxury and splendor of living of the inhabitants thus made richer. These workmen all demand and obtain much higher wages than any other part of the world would afford them, and they are paid in ready money. This rank of people therefore do not, or ought not, complain of hard times, and they comprise a very considerable part of the city inhabitants.

At the distance I live from our American fisheries I cannot speak of them with any certainty; but I have not heard that the labour of the valuable race of men employ'd in them is worse paid or that they meet with less success than before the revolution. The whalemen indeed have been depriv'd of one market for their oil, but another opened up for them. And the demand is constantly increasing for their spermaceti candles, which therefore bear a much higher price than formerly.

There remain the merchants and the shopkeepers. Of these, tho' they make but a small part of the whole nation, the number is considerable, too great indeed for the business they are employ'd in, for the consumption of goods in every country has its limits. The faculties of the people—that is, their ability to buy and pay—is equal only to a certain quantity of merchandise. If merchants calculate amiss on this proposition, and import too much, they will of course find the sale dull for the overplus, and some of them will say that trade languishes. They should, and doubtless will, grow wiser by experience, and import less. If too many artificers in town and farmers from the country flatter themselves with the idea of leading easier lives by turning shopkeepers, the whole natural quantity of business dividend among them all may afford too small a share for each, and occasion complaints that trading is dead; these may also suppose that it is owing to the scarcity of money while in fact, it is not so much from the fewness of buyers as from the excessive number of sellers, that the mischief arises; and if every shopkeeper, farmer and mechanic would return to the use of his plough and working tools, there would remain of widows and other women shopkeepers sufficient for that business, which might then afford them a comfortable maintenance.

No NATION ENJOYS A GREATER SHARE OF HUMAN FELICITY

Whoever has travelled thro' the various parts of Europe, and observed how small is the proportion of people in affluence or easy circumstances there, compar'd with those in poverty and misery; the few rich and haughty landlords; the multitude of poor, abject and rack'd tenants; and the half-paid and half-starv'd ragged labourers; and viewed here the happy mediocrity that so generally prevails throughout these states, where the cultivator works for himself, and supports his family in decent plenty, will, methinks, see abundant reason to bless divine Providence for the evident and great difference in our favour, and be convinc'd that no nation that is known to us enjoys a greater share of human felicity.

It is true that in some of our states there are parties, and discords; but let us look back and ask if we were ever without them? Such will exist wherever there is liberty; and perhaps they help to preserve it. By the collision of different sentiments, sparks of truth strike out, and political light is obtained. The different factions which at present divide us aim all at the public good; the differences are only about the various modes of promoting it. Things, actions, measures and objects of all kinds present themselves to the minds of men in such a variety of lights that it is not possible we should all think alike at the same time on every subject, when hardly the same man retains at all times the same idea of it. Parties are therefore the common lot of humanity, and ours are by no means more mischievous or less beneficial than those of other countries, nations and ages, enjoying in the same degree the great blessing of political liberty.

No revenue is sufficient without economy

Indeed some among us are not so much griev'd for the present state of our affairs as apprehensive for the future. The growth of luxury alarms them, and they think we are, from that alone, on the high road to ruin. They observe that no revenue is sufficient without economy, and that the most plentiful income of a whole people from natural productions of their country may be dissipated in vain and needless expenses, and poverty be introduc'd in the place of affluence. This may be possible; it however rarely happens, for there seems to be in every nation a greater proportion of industry and frugality which tend to enrich, than idleness and prodigality, which occasions poverty, so that upon the whole there is a continual accumulation. Reflect what Spain, Gaul, Germany and Britain were in the times of the Romans, inhabited by people little richer than our savages, and consider the wealth they at present possess, in numerous well built cities, improv'd farms, rich moveables, magazines stor'd with valuable manufactures, to say nothing of plate, jewels, and ready money; all this notwithstanding their bad, wasteful plundering governments, and their mad destructive wars; and yet luxury and extravagant living has never suffer'd much restraint in those countries. Then consider the great proportion of industrious frugal farmers inhabiting the interior part of these American states, and of whom the body of our nation consists; and judge whether it is probable the luxury of our seaports can be sufficient to ruin such a country. If the importation of foreign luxuries could ruin a people we should probably have been ruin'd long ago; for the British nation claim'd a right, and practis'd it, of importing among us not only the superfluities of their production, but those of every nation under heaven; we bought and consum'd them and yet we flourish'd and grew rich.

The agriculture and fisheries of the United States are the great sources of our increasing wealth. He that puts a seed into the earth is recompenc'd perhaps by receiving twenty out of it; and he who draws a fish out of our waters draws up a piece of silver. Let us (and there is no doubt but we shall) be attentive to these, and then the power of rivals, with all their restraining and prohibiting acts, cannot hurt us. We are sons of the earth and seas, and like *Anteus*, if in wrestling with Hercules we now and then receive a fall, the touch of our parents will communicate to us fresh strength and ability to renew the contest. *Be quiet and thankful.*

THE EXTRAVAGANT REJOICINGS EVERY 4TH OF JULY

I think myself happy in returning to live under the free constitution of this commonwealth, and hope that we and our posterity may long enjoy it. The laws governing justice are well administered, and property is as secure as in any country on the globe. Our wilderness lands are daily being bought up by new settlers, and our settlements extend rapidly to the westward. When I read in all the papers of the extravagant rejoicings every 4TH of July, the day on which was signed the Declaration of Independence, I am convinced of the universal satisfaction of the people with the revolution and its grand principles. Their unbound respect for all who were principally concern'd in it, whether as warriors or statesmen, and the enthusiastic joy with which the day of the Declaration of Independence is everywhere annually celebrated are indisputable proofs of this truth.

It was my intention to avoid all public business upon my return to America. I wrote four philosophical papers, which were chiefly speculative and hypothetical, which, except the description of the long arm, a new instrument for taking down books from high shelves, contained little of practical utility. But I had not firmness enough to resist the unanimous desire of my country-folks, and I was plung'd again into public business as deep as ever. They engross'd the prime of my life: they have eaten my flesh and seem resolv'd now to pick my bones. (When I inform'd good friend Dr. Cooper that I was order'd to France being then 70 years old, and made this same observation, that the public having as it were eaten my flesh, seem'd now resolv'd to pick my bones, he replied that he approved their taste, for the nearer the bone the sweeter the meat!) My fellow citizens having in a considerable body express'd their desire that I would still take a post in their public councils, assuring me that it was the unanimous wish of the different parties that divide the state (the constitutionalists and anti-constitutionalists), from an opinion that I might find some means of reconciling them; I had not sufficient firmness to refuse their request of permitting their voting for me as chair of government for the state of Pennsylvania.

I think we are in the right road of improving our governments. I do not oppose all that seems wrong, for the multitude are more effectually set right by experience than kept from going wrong by reasoning with them. And I think we are daily more and more enlightened: So that I have no doubt of our obtaining in a few years as much public felicity as good government is capable of affording. The English newspapers were fill'd with fictitious accounts of anarchy, confusion, distresses and miseries we were suppos'd to be involv'd in, as consequences of the revolution; and the few remaining friends of the old government among us took pains to magnify every little inconvenience. I assur'd my friends in England that all the stories spread in the English papers were as chimerical as the history of my being in chains at Algiers. The great body of our nation find themselves happy in the change, and have not the slightest inclination to return to the domination of Britain. There could not be a stronger proof of the general approbation of the measures that promote change than has been given by the Assembly and Council of this state, in the nearly unanimous choice of me as their governor; the Assembly being themselves the unbrib'd choice of the people. I say nearly unanimous because there were only my own and one other vote in the negative.

As to public affairs, the Congress was not able to assemble more than 7 or 8 states during the whole winter, so the Treaty with Prussia remained unratified until the spring. There were some few faults in our constitutions, which is no wonder, considering the stormy season in which they were made, but these were soon corrected. The disposition to furnish Congress with new powers augmented daily, as people became more enlightened; and I did not remember ever to have seen during my long life more signs of public felicity than appeared at present throughout these states.

"Why don't these damned Americans pay their debts?"

During some years past, the British newspapers were filled with reflections on the inhabitants of America for not paying their old debts to English merchants. And from those papers the same reflections were translated into foreign prints, and circulated throughout Europe, whereby the American character, respecting honour, probity and justice in commercial transactions, was made to suffer in the opinion of strangers, which may be attended with pernicious consequences. At length we were told that the British court has taken up the complaint, and seriously offer'd it as a reason for refusing to evacuate the frontier posts according to the treaty. Yet this same nation has itself run into debt to the amount of two hundred and seventy five millions sterling, much of it to foreigners, which they now confess they never expect or intend to pay, and might therefore, one would think, have a little charity for their own debtors and formerly best customers, whom they themselves have foolishly ruin'd by a most unjust and destructive war. And the heir to the crown, too, is already a bankrupt. But this is the nation which exclaims continually, *Damn these rascally Americans. Why don' t they pay their debts!!!*

Clearly the present inability of many American merchants to discharge their debts contracted before the war is not so much their fault as the fault of the crediting nation who by making an unjust war on them, obstructed their commerce, plundering and devastating their country. We may begin by observing that before the war our mercantile character was good. Our ports were all busy, receiving and selling British manufactures, and equipping ships for the circuitous trade; the seas were covered with those ships and with several hundred sail of our fishermen, all working for Britain; and then let us consider the effect that the conduct of Britain in 1774 and 1775 and the following years must naturally have on the future ability of our merchants to make the payments in question. The first step was shutting up the Port of Boston by an act of Parliament; the next to prohibit by another the New England fishery. An army and a fleet were sent to enforce these acts. Here was a stop put at once to all the mercantile operations of one of the greatest trading cities of America; the fishing vessels all laid up, and the usual remittances by way of Spain, Portugal, and the Straits render'd impossible.

The ships of the fleet employ'd themselves in cruising separately all along the coast. The marine gentry, seldom so well contented with their pay, as not to like a little plunder, they stopp'd and seiz'd under slight pretences the American vessels they met with, belonging to whatever colony. This check'd the commerce of them all. Ships loaded with cargoes destin'd either directly or indirectly to make remittances in England were not spared. Then came another act of Parliament, forbidding any inquisition into those past facts, declaring them all lawful, and all American property to be forfeited whether on sea or land, and authorizing the King's British subjects to take, seize, sink, burn or destroy whatever they could find of it. Before the declaration of open war, General Gage, being with his army in peaceable possession of Boston, shut its gates, and plac'd guards all around to prevent its communication with the country. The inhabitants were on the point of starving. The general propos'd to them a capitulation, in which he stipulated that if they would deliver up their arms, they might leave the town with their families and goods. But when they began to pack up for their departure, the general seized an immense value of all merchant goods. But the cry nevertheless continu'd, *These Boston people do not pay their debts!*

The army, having thus ruin'd Boston, proceeded to different parts of the continent and possessed all the capital trading towns. The troops gorg'd themselves with plunder. They stopp'd all the trade of Philadelphia for nearly a year, of Rhode Island longer, of New York near eight years, of Charleston in South Carolina and Savannah in Georgia, I forget how long. This continu'd interruption of their commerce ruin'd many merchants. The army also burnt to the ground the fine towns of Falmouth and Charles Town near Boston, New London, Fairfield, Norwalk, Esopus, Norfolk (the chief trading city in Virginia), besides innumerable country seats and private farm houses. This wanton destruction of property operated doubly to the disabling of our merchants in making their payments, by the immediate loss they sustain'd themselves, and also the loss suffer'd by their country debtors, who had bought of them the British goods, and who were now render'd unable to pay. The debts to Britain of course remain'd undischarged'd, yet the clamour continu'd, *These knavish Americans will not pay us!*

Our enemies are very industrious in depreciating our national character. Their abuse sometimes provokes me, but this I forbear, though there is abundant room for recrimination, because I would do nothing that might hasten another quarrel by exasperating those who are still sore from their late disgraces. The two separated nations are now at peace, and there can be no use in mutual provocations to fresh enmity.

Taxes and the National Debt

Honesty in money matters is a virtue as justly to be expected from a government as from an individual subject, and therefore I am quite of the opinion that our independence is not quite compleat till we have discharg'd our public debt. Our modes of collecting taxes were yet imperfect, and we needed more skill in financeering; but we improve in that kind of knowledge daily by experience. I am persuaded that the whole will be paid in a few years.

Direct taxes on land are practical in countries that are filled up with inhabitants. But at present we are so sparsely settled, often 5 or 6 miles distant from one another in the back countries, that the collection of a direct tax going from house to house is almost impossible, amounting to more than the value of the tax. Our debt occasion'd by the war being heavy, we are under the necessity of using indirect taxes, i.e., duties on importation of goods and excises, and every method we can think of to assist in raising a revenue to discharge it; but in sentiment we are well disposed to freedom of commerce and to abolishing duties on importation as soon as we possibly can afford to do so. Let the merchants on both sides form treaties with one another. *Laissez les faire.*

Fortunately, our duties are generally so small as to give little temptation to smuggling, as this government affords no protection from the practice. But the people concern'd in smuggling are so dexterous that it is hardly possible for any government to prevent them entirely. Our own laws are daily evaded and transgress'd by them. And when such come hither from foreign ports to purchase provisions, while no compact or treaty subsists that forbids supplying them, our traders do not readily conceive that the commerce with them is not allowable.

THE INSTRUCTION OF YOUTH ESTEEM'D AMONG THE MOST HONOURABLE

It gives me extreme pleasure to find that seminaries of learning are increasing in America, and particularly that the University of Pennsylvania continues to flourish, and the English School in Philadelphia. Having acquired some little reputation among my fellow citizens by projecting the Public Library in 1732 and obtaining subscriptions by which it was established, in 1749 I was encouraged to hazard another project, that of public education for our youth. As in the scheme of the library, I had provided only for English books, so in this new scheme my ideas went no further than to procure the means of a good English education. Before I went about to procure subscriptions, I thought it proper to prepare the minds of the people by a pamphlet, which I wrote and printed, and distributed with my newspapers, gratis: the title was *Proposals relating to the Education of Youth in Pennsylvania.* The instruction of youth is one of the employments which are most useful to the public. It ought therefore to be esteem'd among the most honourable. Its successful exercise does not, however, always meet with the reward it merits, except in the satisfaction of having contributed to the forming of virtuous and able men for the service of their country.

Charitable institutions are often mismanag'd

I also offered the following hints for consideration on the Orphan School House in Philadelphia: Charitable institutions, however originally well intended, and well executed at first for many years, are subject to be in a course of time corrupted, mismanag'd, their funds misapplied or perverted to private purposes. Would it not be well to guard against those by prudent regulations respecting the choice of managers, and establishing the power of inspecting their conduct, in some permanent body, as the monthly or quarterly meeting? Would it not be more reputable for the institution, if the appearances of making a profit from the labour of orphans were avoided, and the dependence for funds rely wholly on charitable contributions? If this should be concluded, then it may be proper to open an account with each orphan on admission, the orphans to have credit for any substance brought in with them, and for the profit made of it, and of their labour, and made debtors for their maintenance and education. At their discharge on coming of age, they may be exhorted to pay the balance against them if ever able, but not to be compell'd. Such as receive a balance may be exhorted to give back a part in charity to the institution that has taken such kind care of them, or at least to remember it favourably if God should bless them with ability either in a benefaction while living or a legacy on decease. When discharg'd, the orphans should receive, besides decent clothing and some money, a certificate of their good behaviour if such it has been, as a recommendation; and the managers of the institution should still consider them as their children, so far as to counsel them in their affairs, encourage and promote them in their business, watch over and kindly admonish them when in danger of misconduct.

I APPLAUD HIS ZEAL FOR PRESERVING THE PURITY OF OUR LANGUAGE

I wrote also a paper entitled *Idea of an English School*, which was printed and afterwards annexed to Mr. Peter's sermon preached at the opening of the school. Although Latin and Greek were to be taught, the original idea of a compleat English education was not to be forgotten, as will appear by the following extracts. On page 1, "The English tongue is to be taught grammatically and as a language." On page 4, in reciting the qualifications of a person to be appointed rector, it is said, "Great regard is to be had to his polite speaking, writing and understanding the English tongue."

Recently I received Noah Webster's *Dissertations on the English Language*, an excellent work that will be greatly useful in turning the thoughts of our countrymen to correct writing. I applaud his zeal for preserving the purity of our language, both in its expressions and pronunciation, and in correcting the popular errors that several of our states are continually falling into.

The Latin language, long the vehicle used in distributing knowledge among the different nations of Europe, is daily more and more neglected; and one of the modern tongues, viz., the French, seems in point of universality to have supplied its place. It is spoken in all the courts of Europe, and most of the literati, those even who do not speak it, have acquired knowledge enough of it to enable them easily to read the books that are written in it. This gives a considerable advantage to that nation; it enables its authors to inculcate and spread thro' other nations such sentiments and opinions on important points as are most conducive to its interests, or which may contribute to its reputation by promoting the common interests of mankind. It is perhaps owing to its being written in French that Voltaire's *Treatise on Toleration* has had so sudden and great an effect on the bigotry of Europe, as almost entirely to disarm it. The general use of the French language has likewise a very advantageous effect on the profits of the bookselling branch of commerce, it being well know that when more copies struck off from one composition of types can be sold, the profits increase in a much greater proportion than they do in making a greater number of pieces in any other kind of manufacture. And at present there is no capital town in Europe without a French bookseller's shop corresponding with Paris.

Our English language bids fair to obtain the second place. The great body of excellent sermons in our language and the freedom of our writings on political subjects have induced a number of divines of different sects and nations, as well as gentlemen concerned in public affairs, to study it, so far at least as to be able to read it. And if we were to endeavour the facilitating its progress, the study of our tongue might become more general. If, therefore, we would have the benefit of seeing our language more generally known among mankind, we should endeavour to remove all the difficulties, however small, that discourage the learning it.

It gave me great pleasure to receive several kind letters of congratulations from my old friends in Boston, that they were not estrang'd from me by the malevolent misrepresentations of my conduct that had been circulated there. Our good God brought us old folks, my sister Jane Mecom in Boston and me, the last survivors of 17 brothers and sisters, to the beginning of a new year. I wrote to her, sending her two volumes of my papers that were printed in London.

One of them was about the new alphabet, which she desired.* I had written several letters in the new spelling to my friends; their objection that rectifying our alphabet will be attended with inconveniences and difficulties is a natural one; for it always occurs when any reformation is proposed, whether in religion, government, laws, and even down as low as roads and wheel carriages. The true question, then, is not whether there will be no difficulties or inconveniences, but whether the difficulties may not be surmounted, and whether the conveniences will not, on the whole, be greater than the inconveniences. To anyone who spells well in the present mode, I imagine the difficulty of changing that mode for the new is not so great, and we might perfectly get over it in a week's writing. As to those who do not spell well, if the two difficulties are compared, viz., that of teaching them true spelling in the present mode, and that of teaching them the new alphabet and the new spelling according to it; I am confident that the latter would be by far the least trouble.

THAT IS WHY I LOVE LIFE!

As to my health, the pains caus'd sometimes by the stone did not augment; my appetite continued good, and my temper generally cheerful; my strength and activity has diminished by slow degrees, as

---

* Franklin had a long-time interest in phonetic spelling reform, and even wrote a pamphlet (unfinished) on the subject, *A Scheme for a New Alphabet and Reformed Mode of Spelling* (published in 1779). See PBF 15:173–78, 216–20.

might be expected at the age of fourscore. I enjoy however the conversation of my friends and my books, my hearing and sight being as good as ever. After long absence in Europe I find myself happily at home in a good and convenient house which I built for myself to retire into some 25 years ago, with a fine family of grand children about my knees who afford me great pleasure, and an affectionate good daughter and son-in-law to take care of me, and in one of the most flourishing cities and best provinces of America, enjoying the universal esteem and respect of the people.

On the whole the stone does not give me more pain than when I was at Passy; and except when standing, walking, or making water, I am very little incommoded by it. I have try'd all the noted prescriptions for diminishing the stone without procuring any good effect. Sitting, or lying in bed, I am generally quite easy, God be thanked, and as I live temperately, drink no wine, and use daily the exercise of the dumb bell (which exercises the upper part of the body without much moving the parts in contact with the stone), I flatter myself that the stone is kept from augmenting so much as it might otherwise do, and that I may still continue to find it tolerable. People who live long drink of the cup of life to the very bottom and must expect to meet with some of the usual dregs; and when I reflect on the number of terrible maladies human nature is subject to, I think myself favour'd in having only three incurable ones that have fallen to my share, viz., the gout, the stone, and old age, and that these have not yet deprived me of my natural cheerfulness, my delight in books and enjoyment of social conversation. There are many sorrows in this life, but we must not blame Providence inconsiderately, for there are many more pleasures. This is why I love life.

I am now surrounded by my offspring, a dutiful and affectionate daughter in my house, with six grandchildren, with whose pretty actions and prattle, and promising tempers and qualities of body and mind, I am extremely pleased and entertained. What their conduct may be when they grow up and enter the important scenes of life, I shall not live to see and I cannot foresee. I therefore enjoy among them the present hour, and leave the future to Providence. He that raises a large family does indeed, while he lives to observe them, as Watts says, *stand a broader mark for sorrow*. But then he stands a broader mark for pleasure too. When we launch our little fleet of barques into the ocean, bound to different ports, we hope for each a prosperous voyage; but contrary winds, hidden shoals, storms and enemies come in for a share in the disposition of events; and though those occasion a mixture of disappointment, yet considering the risk where we can make no insurance, we should think ourselves happy if some return with success.

My daughter lives with me and is the comfort of my declining years, while my son, estrang'd from me by the part he took in the late war, keeps aloof, residing in England, whose cause he espous'd; whereby the old proverb is exemplified,

> *My son is my son till he takes him a wife,*
> *But my daughter's my daughter all days of her life.*

Benny went to college in the next street to compleat his education, while my son's son, Temple, went to look at his lands, a fine farm of 600 acres convey'd to him by his father when we were at Southampton. Temple dropped for the present his views of acting in the political line, and applied himself ardently to the study and practice of agriculture. He seems seriously intent upon a country life, which I much approve. I esteem it the most useful, the most independent, and therefore the noblest of employments. His lands are on navigable water, communicating with the Delaware, and but about 16 miles from Philadelphia, very convenient for bringing his produce to market. He has associated to himself a very skillful English farmer, who instructed him in the business and partakes for a term of the profits.

Building is an amusement in old age

In 1786, I received the pleasing news that Mrs. Polly Hewson and her children had taken passage from England to Philadelphia, accompanied by the mother and sister of John Wilkes. We were extremely happy to see them and enjoy their sweet company again. At about this time, I received an offer from Mr. Daniel Roberdeau to sell me his plantation in this country; but not being in a condition to enjoy a country-seat, since my malady, the stone, does not permit me to ride either on horseback or in a wheel carriage, I have no inducement to purchase land but the prospect of its producing greater profit than money at interest; and having been inform'd of its qualities, quantity of acres, price, and rent it affords, I apprehended the purchase would not suit my views. Jean-Baptiste Leroy provided an account of the progress made in the art of ballooning, by the acquisition of a tight envelope, and the means of descending and rising without throwing out ballast, or letting out air. I have sometimes wished I had brought with me from France a balloon sufficiently large to raise me from the ground. In my malady it would have been the most easy carriage for me, being led by a string held by a man walking on the ground.

I began to build two good brick houses next to the street instead of three old ones which I pulled down. But my neighbour disputing my bounds, I was obliged to postpone till that dispute was settled by law. In the mean time, the workmen and materials being ready, I ordered an addition to the house I live in, being too small for our growing family. The affair involved many good hands, such as bricklayers, carpenters, stonecutters, plasterers, painters, glaziers, lime burners, timber merchants, coppersmiths, carters, laborers, etc. etc., which added not a little to the fatiguing business I went through in the last year. By this addition I have gain'd a large cellar for wood and a drawing room in which we can dine a company of 24 persons. It has 2 windows at each end, the north and south, which makes it an airy summer room, and for winters there is a good chimney in the middle made handsome with marble slabs. Over this room is my library of the same dimensions, with like windows at each end, and lin'd with books to the ceiling, where I can write without being disturb'd by the noise of the children. Over this are two lodging rooms, and overall a fine garret. I hardly know how to justify building a library at an age that will so soon oblige me to quit it; but we are apt to forget that we are grown old, and building is an amusement.

The invention was of some use to the inventor

I found upon my return to this country that the number of lightning conductors has greatly increased, their utility having been made manifest by many instances of their good effect in preserving buildings from lightning. Among others, my own house, in my absence, had receiv'd a great stroke which was visible to the neighbours, who immediately ran in to see if any damage had been done, or any fire commenc'd which might by their assistance be extinguish'd. They found nothing disorder'd, and the family only much frighten'd by the loudness of the explosion. On making the addition to my house, the conductor was taken down to be remov'd, when I found that the copper point, which had been nine inches long, and in its thickest part about one third of an inch diameter, had been almost all melted and blown away. Very little of it remained attach'd to the iron rod. So at length the invention has been of some use to the inventor, and afforded an additional pleasure to that of having seen it useful to others.

The two new houses next to the street are three stories high besides the garrets, and an arch'd passage is left in the middle between them to come thro' down to my dwelling, wide enough for a carriage, so that I have the old passage lot left free to build another house. The two houses are 24 feet from each, and 45 deep. In my new buildings, I have taken a few precautions, not generally us'd, to avoid the risk of fire; to wit, none of the wooden work of one room communicates with the wooden work of any other room; and all the floors and even the steps of the stairs are plastered close to the boards, besides the plastering on the laths under the joints. There are also trap doors to go out upon the roofs, that one may go out and wet the shingles in case of a neighbouring fire. But, indeed, I think the stair cases should be stone, and the floors tiled, as in Paris, and the roofs either tiled or slated.

When I look at these buildings, and compare them with that in which my good parents educated us, the difference strikes me with wonder, and fills me with humble thankfulness to that divine being who has graciously conducted my steps, and prospered me in this strange land to a degree that I could not rationally have expected, and can by no means conceive myself to have merited. I beg the continuance of his favour but submit to his will should a reverse be determin'd.

I SPENT THE TIME SO IDLY... I SHUFFLED THE CARDS AND BEGAN ANOTHER GAME

A long winter passed [1785–86], where I had public business enough to preserve me and private amusement besides in conversation, books, my garden, and cribbage. The companions of my youth are indeed almost all departed, but I find an agreeable society among their children and grandchildren. Considering our well-furnish'd plentiful market as the best of gardens, I turned mine, in the midst of which my house stands, into grass plots and gravel walks, with trees and flowering shrubs.

Cards are sometimes played here in the evenings. It is as they play chess, not for money but for honour or the pleasure of beating one another. I passed a winter agreeably in that manner in Passy a few years ago when Polly Stevenson visited us from London. I have indeed now and then a little compunction in reflecting that I spend time so idly: but another reflection comes to relieve me, whispering, "You know the soul is immortal; why then should you be such a niggard of a little time when you have a whole eternity before you?" So being easily convinc'd, and, like other reasonable creatures, satisfy'd with a small reason, when it is in favour of doing what I have a mind to do, I shuffle the cards again, and begin another game.

As to public amusements, we have neither plays nor operas, but we had recently a kind of oratorio. We have assemblies, balls and concerts, besides little parties at one another's houses, in which there is sometimes dancing, and frequently good music, so that we job on in life as pleasantly as they do in London, where they have plays perform'd by good actors: that is, I think, the only advantage London has over Philadelphia, however.

EXERCISE SHOULD PRECEDE MEALS...

During the long winter, I wrote the following piece, "The Art of Procuring Pleasant Dreams," at the request of Catherine Shipley,* which I print in part:

> As a great part of our life is spent in sleep, during which we have sometimes pleasing and sometimes painful dreams, it becomes of some consequence to obtain the one kind and avoid the other. To this end it is in the first place necessary to be careful in preserving health by due exercise and great temperance; for in sickness the imagination is disturb'd; and sometimes disagreeable and terrible ideas are apt to present themselves. Exercise should *precede* meals, not *immediately follow* them: the first promotes, the latter obstructs

---

* Catherine Shipley and her sister Georgiana, daughters of Jonathan Shipley, were longtime correspondents of Franklin.

digestion. If after exercise we feed sparingly, the digestion will be easy and good, the body lightsome, the temper cheerful, and all the animal functions perform'd agreeably. Sleep when it follows will be natural and undisturb'd, while indolence with full feeding occasions nightmares and horrors inexpressible; we fall from precipices; are assaulted by wild beasts, murderers, or demons; and we experience at times every variety of distress. Observe, however, that the quantities of food and exercise are relative things; those who move much may, and indeed ought, to eat more; those who use little exercise should eat little. In general mankind, since the improvement of cookery, eat about twice as much as nature requires. Suppers are not bad if we have not din'd, but restless nights naturally follow hearty suppers after full dinners. Indeed, as there is a difference in constitutions, some rest well after those meals: it costs them only a frightful dream and an apoplexy, after which they sleep till doomsday. Nothing is more common in the newspapers than instances of people, who after eating a hearty supper, are found dead in a bed in the morning.

Another means of preserving health is having a constant supply of fresh air in the bed chamber. It has been a great mistake sleeping in rooms exactly clos'd and in beds surrounded by curtains. No outward air that may come into you is so unwholesome as the unchang'd air often breath'd of a close chamber. A number of persons crowded into a small room thus spoil the air in a few minutes and even render it mortal, as in the Black Hole at Calcutta. It is recorded of Methuselah, who being the longest liver may be supposed to have best preserved his health, that he slept always in the open air. Physicians, after having for ages contended that the sick should not be indulg'd with fresh air, have at length discover'd that it may do them good. It is therefore to be hop'd they may in time discover likewise, that it is not hurtful to those who are in health; and that we may then be cured of the *Aerophobia* that at present distresses weak minds, and make them choose to be stifled and poison'd, rather than leave open the window of a bedchamber, or put down the glass of a coach.

Correspondence with old friends in Europe

I often think with great pleasure on the happy days I pass'd in England with my learned and ingenious friends, who have left us to join the majority in the world of spirits. Everyone of them now knows more than all of us they have left behind.

The world suffer'd a great loss in the death of Mr. Oswald, who negotiated the peace treaty. Mr. Grand's mention of the malady of M. de Vergennes afflicted me, and much more the news of his death. So wise and so good a man taken away from the station he fill'd is a great loss not only to France but to Europe in general, to America, and to mankind. Being depriv'd of dear friends and relations one after another is a very severe tax we pay for living a great while ourselves.

I wish to hear from my friends by every packet, and presume they may excuse me if I write once a year. The only apology I can make, and that not a very good one, is that indolence is natural to age and that I am too much engag'd in business. Their continued kindness toward me express'd in their letters affects me much; and I never peruse those letters but with fresh pleasure, mix'd with the remembrance of the many delightful hours I pass'd in that sweet society, and the regret with which I find myself forever separated from it.

But tho' I could not leave that dear nation without regret, I certainly did right in coming home. I am here in my niche, in my own house, in the bosom of my family, my daughter and grandchildren all about me, among my old friends or the sons of my friends who equally respect me, and who all speak and understand the same language with me; and if a man desires to be useful by the exercise of his mental faculties, he loses half that force when in a foreign country, where he can only express himself in a language with which he is not well acquainted. I wrote a French letter to Mademoisselle Chaumont, but it cost me too much time to write in that language, and after all 'tis very bad French, and I therefore wrote others in English in hope that it could be interpreted. In short, I enjoy every opportunity of doing good, and everything else I could wish for except repose; and that [repose] I may soon expect, either by the cessation of my office, which cannot last more than 3 years, or by ceasing to live.

THE LAST TWELVE YEARS OF MY LIFE WERE EMPLOYED IN MATTERS OF THE GREATEST IMPORTANCE

I am grown so old as to have buried most of my friends of my youth, and I now often hear persons whom I knew when children called old Mr. such-a-one to distinguish them from their sons, now men grown and in business; so that by living so long I seem to have intruded myself into the company of posterity, when I ought to have been abed and asleep. Yet had I gone at seventy it would have cut off twelve of the most active years of my life, employed too in matters of the greatest importance; but whether I have been doing good or mischief is for time to discover. I only know that I intended well, and I hope all will end well.

I wrote a letter of recommendation to Thomas Jefferson and other friends in France on behalf of Mr. Thomas Paine, the author of the celebrated piece entitled *Common Sense*, published in America with prodigious effect on the minds of the people at the beginning of the revolution. He is an ingenious and skillful artist who carried with him to France the model of a bridge of new construction, his own invention. I requested the Duke de La Rochefoucauld to procure him a sight of the models and drafts in the repository of the Ponts and Chaussees.

I also received a letter from the astronomer Sir William Herschel, together with his catalogue of 1,000 new nebulae and clusters of stars, which I immediately communicated to our Philosophical Society. I congratulated him on his important new discovery of the two satellites revolving round the Georgian planet [Uranus]. Mr. Herschel has wonderfully extended the power of human vision and is daily making us acquainted with regions of the universe totally unknown to mankind in former ages. When free from these bodily embarrassments, I hope to roam through some of the systems he has explored! Had fortune plac'd him in this part of America, his progress in these discoveries might have been still more rapid, as from the more frequent clearness of our air, we have nearly one third more in the year of good observing days than there are in England.

Not having found the cares of government so burdensome as I apprehended, I consented to a second year, and was chosen unanimously by the junction of all parties, so that there was but one negative voice, viz., my own, and that given for modesty sake. The Assembly of this state granted me 3,000 acres of their land, to be located when I can find any vacant.

I also received a letter from William Cocke acquainting me with the honour of naming an intended new state Franklin, having understood at first that it was called *Frank Land*.* Having resided some years in Europe, and being lately arrived from there, I had not had an opportunity of being inform'd of the points of dispute between Mr. Cocke and the state of North Carolina, and said I thought they were perfectly right in resolving to submit them to the decision of Congress, and to abide by their determination.

Shays's Rebellion, that dangerous insurrection

In the state of Pennsylvania, the government, not withstanding our parties, went very smoothly. We had two parties, one for preserving the

---

* Frankland never became a state; it became part of Tennessee.

Constitution as it was, and the other for adding an upper house as a check to the Assembly. But having try'd it seven years, the strongest party was for continuing it as it is. The constitution of Massachusetts is, I think, one of the best in the union, perhaps I might say in the world. But it was disturbed by some disorderly people. Fortunately, Mr. Shays and the insurgents were quelled, and I believe a great majority of that people approved the measures of government in reducing them. I congratulated James Bowdoin, governor of Massachusetts, on the happy success attending the wise and vigorous measures taken for the suppression of that dangerous insurrection. As the president of the Pennsylvania Supreme Executive Council, we proclaimed an act in cooperation with the State of Massachusetts and agreeable to the Articles of Confederation, that rewards the commonwealth in apprehending the proclaimed rebels Daniel Shays, Luke Day, Adam Wheeler and Eli Parsons, that they might be dealt with according to the law.

Too much paper money is mischievous

The rest of the states went on pretty well, except some dissensions in Rhode Island and Maryland respecting paper money. Paper money in moderate quantities has been found beneficial; but when more than the occasions of commerce require, it depreciates and is mischievous, and the populace are apt to demand more than is necessary. In the state of Pennsylvania, we have some, and it is useful, and I do not hear any clamour for more. Our paper money is not well understood. It was made before my arrival, and not being a legal tender,* can do no injustice to anybody, nor does anyone here complain of it, tho' many are justly averse to an increase of the quantity at this time, there being a great deal of real money in the country, and our bank in good credit. I myself purchased ten actions in it, which at least shows my good opinion of it. However, the bank here in Philadelphia [Bank of North America] met with great opposition, partly from envy and partly from those who wish an emission of more paper money, which they think the bank opposes. But it has stood all attacks, and went on well, notwith-standing the assembly repealed its charter, but a new Assembly restored it. The management is so prudent, the dividend has never been less than six percent, and their notes are always instantly paid on demand, and passed on all occasions as readily as silver, because they will always produce silver.

When there is a free government, and the people make their own laws by their representatives, I see no injustice in their obliging one another to take their own paper money. It is no more so than com-pelling a man by law to take his own note. But it is unjust to pay strangers with such money against their will. The making of paper money with such a sanction is a folly, since, although you may by law oblige a citizen to take it for his goods, you cannot fix his prices; and his liberty of rating them as he pleases, which is the same thing as setting what value he pleases on your money, defeats your sanction.

A Constitutional Convention in Philadelphia: Only a virtuous
people are capable of freedom

There seemed to be little thought in the states of mending their par-ticular constitutions, but the Articles of Confederation were generally thought defective and blamed as not having given sufficient powers to Congress, the federal head. That there should be faults in our first sketches or plans of government is not surprising; rather, considering

---

* Federal and state governments passed legal tender laws requiring individuals and businesses to accept government-issued paper money for
  debts and payment of goods and services. During times of inflation,
  such as the American Revolutionary War, citizens were reluctant to
  accept currency unbacked by gold or silver.

the times, and the circumstances under which they were formed, it is surprising that the faults are so few. A convention was first proposed by Virginia, and since was recommended by Congress, to assemble in Philadelphia to revise that constitution, and propose a better one, and the General Assembly desired my assistance in the business of amending the federal Constitution. I noted that France also was engaged in the same project at the same time to have an assembly of notables to consult on improvements of the government, and I expressed the wish that both assemblies would be blessed with success and promote the happiness of both nations. Only a virtuous people are capable of freedom. As nations become corrupt and vicious, they have more need of masters.

Many of the delegates arrived at the convention in Philadelphia in May, 1787. They comprised some of the principal people from several states of our confederation, what the French call *une assemblée des notables*. Gen. Washington was chosen president of the convention. The delegates did me the honor of dining with me, when the cask of port was broached, and its contents met with the most cordial reception and universal approbation. In short the company agreed unanimously that it was the best porter they had ever tasted.

I attended faithfully the business of the convention 5 hours in every day from the beginning, which was something more than four months. My health continued throughout, some telling me I looked better, and they supposed the daily exercise of going and returning from the State House did me good.

Two passions have a violent effect in the affairs of men

I expressed with reluctance a disapprobation on some of the articles of the plan. I happened to differ in particular regarding the salaries to the executive branch. I told the body that I see inconveniences in the appointment of salaries, where I see none in refusing them, but on the contrary great advantages. There are two passions which have a powerful influence in the affairs of men. These are ambition and avarice; the love of power, and the love of money. Separately each of these has great force in prompting men to action; but when united in view of the same object, they have in many minds the most violent effect. Place before the eyes of such men a post of honour that shall at the same time be a place of profit, and they will move heaven and earth to obtain it. The vast number of such positions was one reason the British government was so tempestuous. The struggles for them are the true source of all those factions which are perpetually dividing the nation, distracting its councils, hurrying it sometimes into fruitless and mischievous wars, and often compelling a submission to dishonourable terms of peace. And of what kind are the men that will strive for this profitable pre-eminence, thro' all the bustle of cabal, the heat of contention, the infinite mutual abuse of parties, tearing to pieces the best of characters? It will not be the wise and moderate, the lovers of peace and good order, the men fittest for the trust. It will be the bold and the violent, the men of strong passions and indefatigable activity in their selfish pursuits. These will thrust themselves to this government and be their rulers. And these too will be mistaken in the expected happiness of their situation: for their vanquished competitors of the same spirit and from the same motives will perpetually be endeavouring to distress their administration, thwart their measures, and render them odious to the people.

A CONSTANT WARFARE BETWEEN
THE GOVERNING AND THE GOVERNED

Besides these evils, tho' we may set out in the beginning with moderate salaries, we shall find that such will not be of long continuance. Reasons will never be wanting for propos'd augmentations. And there will always be a party for giving more to the rulers, that the rulers may be able to return to give more to them. Hence as all history informs us, there has been in every state and kingdom a constant kind of warfare between the governing and the governed; the one striving to obtain more for its support, and the other to pay less. And this has alone occasion'd great convulsions, actual civil wars, ending either in dethroning of the princes or enslaving of the people. Generally indeed the ruling power carries its point, and we see the revenues of princes constantly increasing, and we see that they are never satisfied, but always in want of more. I am apprehensive, therefore, perhaps too apprehensive, that the government of these states may in future times end in a monarchy, and a King will the sooner be set over us.

It may be imagined by some that this is a utopian idea, and that we can never find men to serve us in the executive department without paying them well for their services. I conceive this to be a mistake. The High Sheriff of a county in England is an honourable office, but it is not a profitable one. Yet it is executed, and well executed, and usually by some of the principal gentlemen of the county. Another instance is the Quakers. It is an establish'd rule with them that they are not to go to law, but in their controversies they must apply to their meetings. Committees of these sit with patience to hear the parties, and spend much time in composing their differences. In doing this, they are supported by a sense of duty, and the respect paid to usefulness. It is honourable to be so employ'd, but it was never made profitable by salaries, fees, or perquisites. And indeed in all cases of public service, the less the profit the greater the honour. To bring the matter nearer home, have we not seen the greatest and most important of our offices, that of general of our armies, executed for eight years together, without the smallest salary, by a patriot whom I will not now offend by any other praise? I think we shall never be without a sufficient number of wise and good men to undertake and execute well and faithfully the office in question. I only bring the instances to show that the pleasures of doing good and serving their country are sufficient motives with some minds to give up a great portion of their time to the public without the mean inducement of pecuniary satisfaction.*

SINGLE VS. DUAL LEGISLATURE: THE FABLE OF THE SNAKE WITH TWO HEADS

In the debates, I also opposed a legislature with two branches, which I thought would occasion lengthy disputes and delays and great expenses, and promote factions among the people and obstruct the public business. I said to the delegates of Pennsylvania, "Have we not experienced in this colony under the government of the proprietors the mischiefs of a second branch existing in the proprietary-family? What a train of mischiefs, even to the preventing of the defense of the province during several years, when distressed by an Indian war, was caused by the iniquitous demand that the proprietors should be exempt from taxation. Has our present legislature in one assembly committed any errors of importance, which they have not remedied, or may not easily remedy, and more easily probably than if divided into two branches? And if the wisdom brought by the members to the Assembly is divided into two branches, may it not be too weak in each to support a good measure or obstruct a bad one? Has not the famous political fable of the snake with two heads and one body some useful instruction contained in it? She was going to a brook to drink and in her way was to pass thro' a hedge, a twig of which opposed her direct course; one head chose to go on the

---

* Franklin's amendment did not carry.

right side of the twig, the other on the left; so that time was spent in the contest and, before the decision was completed, the poor snake died with thirst."

The important ends of civil government are the personal securities of life and liberty; these remain the same in every member of the society, and the poorest continues to have an equal claim to them with the most opulent, whatever differences of time, chance or industry may occasion their circumstance. I was sorry to see a disposition among some of our people (especially in Pennsylvania) to commence an aristocracy, by giving the rich a predominancy in government, a choice peculiar to themselves in one half the legislature, to be proudly called the upper house, and the other branch chosen by the majority of the people degraded by the denomination of the lower.

REPRESENTATION BY POPULATION OR BY STATE?

During the warm debates on the subject of representation, I expressed my views that the number of representatives should bear some proportion to the number of the represented, and that the decisions should be by the majority of members, not by the majority of states. This was objected to, from an apprehension that the greater states would then swallow up the smaller. I recollected that in the beginning of this century, when the union was propos'd of the two kingdoms, England and Scotland, the Scot patriots were full of fears, that unless they had equal number of representatives in Parliament they should be ruined by the superiority of the English. They finally agreed, however, that the different proportions of importance in the union of the two nations should be attended to, whereby they were to have only forty members in the House of Commons, and only sixteen of their peers were to sit in the House of Lords. A very great inferiority of numbers! And yet to this day I do not recollect that anything has been done in the Parliament of Great Britain to the prejudice of Scotland.

GOD GOVERNS IN THE AFFAIRS OF MEN!

It gave me great pleasure to observe that until the point the proportion of representation in Congress came before us, our debates had been carry'd on with great coolness and temper. For we were sent hither to consult, not to contend with each other, harmony and union being extremely necessary in promoting and securing the common good. However, a contrary kind of discord and division arose, and we made small progress after 4 or 5 weeks of close attendance and continual reasoning with each other. There were different sentiments on almost every question, several of the last producing as many Noes as Ayes. Methinks it was melancholy proof of the imperfection of the human understanding. We indeed seemed to feel our want of political wisdom, since we were running all about in search of it. We went back to ancient history for models of government, and examin'd the different forms of those republics which, having been originally form'd with seeds of their own dissolution, now no longer exist. And we view'd modern states all round Europe, but found none of their constitutions suitable to our circumstances.

In this situation, groping as it were in the dark to find political truth, and scarce able to distinguish it when presented to us, I asked the delegates how it happened that we had not hitherto once thought of humbly applying to the Father of Lights to illuminate our understanding? In the beginning of the contest with Britain, when we were sensible of danger, we had daily prayers in that room for the divine protection! Our prayers were heard; and they were graciously answered. All of us who were engag'd in the struggle must have observ'd frequent instances of a superintending providence in our favour. To that kind providence we owe this happy opportunity of consulting in peace on the means of establishing our future national felicity.

And now, I asked, have we forgotten that powerful friend? Or do we imagine we no longer need its assistance? I have lived a long time; and the longer I live, the more convincing proofs I see of this truth, *that GOD governs in the affairs of men!* And if a sparrow cannot fall to the ground without his notice, is it probable that an empire can rise without his aid? We have been assured in the sacred writings that "except the Lord build the house, they labor in vain that build it." I firmly believe this; and I also believe that without his concurring aid, we shall succeed in this political building no better than the builders of Babel: We shall be divided by our little partial local interests, our projects will be confounded, and we ourselves shall become a reproach and a byword down to future ages. And what is worse, mankind may hereafter, from this unfortunate instance, despair of establishing government by human wisdom, and leave it to chance, war and conquest.

I therefore moved that henceforth prayers, imploring the assistance of heaven and its blessing on our deliberations, be held in that assembly every morning before we proceeded to business; and that one or more of the clergy of this city be requested to officiate in that service. Unfortunately, the convention, except three or four persons, thought prayers unnecessary!!

We continued the debate on representation June 30, 1787. Many expedients had been proposed without effect. I agreed that there ought to be some difference between the first and second branches. But how? I said, "A joiner, when he wants to fit two boards, takes off with his plane the uneven parts from each side, and thus they fit. Let us do the same." I therefore proposed this expedient: Let the Senate be elected by the states equally, and the House by the number of the represented in each state. I have the happiness to report that a similar plan was eventually adopted.*

I consent to this Constitution because this system approaches so near to perfection

The convention finish'd its work on the 17ᵀᴴ of September, 1787. On this final day I arose and made the following speech, which was read to the delegates:

"I confess that I do not entirely approve this Constitution at present, but I am not sure I shall ever approve it: For having lived long, I have experienced many instances of being oblig'd by better information or fuller consideration to change opinions even on important subjects, which I once thought right, but found to be otherwise. It is therefore that the older I grow, the more apt I am to doubt my own judgment, and to pay more respect to the judgment of others. Most men, indeed as well as most sects in religion, think themselves in possession of all truth, and that wherever others differ from them it is so far error. Steele, a protestant, in a dedication tells the Pope that the only difference between our two churches is their opinions of the certainty of their doctrines; that is, the Romish Church is infallible, and the Church of England is never in the wrong. But tho' many private persons think almost as highly of their own infallibility as of that of their sect, few express it so naturally as a certain French lady, who in a little dispute with her sister, said, "I don't know how it happens, sister, but I meet with no body but myself that's always in the right." *Il n'y a que moi a toujours raison.*

"In these sentiments, Sir, I agree to this Constitution, with all its faults, if they are such. Because I think a general government neces-

---

* Franklin's compromise was previously proposed by other delegates,
  especially from Connecticut (the Connecticut Compromise).

sary for us, there is no form of government but what may be a blessing to the people if well administered; and I believe further that this is likely to be well administered for a course of years, and can only end in despotism as other forms have done before it, when the people shall become so corrupted as to need despotic government, being incapable of any other. I doubt too whether any other convention we can obtain may be able to make a better constitution: For when you assemble a number of men to have the advantage of their joint wisdom, you inevitably assemble with those men all their prejudices, their passions, their errors of opinion, their local interests, and their selfish views. From such an assembly can a perfect production be expected? It therefore astonishes me, Sir, to find this system approaching so near to perfection as it does; I think it will astonish our enemies, who are waiting with confidence to hear that our councils are confounded, like those of the builders of Babel, and that our states are on the point of separation, only to meet hereafter for the purpose of cutting one another's throats."

MAY EACH DOUBT A LITTLE
OF HIS OWN INFALLIBILITY

My speech to the Convention continued: "Thus I consent, Sir, to this Constitution because I expect no better, and because I am not sure that it is not the best. The opinions I have had of its errors, I sacrifice to the public good. I have never whisper'd a syllable of them abroad. Within these walls they were born, and here they shall die. If everyone of us in returning to our constituents were to report the objections he has had to it, and endeavour to gain partisans in support of them, we might prevent its being generally received, and thereby lose all the salutary effects and great advantages resulting naturally in our favour among foreign nations, as well as among ourselves, from our real or apparent unanimity. Much of the strength and efficiency of any

government in procuring and securing happiness to the people
depends on the general opinion of the goodness of that government
as well as the wisdom and integrity of its governors. I hope therefore
that for our own sakes, as a part of the people, and for the sake of our
posterity, we shall act heartily and unanimously in recommending this
constitution, wherever our influence may extend, and turn our future
thoughts and endeavours to the means of having it well administered.

"On the whole, Sir, I cannot help expressing a wish that every
member of the convention who may still have objections to it would,
with me, on this occasion doubt a little of his own infallibility, and,
to make manifest our unanimity put his name to this instrument."

Is this a rising or a setting sun?

The motion was made and done by unanimous consent, which was
agreed to and added accordingly. Whilst the last members were signing the document, I looked toward the president's chair, at the back
of which a sun happened to be painted, and observed to a few members near me, that I had often found it difficult to distinguish in their
art a rising from a setting sun. I have, said I, often in the course of
the session and in the vicissitudes of my hopes and fears over the
issues, looked at that sun behind the president, without being able to
tell whether it was rising or setting. But now at length I have the happiness to know that it is a rising and not a setting sun.

The new federal Constitution we propos'd was published in the
papers. The forming of it so as to accommodate all the different interests and views was a difficult task and perhaps, after all, I did not
think it would be receiv'd with the same unanimity in the different
states, that the convention had given the example of, in delivering it
for their consideration. We have, however, done our best.

Chapter Eleven

My Final Years, 1787...

It is a singular thing in the history of mankind that a great people have had the opportunity of forming a government for themselves. After four months of close discussion, the Congress sent copies of the American Constitution of government to the legislatures of the several states, to be submitted by them to the consideration of conventions in each state for approbation. I also sent copies of the new Federal Constitution to my friends in France and England. Our particular state ratify'd the Constitution in early December.

AMERICA IS TOO ENLIGHTENED TO BE ENSLAVED

The propos'd Constitution met with a great deal of opposition in every state, it being difficult to reconcile and accommodate so many different and jarring interests, and jealousy of power. Such opposition strengthens an opinion of mine that America is too enlighten'd to be enslav'd. Though there is a general dread of giving too much power to our governors, I think we are more in danger from too little obedience in the governed. A zealous advocate for the Constitution in a certain public assembly said he believ'd if an angel from heaven were to bring down a Constitution, form'd there for our use, it would nevertheless meet with violent opposition.

But we must not expect that a new government may be formed, as a game of chess may be played, by a skillful hand without a fault. We are making experiments in politics. The players of our game are so many, their ideas so different, their prejudices so strong and so various, and their particular interests independent of the general seeming so opposite, that not a move can be made that is not contested. The numerous objections confound the understanding; the wisest must agree to some unreasonable things, that reasonable ones of the more consequence may be obtained, and thus chance has its share in many of the determinations, so that the play is more like tric-trac with a box of dice. The success of the project, however, means our government will be more energetic, and we shall be in a better condition of being serviceable to our friends on any future occasion.

IN AMERICA, ANOTHER WAR WITH THE INDIANS...

I received news of a war between the state of Georgia and the Creek Indians. During the course of a long life in which I have made observations on public affairs, it has appear'd to me that almost every war between the Indians and the whites has been occasion'd by some injustice of the latter toward the former. It is indeed extremely imprudent in us to quarrel with them for their lands, as they are generally willing to sell, and sell at such good bargains: And a war with them is so mischievous to us, in unsettling frequently a great part of our frontier, and reducing the inhabitants to poverty and distress, and is besides so expensive, that it is much cheaper as well as more honest, to buy their lands than to take them by force.

AND IN EUROPE, ANOTHER WITH...

I heard from Dr. Ingenhousz, physician to the Prussian Emperor, that there was prospect of horrid war with Russia. There is so little good gain'd, and so much mischief done generally by wars, that I wish the imprudence of undertaking them were more evident to princes, in which case I think they would be less frequent. If I were counsellor to the emperor of Russia, and found that she desired to possess some part of the dominions of the Grand Signior, I should advise her to compute what the annual taxes raised from that territory may amount to, and make him an offer of buying it, at the rate of paying for it twenty years purchase. And if I were his counsellor, I should advise him to take the money and cede the dominion of that territory. For I am of the opinion that a war to obtain it will cost her more than that sum, and the event uncertain; and that the defense of it will cost him as much; and not having embrac'd the offer, his loss is double. But to make and accept such an offer, these potentates should both be reasonable creatures, and free from the ambition of glory, &c., which perhaps is too much to be supposed.

An honest heretic

I corresponded with my British friends Benjamin Vaughan, Dr. Richard Price, and the honest heretic Dr. Priestley. I do not call him honest by way of distinction; for I think all heretics I have known have been virtuous men. They have the virtue of fortitude or they would not venture to own their heresy; and they cannot afford to be deficient in any other virtues, as that would give advantage to their many enemies; and they are not like sinners, such as friends who excuse or justify them. Do not, however, mistake me. It is not to my good friend's heresy that I impute his honesty. On the contrary, 'tis his honesty that has brought upon him the character of heretic.

How different was what happened to me!

As it is customary in Europe to make some liberal provision for ministers when they return home from foreign service, during which their absence is necessarily injurious to their private affairs, I did hope that the Congress would at least have been kind enough to have showed their approbation of my conduct by a grant of some small tract of land in their western country, which might have been of use and some honour to my posterity. I saw by their minutes that the Congress allow'd Mr. Lee handsomely for his service in England before his appointment to France, in which services I and Mr. Bollan* co-operated with him and had no such allowance; and since his return he was very properly rewarded with a good place, as well as my friend Mr. Jay. (These were trifling compensations compared with what was granted by the King to M. Gerard on his return from America.) But how different was what happened to me! On my return from England the Congress bestow'd on me the office of Postmaster General, for which I was very thankful. It was indeed an office I had some kind of right to, as having previously greatly enlarg'd the revenue of the post by the regulations I had contriv'd and establish'd, while I possess'd it under the Crown. When I was sent to France, I left it in the hands of my son-in-law, who was to act as my deputy. But soon after my departure it was taken from me and given to Mr. Hazard, when the English ministry formerly thought fit to deprive me of the office. They left me however the privilege of receiving and sending my letters free of postage, which is the custom when a postmaster is not displac'd for malfeasance in the office. But in America I have ever since had the postage demanded of me, which since my return from France has amounted to above £50, much of it occasion'd by my having acted as minister there.

When I took my grandson Temple with me to France, I had purposed, after giving him the French language, to educate him in the study and practice of the law. But by the repeated expectations given me of a secretary, and constant disappointments, I was induced and indeed obliged to retain him with me to assist in the secretary's office;

---

* William Bollan, agent to England for the colony of Massachusetts, 1745–62.

which disappointments continued till my return, by which time so many years of the opportunity of studying the law were lost, and his habits of life become so different, that it appear'd no longer advisable; and I then, considering him as brought up in the diplomatic line and well qualify'd by his knowledge in that branch, took the liberty of recommending him to the Congress for their protection, for the employ of a secretary at least (in which opinion I was not alone, for three of my colleagues, without the smallest solicitation from me, chose him secretary of the commission for treaties, which they were empower'd to do). This was the only favour I ever ask'd of them, and the only answer I receiv'd was a resolution superseding him and appointing Col. David Humphreys in his place; a gentleman who, tho' he might have indeed a good deal of military merit, certainly had none in the diplomatic line, and had neither the French language, nor the experience, nor the address, proper to qualify him in preference for such an employment.

But I would never have made a public complaint; and even if I could have foreseen such unkind treatment from Congress, as their refusing me their thanks, it would not in the least have abated my zeal for the cause and ardour in support of it! For I know something of the nature of such changeable assemblies, and how little successors are inform'd of the services that have been render'd to the corps before their admission, or feel themselves oblig'd by such services; and what effect the artful and reiterated malevolent insinuations of one or two envious and malicious persons may have on the minds of members, even of the most equitable, candid and honorable dispositions, during the absence of the servant in a distant country.

Settling my accounts with Congress

When I was sent to France, I put all the cash I could raise into the loan office. The paper was then of equal value with gold or silver, and indeed part of it had been receiv'd from Congress in discharge of a sum in gold which I had advanc'd to the army in Canada. I saw by the minutes of Nov. 18, 1782, that Mr. Lee's certificates were order'd to be paid in sterling, at the rate of ⅙ a dollar. I supposed there must have been some circumstances attending his certificates which entitled them to such favour, and I wished to know what they were. My certificates, I was told, were worth but about a sixth part of my original loan.

On my arrival in Philadelphia, one of the first things I did was to dispatch Temple to New York to obtain a final settlement of my accounts with Congress. As part of this settlement, I presented a sketch of my services to the United States, but he returned without effecting the settlement, being told that it could not be made till the arrival of some documents expected from France. What those documents were, I was never informed. It is now more than three years that those accounts have been before that honorable body, and to this day no notice has been communicated. But reports have for sometime past been circulating that I am greatly indebted to the United States for large sums that had been put into my hands, and that I avoid a settlement.

My heavy expense in building five houses (which cost much more than I was made to expect) so exhausted my finances that I was in real and great want of money. I therefore sent my son-in-law Richard Bache to New York to make a final settlement of my accounts with my partner, Mr. Francis Childs, printer at New York, to discharge his bond and pay his debt to me.

As I grow older, I find writing more painful

As I grow older, I find writing more painful, and I never have been more burden'd with business than since my return. I was elected a third time by my fellow citizens of Pennsylvania, without a dissenting vote (but my own) to fill the chair of president, the most honourable post in their power to bestow. This universal and unbounded confidence of a whole people flatters my vanity much more than a peerage could do. This however is the last year I can serve, by our Constitution, and so I can enjoy a little leisure before I die.

The Boston manner, turn of phrase, and accent revive me

My malady the stone makes it so extremely inconvenient to me to dine abroad that I have not once done it since my return to America. In February, 1788, I found myself confin'd to my bed by the bruises of a fall on the stone steps into my garden, which sprain'd my wrist and right arm up to the shoulder. This, join'd to that painful disorder the stone, has continu'd to harass me, and disabled me long as to writing. As to my going to Boston, it can no longer be accomplish'd, as such a journey at my age would be attended with much inconvenience and hardship, and might, with the malady I have, be dangerous. I could neither bear walking nor riding in a carriage over its cobbled streets and above all that I should find very few indeed of my old friends living, it being now sixty-five years since I left it to settle here. At present I am in my place, have all my conveniences and comforts about me, and it seems most prudent to stay where I am and enjoy them, without going abroad to give myself and friends a good deal of trouble, which cannot be compensated by our pleasure of meeting, since that will be balanc'd by the pain of parting. But I enjoy the company and conversations of its inhabitants when any of them are so good as to visit me; for besides their general good sense, which I value, the Boston manner, turn of phrase, and even the tone of voice and accent in all please, and seem to refresh and revive me.

I live in a house which I built 25 years ago, contriv'd in my mind, and made still more convenient by an addition since my return. A dutiful and affectionate daughter, with her husband and six children, compose my family. The children are all promising, and even the youngest, who is but four years old, contributes to my amusement.

The oldest, Benjamin, finish'd his studies at our university, and has entered into business I set him up in as a printer and type-founder. Temple has settled on his plantation, but when in town lives with me. I planned to visit my grandson's plantation for a month of leisure to write my friends, free from business and the interruption of visitors, although I am so continually harassed by a painful distemper the stone, and have so enfeebled the old machine, that I think it is not far from the final stop of its motions. My rents and incomes are amply sufficient for all my present occasions, and if no unexpected misfortunes happen during the little time I have to live, I shall leave a handsome estate to be divided among my relatives.

I WISH I HAD BEEN BORN TWO OR THREE CENTURIES HENCE

I have no philosophical news, except that a Mr. Fitch of this country has executed a boat which goes upon rivers against wind and tide by the force of a steam engine; but whether it may be too expensive and troublesome for common use remains to be determin'd by experience. I have sometimes almost wish'd it had been my destiny to have been born two or three centuries hence, for inventions of improvement are prolific, and beget more of their kind. The present progress is rapid. Many of great importance, now unthought of, will before that period be procur'd. I mention one reason for such a wish, which is that if the art of physic shall be improv'd in proportion with other arts, we may then be able to avoid diseases, and live as long as the patriarchs in Genesis.

ABUSE OF THE LIBERTY OF THE PRESS

My gout at length left me after five months confinement, affording me the leisure to read for my amusement the *Pennsylvania Gazette* and other newspapers. I never see any Boston newspapers; my sister mentioned there was something in them to do me honor. I am obliged to them. In January, 1790, I received a kind letter from Rev. Dr. Ezra Stiles, president of Yale College, who propos'd to honour me by placing my portrait in the same room with the portrait of Govr. Yale. I am much obliged to Yale College, the first learned society that took notice of me, and adorned me its honours.

On the other hand, some of our papers here are endeavouring to disgrace me. I take no notice; my friends defend me. I have long been accustomed to receive more blame, as well as more praise, than I have deserved. It is the lot of every public man, and I leave one account to balance the other.

I heard a remark, that on examination of the *Pennsylvania Gazette* for fifty years from its commencement, it appear'd that during that long period scarce one libelous piece had ever appear'd in it. This generally chaste conduct of the paper does much to its reputation: for it has long been the opinion of sober judicious people that nothing is more likely to endanger the liberty of the press than the abuse of that liberty by employing it in personal accusation, detraction, and calumny. The excesses some of our other papers have been guilty of in this particular have set this state in a bad light abroad, for I could not help but notice the *inconsistence* that strikes me between the name of our city, Philadelphia, brotherly love, and the spirit of rancour, malice, and hatred that breathes in its newspapers. I learn from those papers that our state is divided into parties; that each party ascribes all the public operations of the other to vicious motives; that they do not even suspect one another of the smallest degree of honesty; that the anti-federalists are such merely from the fear of losing powers, places, or emoluments which they have in possession or in expectation; that the federalists are a set of conspirators who aim at establishing a tyranny over the persons and property of their countrymen and live in splendor on the plunder of the people. I learn too that our justices of the peace, tho' chosen by their neighbours, make a villainous trade of their office, and promote discord to augment fees, and fleece their electors; and that the Executive Council, with interested or party views, are continually making improper appointments; witness a "petty fiddler, sycophant and scoundrel" appointed Judge of the Admiralty; an old woman and fomenter of sedition to be another of judges; the comptroller and naval officers to prey upon the merchants and deprive them of their property by force of arms, &c. And finally, that I, the President, the unanimous joint choice of the Council and the Assembly, am "an old rogue" who gave his assent to the Federal Constitution merely to avoid refunding money he had purloin'd from the United States.

PENNSYLVANIA IS A GOOD COUNTRY
TO *DIE IN*, THO' A VERY BAD ONE TO *LIVE IN*

There is indeed a good deal of manifest inconsistency in all this, and yet a stranger seeing it in our own prints, tho' he does not believe it all, may probably believe enough of it to conclude that Pennsylvania is peopled by a set of the most unprincipled, rascally and quarrelsome scoundrels upon the face of the globe. I have sometimes indeed suspected that these papers are the manufacture of foreign enemies among us who write with the view of disgracing our country, and making us appear contemptible and detestable all the world over.

There is however one inconsistency that consoles me a little, which is, that the dead are all angels. It is delightful, when any die, to read what good husbands, good fathers, good friends, good citizens and good Christians they were, concluding with a scrap of poetry that places them with certainly everyone in heaven. So that I think Pennsylvania a good country to *die in*, tho' a very bad one to *live in*.

My love of France

It is true that I enjoy here everything that a reasonable man can desire; a sufficiency of income, a comfortable habitation of my own building, having all the conveniences I could imagine; a dutiful and affectionate daughter to nurse and take care of me, a number of promising grand-children, some old friends still remaining to converse with, and more respect, distinction and public honours than I can possibly merit (these are the blessings of God and depend on his continu'd goodness); yet all do not make me forget Paris and the nine years happiness I enjoy'd there in the sweet society of a people whose conversation was instructive, whose manner was highly pleasing, and who above all the nations of the world have in the greatest perfection the art of making themselves belov'd of strangers. And now, even in my sleep, I find that the scenes of my pleasant dreams are laid in that city, or in its neigh-bourhood. I love France, and have a thousand reasons for doing so.

There is one thing wanting to facilitate and augment our inter-course. It is a dictionary, explaining the names of different articles of manufacture in the two languages. When I was in Paris I received a large order for a great variety of goods, particularly of the kind called hardwares, i.e., wares of iron and steel: and when I showed the invoice to their manufacturers, they did not understand what kinds of goods or instruments were meant by the names; nor could any English and French dictionary be found to explain them.

The revolution in France
gives me a great deal of pain

The accounts I have heard of the misunderstandings and troubles that have arisen in the government of that dear country in which I pass'd nine of the happiest years of my life gave me a great deal of pain; but I hope all will tend to its good in the end. When the fermentation is over, and the troubling parts subside, the wine will be fine and good, and cheer the hearts of those that drink it.

The convulsions in France are attended with some disagreeable circumstances and give me great concern; but if by the struggle she obtains and secures for the nation its future liberty and a good constitution, a few years enjoyment of those blessings will amply repair all the damages their acquisition may have occasioned. God grant that not only the love of liberty but a thorough knowledge of the rights of man may pervade all the nations of the earth so that a philosopher may set his foot anywhere on its surface and say, this is my country!

The new Constitution is approved

Our grand machine, the new Constitution of a Federal government, has at length begun to work. Many objections were made to it in the public papers, and answers to those objections. Much party heat there was, and some violent personal abuse. I kept out of the dispute, and wrote only one little paper on the occasion.

At last the first Congress met and General Washington was chosen president. Congress was employed in amending some of the faults supposed to be in the Constitution with some amendments. The first session was conducted with, I think, a greater degree of temper, prudence and unanimity than could well have been expected, and our future prospects seem very favourable. I am grown old, and have now little influence with Congress. The services of a feeble old man rendered inactive by the infirmities of age are scarcely worth offering.

Nothing is certain except death and taxes

My friend Le Veillard was apprehensive about our president's being perpetual. Neither he nor we have any such intention: What danger there may be of such an event, we are all aware of, and shall take care effectually to prevent it. The choice is made every four years, and the appointments will be small; thus we may change our president if we don't like his conduct, and he will have less inducement to struggle for a new election. As to the two chambers, I am of the opinion that one alone would be better, as we have in Pennsylvania, but nothing in human affairs and schemes is perfect, and perhaps that is the case of our opinions.

And thus, our new Constitution is now established, and has an appearance that promises permanency; but in this world nothing can be said to be certain except death and taxes.

I BEGIN TO FEEL MYSELF A FREE MAN

Having now finish'd my term as president of Pennsylvania, and promising myself to engage no more in public business, I begin to feel myself a free man. I amuse myself in reading or writing, or in conversation with friends, joking, laughing, and telling merry stories, as if I were a young man about fifty. My children and grand children, the Baches, are all well, living in my house. And we have lately the addition of a little good-natured girl, whom I begin to love as well as the rest. She had the smallpox very favourably by inoculation and is perfectly recover'd.

I hope to enjoy during the small remains of life that are left to me the leisure I have so long wish'd for. I have begun already to employ it in compleating my personal history. It seems a little like living one's life over again. If my present state of health continues for a few months, I resolve to compleat it by dictating to my grandson.

CONSTANT AND GRIEVOUS PAIN

I have a long time been afflicted with almost constant and grievous pain for which I have been obliged to have recourse to opium, which indeed has afforded me some ease from time to time but then it has taken away my appetite and so impeded my digestion that I am become totally emaciated and little remains of me but a skeleton covered with a skin. I am grown very weak, so that I cannot well sit up to write. In this situation I have not been able to continue my memoirs, and my grandson Benny often takes dictation from me.

The relief of free Negroes
and the abolition of slavery

In the final years of my life, I engaged in a cause of the utmost importance to the honour of the United States of America, and to the happiness and natural rights of mankind. As president of the Philadelphia Society for the Abolition of Slavery, I sent to gentlemen of character and influence, disposed to aid us in exposing the inequity of the slave trade, such as Pierre-Samuel du Pont and Lafayette, copies of the constitution of our society and of the laws that are now in force in Pennsylvania for abolishing Negro slavery. The final purposes of our society are the suppression of the slave trade and the gradual abolition of slavery itself. In the mean time we consider it as our indispensable duty to endeavour by all means in our power to alleviate the miseries of those unhappy people who are doomed to taste of the bitter cup of perpetual servitude.

I found by an old pamphlet in my possession that George Keith, nearly 100 years ago, wrote a paper against the practice of slavery, wherein a strict charge was given to Friends that they should set their Negroes at liberty after some reasonable time of service, &c. &c. About the year 1728 or 29 I printed a book for Ralph Sandyford against keeping Negroes in slavery, two editions of which he distributed gratis; and about the year 1736 I printed another book on the same subject for Benjamin Lay, who distributed the books chiefly among them. By these instances it appears that the seed was sown in the good ground, and 'tis springtime at last, though so late, and is some confirmation of Lord Bacon's observation that *a good motion never dies*, and may encourage us in making such, though hopeless of their taking an immediate effect.

This present age has been distinguished by a remarkable revolution. The human mind has felt its influence. Mankind begin at last to consider themselves as members of one family. The groans of our distressed and injured brethren from the slaves of Africa have at length reached the ears of the citizens of the United States. Most of our legislatures have already abolished the slave trade, and a provision has been made in the general Constitution, which we trust will effect its abolition completely. Great Britain has felt the same spirit of humanity and justice, and her public papers have been filled with the most pathetic and nervous petitions to her Parliament to abolish this iniquitous traffic. But nothing effectual will be done until France concurs in it. We indulge ourselves in the hope that a king, who has so recently distinguished himself by banishing from his dominion religious oppression, will not permit the increase of this most grievous of all civil ones nor continue to pursue this disgraceful commerce in the human species.

THE RELIGION OF JESUS:
THE BEST THE WORLD EVER SAW

Tho' the people of Massachusetts had not in their new constitution kept quite clear of religious tests, we must hope for greater degrees of perfection when their constitution some years hence shall be revised. If Christian preachers had continued to teach as Christ and his apostles did, without salaries, and as the Quakers now do, I imagine tests would never have existed. For I think they were invented not so much to secure religion itself, as the emoluments of it. When a religion is good, I conceive that it will support itself; and when it cannot support itself, and God does not take care to support it, so that its professors are oblig'd to call for the help of the civil power, 'tis a sign, I apprehend, of its being a bad one.

I OPPOSED THE CLAUSE OF RELIGIOUS DECLARATION

I thought the clause in our Pennsylvania constitution, which requires the members of assembly to declare their belief in divine inspiration, had better have been omitted. God governs in the affairs of men, but I often thought of several things in the Old Testament impossible to be given by divine inspiration, such as the approbation ascrib'd by the angel of the Lord, of that abominably wicked and detestable action of Jael the wife of Heber the Kenite.* If the rest of the Book were like that, I should rather suppose it given by inspiration from another quarter, and renounce the whole. I opposed the clause but was overpower'd by numbers, and fearing what might in future times be grafted on it, I prevailed to have the additional clause that no further or more extended profession of faith should ever be exacted. It is proper that the United States consists of thirteen distinct and separate sovereignties, each govern'd by its own laws, in which no one religious sect is established as predominant, but there is a general toleration of all; and should anything be enacted by one of them in favour of a particular sect, it would have no operation in the others.

The Rev. Dr. Ezra Stiles desired to know something of my religion. I endeavoured in a few words to gratify his curiosity, tho' I confided in him not to expose me to criticism and censure by publishing any part of this communication with him. I have ever let others enjoy their religious sentiments without reflecting on them for those beliefs that appeared to me insupportable and even absurd. All sects here,

---

* See Judges chapter 4, especially verses 18–24.

and we have a great variety, have experienced my good will in assisting them with subscriptions for building their new places of worship, and as I have never opposed any of their doctrines I hope to go out of the world in peace with them all.

Nevertheless, here is my creed: I believe in one God, creator of the universe. That he governs it by his providence. That he ought to be worshipped. That the most acceptable service we can render to him is doing good to his other children. That the soul of man is immortal, and will be treated with justice in another life respecting its conduct in this. These I take to be the fundamental principles of all sound religion, and I regard them in whatever sect I meet with them. As to Jesus of Nazareth, my opinion of whom Dr. Stiles particularly desired, I think the system of morals and his religion, as he left them to us, the best the world ever saw, or is likely to see; but I apprehend it has received various corrupting changes, and I have with most of the present dissenters in England, some doubts as to his divinity: tho' it is a question I do not dogmatize upon, having never studied it, and think it needless to busy myself with it now, when I expect soon an opportunity of knowing the truth with less trouble. I see no harm however in its being believed, if that belief has the good consequence, as probably it has, of making his doctrines more respected and better observed, especially as I do not perceive that the Supreme Being takes it amiss, by distinguishing the believers in his government of the world with any particular marks of his displeasure. I shall only add respecting myself that, having experienced the goodness of that Being, in conducting me prosperously thro' a long life, I have no doubt of its continuance in the nest, tho' without the smallest conceit of meriting such goodness; and with regard to future blessings, I cannot help imagining that multitudes of the zealously orthodox of different sects who at the last day may flock together in hopes of seeing the damn'd will be disappointed and oblig'd to rest content with their own salvation.

My sentiments in this regard can be seen in an old letter, copied below, that I wrote in answer to one from a zealous religionist whom I had relieved in a paralytic case by electricity, and who, being afraid I should grow proud upon it, sent me his serious, tho' rather impertinent, cautions.

I MEAN REAL GOOD WORKS, NOT HOLIDAY-KEEPING AND MAKING LONG PRAYERS

To Joseph Huey

Philada. June 6, 1753

Sir,

I received your kind letter of the 2d instant and am glad to hear that you increase in strength; I hope you will continue mending till you recover your former health and firmness. Let me know whether you still use the cold bath, and what effect it has.

As to the kindness you mention, I wish it could have been of more service to you. The only thanks I should desire is that you would always be equally ready to serve any other person that may need your assistance, and so let good offices go around, for mankind are all of a family.

For my own part, when I am employed in serving others, I do not look upon myself as conferring favours, but as paying debts. In my travels and since my settlement I have received many kindnesses from men, to whom I shall never have any opportunity of making the least return, and numberless mercies from God, who is infinitely above being benefited by our services. These kindnesses from men I can therefore only return on their fellow-men; and I can only show my gratitude for those mercies from God by a readiness to help his other children and my brethren. I do not think that thanks and compliments, tho' repeated weekly, can discharge our real obligations to each other, and much less those to our Creator.

You will see in this, my notion of good works, that I am far from expecting (as you suppose) that I shall merit heaven by them. By heaven we understand a state of happiness, infinite in degree, and eternal in duration: I can do nothing to deserve such reward. He that for giving a draught of water to a thirsty person should expect to be paid with a good plantation would be modest in his demands, compar'd with those who think they deserve heaven for the little good they do on earth. Even the mix'd imperfect pleasures we enjoy in this world are rather from God's goodness than our merit; how much more such happiness of heaven! For my own part, I have not the vanity to think I deserve it, the folly to expect it, nor the ambition to desire it; but content myself in submitting to the will and disposal of that God who made me, who has hitherto pre-serv'd and bless'd me, and in whose fatherly goodness I may well confide. He will never make me miserable, and even the afflictions I may at any time suffer shall tend to my benefit.

Doubtlessly, faith has its use in the world; I do not desire to see it diminished, nor would I endeavour to lessen it in any man. But I wish it were more productive of good works than I have gener-ally seen it: I mean real good works, works of kindness, charity, mercy, and public spirit; not holiday-keeping, sermon-reading or hearing, performing church ceremonies, or making long prayers, fill'd with flatteries and compliments, despis'd even by wise men, and much less capable of pleasing the Deity. The worship of God is a duty, the hearing and reading of sermons may be useful; but if men rest in hearing and praying, as too many do, it is as if a tree should value itself on being water'd and putting forth leaves, tho' it never produc'd any fruit.

Jesus tho't much less of these outward appearances and profes-sions than many of his modern disciples. He prefer'd the doers of the word to the mere hearers; the son that seemingly refus'd to obey his father and yet perform'd his commands, to him that profess'd his readiness but neglected the works; the heretical but charitable Samaritan, to the uncharitable tho' orthodox priest and sanctified Levite; and those who gave food to the hungry, drink to the thirsty, raiment to the naked, entertainment to the stranger, and relief to the sick, &c. tho' they never heard of his name, he declares shall in the last day be accepted, when those who cry "Lord, Lord," who value themselves on their faith and great miracles, but have neglected good works, shall be rejected. He profess'd that he came not to call the righteous but sinners to repentance, which imply'd his modest opinion that there were some in his time so good that they need not hear even him for improvement; but nowadays we have scarce a little parson that does not think it the duty of every man within his reach to sit under his petty ministrations and that whoever omits them offends God. I wish to such more humility, and to you health and happiness, being your friend and servant

B Franklin

Old man's wish

I like the concluding sentiment in the old song call'd the *Old Man's Wish*, wherein after wishing for a warm house in a country town, an easy horse, some good old authors, ingenious and cheerful companions, a pudding on Sundays with stout ale and a bottle of burgundy, &c. &c. in separate stanzas, each ended with this burden:

> May I govern my passions with an absolute sway
> Grow wise and better as my strength wears away
> Without gout, or stone, by a gentle decay

he adds,

> With a courage undaunted may I face my last day;
> And when I am gone, may the better sort say,
> In the morning when sober, in the evening when mellow,
> He's gone, and has not left behind him his fellow;
> For he govern'd his passions, &c

I have sung that wishing song a thousand times when I was young, and now find at fourscore that the three contraries have befallen me: being subject to the gout, and the stone, and not being the master of all my passions, I am like the proud girl in my country who wish'd and resolv'd not to marry a parson, nor a Presbyterian, nor an Irishman, and at length found herself married to an Irish Presbyterian parson. You see I have some reason to wish that in a future state I may not only be as well as I was, but a little better. And I hope it: For *I trust in God.* And I observe that there is great frugality as well as wisdom in his works, since he has been evidently sparing both of labour and materials; for by the various wonderful inventions of propagation he has provided for the continual peopling his world with plants and animals, without being at the trouble of repeated new creations. I say that when I see nothing annihilated, and not even a drop of water wasted, I cannot suspect the annihilation of souls, or believe that he will suffer the daily waste of millions of minds ready made that now exist, and put himself to the continual trouble of making new ones. Thus finding myself in the world, I believe I shall in some shape or another always exist: And with all the inconveniences human life is liable to, I shall not object to a new edition of mine; hoping however that the errata of the last may be corrected.

When I was only 23 years of age, I wrote the following epitaph, and gave it to many of my friends:

The Body of

B Franklin,

Printer;

Like the cover of an old book, Its contents torn out,

And stript of its lettering and gilding,

Lies here, food for worms,

But the work shall not be wholly lost:

For it will, as he believ'd, appear once more,

In a new & more perfect edition,

Corrected and amended

By the author.

In 1784, in my 78TH year, I wrote my friends the following entitled "B. F.'s Adieu!"

If life's compared to a feast,

Near fourscore years I've been a guest:

I've been regaled with the best,

And feel quite satisfied.

'Tis time that I retire to rest;

Land lord, I thank ye! Friends, good night.

A man is not completely born until he be dead:

Why then should we grieve?

Thinking of old age and the passing of so many friends and dear valuable relations, I received a letter from my step-niece Elizabeth Partridge telling me that a poor friend was gone, and requesting a copy of a letter I wrote years ago in which I aim'd at consoling her father's friends upon his passing. Mr. Mather Byles once wrote me that many copies had been taken of it from a Boston gazette. Herein is the letter.

To Elizabeth Hubbart

Philadelphia, February 22, 1756

Dear Child,

I condole with you, we have lost a most dear and valuable relation,* but it is the will of God and nature that these mortal bodies
be laid aside, when the soul is to enter into real life; 'tis rather an
embryo state, a preparation for living; a man is not completely
born until he be dead: Why then should we grieve that a new child
is born among the immortals? A new member added to their
happy society? We are spirits. That bodies should be lent us, while
they can afford us pleasure, assist us in acquiring knowledge, or
doing good to our fellow creatures, is a kind and benevolent act of
God. When they become unfit for these purposes and afford us
pain instead of pleasure—instead of an aid, become an encum-
brance and answer none of the intentions for which they were
given—it is equally kind and benevolent that a way is provided by
which we may get rid of them. Death is that way. We ourselves
prudently choose a partial death. In some cases a mangled painful
limb, which cannot be restored, we willingly cut off. He who
plucks out a tooth, parts with it freely since the pain goes with it,
and he that quits the whole body, parts at once with all the pains
and possibilities of pains and diseases it was liable to, or capable
of making him suffer.

Our friend, and we, are invited abroad on a party of pleasure—
that is to last forever. His chair was first ready and he is gone before

---

*John Franklin, brother of Benjamin Franklin. This letter was published
in *The Massachusetts Magazine* (1789), 100. It was also reprinted on
April 17, 1790, the evening of Franklin's death, in *The Federal Gazette
and Philadelphia Daily Advertiser*. PBF 6:407n.

us. We could not all conveniently start together, but why should you and I be grieved at this, since we are soon to follow, and we know where to find him. Adieu.

B. F.

I FEEL A GROWING CURIOSITY TO BE ACQUAINTED WITH SOME OTHER LIFE

The years roll round and the last will come; when I would rather have it said, *He lived usefully*, than, *He died rich*.

I still have enjoyment in the company of my friends; and, being easy in my circumstances, have many reasons to like living. But the course of nature must soon put a period to my present mode of existence: This I shall submit to with less regret, as, having seen during a long life a good deal of this world, I feel a growing curiosity to be acquainted with some other, and can cheerfully with filial confidence resign my spirit to the conduct of that great and good parent of mankind, who created it, and who has so graciously protected and prospered me from my birth to the present hour.

Appendix

The Last Will and Testament of Benjamin Franklin

(17TH *of July, 1788)*

EDITOR'S NOTE: *I have included Franklin's Last Will and Testament because it is also autobiographical. Highlights include his negative feelings about his son William; his gift of the King's portrait with 408 diamonds to his daughter, Sarah Bache; his gift of the crab tree walking stick to General Washington; and the creation of a fund in Boston to finance young artisans.*

I, Benjamin Franklin, of Philadelphia, printer, late Minister Plenipotentiary from the United States of America to the Court of France, now President of the State of Pennsylvania, do make and declare my last will and testament as follows:

To my son, William Franklin, late Governor of the Jerseys, I give and devise all the lands I hold or have a right to, in the province of Nova Scotia, to hold to him, his heirs, and assigns forever. I also give to him all my books and papers, which he has in his possession, and all debts standing against him on my account books, willing that no payment for, nor restitution of, the same be required of him, by my executors. The part he acted against me in the late war, which is of public notoriety, will account for my leaving him no more of an estate he endeavoured to deprive me of.

Having since my return from France demolished the three houses in Market Street, between Third and Fourth Streets, fronting my dwelling-house, and erected two new and larger ones on the ground, and having also erected another house on the lot which formerly was the passage to my dwelling, and also a printing-office between my dwelling and the front houses; now I do give and devise my said dwelling-house, wherein I now live, my said three new houses, my printing-office and the lots of ground thereto belonging; also my small lot and house in Sixth Street, which I bought of the widow Henmarsh; also my pasture-ground which I have in Hickory Lane, with the buildings thereon; also my house and lot on the North side of Market Street, now occupied by Mary Jacobs, together with two houses and lots behind the same, and fronting on Pewter-Platter Alley; also my lot of ground in Arch Street, opposite the church-burying ground, with the buildings thereon erected; also all my silver plate, pictures, and household goods, of every kind, now in my said dwelling-place, to my daughter, Sarah Bache, and to her husband, Richard Bache, to hold to them for and during their natural lives, and the life of the longest liver of them, and from and after the decease of the survivor of them, I do give, devise, and bequeath to all children already born, or to be born of my said daughter, and to their heirs and assigns forever, as tenants in common, and not as joint tenants.

And, if any or either of them shall happen to die under age, and without issue, the part and share of him, her, or them, so dying, shall go to and be equally divided among the survivors or survivor of them. But my intention is that, if any or either of them should happen to die under age, leaving issue, such issue shall inherit the part and share that would have passed to his, her, or their parent, had he, she, or they been living.

And, as some of my said devisees may, at the death of the survivor of their father or mother, be of age, and others of them under age, so as that all of them may not be of capacity to make division, I in that case request and authorize the judges of the Supreme Court of Judicature of Pennsylvania for the time being, or any three of them, not personally interested, to appoint by writing, under their hands and seals, three honest, intelligent, impartial men to make the said division, and to assign and allot to each of my devisees their respective share, which division, so made and committed to writing under the hands and seals of the said three men, or any two of them, and confirmed by the said judges, I do hereby declare shall be binding on, and conclusive between the said devisees.

All the lands near the Ohio, and the lots near the centre of Philadelphia, which I lately purchased of the State, I give to my son-in-law, Richard Bache, his heirs and assigns forever; I also give him the bond I have against him, of two thousand and one hundred and seventy-two pounds, five shillings, together with the interest that shall or may accrue thereon, and direct the same to be delivered up to him by my executors, canceled, requesting that, in consideration thereof, he would immediately after my decease manumit and set free his Negro man Bob. I leave to him, also, the money due to me from the State of Virginia for types. I also give to him the bond of William Goddard and his sister, and the counter bond of the late Robert Grace, and the bond and judgment of Francis Childs, if not recovered before my decease, or any other bonds, except the bond due from — —Killian, of Delaware State, which I give to my grandson, Benjamin Franklin Bache. I also discharge him, my said son-in-law, from all claim and rent of moneys due to me, on book account or otherwise. I also give him all my musical instruments.

The king of France's picture, set with four hundred and eight diamonds, I give to my daughter, Sarah Bache; requesting, however, that she would not form any of those diamonds into ornaments either for herself or daughters, and thereby introduce or countenance the expensive, vain, and useless fashion of wearing jewels in this country; and those immediately connected with the picture may be preserved with the same.

I give and devise to my dear sister, Jane Mecom, a house and lot I have in Unity Street, Boston, now or late under the care of Mr. Jonathan Williams, to her and to her heirs and assigns for ever. I also give her the yearly sum of fifty pounds sterling, during life, to commence at my death, and to be paid to her annually out of the interests or dividends arising on twelve shares which I have since my arrival at Philadelphia purchased in the Bank of North America, and, at her decease, I give the said twelve shares in the bank to my daughter, Sarah Bache, and her husband, Richard Bache. But it is my express will and desire that, after the payment of the above fifty pounds sterling annually to my said sister, my said daughter be allowed to apply the residue of the interest or dividends on those shares to her sole and separate use, during the life of my said sister, and afterwards the whole of the interest or dividends thereof as her private pocket money.

I give the right I have to take up to three thousand acres of land in the State of Georgia, granted to me by the government of that State, to my grandson, William Temple Franklin, his heirs and assigns forever. I also give to my grandson, William Temple Franklin, the bond and judgment I have against him of four thousand pounds sterling, my right to the same to cease upon the day of his marriage; and if he dies unmarried, my will is, that the same be recovered and divided among my other grandchildren, the children of my daughter, Sarah Bache, in such manner and form as I have herein before given to them the other parts of my estate.

The philosophical instruments I have in Philadelphia I give to my ingenious friend, Francis Hopkinson.

To the children, grandchildren, and great-grandchildren of my brother, Samuel Franklin, that may be living at the time of my decease, I give fifty pounds sterling, to be equally divided among them. To the children, grandchildren, and great-grandchildren of my sister, Anne Harris, that may be living at the time of my decease, I give fifty pounds sterling to be equally divided among them. To the children, grandchildren, and great-grandchildren of my brother James Franklin, that may be living at the time of my decease, I give fifty pounds sterling to be equally divided among them. To the children, grandchildren, and great-grandchildren of my sister, Sarah Davenport, that may be living at the time of my decease, I give fifty pounds sterling to be equally divided among them. To the children, grandchildren, and great-grandchildren of my sister, Lydia Scott, that may be living at the time of my decease, I give fifty pounds sterling to be equally divided among them. To the children, grandchildren, and great-grandchildren of my sister, Jane Mecom, that may be living at the time of my decease, I give fifty pounds sterling to be equally divided among them.

I give to my grandson, Benjamin Franklin Bache, all the types and printing materials, which I now have in Philadelphia, with the complete letter foundry, which, in the whole, I suppose to be worth near one thousand pounds; but if he should die under age, then I do order the same to be sold by my executors, the survivors or survivor of them, and the moneys be equally divided among all the rest of my said daughter's children, or their representatives, each one on coming of age to take his or her share, and the children of such of them as may die under age to represent and to take the share and proportion of the parent so dying, each one to receive his or her part of such share as they come of age.

With regard to my books, those I had in France and those I left in Philadelphia, being now assembled together here, and a catalogue made of them, it is my intention to dispose of them as follows: My "History of the Academy of Sciences," in sixty or seventy volumes quarto, I give to the Philosophical Society of Philadelphia, of which I have the honour to be President. My collection in folio of "Les Arts et les Metiers," I give to the American Philosophical Society, established in New England, of which I am a member. My quarto edition of the same, "Arts et Metiers," I give to the Library Company of Philadelphia. Such and so many of my books as I shall mark on my said catalogue with the name of my grandson, Benjamin Franklin Bache, I do hereby give to him; and such and so many of my books as I shall mark on the said catalogue with the name of my grandson, William Bache, I do hereby give to him; and such as shall be marked with the name of Jonathan Williams, I hereby give to my cousin of that name. The residue and remainder of all my books, manuscripts, and papers, I do give to my grandson, William Temple Franklin. My share in the Library Company of Philadelphia, I give to my grandson, Benjamin Franklin Bache, confiding that he will permit his brothers and sisters to share in the use of it.

I was born in Boston, New England, and owe my first instructions in literature to the free grammar schools established there. I therefore give one hundred pounds sterling to my executors, to be by them, the survivors or survivor of them, paid over to the managers or directors of the free schools in my native town of Boston, to be by them, or by those persons or person, who shall have the superintendence and management of the said schools, put out to interest, and so continued at interest forever, which interest annually shall be laid out in silver medals, and given as honorary rewards annually by the directors of the said free schools belonging to the said town, in such manner as to the discretion of the selectmen of the said town shall seem meet.

Out of the salary that may remain due to me as President of the State, I do give the sum of two thousand pounds sterling to my executors, to be by them, the survivors or survivor of them, paid over to such person or persons as the legislature of this State by an act of Assembly shall appoint to receive the same in trust, to be employed for making the river Schuylkill navigable.

And what money of mine shall, at the time of my decease, remain in the hands of my bankers, Messrs. Ferdinand Grand and Son, at Paris, or Messrs. Smith, Wright, and Gray, of London, I will that, after my debts are paid and deducted, with the money legacies of this my will, the same be divided into four equal parts, two of which I give to my dear daughter, Sarah Bache, one to her son Benjamin, and one to my grandson, William Temple Franklin.

During the number of years I was in business as a stationer, printer, and postmaster, a great many small sums became due for books, advertisements, postage of letters, and other matters, which were not collected when, in 1757, I was sent by the Assembly to England as their agent, and by subsequent appointments continued there till 1775, when on my return, I was immediately engaged in the affairs of Congress, and sent to France in 1776, where I remained nine years, not returning till 1785, and the said debts, not being demanded in such a length of time, are become in a manner obsolete, yet are nevertheless justly due. These, as they are stated in my great folio ledger E, I bequeath to the contributors to the Pennsylvania Hospital, hoping that those debtors, and the descendants of such as are deceased, who now, as I find, make some difficulty of satisfying such antiquated demands as just debts, may, however, be induced to pay or give them as charity to that excellent institution. I am sensible that much must inevitably be lost, but I hope something considerable may be recovered. It is possible, too, that some of the parties charged may have existing old, unsettled accounts against me; in which case the managers of the said hospital will allow and deduct the amount, or pay the balance if they find it against me.

My debts and legacies being all satisfied and paid, the rest and residue of all my estate, real and personal, not herein expressly disposed of, I do give and bequeath to my son and daughter, Richard and Sarah Bache.

I request my friends, Henry Hill, Esquire; John Jay, Esquire; Francis Hopkinson, Esquire; and Mr. Edward Duffield, of Benfield, in Philadelphia County, to be the executors of this my last will and testament; and I hereby nominate and appoint them for that purpose.

I would have my body buried with as little expense or ceremony as may be. I revoke all former wills by me made, declaring this only to be my last.

In witness thereof, I have hereunto set my hand and seal, this seventeenth day of July, in the year of our Lord, one thousand seven hundred and eighty-eight.

B Franklin

Signed, sealed, published, and declared by the above named Benjamin Franklin, for and as his last will and testament, in the presence of us.

Abraham Shoemaker, John Jones, George Moore

Codicil

I, Benjamin Franklin, in the foregoing or annexed last will and testament named, having further considered the same, do think proper to make and publish the following codicil or addition thereto.

It having long been a fixed political opinion of mine, that in a democratic state there ought to be no offices of profit, for the reasons I had given in an article of my drawing in our constitution, it was my intention when I accepted the office of President, to devote the appointed salary to some public uses. Accordingly, I had already, before I made my will in July last, given large sums of it to colleges, schools, building of churches, &c.; and in that will I bequeathed two thousand pounds more to the State for the purpose of making the Schuylkill navigable. But understanding that such a sum will do little toward such a work, and that the project is not likely to be undertaken for many years to come, and having entertained another idea, that I hope may be more extensively useful, I do hereby revoke and annul that bequest, and direct that the certificates I have for what remains due to me of that salary be sold, towards raising the sum of two thousand pounds sterling, to be disposed of as I am now about to order.

It has been an opinion, that he who receives an estate from his ancestors is under some kind of obligation to transmit the same to their posterity. This obligation does not lie on me, who never inherited a shilling from any ancestor or relation. I shall, however, if it is not diminished by some accident before my death, leave a considerable estate among my descendants and relations. The above observation is made as merely as some apology to my family for making bequests that do not appear to have any immediate relation to their advantage.

I was born in Boston, New England, and owe my first instructions in literature to the free grammar schools established there. I have, therefore, already considered these schools in my will. But I am also under obligations to the State of Massachusetts for having, unasked, appointed me formerly their agent in England, with a handsome salary, which continued some years; and although I accidentally lost in their service, by transmitting Governor Hutchinson's letters, much more that the amount of what they gave me, I do not think that ought in the least to diminish my gratitude.

I have considered that, among artisans, good apprentices are most likely to make good citizens, and, having myself been bred to a manual art, printing, in my native town, and afterwards assisted to set up my business in Philadelphia by kind loans of money from two friends there, which was the foundation of my fortune, and all the utility in life that may be ascribed to me, I wish to be useful even after my death, if possible, in forming and advancing other young men, that may be serviceable to their country in both these towns. To this end, I devote two thousand pounds sterling, of which I give one thousand thereof to the inhabitants of the town of Boston, in Massachusetts, and the other thousand to the inhabitants of the city of Philadelphia, in trust, to and for the uses, intents, and purposes herein after mentioned and declared.

The said sum of one thousand pounds sterling, if accepted by the inhabitants of the town of Boston, shall be managed under the direction of the selectmen, united with the ministers of the oldest Episcopalians, Congregational, and Presbyterian churches in that town, who are to let out the sum upon interest, at five per cent, per annum, to such young married artificers, under the age of twenty-five years, as have served an apprenticeship in the said town, and faithfully fulfilled the duties required in their indentures, so as to obtain a good moral character from at least two respectable citizens, who are willing to become their sureties, in a bond with the applicants, for the repayment of the moneys so lent, with interest, according to the terms hereinafter prescribed; all which bonds are to be taken for Spanish milled dollars, or the value thereof in current gold coin; and the managers shall keep a bound book or books, wherein shall be entered the names of those who shall apply for and receive the benefits of this institution, and of their sureties, together with the sums lent, the dates, and other necessary and proper records respecting the business and concerns of this institution. And as these loans are intended to assist young married artificers in setting up their businesses, they are to be proportioned by the discretion of the managers, so as not to exceed sixty pounds sterling to one person, nor to be less than fifteen pounds; and if the number of appliers so entitled should be so large as that the sum will not suffice to afford to each as much as might otherwise not be improper, the proportion to each shall be diminished so as to afford to every one some assistance. These aids may, therefore, be small at first, but, as the capital increases by the accumulated interest, they will be more ample. And in order to serve as many as possible in their turn, as well as to make the repayment of the principal borrowed more easy, each borrower shall be obliged to pay, with the yearly interest, one tenth part of the principal; and interest, so paid in, shall be again let out to fresh borrowers.

And, as it is presumed that there will always be found in Boston virtuous and benevolent citizens, willing to bestow a part of their time in doing good to the rising generation, by superintending and managing this institution gratis, it is hoped that no part of the money will at any time be dead, or be diverted to other purposes, but be continually augmenting by the interest; in which case there may, in time, be more that the occasions in Boston shall require, and then some may be spared to the neighbouring or other towns in the said State of Massachusetts, who may desire to have it; such towns engaging to pay punctually the interest and the portions of the principal, annually, to the inhabitants of the town of Boston.

If this plan is executed, and succeeds as projected without interruption for one hundred years, the sum will then be one hundred and thirty-one thousand pounds; of which I would have the managers of the donation to the town of Boston then lay out, at their discretion, one hundred thousand pounds in public works, which may be judged of most general utility to the inhabitants, such as fortifications, bridges, aqueducts, public buildings, baths, pavements, or whatever may make living in the town more convenient to its people, and render it more agreeable to strangers resorting thither for health or a temporary residence. The remaining thirty-one thousand pounds I would have continued to be let out on interest, in the manner above directed, for another hundred years, as I hope it will have been found that the institution has had a good effect on the conduct of youth, and been of service to many worthy characters and useful citizens. At the end of this second term, if no unfortunate accident has prevented the operation, the sum will be four millions and sixty one thousand pounds sterling, of which I leave one million sixty one thousand pounds to the disposition of the inhabitants of the town of Boston, and three millions to the disposition of the government of the state, not presuming to carry my views further.

All the directions herein given, respecting the disposition and management of the donation to the inhabitants of Boston, I would have observed respecting that to the inhabitants of Philadelphia, only, as Philadelphia is incorporated, I request the corporation of that city to undertake the management agreeably to the said directions; and I do hereby vest them with full and ample powers for that purpose. And, having considered that the covering a ground plot with buildings and pavements, which carry off most of the rain and prevent its soaking into the Earth and renewing and purifying the Springs, whence the water of wells must gradually grow worse, and in time be unfit for use, as I find has happened in all old cities, I recommend that at the end of the first hundred years, if not done before, the corporation of the city employ a part of the hundred thousand pounds in bringing, by pipes, the water of Wissahickon Creek into the town, so as to supply the inhabitants, which I apprehend may be done without great difficulty, the level of the creek being much above that of the city, and may be made higher by a dam. I also recommend making the Schuylkill completely navigable. At the end of the second hundred years, I would have the disposition of the four million and sixty one thousand pounds divided between the inhabitants of the city of Philadelphia and the government of Pennsylvania, in the same manner as herein directed with respect to that of the inhabitants of Boston and the government of Massachusetts.

It is my desire that this institution should take place and begin to operate within one year after my decease, for which purpose due notice should be publicly given previous to the expiration of that year, that those for whose benefit this establishment is intended may make their respective applications. And I hereby direct my executors, the survivors or survivor of them, within six months after my decease, to pay over the sum of two thousand pounds sterling to such persons as shall be duly appointed by the Selectmen of Boston and the corporation of Philadelphia, to receive and take charge of their respective sums, of one thousand pounds each, for the purposes aforesaid.

Considering the accidents to which all human affairs and projects are subject in such a length of time, I have, perhaps, too much flattered myself with a vain fancy that these dispositions, if carried into execution, will be continued without interruption and have the effects proposed. I hope, however, that if the inhabitants of the two cities should not think fit to undertake the execution, they will, at least, accept the offer of these donations as a mark of my good will, a token of my gratitude, and a testimony of my earnest desire to be useful to them after my departure.

I wish, indeed, that they may both undertake to endeavour the execution of the project, because I think that, though unforeseen difficulties may arise, expedients will be found to remove them, and the scheme be found practicable. If one of them accepts the money, with the conditions, and the other refuses, my will then is, that both Sums be given to the inhabitants of the city accepting the whole, to be applied to the same purposes, and under the same regulations directed for the separate parts; and, if both refuse, the money of course remains in the mass of my Estate, and is to be disposed of therewith according to my will made the Seventeenth day of July, 1788.

I wish to be buried by the side of my wife, if it may be, and that a marble stone, to be made by Chambers, six feet long, four feet wide, plain, with only a small moulding round the upper edge, and this inscription:

Benjamin And Deborah Franklin 178–

to be placed over us both. My fine crab-tree walking stick, with a gold head curiously wrought in the form of the cap of liberty, I give to my friend, and the friend of mankind, General Washington. If it were a

Sceptre, he has merited it, and would become it. It was a present to me from that excellent woman, Madame de Forbach, the dowager Duchess of Deux-Ponts, connected with some verses which should go with it. I give my gold watch to my son-in-law Richard Bache, and also the gold watch chain of the Thirteen United States, which I have not yet worn. My timepiece, that stands in my library, I give to my grandson, William Temple Franklin. I give him also my Chinese gong. To my dear old friend, Mrs. Mary Hewson, I give one of my silver tankards, marked for her use, during her life, and after her decease I give it to her daughter Eliza. I give to her son, William Hewson, who is my godson, my new quarto Bible, and also the botanic description of the plants in the Emperor's garden at Vienna, in folio, with coloured cuts.

And to her son, Thomas Hewson, I give a set of "Spectators, Tattlers, and Guardians" handsomely bound.

There is an error in my will, where the bond of William Temple Franklin is mentioned as being four thousand pounds sterling, whereas it is but for three thousand five hundred pounds.

I give to my executors, to be divided equally among those that act, the sum of sixty pounds sterling, as some compensation for their trouble in the execution of my will; and I request my friend, Mr. Duffield, to accept moreover my French wayweiser, a piece of clockwork in Brass, to be fixed to the wheel of any carriage; and that my friend, Mr. Hill, may also accept my silver cream pot, formerly given to me by the good Doctor Fothergill, with the motto, Keep bright the Chain. My reflecting telescope, made by Short, which was formerly Mr. Canton's, I give to my friend, Mr. David Rittenhouse, for the use of his observatory.

My picture, drawn by Martin, in 1767, I give to the Supreme Executive Council of Pennsylvania, if they shall be pleased to do me the honour of accepting it and placing it in their chamber. Since my will was made I have bought some more city lots, near the centre part of the estate of Joseph Dean. I would have them go with the other lots, disposed of in my will, and I do give the same to my son-in-law, Richard Bache, to his heirs and assigns forever.

In addition to the annuity left to my sister in my will, of fifty pounds sterling during her life, I now add thereto ten pounds sterling more, in order to make the sum sixty pounds. I give twenty guineas to my good friend and physician, Dr. John Jones.

With regard to the separate bequests made to my daughter Sarah in my will, my intention is, that the same shall be for her sole and separate use, notwithstanding her coverture, or whether she be covert or sole; and I do give my executors so much right and power therein as may be necessary to render my intention effectual in that respect only. This provision for my daughter is not made out of any disrespect I have for her husband.

And lastly, it is my desire that this, my present codicil, be annexed to, and considered as part of, my last will and testament to all intents and purposes.

In witness whereof, I have hereunto set my hand and Seal this twenty-third day of June, Anno Domini one thousand Seven hundred and eighty nine.

B FRANKLIN

Signed, sealed, published, and declared by the above named Benjamin Franklin to be a codicil to his last will and testament, in the presence of us.

FRANCIS BAILEY, THOMAS LANG, ABRAHAM SHOEMAKER

Afterword

"Let all men know thee, but let no man know thee thoroughly."
—Poor Richard

Compiling and editing Franklin's diaries, letters and other papers has provided insight into some of the unresolved controversies that have developed over Franklin. Did Franklin neglect his wife Deborah? Was he a philanderer? Why didn't he forgive his son William after the war? Was Franklin a religious heretic? Politically, was Franklin a libertarian, a conservative, or a radical democrat?

Franklin and his marriage

First, let me discuss his relationship with his wife Deborah and other women. Franklin has been accused of neglecting and abandoning his wife from 1757, the time of his first journey to London as colonial agent, until Deborah's death in 1775. They were separated for all but two of those years, and from all appearances their marriage evolved in a way that satisfied neither of them. Prior to their separation, they had been devoted to each other, even though their interests differed (hers were domestic, his civic and philosophical). Nevertheless, "she prov'd a good and faithful helpmate, assisted me by attending the shop; we throve together, and have ever mutual endeavour'd to make each other happy," Benjamin wrote in his memoirs—after she died, it should be noted. However, when Franklin was appointed agent to London, Debbie was adamant in her refusal to cross the ocean. Franklin mentioned this fact several times, noting that not even friends could change her mind, no matter how hard they tried. William Strahan, his printer friend in London, attempted to draw her overseas by suggesting her husband was being pursued by other women. Nothing worked. Meanwhile, they wrote each other faithfully on household and family matters, local gossip, and national news. In the beginning of their separation, their letters reflected tender thoughts toward one another, especially when Benjamin was ill, but it is clear that with the passage of time his letters became more mundane and sometimes unduly harsh.

In many ways, they outgrew each other. In his letters to colleagues, Benjamin doted on philosophy, science and politics; in his missives to female friends, he put a great deal of energy into making them clever and light-hearted. After Deborah's death, Franklin occasionally expressed a deep sense of loss for his longtime spouse, and he made several attempts to fulfill that loss by proposing various intrigues or marriage with other women in France. When none worked out (as evident from his letters), I suspect he eventually returned to a longing for his devoted companion Debbie as he approached the end of his long life. When he died, he instructed that his body be laid next to his wife's with the simple words on the tombstone, "Benjamin and Deborah Franklin."

As to the rumors of his philandering, the letters to and from Madame Brillon reveal an affectionate relationship of flirtatious but unfulfilled desire, which was probably true of his flirtations with other French women as well. He was, after all, a man in his upper seventies who suffered numerous physical maladies.

RECONCILIATION WITH HIS SON WILLIAM

As to his estranged son, no historian criticizes Franklin's decision to separate from William during the war. Franklin was a rebel; William a royalist. However, some have assailed him for failing to forgive William after the war when his son wrote and asked to reconcile. "It was not Franklin's finest hour," comments one historian.* Yet after suffering through a long vicious war pursued by the British, which Franklin carefully catalogued in his letters, journals, and even on proposed coins and medallions, forgiveness was easier said than done. Franklin felt his bitterness was justified. He lambasted his son for "taking up arms against me, in a cause where my good name, fortune and life were all at stake." Perhaps the fact that William refused to apologize for his fateful decision, even while insisting on a "reconciliation," made it all the harder to forgive.

Why Franklin hated war

The rift between father and son is one reason Franklin often said, "There never was a good war or a bad peace." It destroyed forever a part of his being, his close relationship with his son. Prior to 1776, they had done everything together, and clearly shared a deep affection for each other. The war destroyed this familial bond, as well as his friendships with many other British and American confidants.[†]

Another reason Franklin detested war—all wars—is that it kept him from his first love: scientific pursuits. He constantly complained in England and France of how little time he had to correspond with fellow scientists and to pursue his own creations. When the war ended, he immediately tried to resume his scientific pursuits, working on several inventions, such as the "long arm" to withdraw books from

---

* H. L. Brands, *The First American: The Life and Times of Benjamin Franklin* (New York: Doubleday, 2000), 646.

[†] An entire book has been written on Franklin's long list of enemies. See Robert Middlekauff, *Benjamin Franklin and His Enemies* (University of California Press, 1996).

high up on a shelf. But he felt the war cut short his dreams of technological revolution, and his ability to discover and create new practical innovations. He spoke often of his wish to have been born in the next century or two.

Libertarian, conservative, or radical democrat?

What were Franklin's politics? In many ways, he was a progressive among the Founding Fathers. That he was a radical democrat is clear from his support of a unicameral legislature; that he was a disciple of Adam Smith is evident from his defense of free trade; that he was enamored of the French physiocrats (Turgot, Condorcet, et al.) can be seen by his favorable comments about *laissez faire* and agriculture. He defended the rich, and worried about how incentives for the poor would be affected if the state adopted a welfare system. He opposed a minimum wage law, and wrote in favor of free immigration and fast population growth (he was no Malthusian). He opposed any form of state religion or mandatory religious oaths of office, and demanded that slavery be abolished in the new nation—in 1789. He learned by sad experience (through his son and grandson) that private business would have been more rewarding than public service. His political views can be summed up in a sentence reminiscent of George Washington's farewell address, who in 1796 warned citizens, "The great rule of conduct for us, in regard to foreign nations, is, in extending our commercial relations, to have with them as little political connection as possible." Franklin had said it more succinctly in 1778, nearly two decades earlier: "The system of America is to have commerce with all, and war with none."*

---

* PBF 25:420, "Sir Philip Gibbes: Minutes of a Conversation with Franklin," January 5, 1778.

Yet Franklin was no free-thinking anarchist. In economics, he favored paper money and an inflationary monetary policy beyond specie, though "no more than commerce requires";* easy money would stimulate trade, he wrote, and even rapid inflation during the war paid for itself through its indirect taxation. (His likeness on the $100 bill—the highest current denomination—of an irredeemable American paper currency would greatly please his vanity.) He argued that the state should be actively engaged in the free education of youth and other public services, and in dispelling ignorance of public fads and superstitions. From several sources, it appears that Franklin was in league with Jefferson in emphasizing the defense of "life, liberty, and the pursuit of happiness" as the goal of government, and downplaying the right to "property." Property, he wrote, is purely a "creature of society" and can be legitimately taxed to pay for civil society. This opinion may have been influenced by the fact that large tracts of land in the colonies had been granted by the king to the Penns as proprietaries, not earned through labor or purchase, and thus in Franklin's eyes the government continued to have a claim upon the property. He was quite critical of Americans who were unwilling to pay their fair share of society's "dues."[†]

Franklin was no social libertarian, despite his image as a libertine and religious free thinker. While he is famous for reading books in the nude and playing chess until the late hours while Madame Brillon was taking a bath, he wrote stern letters to his daughter Sally chastising her for wanting to wear the latest fashions, and refused to buy his grandson Benny a gold watch during the war. He dressed plainly and constantly preached economy. Readers might be surprised by Franklin's attack on the growth of taverns in Philadelphia upon his

---

* PBF 44:7599, BF to the Duc de La Rochefoucauld, April 15, 1787.
[†] FPR 46:u344, From Benjamin Franklin: "Hints for the Members of the Pennsylvania Convention," Nov. 3, 1789.

return from England in 1762 (see the beginning of chapter 2, "Return to Philadelphia, 1762–64"). He hated mobs of any kind, and railed against scurrilous newspaper reports. He promoted at all times frugality and industry in both public and private life. In sum, Benjamin Franklin could be best characterized as a social conservative.

Franklin as a religious heretic

When it came to religion, Franklin was more radical. True enough, his letters, essays, and speeches reveal a deep-seated belief in God. "I never doubted...the existence of the Deity, that he made the World, and govern'd it by his Providence," he wrote in his *Autobiography*.* But most of his Christian contemporaries didn't see it that way. They expressed regret that he was an unbeliever and a heretic, or worse, that he doubted the validity of the Bible and the divinity of Jesus. He was not a church-goer, and was a "friend to unlimited toleration," as John Adams put it. That he was a skeptic is not in dispute. He admitted in print that he rejected the principal tenets of Presbyterianism. Yet there is strong evidence in his private writings that he gradually became more convinced of God's active participation in the affairs of men. He was more than just a deist. According to deist philosophy, God made the earth and then let it run its course without any further interference, like a watch that is wound up and left to run itself. According to Franklin, however, the evidence mounted every year that God time and time again intervened in favor of Americans, who were destined by divine decree to win the war and establish a blessed new land of liberty that would prosper like no other. In compiling the *Compleated Autobiography*, I was amazed at how often Franklin spoke of the blessings from Heaven,

---

* *The Autobiography of Benjamin Franklin*, 2nd ed. (Yale University Press, 1964), 146.

Providence's interceding in the American Revolution, and the existence of an afterlife where justice and happiness would prevail. He did not fear death; in fact, he was curious about the next life, which he called a new birth.*

FRANKLIN'S RANKING AS A FOUNDING FATHER

As a Founding Father, how significant was Franklin in the creation of the United States? Over time, his stature has risen. Soon after his death in 1790, only Pennsylvania and France honored him; the U.S. Senate, controlled by his enemies (John Adams, as vice president, was also president of the Senate), waited a year before issuing a eulogy. Even then, the tribute was made by critic William Smith.† Eventually personal antagonisms faded, and with the publication of his *Autobiography* and his celebrated essay "The Way to Wealth," admiration for his accomplishments and philosophy grew. Most historians now agree that without Franklin, the hundreds of millions of dollars (or French livres) so vital to the war effort would not have been forthcoming, and without French military and financial assistance, America could not have won the war, at least not by 1781. General Washington desperately needed French forces to defeat the British at Yorktown. The establishment of an American nation would have been postponed for many more years, perhaps beyond the late 18ᵀᴴ century, without French aid. Moreover, to convince a French monarch to support a rebellion against a fellow monarch was incredible. And yet Franklin, with his prestige and social prowess, accomplished this amazing diplomatic feat.

Franklin's influence may also have a negative side; some have accused him of causing the French Revolution in 1789. The French

---

* PBF 6:406–07, BF to Elizabeth Hubbart, February 22, 1756.
† For the public reaction to Franklin's death, see Gordon S. Wood, *The Americanization of Benjamin Franklin* (New York: Penguin, 2004), 230–35.

spent so much money financing the American revolution that the French Court eventually went bankrupt, which in turn caused the financial minister to depreciate their currency and destroy their economy.* The unintended result of France's financial and military support of America was political and economic chaos at home. Yet the King and the French Court did it willingly, thanks to Franklin's diplomacy.

Thus, it is not surprising that Franklin's life is increasingly studied and appreciated as we complete the third century since his birth. I am hopeful that this long-awaited completion of Franklin's memoirs, an intimate look at the multi-talented "first American," will stimulate a new generation of scholars and admirers.

---

* See the classic essay, "Fiat Money Inflation in France," by Andrew Dickson White (Caxton Printers, 1974).

Sources

PREFACE

Having now done with public affairs.... Franklin Papers Reader (FPR) 46:u201, BF to Catharine Ray Greene, Mar. 2, 1789; FPR 46:u112, BF to the Duc de La Rochefoucauld, Oct. 24, 1788.

I have been persuaded by my friends... FPR 44:u415, BF to Edward Bancroft, Nov. 26, 1786.

The Memoirs has now been brought down to my fifty first year... FPR 46:u112, BF to the Duc de La Rochefoucauld, Oct. 24, 1788; FPR 46:u111, BF to Benjamin Vaughan, Oct. 24, 1788; PR 46:u112, BF to the Duc de La Rochefoucauld, Oct. 24, 1788.

My malady renders my sitting... FPR 46:u320, BF to George Washington, Sept. 15, 1789; FPR 46:u201, BF to Catharine Ray Greene, Mar. 2, 1789.

In writing the memoirs of my life... FPR 46:u312, BF to Louis-Guillaume Le Veillard, Sept. 5, 1789; FPR 46:u352, BF to Louis-Guillaume Le Veillard, Nov. 13, 1789.

Here in hand is a full account of my life.... Carl Van Doren, ed., *Benjamin Franklin's Autobiographical Writings*, p. 673; FPR 46:u320, BF to George Washington, Sept. 15, 1789.

1. FIRST MISSION TO ENGLAND, 1757–62

We safely arriv'd in England... Autobiography 258; PBF 7:244, William Franklin to Elizabeth Graeme, July 17, 1757; PBF 7:243, BF to Deborah Franklin, July 17, 1757; *Memoirs of the Life and Writings of Benjamin Franklin*, 3rd ed., edited by William Temple Franklin (London, 1818), vol. 1, 258n.

My son and I arrived in London... Autobiography 259; PBF 7:364, BF to Deborah Franklin, Jan. 21, 1758.

A Craven Street... PBF 7:368, BF to Deborah Franklin, Jan. 1758; PBF 7:380-81, BF to Deborah Franklin, Feb. 19, 1758.

I found that every time... PBF 7:380, BF to Deborah Franklin, Feb. 19, 1758; PBF 7:272, BF to Deborah Franklin, Nov. 22, 1757; PBF 7:384, BF to Deborah Franklin, Feb. 19, 1758.

My friend Mr. Strahan offered to lay me a considerable wager... PBF 7:359, BF to Deborah Franklin, Jan. 14, 1758; PBF 8:32-33, BF to Deborah Franklin, Mar. 5, 1760.

I mentioned to my wife another of my fancying... PBF 7:383, BF to Deborah Franklin, Feb. 19, 1758; 37:227, BF to Edmund Clegg, Apr. 26, 1782; PBF 19:139, BF to the managers of the Philadelphia Silk Filature, July 29, 1772; PBF 10:321, BF to Peter Templeman, Aug. 12, 1763.

Once recovered from my long illness... And that he said... PBF 8:96, BF to Joseph Galloway, June 10, 1758; PBF 8:101, Isaac Norris to BF; PBF 7:360, BF to Isaac Norris, Jan. 14, 1758.

I reported to the Assembly.... PBF 8:157, BF to Isaac Norris, Sept. 16, 1758; PBF 8:150, BF to Joseph Galloway, Sept. 16, 1758.

I depend chiefly on... PBF 8:133, BF to Deborah Franklin, Sept. 6, 1758.

While at Cambridge... It is but... During the hot Sunday... PBF 8:108-9, BF to John Lining, June 17, 1758.

Billy and I traveled... PBF 8:133-8, BF to Deborah Franklin, Sept. 6, 1758.

While there, I came across... PBF 8:153-55, BF to Jane Mecom, Sept. 16, 1758.

No part of our journey... PBF 9:5, BF to Sir Alexander Dick, Jan. 3, 1760.

The following February... PBF 8:277-80, The University of St. Andrews: Degree of Doctor of Laws, Feb. 12, 1759; PBF 10:311, Ezra Stiles: List of Franklin's Honors, July 11, 1763; PBF 10:76-78, Oxford University: Record of Degree of Doctor of Civil Law, Apr. 30, 1762; FPR 46:u353, Benjamin Franklin: Notes for Continuation of Autobiography.

Returning to London, I was grieved... PBF 7:380, BF to Deborah Franklin, Feb. 19, 1758; PBF 9:159-60, BF to Hugh Roberts, Sept. 16, 1758; PBF 10:202, BF to Caldwallader Colden, Feb. 26, 1763.

In April 1759, it gave me great pleasure... PBF 8:396-7, BF to Isaac Norris, June 9, 1759; PBF 9:280, BF to Hugh Roberts, Feb. 26, 1761.

After my chief business was over... PBF 10:130, BF to Giambatista Beccaria, July 13, 1762; PBF 10:204, BF to Cadwallader Colden, March 2, 1763.

From the summer of 1761... PBF 10:174, BF to Jared Ingersoll, Dec. 11, 1762.

Having seen almost all... PBF 9:356, BF to Deborah Franklin, Sept. 14, 1761; PBF 10:84, BF to David Hume, May 19, 1762.

And thus in the summer of 1762... PBF 9:5, BF to Lord Kames, Jan. 3, 1760; PBF 10:102, BF to Mary Stevenson, June 7, 1762; PBF 10:147, BF to Lord Kames, Aug. 17, 1762.

2. RETURN TO PHILADELPHIA, 1762–64

I left England... PBF 10:166, 167, BF to William Strahan, Dec. 7, 1762; PBF 12:158, June 2, 1765 BF to Lord Kames.

On the first of November... PBF 10:160, 161-62, BF to Richard Jackson and William Strahan, Dec. 2, 1762.

I found the city... PBF 10:209, BF to Richard Jackson, March 8, 1763.

I also found notorious... PBF 11:139, "Explanatory Remarks on the Assembly's Resolves," March 29, 1764.

While I was on the sea... PBF 10:161, BF to William Strahan, Dec. 2, 1762, and
PBF 10:236, BF to William Strahan, March 28, 1763.

In February following... PBF 12:158, BF to Lord Kames, June 2, 1765.

In the spring of 1763... PBF 12:158, BF to Lord Kames, June 2, 1765; PBF 10:276,
BF and John Foxcroft to Anthony Todd, June 10, 1763; PBF 11:20, BF to
Anthony Todd, Jan. 18, 1764.

Having returned home... PBF 10:385, BF to Sir Alexander Dick, Dec. 11, 1763.

I give it my opinion... PBF 12:163, BF to Lord Kames, June 2, 1765.

While home, I also visited the Negro School... PBF 10:395, BF to John Waring,
Dec. 17, 1763.

Just before I left London... PBF 11:89, BF to Jonathan Williams, Feb. 24, 1764.

The assembly sitting through... PBF 11:218, BF to Richard Jackson, June 1, 1764.

Besides my duty as an assemblyman... PBF 11:103, BF to Dr. Fothergill, March 14,
1764; 12:158, BF to Lord Kames, June 2, 1765.

And then in December 1763... PBF 12:158, BF to Lord Kames, June 2, 1765; PBF
11:50-52, A Narrative of the Late Massacres... (1764).

As the rioters... PBF 12:158, BF to Lord Kames, June 2, 1765; PBF 11:103-04, BF
to John Fothergill, Mar. 14, 1764.

But the fighting face... PBF 12:158, BF to Lord Kames, June 2, 1765.

The House however... PBF 11:134, "Resolves of the Assembly," March 29, 1764;
PBF 11:199, Petition to the King, May 23, 1764.

For my own part... PBF 11:148, BF to Richard Jackson, March 29, 1764; PBF
12:158, BF to Lord Kames, June 2, 1765.

When in America... PBF 11:97-98, letter to John Canton, March 14, 1764; PBF
10:169, BF to William Strahan, Dec. 7, 1762; PBF 9:33, BF to Deborah
Franklin, March 5, 1760.

3. Second Mission to England, 1764–75

On sea we had terrible weather.... PBF 12:167, BF to Deborah Franklin, June 4,
1765.

I once more had the pleasure of living at Craven Street.... PBF 11:517, BF to
Deborah Franklin, Dec. 9, 1764; PBF 11:521, BF to Mary Stevenson, Dec.
12-16, 1764; PBF 11:534, BF to Deborah Franklin, Dec. 27, 1764; PBF
12:19, BF to David Hall, Jan. 12, 1765.

Immediately upon arrival.... PBF 12:169, BF to Deborah Franklin, June 4, 1765;
PBF 12:172, BF to John Ross, June 8, 1765; PBF 13:176, BF to Deborah
Franklin, Feb. 27, 1766.

I wrote, God has been very good to us.... PBF 169, BF to Deborah Franklin, June
4, 1765.

*In my younger days, having once some leisure... But not being satisfied with
these.... At Craven Street, in correspondence with friends in Pennsylvania....*
PBF 4:396-401, BF to Peter Collinson, 1752; PBF 12:147-48, BF to John
Canton, May 29, 1765.

As to business, I was immediately engag'd in public affairs... PBF 12:68, BF to John
Ross, Feb. 14, 1765; PBF 12:158, PBF to Lord Kames, June 2, 1765; PBF
12:206, BF to Charles Thomson, July 11, 1765.

At first I was not much alarm'd about Parliament's schemes... PBF 11:19, BF to
    Richard Jackson, Jan. 16, 1764.

As to the true history of the Stamp Act, the fact was this.... PBF 26:95-97, BF to
    William Alexander, Mar. 12, 1778.

I was a member of the Assembly of Pennsylvania .... PBF 26:95-97, BF to William
    Alexander, Mar. 12, 1778.

I took every step in my power to prevent the passing of the Stamp Act.... PBF
    12:256-58, David Hall to BF, Sept. 6, 1765; PBF 12:268, BF to David Hall,
    Sept. 14, 1765; PBF 7:341, "Father Abraham's Speech," Poor Richard's
    Almanac, 1758.

Mr. Thomson tender'd me a response,.... PBF 12:279, Charles Thomson to BF, Sept.
    24, 1765; PBF 13:178, BF to Charles Thomson, Feb. 27, 1766.

In November 1765, I received letters from my wife.... PBF 12:234, BF to John
    Hughes, Aug. 9, 1765; PBF 12:365-66, BF to David Hall, Nov. 9, 1765;
    12:271; Deborah Franklin to BF, Sept. 22, 1765; PBF 12:360, BF to Deborah
    Franklin, Nov. 9, 1765; PBF 13:429, BF to Daniel Wister, Sept. 27, 1766.

I had a long audience at this time with Lord Dartmouth.... PBF 12:362-64, BF to
    William Franklin, Nov. 9, 1765.

During the course of the debate,... PBF 14:62, BF to Lord Kames, Feb. 25, 1767.

What is your name.... *till they can make new ones.* PBF 13:129-59, the
    Examination of Doctor Benjamin Franklin before the Committee of the
    Whole of the House of Commons, 1766.

Two weeks after my examination before the government,... PBF 13:165, BF to Deb-
    orah Franklin, Feb. 22, 1766; PBF 13:233, BF to Deborah Franklin, April 6,
    1766; PBF 13:169, BF to David Hall, Feb. 24, 1766; PBF 13:199, Sarah Frank-
    lin to BF, March 23, 1766; PBF 13:285, Joseph Galloway to BF, May 23, 1766.

As to the reports that spread to my disadvantage... PBF 13:188, BF to Jane Mecom,
    March 1, 1766.

I thank God that I have enjoyed a greater share of health.... PBF 14:72-73, BF to
    Jane Mecom, Mar. 2, 1767.

My enemies were forc'd to content themselves with abusing.... PBF 17:285, BF to
    Jane Mecom, Nov. 7, 1770; PBF 17:314, BF to Jane Mecom, Dec. 30, 1770.

During the course of the Stamp Act affair,.... PBF 13:315-16, BF to Deborah
    Franklin, June 13, 1766; PBF 13:383-84, BF to the Speaker and Committee
    of Correspondence of the Pennsylvania Assembly, Aug. 22, 1766; PBF
    13:429, BF to Daniel Wister, Sept. 27, 1766; PBF 14:64, BF to Lord Kames,
    Feb. 25, 1767.

In December 1766, I was asked to recommend two young sons.... PBF 13:530, BF to
    Benjamin Rush and Jonathan Potts, Dec. 20, 1766.

In 1748, at the age of 42, I took the proper measures for... PBF 3:318, BF to
    Cadwallader Colden, Sept. 29, 1748.

In 1767, my long partnership of the printing business with Mr. Hall expired,.... PBF
    14:192, BF to Deborah Franklin, Jun 22, 1767; PBF 18:91, BF to Deborah
    Franklin, May 1, 1771.

At the same time, Deborah inform'd me that our daughter Sally.... *In December
    1771, I found Mr. Bache at his mother*.... PBF 14:220-21, BF to Richard Bache,

Aug. 5, 1767; PBF 15:185-86, BF to Richard Bache, Aug. 13, 1768; Richard Bache to Deborah Franklin, Dec. 3, 1771; PBF 19:29, BF to Jane Mecom, Jan. 13, 1772; PBF 19:42-45, BF to Deborah Franklin, Jan. 28, 1772; PBF 19:50-51, BF to William Franklin, Jan. 30, 1772.

I was happy to learn from my sister Jane Mecom. . . . PBF 18:185, BF to Jane Mecom, July 17, 1771.

I often wish'd that I were employ'd by the Crown. . . . PBF 6:468, BF to George Whitefield, July 2, 1756.

In 1769, I joined with Thomas Walpole, Richard Jackson, ... PBF 16:167-68, "Petition to the King", June 1769; PBF 16:176, BF to Grey Cooper, July 11, 1769.

The application was raised to twenty million acres in January 1770. . . . PBF 17:8-11, "Petition to the Treasury from Franklin and Others for a Grant of Land"; 17:135n.

We were daily amus'd with expectations that it would be compleated. . . . PBF 20:89, BF to John Foxcroft, Mar. 3, 1773.

The Ohio affair seemed near a conclusion. . . . PBF 18:75-76, BF to William Franklin, Apr. 20, 1771.

The affair of the grant dragged on, but slowly, ... PBF 20:149-50, BF to Joseph Galloway, April 6, 1773.

Years later, in 1774, I was told that . . . . PBF 20:33-34, "Franklin's Ostensible Withdrawal from the Walpole Company", Jan. 12, 1774.

In 1767, some late incidents. . . . *It was a common but mistaken notion in Britain.* . . . *Upon the whole, I had lived so much of my life in Britain,* . . . . PBF 14:62-64, BF to Lord Kames, Feb. 25, 1767.

I stayed too long in London, and made a trip. . . . *There are fair women in Paris who I think.* . . . *Versailles had infinite sums laid out in building it.* . . . *The civilities we every where received gave us.* . . . *Travelling is one way of lengthening life,* . . . . PBF 14:250-51, BF to Mary Stevenson, Sept. 14, 1767, PBF 14:274, BF to Deborah Franklin, Oct. 9, 1767; PBF 15:35, BF to Thomas-Francois Dalibard, Jan. 31, 1768.

I often wished I could procure more attention. . . . PBF 15:98-99, BF to William Franklin, Apr. 16, 1768.

I wrote a piece under the name "Medius". . . . *Besides this tax.* . . . *Much malignant censure.* . . . *If it be said that their wages are too low.* . . *A law might be made.* . . . PBF 15:158, BF to Grey Cooper, June 24, 1768; PBF 15:103-07, "On the Labouring Poor," April 1768.

My piece, along with one I wrote. . . . PBF 15:159, BF to William Franklin, July 2, 1768.

The Parliament was sitting. . . . *Tis really an extraordinary event, to see this Wilkes.* . . . PBF 15:98-99, BF to William Franklin, Apr. 16, 1768.

I was sorry to see in the American papers. . . . PBF 15:224, BF to William Franklin, Oct. 5, 1768.

Even this capital, the residents of the King. . . . PBF 15:128-29, BF to John Ross, May 14, 1768.

The Court of King's Bench postponed giving sentence against them . . . PBF 15:127-28, BF to Joseph Galloway, May 14, 1768.

By summer the tumults and disorders were pretty well subsided....PBF 15:165, BF to Joseph Galloway, July 2, 1768.

Later in 1768 the visit of the King of Denmark engrossed.... PBF 15:225, BF to William Franklin, Oct. 5, 1768.

On the one hand, there was a general disposition in the British nation.... PBF 17:168, BF to Joseph Galloway, June 11, 1770.

Lord Hillsborough, the new Secretary of State,.... PBF 15:76, BF to William Franklin, Mar. 13, 1768.

In January 1771, at the earnest request of Mr. Strahan,.... PBF 18: 12-16, "Franklin's account of his audience with Hillsborough," Jan. 16, 1771.

After this conference between the Secretary and me... PBF 18:24-25, BF to Samuel Cooper, Feb. 5, 1771.

I do not pretend the gift of prophecy, but.... *The resentment of the people will, at times.*... PBF 18:102-04, "To the Massachusetts House of Representatives Committee of Correspondence," May 15, 1771.

Temple came home to us.... PBF 18:74, BF to William Franklin, Apr. 20, 1771; PBF 19:52-53, BF to William Franklin, Jan. 30, 1772.

We had a severe and tedious winter in England... PBF 18:74, BF to William Franklin, Apr. 20, 1771.

In May 1771, I made with friends a journey of a fortnight.... *The next morning the travelers left Manchester.*... *The next day we came to Birmingham.*... PBF 18:118-19, BF to Deborah Franklin, June 5, 1771; PBF 18:114-16, "Journal of Jonathan Williams, Jr. on his Tour with Franklin and Others through Northern England," May 28, 1771.

In June of 1771, I went out of town... PBF 18:137, BF to Jonathan Shipley; Franklin's *Autobiography*, 43; PBF 18:204, BF to Deborah Franklin.

My wife sent to the bishop's family.... PBF 20:58, BF to Deborah Franklin, Feb. 14, 1773; PBF 19:301, BF to Georgiana Shipley, Sept. 26, 1772.

I set out for Ireland, where Mr. Jackson and I were invited to dine... PBF 19:47-49, BF to William Franklin, Jan. 30, 1772; PBF 19:243, BF to William Franklin, Aug. 17, 1772.

In Ireland I had a good deal.... *In Scotland, I spent 5 days with Lord Kames.*... PBF 19:49-50, BF to William Franklin, Jan. 30, 1772.

In Scotland things made a better appearance... PBF 19:7, BF to Joshua Babcock, Jan. 13, 1772; PBF 19:71-72, BF to Joseph Galloway, Feb. 6, 1772.

I return'd again to London from a journey.... PBF 20:315, BF to Benjamin Rush, July 14, 1773.

The cold bath has long been in vogue here.... PBF 19:16, BF to Thomas Cushing, Jan. 13, 1772; PBF 15:180, BF to Jacques Barbeu-Dubourg, July 21, 1768; PBF 18:206, BF to Jonathan Shipley, Aug. 15, 1771.

It is of the greatest importance to prevent diseases;... PBF 19:256, BF to William Franklin, Aug. 19, 1772.

As to my situation in London nothing.... PBF 19:258-59, BF to William Franklin, Aug. 19-22, 1772.

I was fortunate enough not to suffer....PBF 19:315, BF to Richard Bache, Oct. 7, 1772.

The philosophical transactions of the Royal Society...PBF 19:324-25, BF to Horace-Benedict de Saussure, Oct. 8, 1772.

In late 1772, I settled into my new apartment....PBF 19:361, BF to William Franklin, Nov. 3, 1772.

A fifth edition of my book....PBF 20:384, BF to Deborah Franklin, Sept. 1, 1773.

I had when a youth, read and smiled at an account....PBF 20:464-65, BF to William Brownrigg, Nov. 7, 1773.

Two of the only descendants of my grandfather....PBF 18:186, BF to Jane Mecom, July 17, 1771; PBF 19:395, BF to Deborah Franklin, Dec. 1, 1772.

Mrs. Stevenson's daughter Polly married....PBF 17:209, letter to Timothy Folger, Aug. 21, 1770.

In 1774, Mrs. Hewson had the smallpox....PBF 21:205, BF to Deborah Franklin, Apr. 28, 1774; PBF 21:208, BF to Deborah Franklin, May 5, 1774; PBF 21:245, letter to Thomas Coombe, Jr., July 22, 1774.

In 1773, I wrote two pieces in England for the Public Advertiser...PBF 20:437-39, BF to William Franklin, Oct. 6, 1773.

Having been from my youth more or less engag'd in public affairs....I should therefore....Herein is the background: It has long appeared to me....PBF 21:415-17, Tract Relative to the Affair of the Hutchinson Letters, 1774.

At the same time, I am a mortal enemy to arbitrary government...PBF 1:11, "Silence Dogood, No. 2," April 16, 1722; PBF 20:330, BF to John Winthrop, July 25, 1773; PBF 21:418-19, Tract Relative to the Affair of the Hutchinson Letters, 1774.

In 1773, I opposed without success the tax on tea...I sent the original letters to my particular... Carl Van Doren, ed., *Benjamin Franklin's Autobiographical Writings*, 636; PBF 21:420, Tract Relative to the Affair of the Hutchinson Letters, 1774; PBF 20:550, letter of Thomas Hutchinson, Jan. 20, 1769.

*The news being arriv'd in England of the divulging....My answer to the oath was, that the letters in question....It had about this time become evident that....*PBF 21:427-35, Tract Relative to the Affair of Hutchinson's Letters, 1774.

I heard from all quarters that the ministry....PBF 21:334, BF to Joseph Galloway, Oct. 12, 1774.

On the 29th of January 1774 the....PBF 21:80-81, "A letter from London," Apr. 25, 1774; PBF 21:92-94, BF to Thomas Cushing, Feb. 15, 1774; PBF 21:147-48, BF to Jan Ingenhousz, Mar. 18, 1774; FPR 46:u156, Franklin sketch of services to U.S., Dec. 29, 1788.

I wrote my son William in New Jersey to acquaint him that....PBF 20:437, BF to William Franklin, Oct. 6, 1773;PBF 21:75, BF to William Franklin, Feb. 2, 1774; PBF 21:212, BF to William Franklin, 1774 (?); PBF 21:287, BF to William Franklin, Sept. 7, 1774.

During the whole of my time in England.... PBF 21:597-98, Journal of
   Negotiations in London, Mar. 22, 1775.
*During the recess of the last Parliament....From the time of the affront given me....
   When I first came to England in 1757....But toward the end of August 1774....
   He mention'd an opinion prevailing in.... The new Parliament was to meet the
   29th of November, 1774....A time was appointed on which I was to have my
   second chess party....On Christmas day, visiting Mrs. Howe....After some
   extremely polite compliments....Mrs. Howe here offering to withdraw....I
   returned to town the next Wednesday....Lord Howe here took out of his pocket
   a paper....In a day or two, I sent the paper in a cover....On the following
   Tuesday, Jan. 3, 1775....On the Sunday being the 29th of January his Lordship
   Chatham....On Wednesday Lord Stanhope at Lord Chatham's request....To
   hear so many of these hereditary legislators...After this proceeding I expected
   to hear no more....We had not at this time a great deal of....* PBF 21:545-93,
   Journal of Negotiations in London, Mar. 22, 1775.
About this time, I was asked by a nobleman.... PBF 21:599-600, Franklin's
   Purported Answer to a Nobleman's Question on the American Disputes, 1775.
*On the morning of Feb. 20, it was currently...It was during this time I wrote the
   following letter...*PBF 21:512, BF to Jane Mecom, Feb. 26, 1775.
It was at this time in 1775 that I was inform'd.... PBF 21:401-02, Richard Bache to
   BF, Dec. 24, 1774; PBF 21:402-04, William Franklin to BF, Dec. 24, 1774;
   PBF 23:311, BF to Jan Ingenhousz, Feb. 12, 1777; PBF 21:593, Journal of
   Negotiations in London, Mar. 22, 1775.
*Hearing nothing from Lord Howe.... The next morning (March 1)....A little before I
   left London.....Mr. Walpole called at my house the next day...*PBF 21:593-99,
   Journal of Negotiations in London, Mar. 22, 1775.
*The day before I left London....*J. T. Rutt, *Life and Correspondence of Joseph
   Priestley* (London, 1831-32), vol. 1, 209-12.
*That evening I received a note...*PBF 21:538, John Fothergill to BF, Mar. 19, 1775.

4. Congress and the Declaration
of Independence, 1775–76

I arrive at home on the evening of the 5th of May, 1775,.... PBF 22:34, BF to David
   Hartley, May 8, 1775; PBF 22:42, BF to Jonathan Shipley, May 15, 1775; PBF
   22:98, BF to Jonathan Shipley, July 7, 1775; PBF 22:65, BF to William Temple
   Franklin, Jun 13, 1775; PBF 22:100, BF to Mary Hewson, July 8, 1775; PBF
   22:17, "Observations at Sea on Temperatures of Air and Water," April
   10–May 3, 1775; FPR 39:u263, BF to Michel-Guillaume St. Jean de
   Crevecouer, no date; FPR 41:u384, BF to Julien-David LeRoy, Feb. 1784.
I brought over a son with me.... PBF 22:34, BF to David Hartley, May 8, 1775; PBF
   22:42, BF to Jonathan Shipley, May 15, 1775; PBF 22:98, BF to Jonathan
   Shipley, July 7, 1775; PBF 22:65, BF to William Temple Franklin, Jun 13,
   1775; PBF 22:100, BF to Mary Hewson, July 8, 1775.
I found at my arrival all America.... PBF 22:93-94, BF to Jonathan Shipley, July 7,
   1775; PBF 22:108, BF to Margaret Stevenson, July 17, 1775.

The Massachusetts governor call'd. . . . PBF 22:44, BF to Joseph Priestley, May 15, 1775.

The next morning I was unanimously. . . . PBF 22:34, BF to David Hartley, May 8, 1775; PBF 22:36, "Instructions to Its Delegates to Congress," May 9, 1775; PBF 22:94, BF to Joseph Priestley, July 7, 1775; PBF 22:94, BF to Jonathan Shipley, July 7, 1775; *Autobiography*, 211.

The Congress met at a time when all minds. . . . PBF 22:91, BF to Joseph Priestley, July 7, 1775; PBF 22:97, BF to Jonathan Shipley, July 7, 1775; PBF 22:196, BF to David Hartley, Sep. 12, 1775.

Thus, propositions from Britain attempting. . . . PBF 22:50-51, BF to Humphry Marshall, May 23, 1775; 22:91-95, letter to Joseph Shipley, July 7, 1775; PBF 22:198, BF to Jonathan Williams, Jr., Sep. 12, 1775; PBF 22:218, BF to Joseph Priestley, Oct. 3, 1775.

I addressed (but never sent) the following letter to Mr. Strahan. . . . PBF 22:85

Thus, if a temperament naturally cool. . . . PBF 22:98, BF to Joseph Shipley, July 7, 1775.

Great frugality and great industry became fashionable . . . PBF 22:93, BF to Joseph Priestley, July 7, 1775.

On July 21, 1775 my proposed sketch. . . . PBF 22:120-25, "Proposed Articles of Confederation," July 21, 1775.

The Congress adjourned on August 2 to the 5th of September, ... PBF 22:142, BF to Jane Mecom, Aug. 2, 1775; PBF 22:219, BF to William Straham, Oct. 3, 1775.

In addition to muskets, ... PBF 22:343, BF to Charles Lee, Feb. 11, 1776.

We gave up our commerce with Britain. . . . PBF 22:199, BF to Jonathan Shipley, Sept. 13, 1775; Carl Van Doren, ed., *Benjamin Franklin's Autobiographical Writings*, 636.

I observed on one of the drums. . . . *I confessed.* . . . *'Tis curious.* . . . *I communicated.* . . . . "The Rattlesnake as America's Symbol," BF to the Pennsylvania Journal, Dec. 27, 1775; *A Benjamin Franklin Reader*, ed. by Walter Isaacson (New York: Simon & Schuster, 2003), 263-66.

I was as happy as I could be under the fatigue. . . . PBF 22:108, BF to Margaret Stevenson, July 17, 1775; PBF 22:200, BF to Jonathan Shipley, Sep. 13, 1775; PBF 25:78, "Franklin's Description of His Ailments," Oct. 17, 1777.

In October 1775, I travelled with two other delegates. . . . PBF 22:242, BF to Richard Bache, Oct. 19, 1775.

I learned that there were many cheerful countenances. . . . PBF 22:223, BF to Jane Mecom, Oct. 16, 1775; PBF 22:197, BF to Jonathan Williams, Jr., Sep. 12, 1775; PBF 22:241-42, BF to Richard Bache, Oct. 19, 1775.

In early 1776, I received a letter from Gen. Charles Lee . . . PBF 22:357, BF to Charles Lee, Feb. 19, 1776; FPR 44:u599, BF to Duc de la Rochefoucauld, Apr. 15, 1787.

The ancient Romans and Greek orators. . . . PBF 37:472-73, BF to Richard Price, June 13, 1782.

I always valu'd Mr. Paine's friendship. . . . PBF 43:454, BF to Thomas Paine, Sep. 27, 1785; PBF 44:u600, BF to Charles-Henri, Comte d'Estaing, Apr. 15, 1787.

It would be a happiness to me if... PBF 22:367-68, BF to the Speaker of the Pennsylvania Assembly, Feb. 26, 1776.

In Congress, I was made a member.... PBF 22:369-74, "The Committee of Secret Correspondence: Instructions to Silas Deane," Mar. 2–3, 1776.

The Committee then reported that they conferr'd.... PBF 22:352, "The Committee of Secret Correspondence: a Report to Congress," Feb. 14, 1776; 22:382, "Instructions and Commission from Congress," Mar. 20, 1776; 22:379, letter to Philip Schuyler, Mar. 11, 1776; PBF 22:400, BF to Josiah Quincy, Sr., Apr. 15, 1776; PBF 25:78, "Franklin's Description of His Ailments," Oct. 17, 1777.

After some difficulty and delay in getting.... PBF 22:413-15, "The Commissioners to Canada to John Hancock," PBF May 1, 1776; 22:418, "The Commissioners to Canada to John Hancock," PBF May 6, 1776; 22:420, "The Commissioners to Canada to Philip Shcuyler," PBF May 6, 1776; PBF 22:425, "The Commissioners to Canada to John Hancock," May 8, 1776; FPR 46:u156, Franklin sketch of services to U.S., Dec. 29, 1788.

On the 10th of May, five ships of war arrived from Quebec.... PBF 22:427-28, "The Commissioners to Canada to Philip Schuyler," May 10, 1776; PBF 22:432, BF to Philip Schuyler, May 12, 1776; PBF 22:439-40, BF to Charles Carroll and Samuel Chase, May 27, 1776; PBF 25:78, "Franklin's Description of His Ailments," Oct. 17, 1777.

We were obliged to quit Canada... PBF 22:503-04, "The Committee of Secret Correspondence to Silas Deane," July 8, 1776.

I arrived home in Philadelphia,.... PBF 22:443-44, "The Committee of Secret Correspondence: Instructions to William Brigham," June 3, 1776; PBF 22:484-85, BF to George Washington, June 21, 1776.

In June, I was asked to assist in the preparing of a declaration of independence.... PBF 22:486, BF from Thomas Jefferson, June 21, 1776; PBF 20:302, BF to William Franklin, July 14, 1773.

I had written a draft of a resolution.... PBF 22:323, "Proposed Preamble to a Congressional Resolution," 1775.

While recovering from boils and the gout.... Jefferson Papers 18:169, Thomas Jefferson to Robert Walsh, Dec. 4, 1818; PBF 22:486, Thomas Jefferson to BF, June 21, 1776.

The Congress, after mature deliberation.... PBF 22:502-03, "The Committee of Secret Correspondence to Silas Deane," July 8, 1776; BF to Jane Mecom, July 4, 1786.

It is impossible we should think of submission.... *Long did I endeavour with unfeigned and unwearied zeal.*... *Upon arrival in New York.*... PBF 22:606-08, "The Committee of Conference: Report to Congress"; PBF 22:598-605, "Lord Howe's Conference with the Committee of Congress"; PBF 22:575, BF to Lord Howe, Aug. 20, 1776.

I wrote the following letter to Lord Howe.... PBF 22:518-21, BF to Lord Howe, July 20, 1776.

On July 4th, I had been appointed to a committee.... PBF 22:562-63, "Proposal for the Great Seal of the United States," Before Aug. 14, 1776.

At this time, Temple proposed to go to his father, ... PBF 23:314, BF to Jan
Ingelhousz, Feb. 12, 1777; PBF 22:612, BF to William Temple Franklin, Sep.
19, 1776; PBF 22:622, BF to William Temple Franklin, Sep. 22, 1776.

Nothing has ever hurt me so much. ... PBF 42:129, BF to William Franklin, Aug.
16, 1784.

The several colonies approv'd and confirm'd. ... PBF 22:571-75, "Protest against the
First Draft of the Articles of Confederation," before Aug. 20, 1776; 23:118,
"Memoir on the State of the Former Colonies," before Jan. 5, 1777.

The Declaration of Independence was met. ... PBF 22:554, "The Committee of Secret
Correspondence to Silas Deane," Aug. 7, 1776; PBF 22:583, BF to Horatio
Gates, Aug. 28, 1776; PBF 22:585, BF to Anthony Wayne, Aug. 28, 1776.

The fleet under Lord Howe was vastly. ... *It had been previously determined to
abandon.* ... *The only source of uneasiness among us* ...PBF 22:643, "The
Committee of Secret Correspondence to Silas Deane," Oct. 1, 1776.

In September, the Congress appointed me,. ... PBF 22:625, "Instructions to
Franklin, Silas Deane, and Arthur Lee as Commissioners to France";
Lyman H. Butterfield, ed., *Letters of Benjamin Rush* (Princeton, NJ: 1951),
vol. 1, 118.

Our appointment on this business remained. ... PBF 22:649, "The Committee of
Secret Correspondence to Silas Deane", Oct. 2, 1776; PBF 22:625-30, "The
Continental Congress: Instructions to Franklin, Silas Dean, and Arthur Lee
as Commissioners to France," Sep. 24–Oct. 22, 1776; PBF 22:643, "the
Committee of Secret Correspondence to Silas Deane," Oct. 1, 1776.

Before my departure, I ordered all the money. ...PBF 46:u156, Franklin sketch of
services to U.S., Dec. 29, 1788.

Being once more order'd to Europe,. ... PBF 22:670, BF to Samuel Cooper, Oct. 25,
1776.

The manner in which the whole of this business. ... *It was, however, formed and
established in despite of.* ... *In commerce, such profits were offered as tempted.* ...
The consequence was, that in a few months. ... *This is the greatest revolution the
world has ever saw.* ...PBF 25:100-02, "Franklin on the Miracle of the
Revolution", quoted from Richard Henry Lee, *Life of Arthur Lee* (Boston:
Wells and Lilly, 1829), 343–46.

5. Minister to France, 1776–78: The Treaty of Alliance

I arrived in France.. ... PBF 23:23 and FPR 46:u156, "Sketch of services to U.S.,"
Dec. 29, 1788; PBF 25:79, "Franklin's Description of His Ailments," Oct. 17,
1777; PBF 23:33-34, BF to Jane Mecom, Dec. 8, 1776; PBF 23:28, BF to Silas
Deane (Franklin journal), Dec. 4, 1776.

I brought with me two grandsons. ... PBF 23:30, BF to Silas Deane, Dec. 7, 1776;
PBF 23:314, BF to Jan Ingenhousz, Feb. 12, 1777; PBF 25:553, Richard
Bache to BF, Jan. 31, 1778.

I was made extremely welcome in France. ... PBF 23:31, BF to the Committee of
Secret Correspondence, Dec. 8, 1776; PBF 4:466, BF to Jared Eliot, Apr. 12,
1753; PBF 23:32-33, BF to John Hancock, Dec. 8, 1776; PBF 23:29, BF to
Silas Deane, Dec. 7, 1776.

Knowing that all views of accommodation with Great.... PBF 23:50-57, 97-99, "The Committee of Secret Correspondence to the American Commissioners," Dec. 21–23, 1776 and Dec. 30, 1776.

I arrived in Paris in two weeks... PBF 23:113-14, BF to the Committee of Secret Correspondence, Jan. 4, 1777; 23:122, "the American Commissioners to Vergennes", Jan. 5, 1777.

In my opinion the surest way to obtain liberal aid... PBF 36:646, BF to Robert R. Livingston, Mar. 4, 1782.

Consequently my "Memoir concerning the present.... I inform'd the French and Spanish that America .... PBF 23:118-19, "Memoirs on the State of the Colonies," before Jan. 5, 1777.

As to agriculture and commerce,.... PBF 23:120, "Memoirs on the State of the Colonies," before Jan. 5, 1777.

The hearts of the French were universally for us... PBF 23:197, "The American Commissioners to the Committee of Secret Correspondence," Jan. 17, 1777.

In our first conversation with the minister.... Means were proposed of our obtaining a large sum of money... PBF 23:467-69, "the American Commissioners to the Committee of Secret Correspondence," Mar. 12, 1777; PBF 29:142, BF to Joshua Johnson, Mar. 17, 1779.

The desire in France of military officers.... PBF 23:471-72, "The American Commissioners to the Committee of Secret Correspondence," Mar. 12, 1777.

I apprehended that General Washington.... PBF 23:530, BF to George Washington, Mar. 29, 1777.

Baron de Steuben, lately a lieutenant general.... PBF 24:98, letter to George Washington, May 29, 1777; PBF 24:499, BF to George Washington; 24:73, "The American Commissioners to the Committee of Secret Correspondence," Mar. 25, 1777.

Most officers going to America... Oh, how I was harass'd.... PBF 25:20, letter to Barbeu-Dubourg, Oct. 2, 1777.

In response to these persistent requests,... PBF 23:549, "Model of a Letter of Recommendation," Apr. 2, 1777.

By 1779, the Congress expressed extreme embarrassment.... PBF 29:665, BF to Vergennes, June 11, 1779.

All Europe was for us.... PBF 23:473, "The American Commissioners to the Committee of Secret Correspondence," Mar. 12, 1777.

The French fleet was nearly ready.... PBF 23:475, "The American Commissioners to the Committee of Secret Correspondence," Mar. 12, 1777.

In early 1777, we received general alarming accounts... 23:260-62, The American Commissioners: Memorandum to Vergennes, Feb. 1, 1777; 23:288, "the American Commissioners to the Committee of Secret Correspondence," Feb. 6, 1777.

All Europe was on our side of the question... PBF 24:6, BF to Samuel Cooper, May 1, 1777.

Mr. Hartley, a member of the British Parliament... PBF 26:334, BF to Vergennes, Apr. 24, 1778.

In sum: The system of America is.... PBF 25:423, "Sir Philip Gibbes: Minutes of a Conversation with Franklin," Jan. 5, 1778.

I inform'd Mr. Hartley that our prisoners. . . . PBF 25:66-67, letter to David Hartley,
Oct. 14, 1777; 25:275, The American Commissioners to Lord North, Dec. 12,
1777;PBF 25:650, BF to David Hartley, Feb. 12, 1778.

Meanwhile, we had in France above two hundred prisoners, ... PBF 26:526, BF to
David Hartley, May 25, 1778; PBF 26:534, BF to John Paul Jones, May 27,
1778; 27:422-23, The American Commissioners to American Prisoners in
England, Sep. 19, 1778.

Our first applications for exchanging prisoners were. . . PBF 27:576-77, BF to
Wuybert, Lunt and MacKellar, Oct. 20, 1778; PBF 28:169, BF to David
Hartley, Nov. 29, 1778; PBF 28:588, BF to David Hartley, Feb. 22, 1779; PBF
28:415-16, David Hartley to BF, Jan. 23, 1779; PBF 28:461, BF to David
Hartley, Feb. 3, 1779.

It appeared that Mr. Hartley. . . . PBF 29:176, BF to David Hartley, Mar. 21, 1779;
29:550, letter to the Committee for Foreign Affairs, May 26, 1779.

I wished it were in my power to relieve. . . . PBF 29:340, BF to Jonathan Williams,
Jr., Apr. 20, 1779; PBF 29:350, BF to John Adams, Apr. 21, 1779.

The English conduct with regard to the exchange. . . . PBF 32:123, BF to James
Lowell, Mar. 16, 1780.

I believe in my conscience that mankind. . . . PBF 23:238, BF to Joseph Priestley,
Jan. 27, 1777.

I continue amazingly well and hearty. . . . PBF 24:90, BF to Jonathan Williams, Sr.,
May 27, 1777; PBF 23:238, BF to Joseph Priestley, Jan. 27, 1777.

It was with pleasure that we acquainted. . . . PBF 27:525, The American
Commissioners to Domenico Caracciolo, Oct. 9, 1778.

Before his leaving, Mr. Hartley warn'd me to take care. . . PBF 26:374, BF to David
Hartley, Apr. 29, 1778.

Mr. Hartley also warn'd me of French spies. . . PBF 23:211, BF to Juliana Ritchie,
Jan. 19, 1777; PBF 26:472, BF to Edward Bancroft, May 15, 1778.

In financial matters, the total failure of remittances from the Congress . . . . PBF
25:40-41, The American Commissioners to the Committee for Foreign
Affairs, Oct. 7, 1777.

We were much troubled with complaints. . . PBF 25:211, The American
Commissioners to the Committee for Foreign Affairs, Nov. 30, 1777.

On December 4, 1777, a Mr. Austin. . . . "Yes sir," he replied . . . I started to return
to the hotel. . . . We immediately issued a public announcement. . . .
PBF 25:234-36, "The American Commissioners: A Public Announcement,"
Dec. 4, 1777, Letter to Vergennes, Dec. 4, 1777; PBF 25:260-61, the
American Commissioners to Vergennes, Dec. 8, 1777; PBF 25:305, The
American Commissioners to the Committee for Foreign Affairs, Dec. 18,
1777; PBF 25:684, BF to the Massachusetts Board of War: Extract, Feb. 17,
1778.

Within several weeks, we had succeed'd in our negotiations. . . . PBF 25:635, Franklin
and Silas Deane to the President of Congress, Feb. 8, 1778.

The treaties were signed by the plenipotentiaries. . . PBF 25:722, BF to Thomas
Cushing, Feb. 27, 1778; 25:728, "The American Commissioners to the
Committee for Foreign Affairs," Feb. 28, 1778.

On the occasion of the signing of the treaty... Walter Isaacson, *Benjamin Franklin* (New York: Simon & Schuster, 2003), 347, 548.

Several of our American ships,... PBF 25:722, BF to Thomas Cushing, Feb. 27, 1778; 25:728, "The American Commissioners to the Committee for Foreign Affairs," Feb. 28, 1778.

6. Minister to France, 1778–79: An Ambassador's Life

Several months after arriving in Paris.... The extreme hurry.... FPR 42:u127, BF to Mary Hewson, Aug. 15, 1784; FPR 46:u247, BF to George Washington, June 3, 1789.

Mr. De Chaumont.... FPR 43:u24, BF to Richard Henry Lee, Apr. 12, 1785; FPR 46:u156, Franklin's sketch of services to U.S., Dec. 29, 1788.

Valentinois is a fine airy house... FPR 38:u9, BF to Robert R. Livingston, Sep. 3, 1782; PBF 25:28, BF to Jane Mecom, Oct. 5, 1777; PBF 28:421, BF to Margaret Stevenson, Jan. 25, 1779; PBF 31:361, BF to Mary Hewson, Jan. 10, 1780; PBF 34:348, BF to Georgiana Shipley, Feb. 3, 1781.

The clay medallion.... PBF 29:612, BF to Sarah Bache, June 3, 1779.

I had, at the request of friends.... PBF 32:590, BF to Thomas Digges, June 25, 1780.

Think how I must have appeared... PBF 23:298, BF to Emma Thompson, Feb. 8, 1777.

Besides being harass'd with.... FPR 43:u71, letter to Jan Ingenhousz, Apr. 29, 1785.

As to the Latin verse.... FPR 28:t117, Jacques Brillon de Jouy to BF, Nov. 15, 1778; FPR:u551, BF to Felix Nogaret, Mar. 8, 1781.

They told me that in writing.... PBF 23:235-36, BF to Mary Hewson, Jan. 26, 1777.

I found them a most amiable nation.... PBF 29:358, BF to Josiah Quincy, Sr., Apr. 22, 1779.

The desire of pleasing.... PBF 32:518, BF to John Jay, June 13, 1780.

At Passy, I found a little leisure... PBF 23:243-44, BF to Dumas, Jan. 28, 1777; PBF 30:514, BF to Elizabeth Partridge, Oct. 11, 1779.

I had, at the request of friends... PBF 32:590-01, BF to Thomas Digges, June 25, 1780.

France is the civilest nation... PBF 30:514, BF to Elizabeth Partridge, Oct. 11, 1779.

I pitied my poor old sister... PBF 25:732-33, BF to Catherine Green, Feb. 28, 1778.

Madame Brillon is one such friend... PBF 32:543, BF to William Carmichael, Jun 17, 1780; FPR 34:u126, BF to Madame Brillon, Dec. 10, 1780.

Madame Brillon wished to divert me.... FPR 23:t542, Madame Brillon to Le Veillard, March 1777; FPR 27:t397, Madame Brillon to BF, Sep. 13, 1778; FPR 27:t403, BF to Madame Brillon, Sep. 15, 1778; FPR 34:t317, BF to Madame Brillon, Jan. 11, 1781.

Madame Brillion has the honor.... FPR 24:t376, M. Brillion to BF, 30 July 1777.

Upon returning home... FPR 25:t204, BF to Madame Brillon, Nov. 29, 1777.

No, you did not do me any harm.... FPR 25:t218, Madame Brillon to BF.

You were kind enough yesterday.... It is well.... The first is pride.... The second....
The third.... The fourth.... The fifth.... The sixth.... The seventh.... FPR
26:t75, Madame Brillon to BF, Mar. 7, 1778.

I am charm'd with.... People commonly.... And now as I am.... But why should...
PBF 26:85, BF to Madam Brillon, Mar. 10, 1778.

You are a man, I am a woman.... Farewell.... FPR 26:t116, Madame Brillon to BF,
Mar. 16, 1778.

You adopt me..... Yesterday, I forgot.... When I go to paradise.... FPR 27:t476,
Madame Brillon to BF, Sep. 30, 1778; FPR 28:t212, Madame Brillon to BF,
Dec. 10, 1778.

Since you assure me... FPR 28:t214, BF to Madame Brillon, Dec. 10, 1778.

I am thinking about.... I despise the back-biters.... FPR 28:t253, Madame Brillon
to BF, Dec. 20, 1778; FPR 28:t411, 22 Jan. 1779; FPR 29:t169, Mar. 20, 1779;
28:t174, Nov. 30, 1778.

You may remember... It was, says he, the opinion.... PBF 27:430, BF to Madame
Brillon: "The Ephemera," Sept. 20, 1778.

Another friend in France.... PBF 27:670, BF to Madame Helvetius, Oct. 1778; FPR
28:t315, Madame Brillon to BF, 1778; FPR 36:t39, Madame Brillon to BF, Nov.
12, 1781.

I had often noticed.... PBF 34:u639, BF to L'Abbe de la Roche, Mar. 29, 1781;
Claude-Anne Lopez, *Mon Cher Papa* (New Haven: Yale University Press,
1990), 265.

On September 19, 1779, I addressed.... Sadly, she resolved to remain single.... Vexed
by your barbarous resolution.... There M. Helvétius.... "Ah!" said he, "you
make.... At these words.... Offended by this refusal... Walter Isaacson,
Benjamin Franklin: An American Life (New York: Simon & Schuster, 2003),
366–67; Claude-Anne Lopez, *Mon Cher Papa* (New Haven: Yale University
Press, 1990), 265–67.

I often think of the happiness.... PBF 45:u480, BF to Madame Helvétius, Apr. 23,
1788.

It was always with great pleasure to... I rejoice to learn.... Why do never.... PBF
28:421, BF to Margaret Stevenson, Jan. 25, 1779.

I had enjoy'd continu'd health.... PBF 25:77-78, "Franklin's description of his
Ailments," Oct. 17, 1777; PBF 33:429, BF to Sarah and Richard Bache, 1780.

I had not much time to consider... PBF 23:313, BF to Jan Ingenhousz, Feb. 12,
1777.

I have never entered... PBF 25:26, BF to Legegue de Presle, Oct. 4, 1777.

Adventures of all descriptions.... First, a man came to tell me.... Next, a Mons.
Coder came.... Then, a man came with a request.... Finally, I received a
parcel.... PBF 28:224-26, "Extract from Franklin's Journal," Dec. 13, 1778.

An anonymous letter was.... PBF 26:516, *Memoirs of the Life and Writings of*
Benjamin Franklin II:249-50, ed. by W. T. Franklin .

My grandson Temple was well.... PBF 24:63, BF to Richard Bache, May 1777; PBF
24:90, BF to Jonathan Williams, Sr., May 27, 1777.

I had a great deal of pleasure in Ben too... PBF 29:599-600, BF to Richard Bache, June 2, 1779; PBF 29:357, BF to Jane Mecom, Apr. 22, 1779.

After this time I received a report from James Lovell... PBF 26:662, James Lovell to BF, June 20, 1778; FPR 46:u107, letter to Marie-Anne Pierrette Paulze Lavoisier, Oct. 23, 1788; PBF 27:601, Richard Bache to BF, Oct. 22, 1778; PBF 27:604-05, Sarah Bache to BF, Oct. 22, 1778; PBF 29:437, BF to Benjamin Vaughan, May 5, 1779; PBF 32:610, BF to Richard Bache, June 27, 1780; PBF 35:471-72, BF to Richard Bache, Sept. 13, 1781; PBF 27:601, Richard Bache to BF, Oct. 22, 1778; PBF 27:604-05, Sarah Bache to BF, Oct. 22, 1778; PBF 29:437, BF to Benjamin Vaughan, May 5, 1779; PBF 32:610, BF to Richard Bache, June 27, 1780; PBF 35:471-72, BF to Richard Bache, Sept. 13, 1781; FPR 46:u137, BF to Elizabeth Partridge, Nov. 25, 1788.

With the addition... PBF 25:331, BF to Robert Morris, Dec. 21, 1777.

I had always resolved to have no quarrel... PBF 29:608, BF to James Lovell, June 2, 1779.

I frequently received letters... PBF 26:230-35, BF to Arthur Lee, Apr. 4, 1778; PBF 26:249, BF to Silas Deane, Apr. 7, 1778; PBF 26:308, BF to Jonathan Williams, Jr., Apr. 18, 1778.

Herein a correspondence...It was with the utmost surprise....That a measure of such moment...I trust, sir, you will think with me....I trust too, sir, that you will not treat...This is the draft of a letter...It is true I have omitted... PBF 26:220-23, BF to Ben Franklin, Apr. 2, 1778; BF to Arthur Lee, Apr. 3, 1778.

This is the letter I actually sent...Mr. Deane communicated to me...You ask me why....It is true that I have omitted....One more word about the accounts... PBF 26:231-35, BF to Arthur Lee, Apr. 4, 1778.

I was very easy about... PBF 29:601, BF to William Carmichael, Jun 2, 1779.

I trusted in the justice of... PBF 29:599, BF to Richard Bache, June 2, 1779.

My experiences with Lee...There are two sorts of people....An old philosophical friend of mine...I therefore advise these critical... PBF 34:41-44, "The Deformed and Handsome Leg," Nov. 23, 1780.

The body of our people are...We purpose, if possible... PBF 27:5-6, BF to Charles de Weissenstein, July 1, 1778.

I received notice from Congress.... PBF 27:137-38, BF to James Lovell, July 22, 1778.

My colleague... PBF 26:203-04, BF to Henry Laurens, Mar. 31, 1778; PBF 30:548, BF to James Lovell, Oct. 17, 1779; PBF 26:267-68, The American Commissioners to Vergennes, Apr. 10, 1778.

To Mr. Lovell of Congress.... PBF 27:360-61, BF to John Paul Jones, Sept. 6, 1778; PBF 27:139-40, BF to James Lowell, July 22, 1778. (Written at 5 am!).

We had no news.... PBF 27:360-61, BF to John Paul Jones, Sept. 6, 1778.

7. Minister to France, 1779–81: The War Continues

On the 11ᵗʰ of February, 1779... PBF 28:536, BF to Vergennes, Feb. 14, 1779; PBF 29:252, BF to John Adams, Apr. 3, 1779; PBF 28:522, BF to Jonathan Williams, Jr., Feb. 13, 1779; PBF 28:510, Franklin's Diary of Correspondence, Feb. 17, 1779; PBF 28:570, BF to Dumas, Feb. 19, 1779; PBF 28;571, BF to

Horneca, Fizeaux & Cie., Feb. 19, 1779; PBF 29:547, BF to the Committee for Foreign Affairs, May 26, 1779.

After that I constantly attended... PBF 29:548, BF to the Committee for Foreign Affairs, May 26, 1779.

All our letters from... PBF 28:571, BF to Dumas, Feb. 19, 1779; PBF 32:56-57, BF to George Washington, Mar. 5, 1780.

The Marquis de Lafayette spoke of the taking of Savannah....I was glad to see in news from home...I saw by the Virginia papers... PBF 29:235, BF to Stephen Sayre, Mar. 31, 1779; PBF 33:368, BF to Sarah and Richard Bache, Oct. 4, 1780; PBF 29:458, BF to John Adams, May 10, 1779.

At this time I did not totally... PBF 29:429, BF to Ingenhousz, May 4, 1779; PBF 31:456, BF to Joseph Priestley, Feb. 8, 1780.

I rejoiced to hear that....We make great improvements in nature... PBF 31:455-56, BF to Joseph Priestley, Feb. 2, 1780; PBF 31:452-53, BF to Richard Price, Feb. 6, 1790.

In March 1779, I sent letters...I also sent the letter to Holland....It was to be his last voyage.... PBF 31:487, BF to Thomas Digges, Feb. 15, 1780; FPR 42:u148, BF to Sir Joseph Banks, Aug. 21, 1784; FPR 44:u101, BF to Andrew Strahan, May 6, 1786.

My apprehensions of.... PBF 29:358, BF to Josiah Quincy, Sr., Apr. 22, 1779.

With this in mind, I wrote the following letter...I have before me your letters....The clay medallion of me you....When I began to read your account....If you happen again to see General Washington....Present my affectionate regards... PBF 29:61215, BF to Sarah Bache, June 3, 1779.

A merchant of Amsterdam... PBF 29:144, BF to Vergennes, Mar. 17, 1779.

I had in various ways... PBF 29:551-53, BF to the Committee for Foreign Affairs, May 26, 1779.

As to our finances in France,... PBF 29:554-55, BF to the Committee for Foreign Affairs, May 26, 1779.

The Committee of Commerce... PBF 32:185-86, BF to William Carmichael, Mar. 31, 1780.

Our credit and weight... PBF 33:354, BF to John Adams, Oct. 2, 1780.

At length I got over a reluctance... PBF 33:358, BF to John Jay, Oct. 2, 1780.

The principal difficulty.... PBF 26:160, The Committee for Foreign Affairs to the American Commissioners: Two Letters," Mar. 24, 1778; PBF 29:355-56, BF to Samuel Cooper, Apr. 22, 1779.

I took all the pains I could in... PBF 29:355-56, BF to Samuel Cooper, Apr. 22, 1779.

This effect of paper currency.... PBF 29:355-56, BF to Samuel Cooper, Apr. 22, 1779.

An expedition to Canada was... PBF 29:606, BF to John Jay, June 2, 1779.

Correspondence between friends.... PBF 29:602, BF to Charles Carroll, June 2, 1779; PBF 29:597, BF to Richard Bache, June 2, 1779; PBF 33:381, BF to Georgiana Shipley, Oct. 8, 1780.

I did take time to write my old friend Thomas Viny...When all the bustle is over.... PBF 29:431, BF to Thomas Viny, May 4, 1779.

I thought every day of my grandson... PBF 30:241, BF to Benjamin Franklin
   Bache, Aug. 19, 1779.
I received a letter from Madame Brillon.... FPR 29:t417, Madame Brillon to BF,
   May 3, 1779; 29:t450, May 8, 1779; 29:t464, May 11, 1779.
You told me, my dear daughter.... I am aware that.... FPR 29:t465, BF to Madame
   Brillon, May 11, 1779.
*I am charm'd with your description.... You ask what I mean? .... This, however, was
   afterwards.... Yet I ought to have charity....* FPR 31:t73, BF to Madame Brillon,
   Nov. 10, 1779.
*Instead of spending this Wednesday evening.... I was charm'd with your
   description.... When I was a child of seven.... This, however, was afterwards....
   Yet I ought to have charity....* PBF 31:73-75, "The Whistle," Nov. 10, 1779.
I assure you, my kind papa.... Mr. Brillon laughed.... A week from Saturday... FPR
   31:t112, Madame Brillon to BF, Nov. 16, 1779.
*In America, there was an intention to strike.... The other side I proposed to fill
   with....* PBF 30:430, BF to Edward Bridgen, Oct. 2, 1779.
We gave the English a little taste... PBF 30:545-46, BF to the Eastern Navy Board,
   Oct. 17, 1779; PBF 30:559, BF to David Hartley, Oct. 19, 1779; PBF 30:566,
   BF to Jonathan Loring Austin, Oct. 20, 1779; PBF 30:583-84, BF to Jane
   Mecom, Oct. 25, 1779; PBF 30:597-98, BF to Samuel Cooper, Oct. 27, 1779.
Accounts upon oath were taken in America... PBF 31:439, BF to David Hartley,
   Feb. 2, 1780; PBF 32:557, BF to William Hodgson, June 19, 1780.
Meanwhile, the French Court... PBF 30:549, BF to James Lovell, Oct. 17, 1779.
I frequently heard the old generals.... BF 32:57, BF to George Washington, Mar. 5,
   1780.
Messrs. Lee and Izard together... PBF 32:186-87, BF to William Carmichael, Mar.
   31, 1780.
The Alliance was expected to sail... PBF 32:448, BF to Samuel Huntington, May
   31, 1780; PBF 32:488-89, BF to Officers of the Alliance, June 7, 1780; PBF
   32:506-07, BF to John Paul Jones, June 12, 1780; PBF 32:542, BF to William
   Carmichael, June 17, 1780.
I went immediately to Versailles.... PBF 32:448, BF to Samuel Huntington, May
   31, 1780; PBF 32:488-89, BF to Officers of the Alliance, June 7, 1780; PBF
   32:506-07, BF to John Paul Jones, June 12, 1780; PBF 32:542, BF to William
   Carmichael, June 17, 1780.
I learned later that the Landais affair... PBF 32:612, BF to John Paul Jones, June
   27, 1780; PBF 34:107, BF to Samuel Huntington, Dec. 3, 1780.
My time was more taken up... PBF 32:187-88, BF to William Carmichael, Mar. 31,
   1780; PBF 32:516, BF to John Jay, June 13, 1780; PBF 32:187-88, BF to
   William Carmichael, Mar. 31, 1780; PBF 32:615, BF to Jonathan Williams,
   Jr., June 27, 1780.
I received a kind letter... PBF 32:195, Robert Morris to BF, Mar. 31, 1780.
A year later, I received a letter.... have just received your very... PBF 35:311-12, BF
   to Robert Morris, July 26, 1781.
London was in the utmost confusion... PBF 32:541, BF to William Carmichael,
   June 17, 1780; PBF 32:546, BF to Samuel Wharton, June 17, 1780.

The privateers Black Prince... PBF 33:171, BF to Samuel Huntington, Aug. 10, 1781.

In truth England brought itself... PBF 32:452, BF to Samuel Huntington, May 31, 1780; PBF 32:518, BF to John Jay, June 13, 1780.

I received several pleasing letters... I told Sally that her son Ben wrote me... PBF 35:58-59, BF to Richard and Sarah Bache, May 14, 1781; PBF 34:550, BF to Benjamin Franklin Bache, Apr. 16, 1781; PBF 32:611, BF to Sarah Franklin, June 27, 1780.

I sent the following letter to my grandson.... It always gives me pleasure to hear.... You see everywhere two sorts of people.... Take care therefore, my dear child.... I am ever, my dear child.... PBF 33:326-27, BF to Benjamin Franklin Bache, Sept. 25, 1780.

Soon after October... PBF 34:274, BF to John Jay, Jan. 15, 1781; PBF 34:288, BF to Dumas, Jan. 18, 1781; PBF 34:313, BF to John Jay, Jan. 27, 1781.

I received a letter from a friend... PBF 34:290, BF to Dr. Benjamin Waterhouse, Jan. 18, 1781.

Dialogue with the Gout.... Franklin's *Autobiographical Writings,* ed. By Carl Van Doren (Viking Press, 1945), 484–89, Oct. 22, 1780.

In news from America, I received a large and particular account.... PBF 34:90, BF to James Searle, Nov. 30, 1780; PBF 34:142, BF to Lafayette, Dec. 9, 1780; PBF 34:516, BF to John Adams, Apr. 7 1781; PBF 35:65, BF to the Marquis de Lafayette, May 14, 1781; PBF 85:547, BF to Ingenhousz, Oct. 2, 1781.

Mr. Henry Laurens, voted envoy... PBF 34:106, BF to Samuel Huntington, Dec. 3, 1780; PBF 34:211, BF to Jonathan Williams, Jr., Dec. 27, 1780; PBF 34:288, BF to Dumas, Jan. 18, 1781.

Regarding Spain, their long delay... PBF 34:312-13, BF to William Carmichael, Jan. 27, 1781.

I have long imagined that... PBF 34:519, BF to Francis Dana, Apr. 7, 1781.

I heard that a motion was made... PBF 34:312, BF to William Carmichael, Jan. 27, 1781.

By several letters to me..... I was thus charged by Congress... I am grown old... I am with great respect... PBF 34:372-73, BF to Vergennes, Feb. 13, 1781; PBF 34:390, BF to John Adams, Feb. 22, 1781.

This request was well received... PBF 34:446, BF to Samuel Huntington, Mar. 12—Apr. 12, 1781.

In January 1781, I passed my 75th year.... Having long tired of the trade of minister... However, I received dispatches .... PBF 35:398-99, BF to William Carmichael, Aug. 24, 1781; PBF 34:447-48, BF to Samuel Huntington (president of Congress), Mar. 12–Apr. 12, 1781; PBF 34:533, BF to John Jay, Apr. 12, 1781; PBF 35:175, Samuel Huntington to BF, June 19, 1781; PBF 35:365, BF to John Adams, Aug. 16, 1781; PBF 35:59, BF to Richard and Sarah Bache, May 14, 1781; PBF 35:66, BF to Marquis de Lafayette, May 14, 1781; PBF 35:84, BF to John Ada ms, May 19, 1781; PBF 35:365, BF to John Adams, Aug. 16, 1781; PBF 35:382, BF to John Jay, Aug. 20, 1781; PBF 35:474-75, BF to Samuel Huntington, Sept. 13, 1781; PBF 35:551, BF to Dr. Ingenhousz, June 21, 1782.

I had one request more to make... PBF 34:447-48, BF to Samuel Huntington, Mar. 12–Apr. 12, 1781; PBF 34:533, BF to John Jay, Apr. 12, 1781.

At this time I also spoke to.... *Monsieur Brillon raised two*..... *These essential principles*.... *However, Monsieur Brillon may have*.... FPR 34:t736, BF to Madame Brillon, before Apr. 20, 1781.

I was so engag'd in public affairs... PBF 34:380, BF to Beccaria, Feb. 19, 1781; PBF 35:69, BF to Samuel Cooper, May 15, 1781.

It had been a long time since... PBF 35:545, BF to Ingenhousz, Oct. 2, 1781.

"Go on with your excellent experiments... PBF 35:550, BF to Dr. Ingenhousz, June 21, 1782.

Those whom I had heard speak... PBF 35:456-57, BF to Dr. Ingenhousz, June 21, 1782.

The ship having the honour of.... PBF 34:517, BF to John Adams, Apr. 7, 1781; PBF 35:64, BF to the Marquis de Lafayette; PBF 35:68, BF to Samuel Cooper, May 15, 1781; PBF 35:400, BF to William Carmichael, Aug. 24, 1781; PBF 36:17-18, BF to Thomas McKean, Nov. 5, 1781.

The Indiana, as she had been formerly... PBF 35:383, BF to John Jay, Aug. 20, 1781.

I begged Mr. Adams to concur... PBF 34:567-68, BF to John Adams, Apr. 21, 1781; PBF 34:580, BF to John Adams, Apr. 29, 1781; PBF 35:61-62, BF to Samuel Huntington, May 14, 1781; PBF 35:83, BF to John Adams, May 19, 1781; PBF 35:119, BF to the Comte de Vergennes, June 4, 1781.

Mr. Ferdinand Grand... PBF 35:313, BF to Robert Morris, July 26, 1781.

I had no doubt that America... PBF 35:83, BF to John Adams, May 19, 1781.

I have never known a peace made... PBF 35:582, BF to John Adams, Oct. 12, 1781.

The English played a desperate game... PBF 35:65, BF to Marquis de Lafayette, May 14, 1781.

There arose a good deal of misunderstanding... PBF 35:151-52, BF to Durival, June 12, 1781; PBF 29:166, BF to Jonathan Williams, Jr., Mar. 19, 1779.

Thanks to God I still enjoyed health... PBF 35:270, BF to John Temple, July 15, 1781.

I received a letter from Mr. Jay... PBF 35:379, BF to John Jay, Aug. 20, 1781.

By this time.... PBF 31:479, BF to Sartine, Feb. 13, 1790; PBF 37:228, BF to William Hodgson, Apr. 26, 1782.

I received a letter.... PBF 35:237, John Jay to BF, July 9, 1781; PBF 35:380, BF to John Jay, Aug. 20, 1781; PBF 35:477, BF to James Lovell, Sep. 13, 1781.

I received a letter signed by 280 American soldiers.... *The season being cold and blustering*.... *We are very discontented among us*... PBF 31:442-43, BF 280 American Solders to BF, Feb. 3, 1780.

The prisoners did not sign their above mentioned letter.... PBF 29:282, BF to Schweighauer, Apr. 8, 1779; PBF 29:340, BF to Jonathan Williams, Jr., Apr. 20, 1779; PBF 29:550, BF to the Committee for Foreign Affairs, May 26, 1779.

I received a letter.... PBF 35:477, BF to James Lovell, Sep. 13, 1781.

Nevertheless, I ordered another sum... PBF 35:673-74, BF to William Hodgson, Oct. 31, 1781; PBF 37:537, BF to Robert R. Livingston, June 25, 1782.

Mr. Thomas Digges, an American merchant... PBF 35:381, BF to John Jay, Aug. 20, 1781; PBF 34:475, William Hodgson to BF, Mar. 20, 1781; PBF 34:507, BF to William Hodgson, Apr. 1, 1781; PBF 34:572, BF to William Hodgson, Apr. 25, 1781; PBF 35:340, BF to Moses Brown, Aug. 6, 1781.

That very great villian Digges... PBF 37:537-38, BF to Robert R. Livingston, June 25, 1782.

The practice of sending prisoners... PBF 36:14, BF to Thomas McKean, Nov. 5, 1781.

I received a letter from Francis Coffyn... PBF 35:392-93, BF to Francis Coffyn, Aug. 22, 1781; PBF 36:25, BF to John Adams, Nov. 7, 1781.

I found that there were no people.... PBF 35:u423, BF to John Jay, Aug. 20, 1781.

A gentleman arrived from America... PBF 35:381, BF to John Jay, Aug. 20, 1781.

Col. Laurens... PBF 35:399, BF to William Carmichael, Aug. 24, 1781.

Holland did not seem to feel for us... PBF 35:341, BF to Dumas, Aug. 6, 1781; PBF 35:353, BF to Dumas, Aug. 12, 1781.

I was exceedingly embarrass'd.... PBF 35:429-30, BF to John Adams, Aug. 31, 1781; PBF 35:466, BF to Robert Morris, Sept. 12, 1781.

The sentiment expressed by Mr. Robert Morris... PBF 36:20, 22, BF to Robert Morris, Nov. 5, 1781.

I had received a very friendly letter.... BF 35:594, BF to Edmund Burke, Oct. 15, 1781; PBF 36:13, BF to Thomas McKean, Nov. 5, 1781; PBF 36:94, BF to Benjamin Vaughan, Nov. 22, 1781; PBF 36:454, BF to John Jay, Jan. 19, 1782.

Captain Folger, a relation of mine... PBF 36:67, BF to Jonathan Williams, Jr., Nov. 19, 1781.

In the summer of 1781.... Her good neighbors.... FPR 35:t611, BF to Madame Brillon, Oct. 1, 1781; FPR 35:t662, BF to Madam Brillon, Oct. 12, 1781; FPR 36:t415, BF to Madame Brillon, Jan. 6, 1782; FPR 36:t318, BF to Madame Brillon, Dec. 25, 1781.

Being without my good friend.... PBF 35:131, BF to Madam Brillon, Jun 7, 1781; translation by Mary Laure Petipaw and Lesley Skousen-Chio. See also Stacy Schiff, *A Great Improvisation* (New York: Henry Holt, 2005), 279.

Later that year.... FPR 36:u253, BF to David Harley, Dec. 15, 1781.

I wished most heartily that.... PBF 36:102, BF to Thomas Pownall, Nov. 23, 1781.

We have no safety but in our independence.... PBF 37:563, BF to Samuel Cooper, June 28, 1782.

8. Minister to France, 1781–83: Peace Treaty with England

Glorious news! The Duke de Lauzun.... I received a packet.... PBF 36:115, BF to John Adams, Nov. 26, 1781; PBF 36:79, BF to Vergennes, Nov. 20, 1781; PBF 36:454, BF to John Jay, Jan. 19, 1781; PBF 37:87-88, BF to Gen. Washington, Apr. 2, 1782; PBF 36:644, BF to Robert R. Livingston, Mar. 4, 1782.

Madame Brillon complained.... FPR 36:t240, Madam Brillon to BF, Dec. 11, 1781; FPR 36:t318, BF to Madame Brillon, Dec. 25, 1781.

From the English papers.... PBF 36:674, BF to Robert Morris, Mar. 9, 1782; PBF 36:680, BF to John Adams, Mar. 11, 1782.

The French Court was highly disposed.... PBF 36:646, BF to Robert R. Livingston, Mar. 4, 1782.

However, I long feared that.... PBF 36:411-12, BF to Robert Morris, Jan. 9, 1782; PBF 36:434, BF to Ferdinand Grand, Jan. 15, 1782; PBF 36:438, BF to John Jay, Jan. 15, 1782.

I drew a bill on Congress....I had much vexation.... PBF 36:451-52, BF to John Jay, Jan. 19, 1782; PBF 36:438, BF to John Jay, Jan. 15, 1782; PBF 36:651, BF to Robert Morris, Mar. 4, 1782.

The Marquis de Lafayette was very.... PBF 36:467, BF to William Carmichael, Jan. 23, 1782; PBF 36:644, BF to Robert R. Livingston, Mar. 4, 1782; PBF 36:650, BF to Robert Morris, Mar. 4, 1782.

Meanwhile, I received a very long political letter....I was not convinced.... PBF 36:u487, BF to John Jay, Jan. 19, 1782; PBF 37:74, BF to Robert Morris, Mar. 30, 1782; PBF 37:172-73, BF to Silas Deane, Apr. 19, 1782.

I also received a letter from.... PBF 36:477, BF to Benjamin Franklin Bache, Jan. 25, 1782; PBF 39:u422, BF to Benjamin Franklin Bache, May 2, 1783.

A gentleman of Lyons.... PBF 36:478, BF to Samuel Cooper Johonnot, Jan. 25, 1782.

In early 1782, I received the supplication.... FPR 36:t415, BF to Madame Brillon, Jan. 6, 1782.

Despite the victory at Yorktown.... PBF 36:647, BF to Robert R. Livingston, Mar. 4, 1782; PBF 37:79, BF to William Hodgson, Mar. 31, 1782.

I wrote the following letter to Mr. David Hartley.... PBF 37:u14, BF to David Hartley, Apr. 5, 1782.

Soon after this we heard.... PBF 37:229, BF to William Hodgson, Apr. 26, 1782; PBF 37:293, Journal of the Peace Negotiations, May 9, 1782; PBF 37:u30, BF to Robert Morris, Apr. 8, 1782; PBF 37:114-15, BF to Robert Morris, Apr. 8, 1782; PBF 37:116, BF to George Washington, Apr. 8, 1782.

Capt. Barry told me.... PBF 37:41, BF to Jonathan Williams, Jr., and 37:42, BF to Robert Morris, Mar. 30, 1782.

England at length saw.... PBF 37:u364, BF to Jan. Ingenhousz, June 21, 1782.

I was one of five.... PBF 37:78-79, BF to David Hartley, Mar. 31, 1782; PBF 37:536-37, BF to Robert R. Livingston, June 25, 1782; PBF 37:u104, BF to John Jay, Apr. 23, 1782.

I kept a very particular journal.... PBF 37:536, BF to Robert R. Livingston, June 25, 1782; PBF 37:u16, BF to David Hartley, Apr. 5, 1782; PBF 37:250, David Hartley to BF, May 1, 1782.

Great affairs sometimes take.... PBF 37:292-93, Journal of the Peace Negotiations, May 9, 1782.

Soon after this we heard.... PBF 37:293, Journal of the Peace Negotiations, Mar. 22, 1782.

Mr. Oswald came accordingly... PBF 37:294, Journal of the Peace Negotiations, Apr. 16, 1782.

On our return from Versailles... PBF 37:295, Journal of the Peace Negotiations, April 19, 1782.

The next morning when.... PBF 37:295-96, Journal of the Peace Negotiations, Apr. 19, 1782; PBF 37:181, BF to John Adams, Apr. 21, 1782.

I then touch'd upon the affair.... PBF 37:296, Journal of the Peace Negotiations, Apr. 19, 1782.

He then told me that... PBF 37:297, Journal of the Peace Negotiations, Apr. 19, 1782.

By the first opportunity.... PBF 37:297, Journal of the Peace Negotiations, Apr. 19, 1782.

On the 4th of May, 1782, Mr. Oswald.... PBF 37:298, Journal of the Peace Negotiations, May 4, 1782.

Mr. Oswald then show'd me... PBF 37:298-99, Journal of the Peace Negotiations, Apr. 27, 1782.

Mr. Oswald also inform'd.... PBF 37:299, Journal of the Peace Negotiations, May 4, 1782.

Finally Mr. Oswald acquainted me... PBF 37:299, Journal of the Peace Negotiations, May 4, 1782.

Mr. Oswald repeated to me... PBF 37:300, Journal of the Peace Negotiations, May 5, 1782.

Several days later, I had but just sent.... PBF 37:301, Journal of the Peace Negotiations, May 8, 1782.

Vergennes was glad to hear... PBF 37:302, Journal of the Peace Negotiations, May 8, 1782.

"To be sure,".... PBF 37:303, Journal of the Peace Negotiations, May 8, 1782.

"As to our being satisfied with.... PBF 37:303-04, Journal of the Peace Negotiations, May 8, 1782.

The coming and going.... PBF 37:305, Journal of the Peace Negotiations, May 8, 1782.

On May 13, 1782, I received the good news.... PBF 37:362-63, BF to David Hartley, May 13, 1782.

On May 26, Mr. Grenville... PBF 37:313-14, Journal of the Peace Negotiations, May 36, 1782.

Mr. Jay wrote me from time.... PBF 37:310, Journal of the Peace Negotiations, May 13, 1782.

It seems to me that we have.... PBF 37:310, Journal of the Peace Negotiations, May 13, 1782.

The northern princes are.... PBF 37:312, Journal of the Peace Negotiations, May 13, 1782; PBF 37:538, BF to Robert R. Livingston, June 25, 1782.

I have never yet known.... PBF 37:415-16, BF to Henry Laurens, May 25, 1782; PBF 37:609, BF to Benjamin Vaughan, July 10, 1782.

During the negotiations.... PBF 37:316, Journal of the Peace Negotiations, May 27, 1782.

Mr. Grenville came.... PBF 37:318, 323, Journal of the Peace Negotiations, May 25, 1782.

As to the loyalists.... PBF 37:326, Journal of the Peace Negotiations, June 3, 1782; FPR 39:u183, BF to Henry Laurens, Mar. 20, 1783.

He had also, in consequence... PBF 37:326-27, Journal of the Peace Negotiations, June 3, 1782.

On Tuesday June 11, 1782... PBF 37:335, Journal of the Peace Negotiations, June 11, 1782.

In the afternoon of Sunday.... PBF 37:346, Journal of the Peace Negotiations, June 29, 1782.

During these negotiations.... PBF PBF 37:444-46, BF to Joseph Priestley, June 7, 1782.

By resolution of the 14th of June... PBF 37:452-52, Discharge of Cornwallis from his Parole, June 9, 1782.

M. Leray de Chaumont, our landlord.... PBF 37:473-74, BF to Jonathan Williams Jr., June 13, 1782; PBF 37:588-89, Franklin and Chaumont: Agreement for Arbitration by Grand and Dangirard, July 7, 1782; FPR 46:u339, BF to Le Ray de Chaumont, Oct. 31, 1789.

A letter written by James Hutton... I wonder at this.... PBF 37:586-57, BF to James Hutton, July 7, 1782.

In the course of the summer.... FPR 37:u457, BF to David Hartley, July 10, 1782; PBF 37:611-12; FPR 35:t753, BF to Madame Brillon, Oct. 30, 1781.

Congress continued to press.... PBF 37:734-35, BF to Robert Morris, Aug. 12, 1782; PBF 37:731, BF to Robert R. Livingston, Aug. 12, 1782; FPR 35:t753, BF to Mr. & Mrs. Brillon, Oct. 30, 1781.

Tho' the English.... PBF 37:536, BF to Robert R. Livingston; PBF 37:543, BF to Robert Morris, June 25, 1782.

Mr. Grenville returned.... PBF 37:602, letter to La Fayette, July 9, 1782.

During the peace negotiations, I fancied.... What a difference.... You see by this time.... I fancy we shall.... Articles 1.... 9.... Let me know.... PBF 27:164, Exchanges with Madam Brillon de Jouy, July 27, 1778.

Accidents and a long severe.... FPR 38:u363, BF to Robert R. Livingston, Dec. 5, 1782; FPR 38:u119, BF to the American Commissions, Oct. 1, 1782.

My illness, the cruel gout.... FPR 38:u176, BF to John Adams, Oct. 15, 1782; FPR 38:u363, BF to Robert R. Livingston, Dec. 5, 1782; FPR 38u68, BF to La Fayette, Sep. 17, 1782.

Much of the summer was.... FPR 38:u363, BF to Robert R. Livingston, Dec. 5, 1782; FPR 38:u16, BF to de Rayneval, Sep. 4, 1782; FPR 38:u171, BF to Robert R. Livingston, Oct. 14, 1782.

And then we came to the point.... FPR 38:u363, BF to Robert R. Livingston, Dec. 5, 1782; FPR 38:u171, BF to Robert R. Livingston, Oct. 14, 1782; FPR 38:u237, the American Commissioners to Richard Oswald, Nov. 5, 1782.

Everyone of the present British ministry.... FPR 38:u363, BF to Robert R. Livingston, Dec. 5, 1782.

In sum, our independence was.... FPR 38:u237, American Commissioners to Richard Oswald, Nov. 5, 1782; FPR 38:u451, BF to Samuel Cooper, Dec. 26, 1782.

We communicated all the articles.... FPR 38:u416, BF to Vergennes, Dec. 17,
   1782; FPR 38:u363, BF to Robert R. Livingston, Dec. 5, 1782.

I was soon after taken ill... FPR 38:u582, BF to Mary Hewson, Jan. 8, 1783.

The preliminaries of peace.... FPR 38:u633, BF to Robert R. Livington, Jan. 21, 1783.

9. MINISTER TO FRANCE, 1783–85: MY LAST YEARS IN PARIS

At length we were at peace... FPR 38:u668, BF to Mary Hewson, Jan. 27, 1783;
   FPR 38:u363, BF to Robert R. Livingston, Dec. 5, 1782; FPR 38:u731, BF to
   Joseph Banks, Sep. 9, 1782.

It was our firm connection.... FPR 38:u451, BF to Samuel Cooper, Dec. 26, 1782;
   FPR 40:u83, BF to Robert R. Livingston, July 22, 1783.

I heard frequently of.... FPR 39:u183, BF to Henry Laurens, Mar. 20, 1783; FPR
   38:u451, BF to Samuel Cooper, Dec. 26, 1782; FPR 40:u83, BF to Robert R.
   Livingston, July 22, 1783.

I have observed some enemies.... FPR 41:u204, BF to John Jay, Jan. 6, 1784.

The revolutionary war.... FPR 39:u655, BF to Nathaniel Falconer, June 18, 1783;
   FPR 42:u137, BF to William Strahan, Aug. 19, 1784.

I am reminded of..... FPR 42:u137, BF to William Strahan, Aug. 19, 1784.

What was the consequence... FPR 42:u137, BF to William Strahan, Aug. 19, 1784.

But I am not vain enough.... FPR 42:u137, BF to William Strahan, Aug. 19, 1784.

England had lost by this mad war.... PBF 25:562, BF to James Hutton, Feb. 1,
   1778.

A multitude of people.... FPR 39:u337, BF to Robert R. Livingston, Apr. 15, 1783;
   FPR 38:u592, BF to Gaietano Filangieri, Jan. 11, 1783; FPR 38:u169, BF to
   the Earl of Buchan, Mar. 17, 1783.

Mr. Strahan argued that.... FPR 42:u137, BF to William Strahan, Aug. 19, 1784.

There is no doubt but.... FPR 36:u411, BF to Henry Royle et al., Jan. 4, 1782.

Mr. Ingenhousz wrote me.... I was asked about employment... FPR 39:u485, BF to
   Jan Ingenhousz, May 16, 1783.

The cultivators of land.... FPR 42:u617, BF to Georgiana Shipley Hare, Jan. 25,
   1784.

The extravagant misrepresentations... FPR 41:u41, BF to Thomas Mifflin, Dec. 25,
   1783.

I wrote my daughter... FPR 40:u119, BF to Richard and Sarah Bache, July 27,
   1783; *Information to those who would remove to America,* quoted in Claude-
   Anne Lopez, *Mon Cher Papa* (Yale University Press, 1990), p. 205.

I received an account... FPR 38:u667, BF to John Sargent, Jan. 27, 1783.

The departure of my dearest.... FPR 38:u668, BF to Mary Hewson, Jan. 27, 1783.

I received a kind letter of thanks... FPR 43:u63, BF from Mary Hewson, Apr. 26,
   1785; FPR 43:u795, BF to Mary Hewson, May 5, 1785.

That year also carried off.... FPR 38:u668, BF to Mary Hewson, Jan. 27, 1783.

Then, being inform'd that... FPR 40:u119, BF to Richard and Sarah Bache, July
   27, 1783; FPR 40:u321, BF to Mary Hewson, Sep. 7, 1783; FPR 41:u54, BF to
   Mary Hewson, Dec. 26, 1783.

Benny being a very.... FPR 42:u395, BF to Richard Bache, Nov. 11, 1784.

The definitive treaties were.... FPR 39:u106, BF to Robert R. Livingston, Mar. 7, 1783; FPR 39:u337, BF to Robert R. Livingston, Apr. 15, 1783.

We were also totally in the dark... FPR 39:u621, BF to Robert R. Livingston, June 12, 1783; FPR 39:u655, BF to Nathaniel Falconer, June 18, 1783; PBF 40:u24, BF to Henry Laurens, July 6, 1783; FPR 40:u83, BF to Robert R. Livingston, July 22, 1783.

I also received the resolutions.... FPR 38:u657, BF to Vergennes, Jan. 25, 1783.

The finances in France... FPR 39:u337, BF to Robert R. Livingston, Apr. 15, 1783; FPR 39:u112, BF to Robert Morris, Mar. 7, 1783.

The late failure of payment.... FPR 40:u540, BF to Elias Boudinot, Nov. 1, 1783.

Events at length should have... FPR 41:u51, BF to Samuel Cooper, Dec. 26, 1783; FPR 41:u313, BF to John Adams, Feb. 5, 1784; FPR 41:u334, BF to Henry Laurens, Feb. 12, 1784.

If our people who neither paid rents... FPR 40:u114, BF to Robert Morris, July 27, 1783.

The problem is that our people.... FPR 41:u44, BF to Robert Morris, Dec. 25, 1783; FPR 46:u344, From Benjamin Franklin: Queries and Remarks on "Hints for the Members of Pennsylvania Convention," Nov. 3, 1789.

Our merchants complained.... FPR 39:u166, BF to Vergennes, Mar. 16, 1783.

We saw much in parliamentary... FPR 43:u49, BF to Benjamin Vaughan, Apr. 21, 1785.

In transactions of trade.... PBF 21:169-77, Franklin's Contribution to a Pamphlet by George Whatley, March 1774.

It would be better if.... PBF 21:169-77, Franklin's Contribution to a Pamphlet by George Whatley, March 1774.

Let us now forgive and forget.... FPR 39:u168, BF to Jonathan Shipley, Mar. 17, 1783.

It was certainly disagreeable.... FPR 40:u297, BF to Henry Laurens, Sep. 3, 1783; FPR 41:u41, BF to Thomas Mifflin, Dec. 25, 1783.

I rejoiced at the return of peace.... FPR 40:u118, BF to Sir Joseph Banks, July 27, 1783; FPR 40:u343, BF to Josiah Quincy, Sep. 11, 1783.

Nevertheless, it is a pleasing.... FPR 40:u429, BF to Sir Edward Newenham, Oct. 2, 1783.

After the signing of.... It is confidently reported.... It was not my purpose... FPR 40:u336, BF to Henry Laurens and John Jay, Sept. 10, 1783; FPR 40:u343, BF to Josiah Quincy, Sep. 11, 1783.

Lady Dowager Penn... FPR 43:u71, BF to Jan Ingenhousz, Apr. 29, 1785.

In my judgment, when I.... FPR 43:u71, BF to Jan Ingenhousz, Apr. 29, 1785.

The lady's complaints.... FPR 43:u71, BF to Jan Ingenhousz, Apr. 29, 1785.

Our rector of St. Martin's Parish.... FPR 43:u71, BF to Jan Ingenhousz, Apr. 29, 1785.

After the war, in 1783.... FPR 40:u365, BF to Richard Price, Sep. 16, 1783; PBF 41:u47, BF to Benjamin Rush, Dec. 26, 1783; FPR 40:365, BF to Richard Price, Sep. 16, 1783.

The first balloon.... FPR 40:u446, BF to Sir Joseph Banks, Oct. 8, 1783.

The next balloon... FPR 40:u612, BF to Sir Joseph Banks, Nov. 21, 1783.

One of the courageous philosophers... FPR 40:u612, BF to Sir Joseph Banks, Nov. 21, 1783.

This method of filling the balloon.... FPR 40:u612, BF to Sir Joseph Banks, Nov. 21, 1783; FPR 40:u271, BF To Sir Joseph Banks, Aug. 30, 1783.

On several occasions, the new... FPR 40:u642, BF to Sir Joseph Banks, Dec. 1, 1783.

Messrs. Charles and Robert.... FPR 40:u365, BF to Richard Price, Sep. 16, 1783; PBF 40:u653, BF to Henry Laurens, Dec. 6, 1783; FPR 41:u47, BF to Benjamin Rush, Dec. 26, 1783.

It was said by some.... FPR 43:u223, BF to Edward Newenham, June 20, 1785.

I wrote M. de Vergennes that.... FPR 40:u654, BF to Vergennes, Dec. 6, 1783; FPR 43:u71, BF to Jan Ingenhousz, Apr. 29, 1785.

My sitting too much at the desk.... FPR 40:u682, BF to William Carmichael, Dec. 15, 1783; FPR 41:u204, BF to John Jay, Jan. 6, 1784; FPR 41:u688, BF to Thomas Mifflin, June 16, 1784.

The relish for reading poetry.... FPR 37:284, BF to John Thornton, May 8, 1782

Madame Brillon did me the honor.... FPR 41:t493, BF to Madame Brillion, Apr. 8, 1784.

I had promised my dear friend.... FPR 41:t670, BF to Countess d'Houdetot, June 9, 1784.

We had a terrible winter in France.... FPR 41:u334, BF to Henry Laurens, Feb. 12, 1784; FPR 41:u470, BF to David Hartley, Mar. 31, 1784; FPR 36:t415, Jan. 6, 1782.

I received by Capt. Barney... FPR 41:u281, BF to Sarah Bache, Jan. 26, 1784.

I hoped therefore that the Order.... FPR 41:u281, BF to Sarah Bache, Jan. 26, 1784; FPR 43:u149, BF to George Whatley, May 23, 1785.

As to the figure to represent the order... FPR 41:u281, BF to Sarah Bache, Jan. 26, 1784.

In truth, the turkey.... FPR 41:u281, letter to Sarah Bache, Jan. 26, 1784.

I sent Benjamin Webb.... FPR 41:u538, BF to Benjamin Webb, Apr. 22, 1784.

In the same spirit, I flattered myself.... *To the authors of the journal*.... *You often entertain us*.... *I was the other evening*.... *I went home and to bed*.... *I looked at my watch*... *This event has given*.... *I took for the basis*.... *If it should be said*.... *First*... *Second*.... *Third*.... *Fourth*.... *All the difficulty*... *But this sum*.... *For the great benefit*.... FPR 41:u545, From Benjamin Franklin: Proposal re Daylight Saving, Apr. 26, 1784.

I received a kind letter.... *It had been more than 60 years*.... *I longed much to see again my native place*... FPR 41:u587, BF to Samuel Mather, May 12, 1784.

Mr. Jay sail'd for America.... FPR 41:u688, BF to Thomas Mifflin, June 16, 1784; FPR 41:u692, BF to Jane Mecom, June 17, 1784; FPR 42:u73, BF to Comte de Mercy-Argenteua, July 30, 1784; FPR 42:u129, BF to William Franklin, Aug. 16, 1784; FPR 42:u130, BF to Richard Price, Aug. 16, 1784; FPR 42:u155, BF to William Carmichael, Aug. 16, 1784; FPR 42:u636, BF to John Jay, Feb. 8, 1785.

The gout was bad.... FPR 43:140, BF to Jonathan Williams, Jr., May 19, 1785; 43:u71, BF to Jan Ingenhousz, Apr. 29, 1785.

Besides being harass'd.... FPR 43:u71, BF to Jan Ingenhousz, Apr. 29, 1785.

I thought the clause.... FPR 42:u146, BF to John Calder, Aug. 21, 1784; PBF
43:u278, BF to Claudius Crigan, July 5, 1785.

In a letter, George Whatley... FPR 42:u147, BF to George Whatley, Aug. 21, 1784.

My doctor said that my double spectacles.... FPR 43:u149, BF to George Whatley,
May 23, 1785.

We were much amiss'd in France.... FPR 42:u148, BF to Sir Joseph Banks, Aug.
21, 1784; FPR 42:u200, BF to William Temple Franklin, Sep. 8, 1784; FPR
42:t187, From Benjamin Franklin et al: Report on the experiments of animal
magnetism, Sept. 4, 1784.

But one must not be indifferent.... FPR 42:t187, From Benjamin Franklin et al:
Report on the experiments of animal magnetism, Sept. 4, 1784.

The distribution of enlightenment... FPR 42:t115, Secret Report on Mesmerism,
Aug. 11, 1784; FPR 42:t187, From Benjamin Franklin et al: Report on the
experiments of animal magnetism, Sept. 4, 1784.

Mr. Mesmer complain'd about our report.... FPR 42:u148, BF to Sir Joseph Banks,
Aug. 21, 1784; FPR 42:u200, BF to William Temple Franklin, Sep. 8, 1784.

Mesmer still had some adherents.... FPR 43:u71, BF to Jan Ingenhousz, Apr. 29,
1785.

In 1750, I made an experiment... PBF 4:82, BF to John Franklin, Dec. 25, 1750;
FPR 43:u71, BF to Jan Ingenhousz, Apr. 29, 1785.

On another occasion, I had a paralytic.... FPR 43:u71, BF to Jan Ingenhousz, Apr.
29, 1785.

My letters from America.... FPR 42:u628, BF to Richard Price, Feb. 1, 1785;
43:u71, BF to Jan Ingenhousz, Apr. 29, 1785.

The circumstances of the Royalists.... FPR 43:u71, BF to Jan Ingenhousz, Apr. 29,
1785.

Two pamphlets were published.... FPR 42:u712, BF to Benjamin Vaughan, Mar. 1,
1785.

If we really believe.... FPR 42:u712, BF to Benjamin Vaughan, Mar. 1, 1785.

By contrast, privateering has.... FPR 42:u712, BF to Benjamin Vaughan, Mar. 1,
1785.

At length I received from Congress... FPR 43:u425, BF to John Jay, Sept. 19, 1785.

My friends in France were so apprehensive.... FPR 43:u96, BF to Jonathan
Williams, Jr., May 5, 1785; FPR 43:u113, BF to Richard and Sarah Bache,
May 10, 1785.

Having stayed in France.... FPR 43:u310, from Benjamin Franklin's diary, July
12–23, 1785; FPR 43:u349, BF to Benjamin Vaughan, July 24, 1785; FPR
43:u329, BF to Anne-Catherine de Ligniville Helvetius, July 19, 1785,
translated in Carl Van Doren, ed., *Benjamin Franklin's Autobiographical
Writings* (New York: Viking, 1945), 648–49; FPR 43:u338, BF to Thomas
Jefferson, July 21, 1785; FPR 43:u351, BF to Jonathan Shipley, no date but
probably in July, 1785; FPR 43:u316, BF to Jane Mecom, July 13, 1785; FPR
43:u274, BF to Mary Hewson, July 4, 1785.

*The voyage from thence to Southampton.... I read over the writings.... Capt.
Jennings carried down....* FPR 43:u349, BF to Benjamin Vaughan, July 24,
1785; FPR 43:u310, from Benjamin Franklin's diary, July 24–28, 1785.

10. The Creation of a New Nation, 1785–87

We had a pleasant...FPR 43:u526, BF to Mary Stevenson Hewson, Oct. 30, 1785; FPR 43:u362, BF to John Coakley Lettsom, July 26, 1785; FPR 43:u868, BF to Jonathan Williams, Jr., Jan. 27, 1786; FPR 44:u7, BF to Louis-Guillaume Le Veillard, Mar. 6, 1786; FPR 44:u602, BF T Louis-Guillaume Le Veillard, Apr. 15, 1787; FPR 44:u266, BF to Jean-Baptiste Le Roy, Aug. 15, 1786; FPR 44:u266, BF T Jean-Baptiste Le Roy, Aug. 15, 1786.

On September 14, 1785...FPR 43:u310, from Benjamin Franklin's diary, Sept. 14, 1785.

I was continually surrounded...FPR 43:u430, BF to Jane Mecom, Sept. 19, 1785; FPR 43:u427, BF the Justices of the City and County of Philadephia, Sept. 1785; FPR 43:u434, BF to John and Sara Van Brugh Livingston Jay, Sep. 21, 1785.

The vessel from Havre...FPR 44:u5, BF to Rodolphe-Ferdinand Grand, Mar. 5, 1786.

Statuary Mr. Houdon...FPR 43:u432, BF to George Washington, Sept. 20, 1785; FPR 43:u464, BF Thomas Jefferson, Oct. 1, 1785; PBF 43:u579, BF to Houdon, Nov. 30, 1785.

Upon my return, I found...FPR 44:u404, BF to John Hunter, Nov. 24, 1786; FPR 43:u515, BF to David Hartley, Oct. 27, 1785; FPR 44:u5, BF to Rodolphe-Ferdinand Grand, Mar. 5, 1786.

There is a tradition that...*I saw in the public papers*...*The great business of the continent*...*If we enter the cities*...*At the distance I live*...*There remain the merchants*...*Whoever has traveled*...*It is true that in*...*Indeed some among us*...*The agriculture and fisheries*...PBF 43:u781, From Benjamin Franklin: On the Internal State of America, c. 1785.

I think myself happy....FPR 43:u423, BF to the Philadelphia Constitution Society, Sept. 1785; FPR 44:u404, BF to John Hunter, Nov. 24, 1786; FPR 44:u606, BF to Lafayette, Apr. 17, 1787; FPR 44:u617, BF to Abbe Andre Morellet, Apr. 22, 1787.

It was my intention to avoid...FPR 43:u559, BFto John and Susanna Bard, Nov. 14, 1785; FPR 43:u893, BF to Jonathan Williams, Jr., Feb. 12, 1786; FPR 43:u526, BF to Mary Stevenson Hewson, Oct. 30, 1785; PBF 43:u454, BF to Thomas Paine, Sep. 27, 1785; FPR 43:u913, BF to Jonathan Shipley, Feb. 24, 1786; FPR 44:u599, BF to the Duc de La Rochefoucauld, Apr. 15, 1787; FPR 45:u248, BF to Jane Mecom, Nov. 4, 1787.

I think we are in the right road....FPR 43:u913, BF to Jonathan Shipley, Feb. 24, 1786; FPR 44:u7, BF to Louis-Guillaume Le Veillard, Mar. 6, 1786.

As to public affairs....FPR 44:u30, BF to Thomas Jefferson, Mar. 20, 1786; FPR 44:u5, BF to Rodolphe-Ferdinand Grand, Mar. 5, 1786.

During some years past....FPR 44:u479, "A. B.", c. 1786; 44:u481, "A. B.", c 1786; 44:u482, The Retort Courteous, c. 1786; FPR 44:u602, BF to Louis-Guillaume Le Veillard, Apr. 15, 1787.

Clearly the present inability....FPR 44:u482, the Retort Courteous, c. 1786.

The ships of the fleet employ'd themselves. . . . The army, having thus. . . . Our enemies are very. . . . FPR 44:u482, the Retort Courteous, c. 1786; FPR 44:u606, BF to Lafayette, Apr. 17, 1787.

Honesty in money matters. . . . FPR 44:u481, "A. B.," c. 1786; 44:u7, BF to Louis-Guillaume Le Veillard, Mar. 6, 1786; FPR 44:u602, BF to Louis-Guillaume Le Veillard, Apr. 15, 1787.

Direct taxes on land. . . . FPR 44:u617, BF to Abbe Andre Morellet, Apr. 22, 1787; FPR 45:u17, BF to George Whatley, May 18, 1787; FPR 45:u176, BF to Alexander Small, Sep. 28, 1787.

Fortunately, our duties are. . . . FPR 45:u52, BF to Don Diego de Gardoqui, June 11, 1787; FPR 45:u478, BF to Louis-Guilaume Le Veillard, Apr. 22, 1788.

It gives me extreme pleasure . . . FPR 46:u269, Franklin tract relative to the English School in Pennsylvania, 1788; FPR 43:u419, BF to the University of Pennsylvania, Sept. 1785.

I also offered the following. . . . FPR 43:u782, From Benjamin Franklin: Hints for Consideration on the Orphan School House in Philadelphia, c. 1785.

I wrote also a paper entitled . . . FPR 46:u269, Franklin tract relative to the English School in Pennsylvania, 1788.

Recently I received Noah Webster's . . . FPR 46:u378, letter to Noah Webster, Jr., Dec. 26, 1789.

The Latin language. . . . FPR 46:u378, BF to Noah Webster, Jr., Dec. 26, 1789.

Our English language bids . . . FPR 46:u378, BF to Noah Webster, Jr., Dec. 26, 1789.

It gave me great pleasure. . . . One of them was about the new alphabet . . . FPR 43:u828, BF to James Bowdoin, Jan. 1, 1786; FPR 43:u829, BF to Jane Mecom, Jan. 1, 1786; FPR 44:u93, BF to Jane Mecom, May 2, 1786; FPR 15:218, BF to Mary Stevenson, Sept. 28, 1768.

As to my health, the pains. . . . FPR 43:u862, BF to Jane Mecom, Jan. 24, 1786; FPR 44:u285, BF to Jan Ingenhousz, Sep. 2, 1786; FPR 44:u404, BF to John Hunter, Nov. 24, 1786.

On the whole the stone. . . . FPR 44:u602, BF to Louis-Guillaume Le Veillard, Apr. 15, 1787; FPR 45:u18, BF to Thomas Jordon, May 18, 1787; FPR 45:u278, BF to the Comte de Buffon, Nov. 4, 1787; FPR 36:t375, BF to Madame Brillon, Dec. 31, 1781.

I am now surrounded by my offspring. . . . FPR 43:u913, BF to Jonathan Shipley, Feb. 24, 1786; FPR 44:u609, BF to the Comtesse D'Houdetot, Apr. 17, 1787.

My daughter lives with me. . . . FPR 45:u538, BF to Matthew Byles, June 1, 1788.

Benny went to college. . . . FPR 43:u526, BF to Mary Stevenson Hewson, Oct. 30, 1785; FPR 43:u912, BF to Jonathan Shipley, Feb. 24, 1786; FPR 44:u5, BF to Rodolphe-Ferdinand Grand, Mar. 5, 1786; FPR 44:u93, BF to Jane Mecom, May 2, 1786.

In 1786, I received the pleasing news. . . . FPR 44:u33, BF to Daniel Roberdeau, Mar. 23, 1786; FPR 44:u317, John Wilkes to William Temple Franklin, Sep. 18, 1786; FPR 44:u322, BF to John Wilkes, Sep. 21, 1786; FPR 44:u610, BF to Jean-Baptiste Leroy, Apr. 18, 1787.

I began to build two good brick houses...FPR 44:u602, BF to Louis-Guillaume Le
   Veillard, Apr. 15, 1787; FPR 44:u323, BF to Jane Mecom, Sep. 21, 1786; FPR
   45:u39, BF to Jane Mecom, May 30, 1787.
I found upon my return....FPR 45:u204, BF to Marsilio Landriani, Oct. 14,
   1787.
The two new houses....FPR 45:u39, BF to Jane Mecom, May 30, 1787; FPR
   45:u167, BF to Jane Mecom, Sep. 20, 1787.
When I look at these buildings....FPR 45:u39, BF to Jane Mecom, May 30,
   1787.
A long winter passed....FPR 44:u102, BF to Mary Hewson, May 6, 1786.
Cards are sometimes played....FPR 44:u102, BF to Mary Hewson, May 6, 1786.
As to public amusements...FPR 44:u102, BF to Mary Hewson, May 6, 1786.
During the long winter....*As a great part*....*Another means of preserving health*....
   FPR 44:u92, BF to Catherine Shipley, May 2, 1786.
I often think with great pleasure....FPR 44:u536, letter to Alexander Small, Feb.
   19, 1787.
The world suffer'd a great loss...FPR 43:u139, BF to Caleb Whitefoord, May 13,
   1785; FPR 44:u615, BF to Rodolphe-Ferdinand Grand, Apr. 22, 1787; FPR
   45:u22, BF to Richard Price, May 18, 1787.
I wish to hear from my friends....FPR 44:u614, BF to Abbe Martin Lefebvre de la
   Roche, Apr. 22, 1787.
But tho' I could not leave....FPR 44:u617, BF to Abbe Andre Morellet, Apr. 22,
   1787; FPR 44:u342, BF to Jacques-Donatien Le Ray de Chaumont, Oct. 7,
   1786.
I am grown so old....FPR 44:u17, BF to George Whatley, May 18, 1787.
I wrote a letter of recommendation....FPR 44:u599, BF to the Duc de La
   Rochefoucauld, Apr. 15, 1787; FPR 44:u600, BF to Charles-Henri, Comte
   d'Estaing, Apr. 15, 1787; FPR 44:u602, BF to Louis-Guillaume Le Veillard,
   Apr. 15, 1787; FPR 44:u613, BF to Thomas Jefferson, Apr. 19, 1787.
I also received a letter from....FPR 44:u23, BF to Sir William Herschel, May 18,
   1787; FPR 45:u18, BF to Thomas Jordan, May 18, 1787.
Not having found the cares....FPR 44:u615, BF to Rodolphe-Ferdinand Grand,
   Apr. 22, 1787; FPR 44:u600, BF to Charles-Henri, Comte d'Estaing, Apr. 15,
   1787; FPR 44:u602, BF to Louis-Guillaume Le Veillard, Apr. 15, 1787.
I also received a letter from....FPR 44:u253, BF to William Cocke, Aug. 12,
   1786.
In the state of Pennsylvania....FPR 44:u602, BF to Louis-Guillaume Le Veillard,
   Apr. 15, 1787; FPR 44:u553, BF to James Bowdoin, Mar. 6, 1787; FPR
   44:u556, Proclamation of Benjaming Franklin and the Pennsylvania Supreme
   Executive Council, Mar. 10, 1787.
The rest of the states....FPR 44:u604, BF to the Marquis de Chastellux, Apr. 17,
   1787; FPR 44:u599, BF to the Duc de La Rochefoucauld, Apr. 15, 1787; FPR
   44:u602, BF to Louis-Guillaume Le Veillard, Apr. 15, 1787; FPR 45:u17, BF
   to George Whatley, May 18, 1787.
When there is a free government...FPR 45:u406, BF to Louis-Guillaume Le
   Veillard, Feb. 17, 1788.

There seemed to be little. . . . FPR 44:u599, BFto the Duc de La Rochefoucauld, Apr. 15, 1787; FPR 44:u602, BF to Louis-Guillaume Le Veillard, Apr. 15, 1787; FPR 44:u606, BF to Lafayette, Apr. 17, 1787; FPR 44:604, BF to Marquis de Chastellux, Apr. 17, 1787; FPR 44:u605, BF to the Abbes Chalut and Arnoux, Apr. 17, 1787.

Many of the delegates arrived. . . . FPR 45:u18, BF to Thomas Jordan, May 18, 1787; FPR 45:u32, BF to Sir Edward Newenham, May 24, 1787; FPR 45:u32, BF to Sir Edward Newenham, May 24, 1787.

I attended faithfully. . . . FPR 45:u167, BF to Jane Mecom, Sep. 20, 1787; FPR 45:u406, BF to Louis-Guillaume Le Veillard, Feb. 17, 1788.

I expressed with reluctance. . . . *Besides these evils.* . . . *It may be imagined.* . . . FPR 45:u41, Franklin's Convention Speech on Salaries, June 2, 1787.

In the debates, I also opposed. . . . FPR 46:u344, Benjamin Franklin: Queries and Remarks on "Hints for the Members of the Pennsylvania Convention," Nov. 3, 1789.

The important ends of civil government. . . . FPR 46:u344, Benjamin Franklin: Queries and Remarks on "Hints for the Members of the Pennsylvania Convention," Nov. 3, 1789.

During the warm debates. . . . *It gave me great pleasure.* . . . FPR 45:u51, Franklin Convention Speech on Proportionate Representation, 1787; FPR 45:u77, Franklin Convention Speech Proposing Prayers, June 28, 1787.

In this situation. . . . *And now, I asked.* . . . *Unfortunately, the convention* . . . FPR 45:u77, Franklin Convention Speech Proposing Prayers, June 28, 1787.

We continued the debate. . . . Robert Yates, "The Notes of the Secret Debates of the Federal Convention of 1787," in Jonathan Elliot, ed., *Debates on the Federal Constitution* (Philadelphia: J. B. Lippincott, 1863), vol. 1, 470–71.

The convention finish'd. . . . *I confess that I do not.* . . . *In these sentiments* . . . *Thus I consent, Sir.* . . . *On the whole, Sir* . . . FPR 45:u161, Franklin's Speech in the Convention on the Constitution, Sep. 17, 1787.

The motion was made. . . . James Madison, *Records of the Convention* (New York: Oxford University Press, 1920), 2:648.

The new federal Constitution. . . . FPR 45:u167, BF to Jane Mecom, Sep. 20, 1787; FPR 45:u176, BF to Alexander Small, Sep. 28, 1787.

11. MY FINAL YEARS, 1787–

It is a singular thing. . . . FPR 45:u205, BF to Count Castiglione, Oct. 14, 1787; FPR 45:u206, BF to Duc de la Rochefoucauld, Oct. 14, 1787; FPR 45:u229, BF to Rodolphe-Ferdinand Grand, Oct. 22, 1787.

The propos'd Constitution. . . . FPR 45:u396, BF to Charles Vaughan, Feb. 12, 1788; FPR 45:u405, BF to Comtesse d'Houdetot, 1788; FPR 45:u406, BF to Louis-Guillaume Le Veillard, Feb. 17, 1788; FPR 45:u405, BF to Comtesse d'Houdetot, 1788; FPR 45:u463, BF to the Editor of the Federal Gazette, 1788.

But we must not expect. . . . FPR 45:u553, BF to Pierre-Samuel du Pont de Nemours, June 9, 1788; FPR 46:u112, BF to the Duc de La Fochefoucauld, Oct. 24, 1788; FPR 45:u405, BF to Comtesse d'Houdetot, 1788; FPR 45:u463, BF to the Editor of the Federal Gazette, 1788.

I received news of a war. . . . FPR 45:u318, BF to John Sevier, Dec. 16, 1787.

I heard from Dr. Ingenhousz. . . . FPR 45:u395, BF to Jan Ingenhousz, Feb. 11, 1788.

I corresponded with. . . . FPR 46:u111, BF to Benjamin Vaughan, Oct. 24, 1788.

As it is customary in Europe. . . . FPR 46:u157, BF to Charles Thomson, Dec. 29, 1788; FPR 46:u157, BF to Charles Thomson, Dec. 29, 1788.

When I took my grandson. . . . FPR 46:u157, BF to Charles Thomson, Dec. 29, 1788.

But I would never have made. . . . FPR 46:u157, BF to Charles Thomson, Dec. 29, 1788.

When I was sent to France . . . FPR 46:u157, BF to Charles Thomson, Dec. 29, 1788.

On my arrival in Philadelphia. . . . FPR 46:u141, BF to the president of Congress, Nov. 29, 1788; PBF 46:156, Franklin sketch of services to U.S., Dec. 29, 1788.

My heavy expense. . . . FPR 46:u222, BF to Francis Childs, Apr. 27, 1789.

As I grow older, I find . . . FPR 45:u405, BF to the Comptesse de'Houdetot, 1788; FPR 45:u248, BF to Jane Mecom, Nov. 4, 1787; FPR 45:u406, BF to Louis-Guillaume Le Veillard, Feb. 17, 1788; FPR 45:u409, BF to M. Le Roy, Feb. 17, 1788.

My malady the stone. . . . FPR 46:u152, BF to Rev. Colin, Dec. 16, 1788; FPR 45:u469, BF to Jane Collas, Apr. 12, 1788; FPR 45:u535, BF to John Lathrop, May 31, 1788; FPR 45:u393 BF to Eleonore-Francois-Elie, Comte de Moustier, Feb. 10, 1788; FPR 45:u468, BF to Jane Mecom, Apr. 12, 1788.

I live in a house which. . . . FPR 45:u476, BF to Madame Brillon, Apr. 19, 1788; FPR 45:u528, BF to Jan Ingelhousz, May 24, 1788; FPR 45:u548, BF to Rodolphe-Ferdinand Grand, June 7, 1788; FPR 45:u573, BF to William Caslon, 1788; FPR 45:u318, BF to John Sevier, Dec. 16, 1787; FPR 46:u49, BF to John Anderson, Aug. 18, 1788.

I have no philosophical news. . . . FPR 45:u409, BF to M. Le Roy, Feb. 17, 1788; FPR 45:u535, BF to John Lathrop, May 31, 1788.

My gout at length left me. . . . FPR 45:u447, BF to the editor of the Pennsylvania Gazette, Mar. 30, 1788; FPR 46:u138, BF to Jane Mecom, Nov. 26, 1788; FPR 46:u400, BF to Ezra Stiles, Mar. 9, 1790.

On the other hand, some of our papers. . . . FPR 45:u447, BF to the editor of the Pennsylvania Gazette, Mar. 30, 1788; FPR 46:u138, BF to Jane Mecom, Nov. 26, 1788.

I heard a remark. . . . FPR 45:u446, BF to Hall & Sellers, Mar. 30, 1788; FPR 45:u447, BF to the editor of the Pennsylvania Gazette, Mar. 30, 1788.

There is indeed a good deal . . . FPR 45:u447, BF to the editor of the Pennsylvania Gazette, Mar. 30, 1788.

There is however one inconsistency . . . FPR 45:u447, BF to the editor of the Pennsylvania Gazette, Mar. 30, 1788.

It is true that I enjoy here. . . . FPR 46:u107, BF to Marie-Anne Pierrette Paulze Lavoisier, Oct. 23, 1788; FPR 46:u112, BF to the Duc de La Rochefoucauld, Oct. 24, 1788.

There is one thing wanting . . . FPR 45:u553, BF to Pierre-Samuel du Pont de Nemours, June 9, 1788.

The accounts I have heard... FPR 45:405, BF to Comtesse d'Houdetot, 1788; FPR 46:u115, BF To Louis-Guillaume Le Veillard, Oct. 24, 1788.

The convulsions in France.... FPR 46:u368, BF to David Hartley, Dec. 4, 1789; BF to Benjamin Vaughan, Nov. 2, 1789, in *Franklin's Autobiography Writings* (Viking, 1938), ed. By Carl Van Doren, 775.

Our grand machine.... FPR 46:u111, BF to Benjamin Vaughan, Oct. 24, 1788; FPR 46:u115, BF to Louis-Guillaume Le Veillard, Oct. 24, 1788.

At last the first Congress met.... FPR 46:u149, BF to Louis-Guillaume Le Veillard, Dec. 10, 1788; FPR 46:u112, BF to the Duc de La Fochefoucauld, Oct. 24, 1788; FPR 46:u114, BF to Thomas Jefferson, Oct. 24, 1788; FPR 46:u237, BF to Charles Carroll, May 25, 1789; FPR 46:u312, BF to Louis-Guillaume Le Veillard, Sep. 5, 1789; BF to Benjamin Vaughan, Nov. 2, 1789, in *Franklin's Autobiography Writings* (Viking, 1938), ed. by Carl Van Doren, 776; FPR 45:u318, BF to John Sevier, Dec. 16, 1787; FPR 45:u393 BF to Eleonore-Francois-Elie, Comte de Moustier, Feb. 10, 1788.

My friend Le Veillard was.... FPR 46:u115, BF to Louis-Guillaume Le Veillard, Oct. 24, 1788.

And thus, our new constitution... Thomas Fleming, ed., *Benjamin Franklin, A Biography in his Own Words* (New York: Harper & Row, 1972), 403.

Having now finish'd my term.... FPR 46:u147, BF to Abbe Andre Morellet, Dec. 10, 1788; FPR 46:u112, BF to the Duc de La Fochefoucauld, Oct. 24, 1788; FPR 46:u137, BF to Elizabeth Partridge, Nov. 25, 1788; PBF 46:u137, BF to Elizabeth Partridge, Nov. 25, 1788; FPR 46:u366, BF to Jane Mecom, Nov. 30, 1789.

I hope to enjoy.... FPR 46:u112, BF to the Duc de La Fochefoucauld, Oct. 24, 1788; FPR 46:u137, BF to Elizabeth Partridge, Nov. 25, 1788; FPR 46:u147, BF to Abbe Andre Morellet, Dec. 10, 1788; FPR 46:u148, BF to the Duc de La Rochefoucauld, Dec. 10, 1788.

I have a long time.... FPR 46:u312, BF to Louis-Guillaume Le Veillard, Sep. 5, 1789; FPR 46:u348, letter to Sir Edward Newenham, Nov. 5, 1789.

In the final years of my life.... FPR 45:u533, BF to Pierre-Samuel du Pont de Nemours, May 27, 1788; FPR 46:u6, BF to Lafayette and Dupont, 1788; FPR 46:u6, BF to Lafayette and Dupont, 1788.

I found by an old pamphlet.... FPR 46:u345, BF to John Wright, Nov. 4, 1789.

This present age has been distinguished.... FPR 46:u6, BF to Lafayette and Dupont, 1788; FPR 45:u550, BF to John Bondfield, June 7, 1788; FPR 45:u551, BF to Louis-Guillaume Le Veillard, June 8, 1788.

Tho' the people of Massachusetts.... FPR 33:390, BF to Richard Price, Oct. 9, 1780.

I thought the clause in.... FPR 42:u146, BF to John Calder, Aug. 21, 1784.

The Rev. Dr. Ezra Stiles desired.... FPR 46:u400, BF to Ezra Stiles, Mar. 9, 1790.

Nevertheless, here is my creed.... FPR 46:u400, BF to Ezra Stiles, Mar. 9, 1790; FPR 46:u137, BF to Elizabeth Partridge, Nov. 25, 1788.

My sentiments in this regard.... I received your kind letter.... As to kindness... For my own part.... You will see in this... Doubtlessly... Jesus tho't much less.... FPR 4:503-04, BF to Joseph Huey, June 6, 1753.

I like the concluding sentiment....I have sung that.... FPR 43:u149, BF to George
  Whatley, May 23, 1785.
When I was only 23 years of age, I wrote....In 1784, in my 78th year, I wrote....
  FPR 46:u400, BF to Ezra Stiles; 41:u539, Franklin's epitaph and adieu, Apr.
  22, 1784.
Thinking of old age.... FPR 46:u137, BF to Elizabeth Partridge, Nov. 25, 1788.
I condole with you....Our friend, and we.... PBF 6:406-07, BF to Elizabeth
  Hubbart, Feb. 22, 1756.
The years roll round.... PBF 3:475, BF to Abiah Franklin, Apr. 12, 1750.
I still have enjoyment in the company.... FPR 43:u913, BF to Jonathan Shipley,
  Feb. 24, 1786.

Important Dates

1751 Founds with others the Academy for Education of Youth (now University of Pennsylvania); founds Philadelphia City Hospital. His *Experiments and Observations on Electricity* published in London.

1751 Representative at the Pennsylvania Assembly (until 1764)

1752 Fire insurance company formed, with Franklin as president

1754 Proposes the Albany Plan to unite the colonies

1757 Sails to England as colonial agent of the Pennsylvania Assembly

1759 Receives honorary degree from the University of St. Andrews (thereafter referred to as "Dr. Franklin")

1762 Receives honorary degree from Oxford University; returns to Pennsylvania

1763–64 Paxton Boys attack Indians

1764 Sails to England for second mission as colonial agent

1765 Opposes the Stamp Act

1766 Stamp Act repealed

1769 Elected president of American Philosophical Society

1771 Begins autobiography

1773 Boston Tea Party, December 16

1774 Censored by the Privy Council for the Hutchinson Letters scandal; dismissed as deputy postmaster general; Boston port closes; wife Deborah dies

1775 Battles of Lexington and Concord in April; returns to America; elected member of the Second Continental Congress; named postmaster general; submits Articles of Confederation for United Colonies

1776 Mission to Canada in spring; serves on committee to draft the Declaration of Independence; signs the Declaration of Independence; elected delegate to Pennsylvania Constitutional Convention; goes to France as one of three American commissioners to negotiate a treaty

1777 In December, receives news of British General Burgoyne's surrender at Saratoga

1778 Negotiates treaties of financial and military aid from France; appointed sole plenipotentiary in France

1781 In November receives news of surrender of British General Cornwallis at Yorktown on October 19; appointed with John Jay, John Adams and others to negotiate a peace with Great Britain

1783 Signs Treaty of Paris with Great Britain

1785 Replaced by Thomas Jefferson as ambassador to France; returns to the United States

1785 Elected president, Supreme Executive Council of Pennsylvania (through 1788)

1787 Represents Pennsylvania at the Constitutional Convention

1790 In February, signs his last public document as president of the Pennsylvania Society for Promoting the Abolition of Slavery

1790, Apr. 17 Dies and is buried next to his wife in Philadelphia, Pennsylvania

Cast of Characters

John Adams (1735–1826), lawyer and Massachusetts delegate to Congress who later joined Franklin as a joint commissioner in France; became the second president of the United States.

Conde de Aranda: Pedro Pablo Abarco de Bolea Aranda (1718–83), Spanish ambassador to France who had little influence with the Spanish court.

Benedict Arnold (1741–1801), general in the Continental Army who defected to the British side in 1780.

Benjamin Franklin Bache (1769–98), known as Benny; son of Richard and Sally Franklin Bache; accompanied his grandfather to France in 1776; returned in 1785 to become publisher of the *Aurora*.

Richard Bache (1737–1811), English merchant who, after marrying Franklin's daughter Sally, became Postmaster General of the United States in 1776–82. The Baches had eight children.

Sally Franklin Bache (1769–98), Franklin's only daughter, who married Richard Bache in 1767.

Edward Bancroft (1745–1821), unofficial secretary to Franklin and the American commission to France, 1776–83, and an American-born British spy.

David Barkley, Jr. (1729–1809), London merchant who, with his brother John, established Barclay's Bank.

Pierre-Augustin Caron de Beaumarchais (1732–99), French playwright famous for "The Marriage of Figaro" (1775) who became an arms dealer in the American cause.

Matthew Boulton (1728–1809), English engineer whose Birmingham factory manufactured the revolutionary steam engines of partner James Watt (1736–1819).

Anne-Louise Brillon de Jouy (1744–1824), wife of Jacque Brillon, was Franklin's friendly neighbor in Passy, a pianist and composer.

Comte de Buffon (1707–88), Georges-Louis Leclerc, French naturalist and director of the Jardin du Roi.

John Burgoyne (1723–92), member of Parliament and a British general in the American Revolution.

Edmund Burke (1729–97), member of Parliament friendly to the American cause, but later critical of the French Revolution.

Mather Byles (1707–88), Boston preacher and grandson of Increase Mather.

William Carmichael (?–1795), member of Congress, 1778–79; accompanied John Jay to Spain in 1780, where he served as secretary.

Charles Carroll of Carrollton (1737–1832), signer of the Declaration of Independence and U.S. Senator from Maryland.

Lord Chatham: William Pitt the Elder (1708–78), First Earl of Chatham, a Whig statesman, war minister during the Seven Year War against France, and later prime minister; father of William Pitt the Younger (1759–1806), who also became prime minister.

Samuel Chase (1741–1811), Maryland delegate to Congress and U.S. Supreme Court justice.

Jacques-Donatien Le Ray de Chaumont (1725–1803), merchant who purchased the Hotel de Valentinois in Passy, which served as the American embassy in France and Franklin's headquarters. Chaumont was the first to offer military aid to the Americans, but eventually went bankrupt.

King Christian VII (1749–1808), king of Demark and Norway.

Peter Collinson (1694–1768), London Quaker merchant and botanist who was responsible for the first publication of Franklin's *Experiments and Observations on Electricity* (1751).

Marquis de Condorcet: Marie-Jean-Antoine-Nicolas Caritat (1743–94), French mathematician and economist; poisoned in the French revolution.

Rev. Samuel Cooper (1725–83), Boston politician and clergyman.

Charles Cornwallis (1738–1805), member of Parliament and British Major General in the American Revolution, 1775–81; after the defeat at Yorktown, he returned to England and later became commander in chief in India.

Thomas Cushing (1725–88), Speaker of the House in Massachusetts (1766–74) and recipient of the Hutchinson letters.

Silas Deane (1737–89), lawyer, merchant, and delegate to Congress; commissioner with Franklin in France, 1776, but recalled by Congress in 1778 for alleged embezzlement; ultimately vindicated.

John Dickinson (1732–1808), Philadelphia politician and author of *Letters from a Pennsylvania Farmer*, which Franklin helped publish in 1768.

Denis Diderot (1713–84), French philosopher and editor of the popular *Encyclopedie* (35 volumes were published between 1751 and 1780).

Pierre-Samuel du Pont de Nemours (1739–1817), French physiocrat, politician and founder of Du Pont de Nemours in the United States.

Lord William Dartmouth (1731–1801), named William Legge, Earl of Dartmouth, Secretary of State for the American Colonies in 1772–74.

Comte d'Estaing: Charles-Henri d'Estaing (1729–1794), Franklin's neighbor and French admiral who fought in the American Revolution.

Alleyne Fitz-Herbert (1753–1839), British peace negotiator sent by Lord Shelburne to Paris.

Dr. John Fothergill (1712–80), Quaker physician in London.

Charles James Fox (1749–1806), secretary of state for foreign affairs in 1782–83 and British statesman favorable to the American cause.

Abiah Folger Franklin (1667–1752), wife of Josiah Franklin and mother of ten children, including Benjamin.

Deborah Read Franklin (1705?–1774), Franklin's wife, and mother of two children, Francis and Sarah (Sally).

Francis Folger Franklin (1732–36), second son of Franklin, died at age 4 of smallpox.

John Franklin (1690–1756), Benjamin's favorite brother; soap maker and postmaster of Boston.

Josiah Franklin (1657–1745), Benjamin's father, who moved to Boston in 1683. He had seventeen children, seven from his first wife Ann Child, and ten by his second, Abiah Folger.

William Franklin (c. 1731–1813), illegitimate son of Benjamin Franklin, was raised by Franklin and his wife Deborah; appointed royal governor of New Jersey in 1762, and remained a loyalist during the war.

William Temple Franklin (c. 1760–1823), illegitimate son of William Franklin and an unknown mother. Born in London; accompanied his grandfather to France, 1776–85, where he served as secretary.

Thomas Gage (1721–87), commander in chief of the British Army in the American colonies, 1763–75.

Joseph Galloway (c. 1731–1803), Pennsylvania assemblyman who worked closely with Franklin against the proprietary government, but remained loyal to the Crown during the American revolution.

King George III (1738–1820), king of England during the American Revolution; succeeded his grandfather George II and was crowned at the age of 22.

Conrad-Alexandre Gerald (1729–90), lawyer and diplomat, first foreign minister to the United States, 1778–79.

Radolphe-Ferdinand Grand (1726–94), America's banker and financial agent in France.

Catherine Ray Greene (1731–94), friend and correspondent of Franklin since meeting in Boston in 1754; married William Greene, governor of Rhode Island, and had six children.

George Grenville (1712–70), Lord Secretary of the Treasury and author of the Stamp Act.

Thomas Grenville (1755–1846), second son of George Grenville, peace negotiator in 1782, and later First Lord of Admiralty in 1806–07.

David Hall (1714–72), Franklin's printing partner until 1767.

David Hartley (c. 1730–1813), British statesman and scientist, and a member of Parliament; helped negotiate the peace and exchange of prisoners.

Anne-Catherine de Ligniville d'Autricourt Helvétius (1719–1800), widow who lived in Auteuil (next to Passy) following the death of her husband, Claude-Adrien Helvétius, in 1771.

Mary "Polly" Stevenson Hewson (1734–95), daughter of Margaret Stevenson; married William Hewson in 1770, and was widowed 4 years later.

Countess d'Houdetot: Elisabeth-Francoise-Sophie de La Live de Bellegarde (1730–1813), wife of Claude-Constance-Cesar, comte d'Houdetot, a witty and charming neighbor who was made famous by Rousseau in his *Confessions*.

Jean-Antoine Houdon (1740–1828), French sculptor who made busts of Franklin (1778), Washington, Voltaire, Rousseau, and other notables.

Caroline Howe (c. 1721–1814), sister of Lord Richard Howe; married to John Howe.

Lord Richard Howe (1726–99), British politician, and commander in chief of the British Navy (1776–78).

William Howe (1729–1814), commander in chief of the British Army in the American colonies from 1775 until 1778; brother of Lord Richard Howe.

Thomas Hutchinson (1711–80), lieutenant governor of Massachusetts; his letters to friends caused a scandal for him and Franklin in 1773–74.

David Hume (1711–76), philosopher and economist of the Scottish Enlightenment.

Jan Ingenhousz (1730–99), Dutch physician to the Austrian Court, scientist, and correspondent with Franklin.

Ralph Izard (1741–1804), American diplomat appointed commissioner to Tuscany in 1777, but remained in Paris because Tuscany refused to recognize the United States. Recalled in 1779, and later became a U.S. Senator (1789–95).

Richard Jackson (c. 1721–87), British scientist and member of Parliament; was co-agent with Franklin representing Connecticut, Pennsylvania, and Massachusetts.

Abel James (c. 1726–90), Philadelphia Quaker merchant who, along with Franklin, encouraged silk production in America; he obtained possession of the first part of Franklin's *Autobiography* through the estate of Mrs. Joseph Galloway.

John Jay (1745–1829), American ambassador to Spain (1780–82), and later Chief Justice of the U.S. Supreme Court and Governor of New York.

Thomas Jefferson (1743–1826), Virginia delegate to Congress and the chief composer of the Declaration of Independence; succeeded Franklin as ambassador to France and later became the third president of the United States.

Dr. Samuel Johnson (1709–84), English essayist and critic made famous by James Boswell's *Life of Johnson* (1791).

John Paul Jones (1747–92), famed American naval captain and commander of the *Bonhomme Richard* in 1779; returned to America on the *Alliance* in 1781.

Lord Kames (1696–1782): Henry Home, Scottish judge.

Marquis de Lafayette (1757–1834): Marie-Joseph-Paul-Yves-Roche-Gilbert du Motier, French captain American revolutionary general. Franklin and Lafayette remained friends throughout their lives.

Henry Laurens (1724–92), president of the Continental Congress in 1777–78, and commissioner to France to help negotiate the peace treaty with England.

John Laurens (1754–82), son of Henry Laurens; envoy in 1781 to France to seek additional aid.

Antoine-Laurent Lavoisier (1743–1794), French chemist and one of Europe's most influential scientists, and director of the Academy of Sciences. He died on the guillotine in 1794.

Arthur Lee (1740–92), Virginia-born lawyer, soldier, and commissioner with Franklin to France, 1776–79; a bitter critic of Franklin.

Charles Lee (1731–82), English-born American revolutionary general.

William Lee (1739–95), brother of Arthur and Richard Henry Lee; appointed commissioner to Berlin and Vienna, but these courts refused to recognized the United States, forcing Lee to stay in Paris.

Le Roy, Jean-Baptiste (1720–1800), French scientist and loyal friend to Franklin.

Robert Livingston (1746–1813), New York politician and foreign secretary of the United States, 1781–83.

King Louis XV (1710–74), king of France; married Queen Marie, a polish princess, in 1725.

King Louis XVI (1754–93), king of France at age 20 upon the death of his grandfather Louis XV; married Marie Antoinette in 1770.

James Lovell (1737–1814), Massachusetts delegate to Congress (1777–82) and member of the committee of foreign affairs.

Cotton Mather (1663–1728), famous Puritan minister, son of Increase Mather. Franklin was influenced by his *Essays to Do Good* (1710), and corresponded with his grandson Samuel Mather.

Jane Franklin Mecom (1712–94), youngest daughter of Josiah and Abiah Folger Franklin, and favorite sibling of Franklin, the youngest of ten sons. They were the last surviving of 17 children.

Franz Anton Mesmer (1734–1815), Viennese psychiatrist whose techniques created a sensation in France; later discredited by Franklin and others.

Abbe Andre Morellet (1727–1819), French economist and contributor to Diderot's *Encyclopedie*.

Robert Morris (1734–1806), patriot and financier.

Jacques Necker (1732–1804), banker and French finance minister (1777–81).

Isaac Norris (1701–66), Quaker merchant and speaker of the Pennsylvania Assembly, 1750–64.

Lord Frederick North (1732–92), British prime minister during the American Revolution, from 1770 to 1782.

Richard Oswald (1708–84), Scottish-born merchant and British politician who helped negotiate the peace treaty, but was recalled before the Treaty of Paris was signed in 1783.

Thomas Paine (1737–1809), English-born journalist and author of *Common Sense* (1776) and other pamphlets favoring American independence.

Governor John Penn (1729–85), grandson of Pennsylvania founder William Penn; served as governor from 1763 until 1776.

Thomas Penn (1702–1775), son of William Penn, Quaker founder and proprietor of Pennsylvania.

William Penn (1644–1718), Quaker founder and proprietor of Pennsylvania.

Joseph Priestley (1733–1804), English scientist and theologian, and discoverer of oxygen.

John Pringle (1707–82), Scottish physician and Franklin's traveling companion.

The Duke de la Rochefoucauld-Liancourt (1747–1827), a French aristocrat who supported liberal democratic reforms during and after the French Revolution

Jean-Jacques Rousseau (1712–78), French philosopher and author of *The Social Contract* (1761).

Benjamin Rush (1746–1813), physician and signer of the Declaration of Independence.

Edward Rutledge (1735–1826), South Carolina lawyer and signer of the Declaration of Independence.

Lord Sandwich: John Montagu (1718–92), 4th Earl of Sandwich; Secretary of State; First Lord of Admiralty; member of the House of Lords.

James Searle (1733–97), merchant and Pennsylvania delegate to Congress sent to Europe in 1780 to obtain a loan to purchase supplies.

Captain Daniel Shays (c. 1747–1825), farmer and war veteran who led an armed uprising in Massachusetts to protest the jailing of debtors during depressed economic conditions in 1786–87. Shays was captured and sentenced to hang, but was pardoned by new Governor John Hancock.

Earl of Shelburne (1737–1805): William Petty, colonial secretary and British prime minister during 1782–83.

Rev. Jonathan Shipley (1714–88), Bishop of St. Asaph; Franklin's lifelong friend and correspondent; it was at his house in Twyford, near Winchester, that Franklin began his memoirs. Daughters Catherine and Georgiana corresponded frequently with Franklin.

Adam Smith (1723–90), Scottish economist and author of *The Wealth of Nations* (1776).

Reverend William Smith (1727–1803), an Anglican minister in Philadelphia, was one of Franklin's critics.

Margaret Stevenson (c. 1706–83), landlady of the Craven Street residence where Franklin lived in London, and mother of Mary "Polly" Stevenson Hewson.

Rev. Ezra Stiles (1727–95), Connecticut clergyman and president of Yale College (1778–95).

David Murray Stormont, Earl of Mansfield (1727–96), Scottish aristocrat and British ambassador to Versailles during the American Revolution.

Henry Strachey (1737–1810), undersecretary of the Home Department in 1782–83.

William Strahan (1715–85), English printer and a member of Parliament, publisher of such renowned works as Edward Gibbon's *Decline and Fall of the Roman Empire* and Adam Smith's *Wealth of Nations*, both in 1776.

Rev. William Sturgeon (c. 1722–70), Anglican clergyman.

Charles Townsend (1725–67), chancellor of the exchequer, author of the Townshend Acts of 1767.

Thomas Townshend (1733–1800), Secretary of War under Rockingham in 1782 and Secretary of the Home Office in 1783–89, and a cousin of Charles Townshend.

Anne-Robert-Jacques Turgot (1727–81), French economist and finance minister to Louis XVI. Wrote the famous epigram: *Eripuit celo fulmen sceptrumque tyrannis*: He snatched lightning from the sky and the scepter from tyrants.

Benjamin Vaughan (1751–1835), British diplomat who helped Franklin negotiate the peace treaty with England, and published Franklin's works in 1779.

Comte de Vergennes: Charles Gravier Vergennes (1717–87), highly influential French minister of foreign affairs under Louis XVI.

Louis-Guillaume Le Veillard (1733–94), neighbor and friend to Franklin; died on the guillotine.

Voltaire (1694–1778), pen name for Francois Marie Arouet, French author and philosopher; Franklin and Voltaire met in Paris in 1778, the final year of Voltaire's life.

Thomas Walpole (1727–1803), British merchant, banker, and member of Parliament who led a group of investors, including Franklin, to seek from the crown a land grant in Ohio.

George Washington (1732–99), commander of the Continental Army from 1775 until the end of the Revolutionary War, and first president of the United States.

Alexander Wedderburn (1733–1805), British solicitor general who interrogated Franklin in the Cockpit in January 1774 regarding the Hutchison Letters scandal.

George Whatley (c. 1709–91), London merchant and author of a pamphlet on trade in which Franklin wrote annotations supporting free trade. No relation to George Whately of Hutchinson Letters fame.

George Whitefield (1714–70), Anglican priest and Methodist evangelist who was one of the most successful preachers in America.

Jonathan Williams, Jr. (1750–1815), Franklin's grand nephew who served as the American agent at Nantes, France, procuring supplies for the war, etc. He returned with Franklin to America in 1785, and became the first Superintendent of West Point (1801–03, 1805–12).

John Wilkes (1725–98), controversial member of Parliament and Lord Mayor of London who defended English rights.

About the Compiler and Editor

Mark Skousen, Ph. D., is a professional economist, university professor, and author of more than 20 books on economic and financial
topics. He has taught economics and economic history at Columbia
Business School, Barnard College, and Rollins College. He earned
his Ph. D. in monetary economic history in 1977 from George Washington University. Since 1980, he has been editor of *Forecasts &
Strategies*, an award winning economic/financial newsletter (www.
markskousen.com). He is past president of the Foundation for Economic Education (FEE) and a former columnist for *Forbes* magazine. His books include *The Making of Modern Economics* (M. E.
Sharpe, 2001), *The Power of Economic Thinking* (FEE, 2002), and
Vienna and Chicago, Friends or Foes? (Capital Books, 2005). In honor
of his work in economics, finance, and management, Grantham University renamed its business school, "The Mark Skousen School of
Business" in 2005.

Websites: www.markskousen.com; www.mskousen.com
Email: mskousen@mskousen.com

Index